Whatever happened to Lady Justice?

Copyright © 2010 Vincent Carraher

Typeset in Calibri

Self published by Vincent Carraher & Andre Duke

ISBN 978-0-615-36422-3

Contents

1. Foreword i
   Some guiding principles that seem to have been forgotten
2. Introduction 5
3. The Congdon-Pietila Homicide 13
   The Case
   Investigations
   Candy is dandy
   More witnesses
   Nasty, Nasty
   Reflections
4. Numero Uno: Ronald Meshbesher, Esq. 33
5. More homicide: T. Eugene Thompson 59
   Working the streets
   People, papers and publicity
6. The Judges: three wise men 73
   Judge Jack Nordby
   Judge James Gilbert
   Judge Paul Anderson
7. Ralph Chavez Duke 95
   Interviews
   Trial transcript
   Argument
   Letter from Duke
8. 'Broadway' Joe Friedberg, Attorney 119
9. Sex Crimes & False Accusations 135
   Sex Crimes
   Scott County
   Summary
10. Unsportsman-like conduct 151
    Interview with Jerry Thomas
    Big Time Athletics
    The Academic World
    Marvelous Marty

11. King of the Sex Cases 193
   Robert Sicoli
12. The Police (part one) 209
   Anthony Bouza
13. The Police (part two) 221
   Michael Young
   Roger Concannon
14. Snitches 237
   Informants
   Snitch Culture - by Jim Redden
   Red Adams
   Mike Montana
   Scoundrels
   Andrew Chambers
   A favored kingpin
15. More Attorneys: Peter Thompson 253
16. Even more attorneys: Joseph Margolis 275
17. Women and the Law 287
   Nancy Berg-The Polish Cannon
   Karen Hanson
   Pamela Spaulding
   Christine Friendt
   Summary
18. Hold that tiger! 317
   Concluding remarks
19. Conclusion 325
20. Appendix: Images and articles 329
21. Appendix: Duke Evidence 348

Acknowledgements

Liz Arms, John Arms, Bob Andrus, Judge Paul Anderson, Howard Bass, Nancy Berg, Tony Bouza, Nancy Bakeman, Lori Carraher, Chris Carraher, Roger Concannon, Christo's Restaurant, Marty Dworkin,

Andre Duke, Ralph Duke, Tracy Demmick, Joe Friedberg, Christine Friendt, Georgine Ganson, Judge James Gilbert, Daniel H...., Judge Bruce Hartigan, Karen Hanson, Mary Hartman, Kenneth Keller, Richard Kyle, Renee Kinney, Jill Lindaman, Tom and Audra Mc Alpine,

Ronald Meshbesher, Ken Meshbesher, Libby and the team, Sara McGilles, Judge Jack Nordby, Dick Passine, Melissa Olson, Jackie Stone, Bob Sicoli, Otis Smith, Patti and David Smith, Pam Spaulding, Jody Spaude, Jerry Thomas, Peter Thompson, Beth Van Buren, Kathleen Weiker, Michael Young.

I am indebted to all of you who helped me put this book together, and I cannot but thank each and every one of you for your time and concern in getting "Whatever Happened to Lady Justice" published.

Dedication

To Lori, Chris, Jean, Matt and Megan, Gina, Lauren and Keighty with love and kisses.

Unfortunately the criminal law was never equipped to prove innocence. It was crafted to established one thing only; Guilt in the eyes of the public, which holds the collateral to all of our reputations, the absence of guilt is seldom seen as the equivalent of innocence.

Steve Martini

Foreword

Before you start this exciting trip into Vinnie's life, I would like to say a few words.

In the legal system it is the lawyers, judges and police that get all the recognition. As you will find out; it is men like Vinnie that are the glue that hold together the justice system.

It is important to understand that this is more than a book. It really is a window into the life of an incredible man. A man who has spent more than 40 years helping people. A man who is a hero.

Vinnie would never admit nor accept such terms about his life. This is a man who has been a father, husband and a survivor. He would not want you to know that he beat cancer. This book is the culmination of Vinnie's journey for truth and justice. In these times; these words are thrown around so much that they have lost their meaning. Well as you will find out from Vinnie; words have meaning.

Truth and justice are not just words to Vinnie. It is not exaggerating to say that he has put his life on the line for these words.

I would like to sincerely thank Vinnie and his wonderful wife Lori for the opportunity to work with him on this project.

Andre Duke

Some guiding principles that seem to have been forgotten

It is desirable that criminals should be detected, and to that end that all available evidence should be used. It also is desirable that the government should not itself foster and pay for other crimes, when they are the means by which the evidence is to be obtained.

Holmes, J., Olmstead v. United States. 277 U.S. 438, 470 (1928).

Nothing can destroy a government more quickly than its failure to observe its own laws, or worse, its disregard of the charter of its own existence.

Clerk, J., Mapp v. Ohio, 367 U.S. 643, 659 (1961).

We have to choose, and for my part I think it a less evil that some criminals should escape than that the government should play an ignoble part.

Holmes, J., Olmstead v. United States. 277 U.S. 437, 470 (1928).

Introduction

> "First they came for the Communists, but I was not a Communist so I did not speak out. Then they came for the Socialists and the Trade Unionists, but I was neither, so I did not speak out. Then they came for the Jews, but I was not a Jew so I did not speak out. And when they came for me, there was no one left to speak out for me."
>
> Pastor Martin Niemoeller

Would there even be a United States of America had not the founding fathers revolted against England and the crown? Where would we be without leaders like Jefferson, Washington, Adams, Franklin, and inflammatory Tom Paine? It has been said that Thomas Jefferson proclaimed we need a revolution every ten years. I believe Jefferson was not suggesting a violent revolution, but rather shaking up the system and the status quo. This is exactly what is needed today.

Standing up and speaking out is the primary motivation for this book. Another motivational factor was suggestions from friends and acquaintances over the years that I write about cases I investigated that are interesting to the public and involve high profile attorneys in the State of Minnesota. I will focus primarily on the legal system and the criminal justice system in particular. The cases I cite illustrate governmental abuse of power by police, prosecutors, government informants and various state and federal agencies. In support for my position I have interviewed law enforcement officials, lawyers, judges, and people outside of the legal system to get their views and analyses of what is taking place in this country. It is an unfortunate reality that many citizens do not truly understand what is going on in our legal system, and cannot even name their local representatives, let alone name the member of the Supreme Court.

In 1989 and 1990 my wife Lori and I volunteered for the Christian Brothers as teachers on the Islands of St. Vincent and the Grenadines. The Christian Brothers are a Catholic teaching order which operates schools in the United States, Canada, and many

Introduction

foreign countries. Their mission is to teach, and not to proselytize. Through their volunteer program we were assigned to the secondary school of St. Martins on St. Vincent Island. Although neither of us were certified teachers, we did both have degrees, which qualified us to teach. Lori taught art and home economics, and I taught morals and ethics. One of the things I stressed in my classes was the importance of reviewing various sources before coming to a conclusion on a topic.

Every Monday in class, I conducted an exercise I called "What's New?" I asked my students to comment on something they learned over the weekend that pertained to a moral or ethical issue. One morning a student offered that he read a story in the newspaper about a woman giving birth to a goat. Although I went to great lengths to explain why this was impossible, he insisted it was true because he read it in the local newspaper. I ultimately had to send him to the science teacher for an explanation of why a human could not give birth to a goat before he believed me.

As this story illustrates, it is easy to accept the written word as the truth, without challenging this assumption, simply because many magazines and newspapers have a certain sense of authority. Although it is easy to see that this would be a problem in an unsophisticated culture, it is also more problematic in more advanced cultures like ours. Too often people accept what they read at face value, and do not bother to check sources or otherwise make sure the facts are accurate. Often people read about a sensational case in the news, — perhaps a homicide or charges against a prominent person — and assume the person is guilty based on what they read. The notion of "innocent until proven guilty" does not occur to most people in this situation. People should bear in mind that while it is rare for a defense attorney to present information to the media, the prosecution is typically eager to do so. This creates an immediate bias in the news that is presented, and can make it difficult to find an impartial jury. The U.S. might benefit from a system similar to that in Great Britain and Canada, which minimizes the release of any information about a crime until a verdict is reached. It is unlikely, however, that our news media would accept this approach.

Even without biased pretrial publicity, juries are difficult to select. Whole categories of people are almost automatically excused from the jury pool because they have the right connections, or jobs which do not allow them to be away, like stay at home parents. Attorneys tend to have specific opinions as to who they want on their jury, for instance not picking people who are too knowledgeable, or are more educated than average. Finally, many people have personal experiences which make it unlikely that they will be picked for a jury. An insurance defense attorney in a personal injury case, for instance, is unlikely to want a juror who has made a past personal injury claim. I am unlikely to ever be chosen to sit on a criminal jury because of my experience investigating criminal matters for the defense. As a result, the jury pool is often not a very representative cross segment of society.

The great English jurist William Blackstone said, "Better that ten guilty persons escape than that one innocent suffer." Nonetheless, as historian Howard Zinn has pointed out, there is a difference between law and justice.

Corruption and crime can also be two different issues. In an October 2008 issue of the New Yorker magazine, there is an article about the Enron scandal, which I'm sure everyone has heard about, and the author points out that Kenneth Lay, Bush's dear friend, may skate without any criminal charges. Several others on a high level may also slide by, but isn't it a fact that they're all involved in some form of corruption resulting in 10,000 people losing their jobs, bogus loans, phony accounting, etc., etc. Everyone can agree corruption went on, but technically, are some of these people guilty of a crime? This also takes place on the big time sports level, government contracts in the private sector without bids being put out (I give you Halliburton), offshore headquarters for about 70 major companies limiting tax liability and God knows what else. Many times these corporations and individuals are engaging in unethical and immoral behavior, but they are not violating the law.

I suppose I should make some mention of how I became an investigator working for criminal defense lawyers. Actually, I think of myself more as an interviewer of witnesses. I have no background in forensics. Basically what I do is interview witnesses, and that means

Introduction

prosecution witnesses and witnesses that the defense may locate. The defense lawyer wants to know the good, bad and indifferent to properly prepare her or his case.

I started out as an insurance adjuster and investigator for the Hartford Insurance Company. At the time we were located on 9th Street, right off Hennepin Avenue in downtown Minneapolis. Originally, it was not my intent to make a career in the claim department of any insurance company, but I actually liked my work and liked interviewing people and trying to piece together the liability pertaining to personal injury cases. I also worked on some bond losses, in that Hartford insured a number of saloons and liquor stores which were sometimes robbed.

I make a continued effort to read various magazines and newspapers and to watch in-depth analysis of issues on television in order to broaden my understanding. I believe it is important to associate with people from various walks of life in order to give your own viewpoint better balance. You won't learn any new ideas by exclusively associating with people who think the same way as you.

Much has already been written about the tragedy of September 11, 2001. The events which took place that day have forever changed numerous aspects of American life, including its criminal justice system. People living in the United States who are of Middle Eastern descent have become suspects, been investigated, been detained, and, in many instances, have had their civil rights trampled on. This is not the first time that people in America have been singled out for unfair treatment based on the color of their skin, and the country of their origin. I am old enough to remember the internment of the Japanese during World War II when all were suspected of being spies or potential threats against the US and herded off to American concentration camps. A civilized nation must respect all individuals and tread with caution rather than overreact, and violate the rights of certain ethnic groups. However, within that framework, neither the government nor individuals should support terrorism or violence in any form.

In my over 40 years as an investigator, I have seen a number of cases where there has been abuse by the prosecution and or the police, ranging from manipulation, to promises and inducements to snitches, to threats of witnesses. In this book I will set out examples of these based on cases I investigated for respected Minnesota criminal defense attorneys. Some of the blame for current problems in the criminal justice system should be laid at the feet of the Bush administration. Former President George W. Bush appointed John Ashcroft as our nation's Attorney General. Ashcroft's history involves losing a political race in Indiana to a deceased opponent, and refusing to, give press conferences at the US Justice Department in front of the female art-deco "Spirit of Justice" statue, which has one breast exposed, until curtains were added to cover the statue's partial nudity. Such narrow-mindedness sets the stage for a puritanical fear and intolerance. Such an attitude underscores the conservative right's attitude and understanding of what is right and wrong in society, societal behavior, different points of view by citizens, tolerance, and last, but not least, the Constitution of the United States. Those who do not share the views of the extreme right, include middle easterners and liberals, are suspect. This attitude is also highlighted in the conservative law and order theme that we must be tougher on criminals or suspected criminals and bring them to "justice", regardless of the consequences.

Undoubtedly there will be many who read this book who will dismiss me as a wild-eyed liberal who attacks anyone with a conservative bent. They might be surprised to learn that I have a number of conservative and ultra-conservative friends. Many people whose views fall on the extreme right are guilty of only getting their news and commentary from right wing radio hosts, such as Rush Limbaugh, and right wing newspapers, such as the Wall Street Journal. As discussed earlier, however, your views are unlikely to grow, if you never open your eyes to anyone's position but your own. It is both healthy and wise to stay in tune with those that do not support your personal political philosophy.

Both sides of the political spectrum argue that the news media is biased. Certainly there are numerous right-wing radio broadcasts in this nation, controlled by the right. The left's only counter to these stations is Air America. In addition, most of the TV stations, newspapers and magazines are owned and run by individuals and companies which ultimately have a conservative bias.

Introduction

Whether there is a left or right leaning bias in the news, it goes without saying that much of the information which is disseminated by these sources cannot be completely trusted on its face. For a variety of reasons this information can be flat out wrong, or, short of this, biased in its presentation. In addition to biases from the sources, biases inherent in the people to whom the information is being presented also plays a role. Often a newspaper will contain details about a terrible murder or sexual assault and go so far as to identify a suspect. The natural human response is to think, "I hope they get that son of a bitch." It is not uncommon, however, to later learn that the suspect may not have been involved at all. I know this from personal experience, as I have worked on cases I first read about in the newspaper, or heard about on the evening news. In at least some of these cases, after I became involved and additional facts were uncovered, it became clear that the actual situation was different than that depicted by the news media.

People often want to know how I became an investigator, and how I can possibly work on behalf of someone who is guilty. I'll start with the second question. Everyone has the right to counsel, which includes the right to an investigation. I approach each case I work on with the premise that the question of guilt is a jury question, and is not my judgment to make. My role as a criminal defense investigator is to assist the attorney in presenting a legal defense for his or her client. My job is to look for exculpatory evidence. This is evidence that helps prove the accused is not guilty, or, at the very least, evidence which creates reasonable doubt. Reasonable doubt is sometimes explained as being convinced "to a moral certainty."

If the evidence I uncover through interviews and document review makes it more likely that the accused will be found guilty, then it is up to the attorney to so advise the accused. In addition to the evidence I uncover, expert witnesses are often called in to present evidence on fields such as forensic, pathology, ballistics and reconstruction.

If the evidence weighs heavily against the accused, the attorney will typically try to negotiate some type of settlement. It is the client who ultimately makes the decisions about whether to go to trial, however, regardless of how the evidence looks.

To my knowledge I have never worked on behalf of a suspect who confessed to the crime in question to his or her attorney but still expected the attorney to proceed as if the suspect was totally innocent. An attorney has a duty to represent a client, but cannot allow him or her to take the witness stand and lie. The only admissions of wrongdoing which I have heard from clients involve self-defense claims. As an investigator for the defense, I stay in close contact with the attorney, since the defense theory may change based on information I provide, or other new information.

As for the question of how I became an investigator, this was not how I originally started my career. When I was starting out, I was friends with Mike O'Connor, who was a vice president with the Minneapolis Gas Company. Mike suggested I take a written exam for a sales position with his company. When I passed the exam but there were no positions available, Mike suggested I consider being a claims adjuster for an insurance company. Soon after this I was hired on with the Hartford Insurance Company as an adjuster. After about three and half years in this position I was contacted by Russ Spence, a former adjuster who was now an investigator with Robins, Meshbesher & Kirschbaum, about performing investigations of plaintiff claims for his firm. Soon after I started, I was given a homicide case to investigate by Ron Meshbesher and from then on I was hooked on criminal investigation. My career went forward in the criminal area right after my first homicide case.

I enjoyed the criminal defense investigations, and liked the idea of working on behalf of a client who may have been overcharged, or wrongfully charged with a crime. On my first case Ron and F. Lee Bailey were co-counsel. I worked with Bailey's investigator, Andy Tuney. Tuney had worked on the Boston Strangler case, among others, and I was more than a little bit in awe of him.

Chapter 1

The Congdon-Pietila Homicide

As the Irish would say, Marjorie Congdon Caldwell is a caution.

However, as the investigator for Ronald Meshbesher, who represented Marjorie for allegedly orchestrating the murder of her mother and her mother's night nurse, I do not believe that she or her husband were responsible for this horrendous double murder. My convictions are based on the investigation I conducted along with attorney Frank Berman, and the absence of an explanation of how Roger and Marjorie could have pulled off this caper. The prosecutor focused only on Marjorie Congdon Caldwell and her husband Roger all along. They were myopic and prejudicial from the time the murders were discovered. The cops ignored any possibility someone other than bad Marjorie committed this crime.

There have been a number of books written about this case and of course a great deal of media attention was devoted to this horrible murder. But the latest book "Will to Murder" is very troubling to me. The book by Gail Feichtinger was extremely well written with prosecutor John DeSanto and his lead investigator Gary Waller as the contributors. I can only think of two reasons for writing such a book. One would be the motivation of making some money, and the second would be DeSanto and Waller cannot accept that they lost one of the most celebrated cases in the State of Minnesota. The book is worth reading. It is not my position to be a public relations person for these people, but in reading this book, I not only found many important bits of information minimized, excluded, or not explained. I also found a degree of whining. In fact, DeSanto, to me, projects the image of a guy who got screwed by the jury without even being kissed. Balderdash, or to be more emphatic, Bullshit! Another book, "Glensheen's Daughter" was far more fair and objective about the murder case. The author went beyond the homicide cases, covering Marjorie's life of chaos and her conviction in Arizona of arson. My concern in this book deals only with the murders of her mother and the nurse in Duluth.

Chapter 1 - The Congdon-Pietila Homicide

There are people who rob banks who do not kill. There are politicians such as Duke Cunningham of California now doing prison time for taking contractor kick-back, who do not beat children. There are pickpockets that are not violent. However, if any of those I just mentioned did commit a murder, their entire life would be exposed. One can be sure the prosecutors would feed the press by leaking every character flaw the defendant has. Poison the well. I have seen this happen and so have you.

I give you the Jonbonet Ramsay case. The police and prosecutors fucked up that case completely to the detriment of the parents. All the leaking to the press led the public to believe the family was responsible for the child's death. There would have been no way in hell to select a jury that had not read or heard something that pointed to culpability on the part of the family for the dear child's death.

And what about the Duke University lacrosse players who were tried and convicted in the press for abusing a black stripper? Not too smart to hire two women to prance around in the buff, but young men often do this at stag parties. Old men have been known to engage in this activity also. As we know now, the night of this strip party went awry. Ultimately the lads were accused of sexual assault and racism. Protests took place against the lacrosse team and the school administrators. The coach was fired, season cancelled, the shit hit the fan. Personally, I didn't give a rat's ass if the defendants were rich but that was a big issue with the media. The concept of innocent until proven guilty was down the toilet for far too many people in the Duke community and the national public. The ambitious and stupid prosecutor in this case ignored and buried exculpable evidence. Fortunately for the Duke lads charged, their parents had the money to put on a vigorous defense. The facts ultimately surfaced but serious damage was done to all involved. Had the defendants been poor, not able to hire high powered lawyers, the possibility of some convictions may have occurred. If you got the dough, away we go. Justice is expensive.

In Marjorie's case, Ron Meshbesher took a gamble. His firm could bear the expense of taking her case with the promise of being paid when the case was over. I also took a chance because, I was not paid a fee until long after the not guilty verdict came in. The firm did pay travel, lodging and meals for me and interest on my hourly fee. I had other cases I worked on during this time so I had some money coming in to my humble household. Darling Lori, my patient wife, a/k/a roommate, was working so we did just fine. Like the cases I mentioned, the media made things look pretty grim for Marjorie and Roger.

The Case

I'll start from the beginning.

My first involvement with Marjorie Caldwell after receiving the assignment from Ron Meshbesher was an interview with her at my residence. We were living on Dupont Avenue, in southwest Minneapolis, up the hill, east of Lake Harriet. This was shortly after her husband Roger Caldwell had been indicted for the crime. We went through some routine matters, family history, her and Roger's activity in Colorado, what she and Roger were doing over the weekend of the homicide which took place June 26, 1977. I was able to obtain from Marjorie enough information for me to proceed on the defense investigation but when, I finally moved forward, I found that much of what she told me was not accurate. Although I do not believe she was sending me on a wild goose chase, I believe she had some of her dates, times, and even places mixed up. At a later point in time, I had a sense that she was also making an attempt to cover-up Roger Caldwell's alcoholism.

In the final analysis, I found Marjorie Congdon Caldwell to be eccentric or beyond that, not totally playing with a full deck. Admittedly, I am not a psychologist but I believe she would have been the delight of any shrink because she was a complicated person.

She told me some things that I have no way of verifying. For instance, she stated that she was the Cinderella of the family, given hand me down clothing and that with the exception of her mother, the other members of the family looked down upon her. She emphasized that she believed she did have a very good relationship with her mother but I have no way of documenting this. Marjorie once told me that

Chapter 1 - The Congdon-Pietila Homicide

she believed she was the biological child of sharecroppers in one of the Carolina states, but she claimed she had no idea of the background of her adoption. There were also rumors that Marjorie was actually the biological child of Elizabeth Congdon but again, only the immediate family would have this information.

I also learned during the course of my investigation that Marjorie had no idea what-so-ever how to deal with money. For example, I interviewed a husband-wife team who dealt in rather expensive horses, and Marjorie had purchased a horse from these people for $20,000.00. She couldn't rub two nickels together so why in the world would someone do such a thing? She also spent money in other areas and certainly had to know the piggy bank was empty. Her credit was horrendous.

Many years back, it must be noted, Marjorie and her family that included Mr. LeRoy, an insurance agent, lived quite well in south Minneapolis, on Emerson Avenue, east of Lake Harriet. I had interviewed her one time. She was a possible witness in a civil case involving an ice-skating club that one or more of her children belonged to. Many of the people in this club were show-biz type mothers and there was one woman suing the club because her child wasn't getting sufficient ice time. Marjorie didn't remember me but I ultimately moved into that neighborhood and on occasion would walk by her house which reminded me of the ice skating case. On my level, that of a criminal defense investigator, Marjorie was not a great deal of help to me. She may have been a greater help to Ron during the trial, I have no way of knowing because I was sequestered throughout the entire proceedings.

Roger Caldwell was by definition a near-do-well. He was fairly tall, and seemed to be a bright person, yet he had what we call the Irish Disease. The man had virtually no tolerance for alcohol and when he did drink, his personality changed drastically. He suffered from frequent black-outs from his binges. Attorney Bruce Myers who was assisting the late Doug Thomson in Duluth, Minnesota had visited Roger who was in the St. Louis County Jail. Bruce is also the brother-in-law of the well known attorney John Cochrane of St. Paul. I met with Bruce on my first trip to Duluth and we went to the county jail and had a lengthy interview with Roger Caldwell.

Bruce Myers who is a very interesting person is low-key and he had a very friendly manner about him. It was apparent that Bruce could get along with anyone. He had a rather diverse background in that he practiced law, but not on a continuous basis. He also drove a truck out west, was extremely well-read and lived in a cabin a short distance north of Duluth. He told me some funny stories about the bears attacking his home along with trucker's stories. We spent a great deal of time with Caldwell and both of us agreed that this man didn't know what the hell was going on. It was really perplexing interviewing Roger. We came out of the jail, went to a restaurant and tried to make some sense out of the answers that Roger had given us concerning his activity and whereabouts in Colorado preceding the homicide. He admitted one time traveling to Duluth in an attempt to meet with Elizabeth Congdon and secure a loan. He was totally rejected in that effort. He also denied being in Minnesota during the time of the murders. He claimed he was not familiar with the interior of the Congdon Mansion.

Investigations

People who have followed this case know that Roger Caldwell was convicted of this double homicide prior to his trial. Attorney Bruce Myers and I had contacted a political science professor at the University of Minnesota in Duluth. He was experienced in political polling and putting together survey information. I forget this professor's name but he had some of his graduate students do a survey in Duluth for the purpose of getting a change of venue. Doug Thomson was successful in getting a change of venue to Brainerd, Minnesota, but of course, he had hoped to have the case tried perhaps in Minneapolis or St. Paul. On behalf of Doug Thomson, Bruce Myers continued to do what he could in the Duluth area. It must be noted that Roger had no money to pay Thomson. It's none of my business what type of an agreement they made but Doug Thomson was strapped for funds. Ron Meshbesher shared with Thomson the investigation by Mr. Berman and me. The timing was not good, Marjorie's case came up after Rogers and much of the evidence had not yet been mined by us. Marjorie was arrested on July 11, 1978 and I was still in the field looking for information. She was indicted in August 1978 and it wasn't until April 3, 1979 that Marjorie's case began with jury selection.

Chapter 1 - The Congdon-Pietila Homicide

Obviously, it is not my intention to write a book on this particular case. My intent here is to go back to the beginning and point out some facts that presented so much reasonable doubt. First of all, there was never an explanation by the police and prosecutors how Roger Caldwell could possibly have gotten to Minnesota and committed this double homicide. Consider this. He and Marjorie were flat ass broke. There is no contract a killer would take for a case on the come. There must be a down-payment at least. It's just the way it works. Read any books on organized crime and you will know this to be a fact. So, there was no information that came forward that Marjorie and Roger put a contract out on Elizabeth Congdon.

The prosecutor and his investigators left no stone unturned considering flights to and from Colorado to Duluth. Every possibility was checked. For example, maybe one could fly to Los Angeles then get a flight to Minneapolis or one could hire a private plane to fly up to Duluth. Trust me, all of these possibilities were looked into by the authorities. In addition, back in the 70's, the U.S. Air Force had a presence in Duluth and they had radar that could spot low flying aircraft. It would be virtually impossible for someone to sneak in and land, and besides that, you have to file a flight plan. I am sure the prosecution team checked for small craft coming into Minneapolis/St. Paul International or the smaller airports in the Twin Cities vicinity.

If someone did fly in somehow, someway, then of course, he would have to proceed by vehicle to reach the Glensheen Mansion. Rental cars were checked out and cab companies. I suspect someone could go by bicycle or on foot to the Mansion, but it is one hell of a long walk from the airport. In the final analysis, there was no evidence that Roger somehow was in Duluth, Minnesota on Sunday, the day of the murders. His whereabouts the week prior were documented. I will tell you about the eyewitnesses who saw him on Sunday.

But first I will mention the return flights from the Minnesota/St. Paul International airport to Denver at that time showed the flight would leave Minneapolis at 7:30 a.m. I have no idea what the schedule would be today. But then of course, one would have to have transportation to drive to Golden, Colorado. There is no evidence that Roger picked up a vehicle or had a ride waiting for him at the

Denver Airport. The prosecution claimed he was identified in the Minneapolis/St. Paul International Airport at a kiosk making a purchase before he boarded a 7:30 a.m. flight to Denver. The identification was wrong! According to the banker that had repossessed vehicles from Marjorie and Roger, he was allowed to pick up a vehicle in the daytime sometime between 9:00 and 9:30 a.m. Logistically, he could not have gotten from the Denver Airport (the old airport) to the bank in Golden, Colorado within that period of time. The banker verified that Roger did come in on Monday morning to get a vehicle. Concerning the kiosk identification of Roger Caldwell and the garment bag that he allegedly had with him, the female witness at the kiosk stated the man was wearing turquoise jewelry and she talked about a turquoise belt buckle. The fact remains that Roger had pawned all of his turquoise jewelry months before this horrible incident occurred in Duluth. I interviewed the person who ran a coin pawnshop business in Colorado and he verified the transaction between him and Roger regarding jewelry. This is the same individual who priced the Byzantine coin that was allegedly stolen from the mansion by Roger and mailed to Colorado in a Radisson Hotel envelope. The coin, incidentally, was valued at about $400.00. Nancy Berg brought photographs to the kiosk at the International Airport. She ran a photo line-up for the witness. They could not identify Roger in the set of photographs. However, in court, the witness pointed Roger out at the defense counsel table. Give me a fuckin' break! He certainly didn't look like a lawyer at counsel table. His description had been reinforced obviously. Isn't it interesting the witness could not identify Roger for my pal Nancy, but was able to point him out in court.

I interviewed Richard LeRoy on August 20, 2007 at Ron Meshbesher's office where I work out of on a part-time basis. Richard goes by Rick and he works at the neighborhood justice center on 16th and Park Avenue. He was 17 years of age at the time of the murders but still had a clear memory of how he heard about the event, the whereabouts of his mother and step-father and his own activities at the time. At the present time, Rick represents indigent people and he is often in criminal court so he knows the procedure of that arena. He confirmed much of what was discovered during the course of defense investigation.

Chapter 1 - The Congdon-Pietila Homicide

Rick drew me a diagram of their rooms at the Golden Hotel in Golden, Colorado. There were two bedrooms and in between the rooms there was an area where a light was on all the time. He thought it was a fluorescent light over a sink. There was a door from the outside hallway for Marjorie and Roger's room and also a door for Rick's room. Rick came into his room Sunday night, the 26th. There was enough light to lead him to the sink area and he looked into his mother's bedroom. He stated they always left their door open and his bedroom door was frequently open. There were two beds in Rick's room and a queen size bed for Marjorie and Roger. Rick stated his mother was in bed. He could see her hair on the pillow. To his mother's left, he saw a form under the covers. He stated Roger always slept with the covers over his head. He believed it to be Roger under those covers. It would be highly unlikely Marjorie would be sleeping with someone else. Rick went about his business and went to bed. He stated he got up late the next morning which would be Monday and he stated that a man came to his mother's door. Rick paid no attention to that. I asked Rick could the man have been the wild life artist who had been trying to negotiate a sale with Marjorie? He wasn't sure about that, it meant nothing to him at the time. Rick also confirmed that there was maid service, and ultimately I did interview the hotel maid. The maid recalled servicing both Marjorie and Rick's rooms on that particular Monday. She stated that this was routine. She was an experienced maid. She would make up the beds and stated that it appeared to her that two people had slept in the queen size bed in Marjorie's room. She stated that there was an indentation on both sides of the bed. The pillows were in their normal location where the head would rest. Based on her experience, that bed had been slept in by two people.

The key witness was Mrs. Byers, but I will come to her shortly.

Attorney Rick LeRoy spoke to me about some marks on Roger Caldwell's face, that the prosecution claim were defensive marks indicating that the nurse had fought back when he killed her. Rick stated that Marjorie and Roger had intended to purchase some acreage, nearby at Bailey, Colorado. Rick said, of course, they had no money. Everything was on paper but they had access to the place. Roger had a dog out there, and he claimed he was kicked by a horse. However, these marks were on Roger prior to the homicide according to Rick. It's a distinct possibility that Roger may have fallen down drunk. Considering Roger's alcoholism, Rick stated that you could not miss this guy after he had been drinking. He was obnoxious and a gross pain in the ass. Rick confirmed what I had already found out about Roger. Rick stated that his drinking was progressive and it got to a point where he would negotiate with Marjorie about his drinking. For example, he would say he'd only drink a certain amount of wine or a certain amount of beer, but that never worked, obviously. Ask any AA member about controlled drinking. He had gone into treatment. Rick had had some "go arounds" with him when he was drunk and once Roger was arrested on the street intoxicated. Rick stated he was with Roger and Marjorie consistently and knew how they behaved. They lived in adjoining rooms. He was a 17 year old boy at that time, and certainly quite bright. He said they had three vehicles that were repossessed, but once in a while he was allowed to use his mother's repossessed car. He stated that Roger at a point in time had rented a yellow Cordoba Chrysler. No such vehicle was ever seen in Duluth or no one ever claimed that a yellow Chrysler was involved in this case. I informed Rick about my interview with the manager of the alcohol treatment center and also the interview with Roger's boss. Roger's boss has what he called the "Roger Rule", that being no one was allowed to drink at lunch and return to work. Roger at one time, over lunch, drove down a blacktop road and his tire fell off but he kept driving on the rim. He was unaware of the tire falling off. He was stopped by a police officer. He didn't understand what was going on. The treatment center manager informed me that they had an aversion program and confirmed that Roger, based on their evaluation, was an alcoholic. I do not agree with the aversion method of alcohol treatment but the point is he was evaluated by knowledgeable people who concluded Roger was an alcoholic.

My contention is Roger was drunk again the weekend he allegedly went to Duluth, Minnesota for the purpose of killing Elizabeth Congdon. I also believe Marjorie may have been covering up his drunken behavior. She was vague and seemed confused when I questioned her about the entire week's activity on the part of Roger. It is not the least bit uncommon for a spouse to cover up for an alcoholic partner. One would find it implausible to imagine a person

Chapter 1 - The Congdon-Pietila Homicide

such as Roger fortifying himself with a few drinks and heading off to commit a murder. A drunk such as Roger would not be able to function.

Frank Berman assisted in the defense of Marjorie along with Carol Grant. Frank is a tenacious business lawyer and long time friend of Ron Meshbesher. His expertise is contracts, insurance, estate issues, and of course, he is noted as a litigator and tough negotiator.

Frank and I met in Denver, my second trip to that lovely state, to continue our investigation. We had a witness list but I must say, most of the folks we interviewed were not much help to us. They were only helpful to the prosecution in the area of Marjorie's and Roger's convoluted business matters. If this makes one a killer, beware of anyone who has serious credit card debt or gone bankrupt. I had already interviewed the hotel maid and Rick LeRoy established Roger slept in his own bed over the weekend. Now as a matter of routine, we interviewed witness Candace Byers.

Candy is dandy

Candy Byers was a waitress at the hotel where Marjorie, Rick and Roger were living. She had given a 3/4 page statement to the police that was truly a piss poor piece of work. Candy was on duty as a server in the coffee shop she told us when three cops came in to the shop and questioned her about Roger. She told us this not only frightened her, it was embarrassing. Customers were occupying a table and booths at the time and being interviewed in public was quite unsettling to her. In her brief little statement, lacking any detail, she said she did not see Roger that weekend. Bingo-bango, end of story the cops thought.

As with any witness, Frank and I had an in depth, thorough interview with his very nice woman. We went to her residence, a mobile home in a country setting. She was married to a young student. At about 8:00 PM she recalled taking a beer out of the cooler to drink in the lobby during her break. It was an out of character thing for her to do. She felt guilty about what she had done. She saw Roger Congdon walk down the staircase to the lobby. They greeted each other. Byers had waited on Roger frequently and they knew each other.

Her placing Roger that Sunday evening at the hotel unbeknown to her was extremely important. Mrs. Byers stated with emphasis that she had never in the past snuck a beer out of the cooler. This woman was very credible. We now had Byers, Rick LeRoy, and the hotel maid supporting our position that Caldwell was in Colorado on Sunday and Monday morning. Ultimately there was zero evidence that Roger Caldwell ever traveled to Minnesota and committed this horrendous crime.

When I returned to Minneapolis after the Byers interview, I met with Ron Meshbesher, gave him a verbal report, then a written report. Now the rules of discovery in a criminal case require the defense to provide to the prosecution any reports or statements of witnesses that the defense will call to testify. There was a holiday the day I met with Ron Meshbesher concerning Mrs. Byers and Meshbesher called prosecutor DeSanto to inform him that his investigator interviewed Byers. Ron offered to send a copy of my report by messenger to DeSanto's office. This took place, of course, prior to advance technology that all offices now have such as fax machines and e-mail by computer. DeSanto told Ron he would get the report from him at court when they reconvened later that week.

When Ron and DeSanto met again at court, my report was turned over to the prosecutor pertaining to Candace Byers. I was not present, I was sequestered throughout the trial so I did not witness DeSanto's response to receiving the Byers report. I was told later that he was apoplectic, accused Ron of sandbagging him, not playing by the rules, etc. DeSanto made every effort possible to turn the Byers situation around, but to no avail. Mrs. Byers ultimately testified and I was told by attorney Carol Grant that Byers was an excellent witness and she appeared to be very credible. She did not waiver from what she had told Frank Berman and I in Colorado.

After Byers testimony that seriously damaged DeSanto's case, I learned she became the target of a rather nasty investigation by the government. When I say the government, I mean the prosecution and their investigators. She and her husband's finances were looked into, investigators contacted her friends, neighbors and people and work and in essence gave her the " full monty." Naturally, DeSanto was hoping to find evidence of wrongdoing on the part of Mr.

Chapter 1 - The Congdon-Pietila Homicide

Berman and me. Obviously they were looking for information that would reveal intimidation, coercion or bribery on our part, but their search was in vain. In checking the Byers finances, they would be looking for a sudden bump in a bank account, or checking account. There was absolutely nothing to find. I am sure this was disheartening for the prosecution team, but that is life in the big leagues.

It's very difficult for prosecutors to accept that the defense plays by the rules, behaves in an ethical way and treats witnesses with the utmost respect. Prosecutors and many government investigators take the position that only they are the ones who are interested in truth and justice. You see this on television programs, in movies, but we all know there have been serious cases where the prosecution failed to act in an honest, ethical way. There have been numerous cases of prosecutorial misconduct and police misconduct or outright incompetence. I have already cited the Jonbonet Ramsey case and the Duke University Lacrosse players' case.

Thanks to the Northwestern University School of Journalism, students investigated several criminal cases that took place in Cook County, Illinois. At least five of these cases were overturned due to the efforts of these journalist students and these were cases involving homicide or rape where it turned out the wrong people had been convicted. The cases were overturned. The journalists found corruption among some police investigators and prosecutors along with a degree of incompetence with some public defenders. It must be noted that public defenders offices do not have the resources to present a very strong defense because they cannot retain experts, DNA, reconstruction scenes, and they are limited on what they can spend interviewing witnesses. All I can say is Hooray for the Northwestern School of Journalism.

A key player in the Congdon-Pietila homicide case was a rather unsavory investigator by the name of William Furman. During his testimony, he took the Fifth Amendment over fifty times and I'm certain the jury found this individual to be quite disgusting. This Furman is the person that Marjorie's cousin, Tom Congdon, who resided in Colorado, hired for the purpose of protecting him. The following is my experience with one of the most untrustworthy people imaginable.

More witnesses

During my first trip to Colorado, I was calling potential witnesses from my hotel room hoping to line up people that may have had information about Roger and Marjorie's background. Not only was I concerned with Marjorie and Roger's whereabouts over the weekend of the homicides, I was concerned with their behavior and demeanor while living in the Golden, Colorado community. I had a list that I made of witnesses and Tom Congdon certainly would have been able give us some family history so I called him hoping for an interview. Mr. Congdon dismissed me in about 30 seconds stating he was leaving on a six month tour around the world and he didn't have time to see me. After hanging up the phone, I wondered if he was really taking this world tour or if he was, like many people you run in to, just did not wish to be interviewed. I soon found out that Mr. Congdon, who I refer to as "Tommy Tinker Congdon", had indeed been tinkering around with this case having hired William Furman to do his bidding.

About an hour and a half after Congdon's rejection, while still in my hotel room, I took a call from Furman. He told me he was a private investigator hired by Thomas Congdon to protect Mr. Congdon because his client felt he may have been in danger. This I found rather questionable, but Furman went on to state he wanted to meet with me at my hotel coffee shop. I readily agreed to a sit down with this guy because I became suspicious of why Congdon felt threatened and why in the world would he hire an investigator when this was a police matter. The Colorado Police agencies and the Minnesota-Duluth Department had been working on the case, so why would Congdon have someone involved. Certainly I didn't think his welfare was in jeopardy, there was no mad-dog revenge killer on the loose and Roger Caldwell, by this time was in jail. Certainly Marjorie Caldwell, who the police were keeping an eye on, was not a threat to anyone and she was not in contact by telephone or mail with Thomas Congdon.

Chapter 1 - The Congdon-Pietila Homicide

William Furman appeared at the motel I was staying at and we proceeded to the coffee shop and sat in a booth. As I remember Furman, he was rather stout, dark haired with a mustache and was wearing a sport coat. He put both of his arms on the back of the padded booth. I was sitting, as I remember, to the right of him, perhaps three feet away. When his arms went back, his sport coat went open and I could see he was carrying a holstered gun under the left arm. My immediate thought was this was out of a "B" movie or some ridiculous television police show? It was of course his attempt to impress me. This kind of crap does not impress me in the least, it's so staged and bogus that it's almost laughable. I bit my tongue and refrained from any smart-ass remarks and Furman wanted to know if I found anything out it would shed light on the homicide case. Needless to say I told him thus far the attorneys and I had very little to go on, and certainly I wasn't about to give this guy the time of day. My physical makeup is such that I do not look very intimating or threatening or tough, and I've always been friendly and polite. That just happens to be my nature. It is possible Furman took me for some hick living in the north woods next to Canada. I neither know nor care what his take on me was. It's been my philosophy that you catch more flies with honey than vinegar so I just kind of went with the flow. Furman liked to brag, told me about all the important big time cases he worked on that took him to California, Las Vegas, and basically all over western United States. He certainly let me know that he was a tough, rough and tumble private investigator and I of course went into my "gee whiz, holy smoke" mode and let this asshole play out his role.

Furman flapped his tongue for about a half an hour, and we exchanged calling cards. And the meeting obviously was not fruitful for either party. However, it did raise my antenna to the point where I felt I had to obtain information about Furman and try and determine what the hell his real role in this case was. He did call me a few times later when I had returned to Minnesota but I just schmoozed him and we did not learn anything from each other.

After that meeting with Furman, I returned to my room at the hotel, went to the yellow pages and started looking for this dog under investigators. I could find nothing so I began calling other private investigative and security firms to determine if someone knew of

Whatever happened to Lady Justice?

this, William Furman. I hit a home run when I called the Thomas and Visser firm, spoke to a secretary at their Denver office and she stated that a partner, Jim Visser had a case that involved Furman. She stated it was a negative experience that Mr. Visser had been involved in, but he wasn't in the office at that time to speak with me. The woman stated that Mr. Visser was expected to return momentarily and I plead with her tell him I called, that it was urgent and that I was in route to his office.

I have a bit of the Irish luck, perhaps a guardian angel, but in meeting Mr. Visser at his office, I had a feeling that I struck pay dirt. Jim Visser was a very gracious, professional, intelligent man, tall, slender, quite handsome, and he immediately became interested in Marjorie Caldwell's case. I had Ron Meshbesher's office send a Retainer to him as a good-faith gesture and he agreed to do a thorough background check on Furman. He had already had an experience in dealing with Furman and it was a case where Furman made an attempt to sell information on his own client to a prosecutor. Visser described Furman in a very negative way. He further explained that in the state of Colorado, one did not need a license to open a private investigative firm. The reason, Jim explained, is the legislature couldn't get together on the requirements. Visser worked only for attorneys as I did and of course, in the state of Minnesota if you work for a lawyer, you don't need a private investigative license. At the time, however, I did have a Minnesota license.

Visser and his partner, Ron Thomas, provided a great deal of background information regarding Furman and, during the course of the trial, Furman was called to the witness stand. As previously mentioned, he took the Fifth Amendment over fifty times, and in court, Mr. Meshbesher brought out that Furman had stolen $15,000.00 from his employer, Tom Congdon. This is absolutely outrageous and it would have been interesting to hear what the jurors said about Furman. Ron Meshbesher also, in his excellent summation, informed the jury that Furman had every opportunity to plant evidence, such as the items that were allegedly stolen from the Congdon mansion by Roger after the murders. Furman's involvement may have given rise to the jury why Tom Tinker Congdon would have hired the likes of Furman. It would have been so simple for Tom Congdon to go to his attorney for a referral to a protection agency or

Chapter 1 - The Congdon-Pietila Homicide

private investigator or else go to the yellow pages as I did. I don't know. Tom Congdon hired one of the most devious, degenerate people he could find which leads me to believe Congdon and perhaps others wanted some unethical creep to work on the edges of the law in an effort to hang a jacket on Roger and Marjorie for the murders. This case was a police matter and there was something very questionable concerning Furman's involvement. It would be interesting to know if Congdon coordinated Furman's activities with the various police agencies and exactly what did the police agencies and the prosecutors know about Furman? Marjorie was under surveillance by private investigators from Minnesota when she was in her home state and she was often surveyed by Colorado police agencies when she was in the Golden, Colorado area. Furman would be reporting to Tom Congdon, but my question would be, did he ever report to DeSanto or the Duluth and Colorado police agencies. One will never know and one will never know how much he lied to Congdon and again having taken the Fifth Amendment to protect himself against self incrimination, we can only surmise that Furman was up to no damn good.

In Sharon Hendry's excellent book "Glensheen's Daughter" the author presented a fair and accurate presentation of the trial. She quoted from evidence that was presented, and she quoted at length excerpts from Ron Meshbesher's final argument. There was also an interesting point that came out in the book regarding attorney Frank Berman going to the evidence room at the courthouse for some purpose. DeSanto claimed that a piece of evidence was missing sometime after Berman had visited the room and the inference was Mr. Berman had taken a wallet that was logged in this evidence room, belonging to Roger Caldwell. A big issue was made over this and of course, search took place and the wallet just did not appear. What is puzzling to Meshbesher and the rest of us, why was the wallet even going to be in evidence because it was never used in Roger's trial up in Brainerd, Minnesota? I found the inference that Frank would do anything unethical, even illegal, to be rather appalling. But it is not uncommon for prosecutors to suggest, infer, and even accuse defense lawyers and defense investigators of engaging in unethical, even criminal behavior. The whole idea of throwing mud on the wall hoping some will stick and that a judge or jury may buy into the bullshit. Ms. Hendry's book, of course, covered more than just the trial. Marjorie Caldwell continued to make news in a negative way after she was acquitted. My concern in this book deals only with the homicide case, her post murder trial activity is not what I'm writing about.

Nasty, Nasty

I did not attend Roger Caldwell's trial in Brainerd, Minnesota, but I do believe one of the people at Meshbesher's office monitored this trial. In addition, Ron would have been speaking with Doug Thomson who was representing Roger, and Doug would have apprised Ron of what was taking place.

Rick LeRoy, Marjorie's son, who I mentioned is now working with the neighborhood justice center as a trial, lawyer, told me a story that didn't surprise but gave me a bump in my temperature.

Rick had informed me during our interview that his mother obtained an attorney to escort him to court in Brainerd, Minnesota. Rick was a very young guy at that time, 17 years of age, and no doubt the attorney prepped him about procedure and what takes place on the witness stand. I choose not to mention the attorney's name because I think he dropped the ball in this matter. He was a civil lawyer, not a criminal defense lawyer, and he allowed Rick to accompany a female prosecutor to a private room for an interview. Rick's attorney did not accompany Rick to that room. Rick informed me, this was all somewhat disconcerting and he was nervous over this but he cooperated with the prosecutor. He stated he was taken to a room at the Crow Wing County Courthouse in Brainerd, Minnesota, and the door was closed and locked behind him. He stated that also in the room was a police officer. Rick again reminded me that he was a juvenile at the time and certainly never experienced anything quite like this in his brief life. Rick stated that now as an adult he finds that entire incident outrageous. He stated the attorney that was supposedly babysitting him should have known better and that the prosecutor's office damn well could have treated him properly instead of verbally pushing him around. He was still a minor, and as I understand the law, you must have an adult with you under circumstances such as this if not, then actually appointed counsel. It's

Chapter 1 - The Congdon-Pietila Homicide

another example of prosecutors bullying people and taking advantage of the vulnerable who are in difficult situations. I have a number of examples I can present and will do so later on in this book.

Naturally, this female inquisitor did her utmost to manipulate young Rick and she particularly zeroed in on trying to get him to contradict himself. Rick stated in retrospect that he held up pretty well on the witness stand, told the truth, and in fact even landed a few blows for the defense. This did not surprise me. He is a bright man and did go through college, law school, passed the bar, and is now a practicing lawyer.

The burden of proof is on the Plaintiff, which means the State. The State did not and could not prove their case against Marjorie Caldwell. Concerning Roger, the poor soul who was a drunk, DeSanto knew Roger Caldwell would get a new trial and DeSanto could never face another ass kicking from Ronald Meshbesher. Are the grapes still sour in Duluth, Mr. DeSanto?

An incident that has come to mind pertaining to police conduct occurred when I was in Colorado on one of my trips to interview witnesses. I had lined up a man who was a wildlife artist and he had hoped to sell some of his work to Marjorie and Roger Caldwell. Apparently he didn't know that they had no funds, but this man was for certain a struggling artist. We met at the hotel coffee shop, and had barely settled in at booth when three police officers approached us. One of the officers announced that they were going to take this man down to the police station and interview him and that he would be back later. This was somewhat audacious: he and I were just beginning an interview when these cops approached. One police officer was left behind with me; God knows what they thought I would do if they left me alone.

This was all rather tacky and rude. Certainly the police would not stand for me announcing myself at the police station when they were interviewing someone and informing them that I would be taking that person off for my own interview. They would probably chuckle and then throw my body right out on the curb. It's disconcerting to think the cops may have had me under surveillance, tapped my phone or maybe had a spy in the hotel to keep tabs on anything pertaining to Marjorie and Roger Caldwell. Whatever, I remained with this Colorado detective for approximately 15 minutes and finally told him I was going down to the police station. I don't think I showed visible anger and I asked him no questions so he could tell me no lies.

I proceeded to the police station when our Van Gogh of the West was coming out of the interrogation room. He looked rather shaken up and we then met for a second time at the hotel coffee shop where I conducted my interview. This gentleman really didn't have a great deal to offer to either the prosecution or the defense. It was apparent he was not an affluent individual and the routine questions were asked of him. He's another one that ruled out Roger wearing turquoise jewelry in the last months prior to the murders and he also did not fly an airplane. We now had another person to refute the people at the kiosk in the Minneapolis/St. Paul Airport who claimed to identify Roger. The wildlife artist supported the pawn shop owner who in turn supported Rick who in turn supported Marjorie and Roger. There was also the Mahoganite carry-on bag that the kiosk witness mentioned. I had contacted all of the travel stores, luggage stores in the Duluth area to see if such a bag was in their inventory. I hit pay dirt at a store in the Miller Hill Mall, they had records showing that a couple of weeks before the homicides at the Glensheen Mansion, a Mahoganite bag was sold for cash. They had no name, but they had another bag in stock which I purchased. Was this just a coincidence? Nevertheless, Ron Meshbesher used the bag I purchased as demonstrative evidence in court. By the way, there was no such bag discovered to be owned by Roger, Marjorie or Rick and their residence was searched along with hotels they had stayed in.

Reflections

In a final analysis, the prosecution in the Congdon-Pietila case was not able to prove their position. There was a great deal for the jury to consider. Mr. Meshbesher brought forth so much reasonable doubt as to whether Marjorie Caldwell had orchestrated this terrible crime, the jury just could not convict, and Roger Caldwell was released from prison after admitting to the crime. He returned to his home state of Pennsylvania and told some reporters that he admitted to guilt just to get the hell out of prison. Roger then left a suicide note and, again, stated that he did not commit this terrible homicide.

Chapter 1 - The Congdon-Pietila Homicide

Marjorie Caldwell may have many character flaws, be eccentric or even suffering from some type of mental disorder, but that in itself does not mean she is a murderer. As I stated earlier in this chapter, it is not within my province to comment on the parts of Marjorie Congdon Caldwell's behavior that have nothing do with her homicide case.

Enough said. Time for something different: the rainmaker, Ronald Meshbesher.

Chapter 2

Numero Uno: Ronald Meshbesher, Esq.

I had never met a criminal defense lawyer until I went to work for the Robins, Meshbesher & Kirschbaum when they were in the First National Bank building, and then at 1616 Park Avenue in Minneapolis, Minnesota. My coworker and friend, Russell Spence, and I were working as insurance adjusters and investigators. Russ Spence was in law school at William Mitchell and was hired by the Robins, Meshbesher & Kirschbaum firm to act as their full-time investigator. When he graduated from William Mitchell School of Law, he called me to inquire if I was interested in replacing him as their staff investigator. At that particular time, I was not interested in making a change, but Russ, who was hired by the firm as an associate personal injury lawyer, called me back at a later date.

Naturally, I am elated and always will be with the call back because, in the meantime, the claims manager at Hartford offered me a job as the claims manager in their Duluth office. This may sound like it would be a terrific offer, but it was a one man office with a secretary and I was going to get a raise of approximately $75 per month. I turned that down and it occurred to me that when you turn down a corporate promotion, chances are it will not enhance your career.

I interviewed with the Meshbesher law firm and agreed to start work in November of 1964. I was given a modest raise and the promise of a raise in January and they honored their promise. In approximately July of 1965, Michael Robins, the senior partner, came into my office, asked how long I had been on staff and then gave me a $200 per month raise, which was overwhelming in those days. Ultimately, Michael Robins retired and moved to California. Jerry Singer joined the firm as did Thomas Kelly. The firm was growing and with the growth and increased responsibility, I found that if you did good work and were loyal you were rewarded not only monetarily, but in other ways.

Ron and Ken Meshbesher involved me in family events and, in fact, my wife and I were like their adopted relatives. Even when I became

Chapter 2 - Numero Uno: Ronald Meshbesher, Esq.

an independent contractor in approximately 1977, the family still included me in social gatherings. I have often thought how wonderful it was for my wife and I to be "adopted" by a fantastic Jewish family. I am most grateful.

Ron Meshbesher obviously is the rainmaker at the firm of Meshbesher & Spence because of his well-known name. I would say that perhaps 90% of people that I have interviewed know of Ron Meshbesher and respect his skills as an attorney. They all want to know what Ron is like. This is not to say that everybody loves him, some people have said that "he's the guy that gets those criminals off." That doesn't mean they hate him. My response to people asking what he is like is that he is the same person that I met over 43 years ago. He treats everyone, from the cleaning staff to a Supreme Court justice with courtesy and respect, he's generous, comfortable with himself and he has a terrific sense of humor. In the field of criminal law having a sense of humor is almost necessary because of the psychological stress. If you are going to make a career as a criminal defense lawyer, humor helps the stress. These lawyers are representing people who are going through possibly the worst period of their life and this is very serious business.

Often when I meet people and they find out what I do for a living, they want me to rate the criminal defense lawyers that I have worked for. I find that impossible to do and not really fair, although I will say that Ron Meshbesher is considered the dean of the defense attorneys by his peers. Naturally, since I have been with him for so many years, I consider him "numero uno." This, in no way diminishes the outstanding ability of the other notable criminal defense lawyers that I have had the pleasure to work with. Certainly I can name these people, but I absolutely refuse to rate them because each has a different personality and a different approach to juries, but all of them should be rated excellent.

Ron Meshbesher has a powerful intellect, an instant grasp of the facts and he seems to set the tone in the courtroom. By that I mean that he has an ability to get the jury to like him and it is all sincere. He has the ability to set up a witness for an explosive question and he always seems to be a step ahead of his opponent. Ron's cross-examination can sometimes be brutal, but without pissing off the jurors.

Many times after Ron has been successful in gaining an acquittal for a headline client, he will have a social gathering. It is not necessarily a celebration, but a get- together. He has often invited juries to these get-togethers to learn more about what jurors are interested in and to answer their questions. Often a juror will not hear the answer to a question that has been objected to and they remain curious. So this is really a two-way learning experience and it is also supportive of the jurors' decision.

Peter Thompson, after the Dr. John Najarian's acquittal, invited the jurors to a get together sponsored by the doctor's friends at his personal residence. He had me bring statements from witnesses that the jurors did not know about because there were 14 counts against Dr. Najarian that were dismissed by the judge. This involved all of my interviews, which were numerous. Peter wanted these jurors to know what these witnesses had to say. They would have testified, but their portion of the case was dismissed by the judge.

I interviewed Ron Meshbesher on April 1, 2004, at his office at 1616 Park A venue, Minneapolis, Minnesota where he has graciously provided space for me to work. He provided me with a copy of his biography which I have enclosed in this chapter. His credentials would knock the socks off an Italian Cardinal.

My questions to Ron were as follows:

Vinnie: What motivated you to enter the law profession as opposed to medicine, engineering or something else?

Ron: You know, the definition of a lawyer, Vinnie, is a Jewish kid who couldn't stand the sight of blood. But I don't think that applies to me. I've always wanted to be a lawyer as far back as I can remember. My Uncle Cy was a very successful lawyer. He was the rich uncle in the family and everybody sort of looked up to him. He was a pretty nice guy, and I don't know if that was it or not, but my dad, I think, was a frustrated would-be lawyer.

Chapter 2 - Numero Uno: Ronald Meshbesher, Esq.

He and his twin brother helped put their older brother Cy through law school. I think my dad sort of envied his older brother and always wanted to be a lawyer, and I think either directly or indirectly my dad influenced my decision to become a lawyer at a very early age.

My first legal job after law school was acting as a law clerk to the Hennepin County District Court Bench. In those days, each judge, and I only think there were only about 11 or 12 of them in the whole Hennepin County District Court, would rotate on what was called 'special term calendar.' The special term calendar would handle motions— all civil stuff at that time. There was another judge that rotated on the criminal calendar. But they needed a law clerk to do the research, and more often than not I wrote the legal opinions for the judges. They reviewed them, but most of them just accepted them as written. I did that for about eight or nine months. It was a good job because I worked for a different district court judge every month, got to see them in action, got to see how personalities play a role in decision making, and some judges were sharper than others, but even the ones I didn't think were as sharp as others taught me a lot. A lot of it has to do with your disposition and some of it common sense. Since I worked in the courthouse I had an opportunity to watch the better lawyers try cases, and every chance I had at every moment I would go down and watch a case. Even in law school I remember standing in line to watch the Axelrod murder case.

There was a big line, but I waited in line as a second-year law student and watched a lot of that case. There were some good lawyers on the case. Sid Goff was defending, and he had a reputation as one of the best criminal defense lawyers in the Twin Cities and he had an office in St. Paul, and he was a very, very good lawyer. I was very impressed with him. The guy was convicted of manslaughter as opposed to first degree murder, which I think was a pretty good verdict. I don't know if you remember the Axelrod case, Vinnie, but you and I are close to each other in age, but that was a case where a dentist by the name of Axelrod was accused of killing one of his patients. The motive being that he had impregnated her and she was going to blow the whistle to his wife and he denied it, but he was convicted of it. I remember one of my colleagues in law school was saying that the guy was just filling the wrong cavity. Her body was found in the Lake of the Isles district behind the home, in an allyway, near the home of Cowles, one of the owners of the local newspaper. It was quite a front page story.

As I started to tell you, working around the courthouse I not only saw and watched good lawyers at work, but I met a few people in the county attorney's office and I knew there was an opening there. One of the old timers was retiring and I applied for the opening, and actually, I probably got it through the assistance of my cousin Cy Weisman, who was married to my cousin Charlotte. Cy was active in the DFL. George Scott was very active in the DFL and he was a newly appointed county attorney. He had been appointed right before the Axelrod case, so he tried the Axelrod case along with two people in his office. He hired me in 1958 so I went right from the law clerk's job to the county attorney's office in March of 1958 as a young lawyer. I increased my wages. As a law clerk for the district court judges I was paid $400 a month, and working at my first job as an assistant Hennepin County attorney, criminal division, I got $500 a month. When I left the Hennepin County Attorney's Office, about three and a third years later in June of 1961, l was making a grand total of $8,900 a year.

I spent three-and-a-half years, almost — three years, three months actually— and tried every case I could get my hands on. I was fortunate because I was the young eager beaver in the office. Most of the guys had been there many years and frankly, had felt a little too comfortable in their positions. I went around saying."Hey, anybody got a case you want me to try?" They were more than happy to give it to me. And sometimes I second chaired some very good lawyers and like Judge Bruce Stone who became Chief Deputy, George Scott, Paul Jones who was the original one when I started. Bruce was a very good trial lawyer, very methodical. I worked with old Pare Larson who was a venerable lawyer in that office and highly regarded. He was practicing prior to bootleg days. He was telling me stories about breaking down houses of prostitution and prosecuting people under prohibition laws, and it was interesting working with him because he, too, was a very methodical lawyer in preparation. He never missed dotting an "i" or crossing a "t." Sometimes I thought he was being a little bit too careful, and it was kind of unnecessary, but he taught me that those things are extremely necessary. Even though they seemed silly at the time, every little fact has to be supported, has to be accurate. So I learned some good lessons, and in so doing I tried approximately 45 felony jury trials in the space of a little over three years.

Vinnie: That's quite a number of trials.

Ron: It was. When I left the county attorney's office I was 28 years old and was a seasoned trial lawyer. There weren't too many old time lawyers in town that had tried 25 jury trials. So it was probably the best experience I could have had.

I had wonderful mentoring. I mean, I started out being a real loser. I lost the first two or three cases and I said, " Hey, this is the wrong business for me," and I got the encouragement. They would say, "Hey, Ron, you're just starting out, give it a shot." Then after that I had a long string of victories. I won 40 or 41 out of the 45 cases I tried.

Vinnie: Well, having worked with you for close to 43 years, I know you were always meticulous and extremely well-prepared, and it's a pleasure to work for a lawyer who is so highly competent.

Ron: Well, I think I probably learned it in the county attorney's office. I also worked with the cops and sometimes the cops were very good in preparing the reports, sometimes they weren't. I learned from the old timers that if the cop didn't do it right: send it back, interview this witness, get that, and the cops realized I demanded the best from them, and, as a result, I had a very good rapport because some of the guys wanted an open and shut case. I was willing to take a gamble if I thought the defendant was guilty, or the suspect was guilty. So I took more risks with the cases. As a result, a lot of the cops sought me out with what they thought their tougher cases were. So I tried cases from auto — then it was called using auto without the owner's permission — auto theft, auto theft to first degree murder cases, and even tried a few civil cases. In those days we used to try paternity cases. They didn't have DNA and they didn't have real sophisticated blood testing. All they had was an exclusionary blood test. So I tried a number of paternity cases, which was fun. I had a wide variety of cases. I remember some very interesting cases.

Vinnie: Well, of course, we both know Russ Krueger. Was he on the force when you were there?

Ron: Russ was on the moral squad. I think at one time he was head of the moral squad. So I knew they also did a lot of drug stuff and I did prosecute some drug cases when Russ was there and these guys used to bring me some of the tough cases. Russ was a good buddy of mine in those days.

He's mellowed out over the years. And even gave me some help in the Wortnik case. The <u>Knotsheim v. Wortnik</u> case. He became my witness in the case and was very helpful. When I got a plaintiffs verdict in that case, which was a murder case where Russ couldn't even get an indictment, he treated it as though he had won his case. It finally vindicated him. So he became friendly with me after that time and then he got cancer and I think he sort of realized that life was too short and he became extremely friendly to me and very pleasant. I don't see him very often, but time heals a lot of wounds. He did some things in the Hayes case that I was very upset with. But I more or less forgave him.

Vinnie: Well, anyway, that was an interesting case, resulting in me suing the Star, as you know. You were a public figure so you didn't join that. They settled with me, which means I won, in my book. So when did you hook up with Mickey Robbins?

Ron: Well, I left the county attorney's office. Mickey Robbins was leaving his law firm and he had a pretty good inventory of

Chapter 2 - Numero Uno: Ronald Meshbesher, Esq.

personal injury cases — plaintiff's personal injury cases. And Mickey at that time was going almost exclusively in the securities business. He got involved in the hot dollar stock thing and it was a rave stock market. Stocks back in the late 50's, early 60's, but he didn't want to give up that inventory of cases and somebody recommended that maybe Ronnie might want to leave the county attorney's office as an experienced trial lawyer and we could probably give him some quick education in trying PI cases. So I went to work for Mickey. He guaranteed me $8,900 a year, otherwise I wasn't going to leave, and I got it in writing. I still have the letter. And he said I guarantee you $8,900 a year but I know you're going to make more. Well the first year with Mickey I made $18,000. So that was a big deal that I doubled my salary and it took off from there. But I did try a number of personal injury cases and had a good deal of success. He gave me some serious cases. In those days, if you got a $20,000-$25,000 verdict that was big money. And I had several of those in a row, so it was big money.

Vinnie: I don't know if you remember I did a little moonlighting for you folks when you were in the First Bank serving some subpoenas and stuff like that.

Ron: I do remember that. That's when we used to call you Vince.

Vinnie: Well, and of course, you know, your firm grew and you took on a number of other lawyers.

Ron: Well, what happened is Kenny was practicing law with his law school classmate, Joel Kirschbaum. They actually were in the same building we were in, the old First National Bank Building, which is now One Financial Plaza, but that was the newest office building in town. Dorsey was in the top. They were on the 22nd and 23rd and Mickey and I were on the 18th. So I went with Mickey in 1961. I think in 1964 Kenny and Joel and Mickey and I merged our practices. Even when I got out I started doing some criminal defense work. I thought it would be hard but it was easy. I went up to the jail, I think even the first month I got in private practice and I got a call from the

Whatever happened to Lady Justice?

jail from somebody who wanted me to represent them on an assault case. And I walked up to the old jail, which is under the clock in the Hennepin County Courthouse in City Hall, and I remember looking at all those guys in the cell blocks, the same guys that just a month before looked guilty as hell, all looked innocent to me. That was my first offense, it was an assault case. Assault in the first degree with a weapon, a gun, and the guy was acquitted: self-defense. And even though it was self-defense, the judge ordered that the weapon, which was Exhibit A in the case, be returned to the defendant's lawyer, who shall not turn it over to the defendant. I still have that thing.

Vinnie: Judge Tom Bergen was on the bench.

Ron: Hanging Tom. Well he was a good friend of my dad's. He was a better friend of my Uncle Benny.

Vinnie: They called him Hanging Tom?

Ron: Oh; yeah, he was a tough judge, especially on drunk driving cases. Of course, in those days they were doing— I'm not sure when it ended, but you couldn't get a jury trial in drunk driving cases. They used to charge it as a city ordinance. Finally, I think in 1955, the Minnesota Supreme Court said the Constitution requires a jury trial. So the city attorney's office had to change. They had these guys that had never tried jury trials before, and they got nervous. Everybody was demanding jury trials. In those days juries were acquitting a lot of alleged of drunk drivers, and the theory that was set back in those days was, that but for the grace of God go I. The juries could relate to somebody drinking and driving. They couldn't relate to a rapist or murderer, of course, but that's why those cases in those days were easy to win. Now, with all of the publicity and groups like MADD, which do good work, it's much harder to get acquittals in drunk driving cases. I never did a lot of drunk driving cases. I did mostly felonies. My brother Kenny became the specialist at drunk driving, and he used to win them right and left.

Chapter 2 - Numero Uno: Ronald Meshbesher, Esq.

Vinnie: I know. He excelled in that area. He was very well known in the community.

Ron: I think I only tried a couple drunk driving cases. But it was good to get a jury trial because people could go to jail. I think if you go to jail you're entitled to a jury trial.

There have been a number of changes, not just in the criminal justice system, but I think tremendous change just in the bar. The number of women practicing law has increased many, many folds. When I went to law school we had one woman graduate with us. Now, I understand the law schools are at least 50/50 of women and men. That's a major change, and a lot of them are getting involved in trial law. When I first started out there was only one woman trial lawyer that I knew and she was doing defense work. There were no female lawyers in the county attorney's office at that time. There are a lot of them now, and some damn good ones. So I think in terms of apparent change, that really was a major change. And in the criminal justice system, there have been a number of changes. I also should mention too when I'm talking about women's rights, that there was an increase, not as great an increase in minority lawyers. I mean you seldom saw a black lawyer in my day. There were a few of them but not too many. But now there are a lot of them and they're working with some big firms and on their own.

There was one African-American judge who was appointed when I was a young lawyer. I don't know if I was a prosecutor or defense lawyer at the time. It was either late 50's or early 60's. That was L. Howard Bennett, and there was a lot of prejudice in those days. People didn't say it; they found other reasons to dislike Howard Bennett. Bennett was a good judge, a very impressive judge on the bench. He was— I don't know how you put it— he used to irritate a lot of people because he was so dogmatic. I think that's the way to put it. But the Bar Association got together and ran Elmer Anderson against him and Elmer beat Howard Bennett. Elmer was a nice guy. I was sad to see that happen, but fortunately, since those days we've had many, many black lawyers. I don't know of a single black lawyer that's been defeated at the polls. Times have changed in that regard for the better.

Vinnie: Mike Davis is on the federal bench, Pam Alexander is District Court, and throughout the country there are minority judges. Good stuff.

Ron: Other changes in the criminal justice system, I think there's been a big emphasis on victim's rights, which is good now. We've had more thorough pre-sentence investigations. We always had them but I think they're much more thorough and judges get a better idea of the background of the defendant who's about to be sentenced. Also, in the early 1960's was the criminal revolution when the Warren court set out the constitutional rights that applied to the states for the first time. You had the Miranda warning, the search and seizures laws. Everybody thought the world was going to go to hell in a hand basket. The cops will never prove a case anymore. So I got involved in that at the early stages. And to be honest with you, we used to win a lot more suppression cases when those cases first came out because the decisions hadn't been honed down with the nuances that you see nowadays. Nowadays, actually, the Supreme Court over the years has whittled away on the search and seizure laws to the point where it's pretty difficult to get evidence suppressed today. There are many exceptions to it. So we've come almost full circle from the criminal law revolution, and that's because of the perceived and actual increase in crime and the government's war on crime, which essentially was a war on the rights of individuals.

I think it is a failure. In Minnesota we enacted a whole new set of rules of criminal procedure. I was on the committee for 20 years. We started in '71 with a pretty broad range group of lawyers covering all aspects of the law, not only criminal law, but some civil lawyers who were more neutral. In fact, Frank Clayborne, who I don't think tried a criminal case in his life, became chairman of procedure. "I said how come you're chairman, Frank, you never tried a criminal case?" "He said, well, they figured they needed some smart guy to handle you dumb criminal defense lawyers." But he did a hell of a job,

Chapter 2 - Numero Uno: Ronald Meshbesher, Esq.

and that's why we're very successful. In four years we put together probably the best rules of criminal procedure for any state in the country. And they're still in effect today, with some minor changes.

Vinnie: Is this a model you used when you went to Czechoslovakia?

Ron: Yes. When I went to Czechoslovakia with the bar association to discuss preparation of a code of criminal procedure, I left a copy of the Minnesota Rules of Criminal Procedure with them to give them an idea of how it worked. I said it may not work in your society, but I think some of the general principals can apply anywhere because the Czech Republic was fascinated with the idea of presumption of innocence. They lived in a communist country and they were determined to make the presumption of innocence the cornerstone of their criminal justice system and they wondered how it worked, and I was one of two American lawyers. The other one was Professor Goldstein from Yale University, a distinguished professor who was there. And then there was a Barrister from Canada. The three of us were the western advisors to the Czech Republic Committee which consisted of judges and the attorney general and their equivalent to the FBI. We had an interesting panel.

Vinnie: That's quite a feather in your cap. Have you heard what has developed since you were there?

Ron: I really haven't heard much. That was about 10 years ago. I've been remiss in not following up on what they did. I know it took them a while. Most of those people had to communicate through interpreters. There were a couple of professors of law that spoke very good English.

Vinnie: Nowadays people are nastier to each other. In the old days it seemed you could go out and have a cocktail with the prosecutor, and nowadays it's kind of harsh, almost uncivilized in certain respects.

Ron: Well, I think that's a good point. When I first started as a young prosecutor it was a custom for the defense lawyer and the prosecutor to go out and have a drink or what have you to await the jury verdict. We did it as a team, and that continued when I became a defense lawyer for a long period of time, and I knew all the prosecutors. We were friendly, we had drinks together, we socialized together, and to a great extent that's gone now. There's been a change and I think that some of the change is accounted for by the growth of the bar. I mean I think there were only about 3,000-4,000 lawyers in the whole state of Minnesota. Now there's close to 25,000 lawyers.

I think we have too many law schools. I thought that two law schools for the size of this state were sufficient. Then we had a third and now we've got a fourth in St. Thomas. I think the law school is unnecessary and I think we're going to turn out too many lawyers and there may not be enough work for all the lawyers. When that happens, you get lawyers who are fighting for a buck and sometimes will take shortcuts in the practice of law that they wouldn't otherwise.

Vinnie: That's exactly my feeling, and I was offended when St. Thomas came out with a law school with their sanctimonious attitude that we are going to be the ethical moral school. I mean that was a lot of crap.

Ron: Yeah, I know their dean who's a pretty nice guy. I've talked to him in a court meeting and I asked that question. I said, you know, I was offended by that too, and he well, perhaps I didn't phrase it properly. I said, you know, I think by the time you get somebody in law school if they don't know right from wrong, you aren't going to teach it to them. I mean that's all ethics is, is right from wrong. And I'm sure— you might be able to teach some cordiality, geniality among the bar that's lacking, and I wish you luck in that endeavor, but I said you're not going to teach ethics to people who are— the vast majority of them are close to 25 years old. By that age they are either ethical or dangerous. I mean, where have they been all their lives? But I wish them well. I think they've got a first grade law school and they've got some top people there teaching. Who knows? I just feel that we're going to have too

Chapter 2 - Numero Uno: Ronald Meshbesher, Esq.

many lawyers now. I think contrary to what the public thinks, most of these lawyers don't make a lot of money. Some of them are even scrambling now.

Vinnie: What about the sentencing guidelines now? I'm thinking about what's happened to Judge Rosenbaum.

Ron: The sentencing guidelines in Minnesota are basically guidelines, and the judge can usually find a reason to depart and order downward from the guidelines in any given situation as long as he articulates the reason and there's a factual basis for it. So you see judges here giving guys breaks and getting tough on guys who deserve it. The federal practicing guidelines are not just guidelines; they're basically mandatory sentencing requirements. A judge has a limited range of choice. Sometimes they'll say the guideline range is between 26 and 33 months. The judge can go as low as 26 and as high as 33. They can deviate but they have to have specific reasons that are approved by the guidelines. They're hard to come by. Usually the prosecutor has complete control of that, because if you want to become a witness for the government the prosecutor will give you credit for acceptance of responsibility, they have a right to make this notice of 5k1 motion to have your sentence reduced. The judges invariably go along with it because they want to encourage people to become snitches and informants, and so the prosecutor has the advantage. The defense lawyer cannot move for a downward departure, it's not countenance by the guidelines. What the guidelines have done, they have shifted the sentencing power from the federal judge to the prosecutor. The prosecutor basically controls the sentence by what crime he charges and what kind of deal he can make with the co-defendants. That's just the way it goes.

Vinnie: I understand there are a lot of judges that are very upset about this, and it's surprising that they're going after Judge Rosenbaum who is a republican. What is your sense about it?

Ron: Well, I think this present administration is getting bizarre. They have actually criticized Judge Rosenbaum for sentencing somebody to a 121 sentence in a drug case when the guidelines called for 121. He was called before the sentencing commission and I think they're trying to use him as a scapegoat to force judges to not only beholding the prosecutors, but to behold them to congress. Now there's a separation of powers, and they're keeping track now with judges who go below the guidelines without proper reasons. It's an intimidation factor. Almost every judge I know is against it. We recently had Judge Rosenbaum, who was never a bleeding heart liberal, and I told him so and he laughed. But Judge Rosenbaum spoke at our Inns of Court meeting a couple weeks ago and he got a standing ovation from about 150 lawyers who were there to show the support that the lawyers had for his stand in this situation. But he's concerned about it, and it has affected him emotionally. I said," Judge, it's not that it's just politics," and he said, " Yeah, Ron, you're not on the receiving end of it." I said," Hey, you're going to be okay."

Rosenbaum's a pretty good judge. He's never been one to issue a soft sentence, and the irony of it was, shortly after he got criticized by congress, the 8th Circuit reversed an insider trading sentence of his on the grounds that it was too high. They told him he had to cut it down by a couple years.

Vinnie: Well, it's gotten crazy, and my feeling about Ashcroft is he's a very dangerous person. Any guy that covers up a naked work of art has to be a little nutty.

Ron: Yeah, he did cover up the breasts of the Lady Justice at the Justice Department. I saw a cartoon once that showed a picture of the woman covered up and it showed a picture of Ashcroft and I think it said, "Which one is the boob?"

Vinnie: You know you mentioned informants, and that's been of great interest to me, having dealt with a number of them. It was an informant in the Long Cadillac case.

Ron: He was completely discredited years later.

Chapter 2 - Numero Uno: Ronald Meshbesher, Esq.

Vinnie: I think Peter Thompson went after him on his taxes, etc., and then in the Ralph Duke case, Jack Nordby, you probably remember, handled that appeal.

Ron: Wasn't it the same informant in that case too? The same guy that was in the Long Cadillac case is Chambers.

Vinnie: Yeah. He had been paid over two and half million dollars.

Ron: Oh, yeah, which he didn't declare on his taxes. I cross-examined the guy too.

My sense of it is that the government probably couldn't prove half those cases without these informants, and the incentive for these people to lie is tremendous. You're not only paying them money, but usually you're giving them their freedom. Now what's worth more than your freedom? If I gave a guy a $100 to testify, I'd go to jail for bribery, but the government can not only give him money, but they can also say instead of getting 10 years, we're going to give you probation and we're going to dismiss the charges against you. Now what's the motivation of this guy to do the bidding in the government? That's the problem with informants. And there have been federal prosecutors, one guy in particular, Steven Traut, who's now— I don't know if he's on the 9th Circuit Court of Appeals or a district judge in the San Francisco area, but he wrote a wonderful article talking about lectures he gives to prosecutors saying informants are the most dangerous witness you can have. He says they're notoriously unreliable, and you've got to proceed with caution when you're using a paid informant or someone who's getting a big break from him. And in fact, I copied one of his quotes in an article I wrote years ago about the misuse of informants.

This was in the Champion, which is the official magazine of the National Association of Criminal Defense Lawyers. I wrote my presidents column between '84 and '85. It's in one of those issues. I probably have a copy of that hanging around here I could dig up for you. You've got to remind me.

Vinnie: Yeah, I had one informant, you know, lie about me on the stand. It was very upsetting.

Ron: Well, wait a minute. Remember I had the Kenny Hayes case? Is that the one the informant lied about you?

Wayne Newcomb — God rest his soul — he got killed in a car accident in Arizona. But he actually flip-flopped on me. He was a witness for me and then the government got to him. I think— what's his name— Johnson, and maybe perhaps Krueger too, but he turned around, and then he had the audacity to say that I had driven up in my Cadillac to some place in northern Minnesota where he was staying and I paid him money to testify that way. I pinned him down on the date and place. Number one, I didn't have a Cadillac, I was driving a Lincoln at that time. It was not a question of being in court. What he said about the time I came up there, I had a number of witnesses, including Peter Dorsey, I was at dinner with him at McCarthy's Cafe and I had about five or six respectable witnesses. Had I not had those witnesses, I may have been sitting in jail today, because they wanted to believe this son-of-a bitch. He was lying through his teeth.

Vinnie: As you remember, he called me and I called him back and taped him and he was in jail in Dakota.

Ron: He was in jail?

Vinnie: Yeah, he said I owed him money or something. It was just bizarre. He was trying blackmail you. Then the Star did that dumb article. Had you ever seen any blatant examples of police misconduct?

Ron: Well, that case was. That case, because the cops turned this guy against me, and they threatened him with jail. He was drug addict. I don't know what they did, but, basically, his story was essentially corroborated, at least where he was at the time of the shooting, in the bathroom, he was the only guy there. That was corroborated by independent witnesses.

Chapter 2 - Numero Uno: Ronald Meshbesher, Esq.

Vinnie: I ran an ad, and that's how Newcomb showed up. His supervisor in the 180 degree house, Bill Rankin, brought him over.

Ron: And the guy that he said told him that, we subpoenaed him and he admitted he was in the bathroom at the time of the shooting. In fact, I was not going to call Newcomb because I don't know whether to believe the son-of-a-bitch or not, but after Strusand testified that he was there at the time and he ran out — he was on a parole violation and that he knew Newcomb and he had talked to Newcomb and the day of the funeral of the deceased in that case, Jerry Strusand lied and this corroborates almost everything that Newcomb told us, and after that I called Newcomb.

Vinnie: I tell you this; there was a so-called private investigator that was doing some background on behalf of Krueger. He called me all the time. They had no idea. They thought you were going to present a self-defense. They had no idea of your tactic. It knocked them right on their ass.

Ron: You take the witness where you find them. That's what the prosecution always says. By the way, there was another significant case of prosecutorial misconduct, or maybe police misconduct. I don't think the prosecutor was aware of it in the Piper kidnapping case where they— after having the FBI look at the fingerprint of the co-defendant, a guy named Larson, which was the key bit of evidence against the fingerprint on the bag that was found in the kidnap car, and they looked at it three times and said it wasn't Larson's, it wasn't Callahan's. Then two weeks before the statute of limitations was about to run on a five-year statute, they indict these two guys. And low and behold, their new witnesses— the FBI agent now says he made a mistake and he misidentified it three times and now he can identify it positively. I knew something was amiss, and I didn't find that out until those guys got convicted. Fortunately, we got him a new trial. At the new trial I had found a fingerprint expert who told me that that fingerprint is not Larson's, but the fingerprint has been what he called enhanced. I said what does that mean, does that mean it was forged? He said well, you can say that, I said well, use the language that the jury understands. I said please use it. Enhanced is the same as forgery in your mind? He says yeah, they doctored the fingerprint up to make it look like his to create points of identification. Now that's clear cut. I've got the transcript and I had a photographer to testify how they did it, and the reason my expert found out about it because the negative that they gave me of the print was blurred on the edges. These are contact prints. It should be completely in focus or completely out of focus. He said there's something amiss, this is not the original negative, this thing has been tampered with. A photographer backed him up on that. The U.S. attorney did not call a single witness in rebuttal of that testimony.

Vinnie: Who was the U.S. attorney?

Ron: Thor Anderson, and I don't think he had anything to do with it. He couldn't call a witness because they knew that our people were telling the truth. The jury acquitted these guys of the biggest kidnapping in the history of the state of Minnesota. Probably one of the biggest in the country where there's still a million dollars in unrecovered ransom money, and that was FBI misconduct. I know Thor Anderson, he's a man of great integrity, and I don't think he could believe it either. I just don't think he could believe it.

Vinnie: Well, how about the Congdon case with the fingerprint? Well, that was just carelessness. That was just dumb. They fired the expert?

Ron: He was incompetent. He didn't forge anything, he just completely misidentified it, and I used the same fingerprint expert who came in and said, "Hey, this is not only not his fingerprint, it's too big to be a fingerprint. It has to be a thumb print." They claimed it was a middle finger or something on and he said there are no points of identification here. There are three or four differences. You cannot make a case from that. That just blew the case out of the water.

Chapter 2 - Numero Uno: Ronald Meshbesher, Esq.

Vinnie: Well, I know you weren't involved in the Duke case. I was not involved in that case. They prohibited you from representing him. I worked on the appeal.

Ron: No, Kenny had done some legal work for him at one time and they said it was a conflict of interest. They claimed they were going to use Kenny as a witness but they never did. So Joe Friedberg got appointed, I think, or took over the case.

Vinnie: It was found out that the prosecutors, Denise Reilly and Hopeman, they knew the informant's background. It was never divulged to the defense and they let him testify. Jack Nordby did that wonderful appeal. He won the battle but lost the war, and then, of course, you know Howard Bass and I got involved *pro bono* and Bass wrote a wonderful document. It was sent back with no comment denying it. Is that unusual that they wouldn't comment on it?

Ron: Well, they do a lot of those on post-convictions.

Vinnie: I was disappointed because I had statements from about 23 witnesses.

Ron: These courts are getting very much conservative, and, as a result, you're seeing innocent people go to prison. Years ago, at least in those numbers, you didn't see.

Vinnie: Maybe Duke did a lot of things, but I don't think he did that case. I mentioned to you in this questionnaire some of the high profile cases you tried. We talked a little bit about Hayes. We haven't talked about Kronholm. That was an outstanding criminal case also that you won on a state level, which I almost fainted. I was in Chicago when I heard the results.

Ron: Actually the defendant's wife actually did faint when the jury said not guilty. That was in Anoka County. This guy admitted that he was the kidnap guy and that they — because they found two hundred grand in cash that was dumped on a freeway--and he went to pick it up. But he claimed that he acted under duress and he met Big Mike in a bar and I think the Black Angus bar in Minneapolis, who said that he was going to do this job for them and the boys from Chicago had to take care of him. So we called him Big Mike from Chicago and we thought it was all bullshit. And this guy — actually I had a pretty good plea bargain for the guy. He would have only had to do about three or four years and he would have got out but he wouldn't take it. He insisted on going to trial and he testified about Big Mike from Chicago, and I'll be damned, he was acquitted.

Vinnie: I'll never forget. Remember we were looking for that police officer. Johnson had crashed his car into the restaurant, fell out, and made a dying declaration and said Mike's boys — the cop thought he was dying. He was bleeding all over. He got shot in, the head. Do you remember that?

Ron: They claim he did it himself.

Vinnie: Well one of the FBI guys said I did it. It was out in Lakeville.

Ron: I think they claimed that Johnson did it as a setup for himself. I think he didn't intend to hit himself. He was going to shoot it through the car window and it ricocheted. I forgot about that. You've got a better memory than I do.

Vinnie: I can't believe the cop. I found him about one in the morning and he agreed to meet me and he came in and testified. I had a subpoena for him. But I asked him specifically, when you arrived on the scene, what did it look like to you? He said geez, there was blood all over. I said you think the guy was maybe dying? He said yeah, and what did he say to you? He said well, Mike's boys, you know, because the cop was well, who did this? He said Mike's boys. I couldn't believe it. Did the cop ever testify?

Ron: Yes, he came up and testified for you. He was a real straightforward honest guy.

Vinnie: He was a terrific guy. We got lucky on that. He could have easily told me get out of here. But that was a fascinating case. The one that, you know, I got really deeply involved — well I

Chapter 2 - Numero Uno: Ronald Meshbesher, Esq.

got involved with all of them — but that Congdon murder case.

Ron: Well, the Congdon murder case, according to media people, is Minnesota's case of the 20th century.

Vinnie: I thought the evidence was lacking. This is my personal feeling. Marjorie Caldwell is — to use a medical term — a nutcase. I just did not think that her husband was capable of coming up here and doing it, but there's been a book written about it.

Ron: They had a pretty strong case against the husband. I defended Marjorie and she was acquitted. The case against Marjorie was substantially weaker, especially when I disproved the fingerprint, and as a result of that fingerprint expert I dug up, who was a legitimate guy, one of the best guys in the country, and the FBI supported him and his opinion. Roger got a new trial. He had been convicted a year prior, and because the fingerprint was used to convict him he got a new trial. He ended up getting a helluva deal from the prosecutor. I didn't represent Roger because I represented his wife who was a conflict, but Doug Thomson did, and they allowed him to plead guilty. They said if you admit to the crime we'll give you time served. He was doing life. Double life in Stillwater. He had done five years by the time his conviction was reversed, so he said hell, I'll take that deal. He admitted it and as soon as he got out of court he said I didn't do it, and the only reason I admitted guilt was because I couldn't take a chance of going back to prison for something I didn't do.

Vinnie: Yeah, I remember that. He also left a suicide note and said he never did it. But anyway, that case is a book in itself. We talked a little bit about the Hayes case. There was kind of an emotional case — do you remember Sykes?

Ron: That was a very important case. In that case they accused Mr. Sykes of murdering his wife. That happened in Anoka too. And I think the case was in front of Pare Larson who was known as kind of a conservative judge. It turns out he was a terrific judge. I'd try anything in front of Larson but he's no longer with us. But the Sykes case, they claimed that the powder bums — that the swipes showed powder bums on his hand, a great amount, and he said I never had the gun, and I had nothing to do with the gun and denied it. There was the one guy I believed for sure because he said that they can give me the electric chair, but I'm not going to admit I did do it. I said they don't have capital punishment in this state. He didn't even understand that. He thought he was done for and going to the electric chair. So, anyhow, I dug up — I don't know if you remember the guy's name? Do you remember his name — the expert on neutron activation analysis?

Dr. Vince Gwen at the University of California Irvine. He did the analysis of the weapon and he said that the amount of gun powder on this guy's hand was so great that he had to have been firing a cannon. He tested the gun and the gun wouldn't have left that much. Gun powder was a small amount. He thinks that the police just screwed up the swabbing procedure or whatever they did and he was the key. He was the cornerstone of the acquittal in that case because we disproved the key bit of evidence. Dr. Vince Gwen, I'll never forget him. Terrific guy. I remember we went out to dinner with him at Charlie's Cafe in downtown Minneapolis after he testified. He was an expert on wine. He was giving us a tutorial on all kinds of wine. Not just California but French wines too. I probably over did it and didn't remember much about that. That case was back in 1965?

Vinnie: What about civil cases?

Ron: Unfortunately, a lot of states have put caps on civil damages. The Supreme Court certainly has put caps on the punitive damages. I'm more concerned about compensatory damages. I think because that really takes true compensation away from people who deserved it because of the wrongful act of a defendant when someone's loved ones are maimed or oftentimes killed. You look at it this way, a jury traditionally decides, and granted their intangible, but the jury is in the best position using all its discretion and the common sense, to award money damages commensurate with the injuries and the legislatures are putting arbitrary caps on them. So no matter how severely injured you are, you will never get more than a certain amount for your pain and suffering, things of that sort, we call that intangible damages. If you can prove economic damages, you can get that. But, for example, somebody is rendered a quadriplegic because some drunk driver goes through a stop sign, a young kid ruins his life and puts him in a wheelchair, that person will never get more in some of these states of $200,000 or $250,000 in pain and suffering, emotional distress damages. Never. Yet, somebody who perhaps can have a back operation, but he's still working and doing things, he's not completely disabled, he can drive a car and get around, the jury could give that person $250,000. You would be entitled to get the same amount as a paraplegic. Justice, as someone used to say, half of justice is half of injustice. It's like it's the half truth, and the other half is half lie. It's wrong, it's unfair, it sets the civil justice system back. In fact, it never was that bad. It puts a governor on the civil justice system that prevents full justice from being awarded to severely injured people. Perhaps if they even said well, in catastrophic injuries there's not going to be any cap, but they won't even say that.

Vinnie: And you've had a couple of these cases here. Here's one thing that the right doesn't bring up. There's risk often, you know, you're taking on a very expensive case and there's always a possibility you can lose it.

Ron: They're always critical of the contingent fee system. But the contingent fee system has always been thought of as the poor man's key to the courthouse, because if they have to pay a lawyer even a minimal amount to take the case, these people usually couldn't afford to do it. To pay them an hourly rate, they wouldn't want to take the risk. You know, many times I've offered injury people the opportunity, if you want to hire me by the hour, I'll give you this by the hour, or else I can take it on a contingency, where if I win, I get one-third of the amount, usually one-third, sometimes less. Never more than a third and we'll share it together. Otherwise, I'll just take it by the hour and if you win it all goes in your pocket plus the hourly rate. No one, in over the 40 years I've practiced law, has ever accepted my offer of an hourly rate.

They don't want to take the risk. They want me to take the risk, and so I'm the one that fronts the money for the case. Sometimes these cases involve three or four hundred thousand dollars in out-of-pocket expenses for expert witnesses, reconstructions experts, medical experts, you know, what have you. So the civil justice system is very important getting justice. The insurance companies, major corporations, are trying to limit people's right to justice, all for the almighty pocket. You know, these companies can spread the risk. They make up these phony figures on how much it's costing each individual tax payer. It's all bullshit. And they have this powerful lobby. And what happens, the average guy doesn't get in these situations so they think it's good they're saving a buck on their insurance premium which is phony anyhow, and they don't understand it, but when one of their loved ones or they get hurt in an accident, oh, I didn't realize the law was that bad. Then they don't realize it. Well how did it get that way. I said it got that way because people like you weren't alert to it and you believed the propaganda that was being fed to you by the insurance industry and corporate America, including the Chamber of Commerce.

Vinnie: Yeah, it's a great injustice. Regarding jurors, I have mixed feelings myself about jurors. I've seen — well, it was that one case down here your nephew handled. I thought that was such a terrible decision to convict that woman. I know most lawyers prefer a jury. They don't want to go in front of just a judge. Do you think maybe a panel of judges would be a better system?

Ron: The whole beauty of the justice system in this country is the jury. But putting caps, putting limitations on evidence, can basically take away the jury's power, which is a big mistake. When you get eight, ten, twelve people on a jury, there's twelve in a criminal case, and civil cases. It should be twelve I think. But twelve people from all walks of life will reach a

Chapter 2 - Numero Uno: Ronald Meshbesher, Esq.

much better decision than any given judge in any given case. Sure juries make some mistakes, but judges make more mistakes than jurors do.

Vinnie: It's hard to get a good jury, isn't it?

Ron: No, I have complete trust in juries. I've seen juries make mistakes and sometimes we're able to remedy it by getting a new trial, but I think the vast majority of times, juries, day in and day out do a wonderful job of meeting justice, both in the civil arena and in the criminal arena. Judges in my opinion make more mistakes. Judges become cynical, they become case hardened. Juries come in with no acts to grind, they don't have to run for reelection, they don't have to answer to the community, they sit on the case, they go home, and they've done their job. There's no pressure on them to reach a decision. They come together as a group. You can get a runaway jury one way or the other sometimes, but in the main I have great respect and confidence in the American jury system. It is the keystone of our justice system, and I'm fearful that the more they tamper with it, the less our justice system will be a justice system.

Vinnie: Well, I guess I just let a couple of cases bother me. One, of course, was the OJ Simpson case, and the other is the Martha Stewart case. Maybe you read there was a juror that lied. She may get a new trial over that.

Ron: Who knows?

Chapter 3

More homicide: T. Eugene Thompson

After that lighter interlude, something more gruesome: another homicide case. This time the defendant was one T. Eugene Thompson.

A recent book on the homicide of Carol Thompson has come on the market, but I have not read it nor do I intend to read it. My reason for not wishing to read this book is simply because of my involvement in the case doing a reinvestigation on behalf of Ron Meshbesher and F. Lee Bailey. Other books have been written about this matter, but I do feel an urge to present my findings in the course of my assignment by Mr. Meshbesher and Mr. Bailey.

I cannot say that I knew a great deal about T. Eugene Thompson. He was older than I and practicing law in St. Paul when I was an insurance adjuster for the Hartford in Minneapolis, Minnesota. The community knows that Mr. Thompson was tried and convicted for arranging the murder of his wife. After his conviction, he was incarcerated at Stillwater Prison in Minnesota. He made contact with F. Lee Bailey who agreed to visit him and ultimately represent him. When an out-of-state attorney comes to another state in which he is not licensed, he is required to obtain co-counsel, and F. Lee Bailey brought in Ron Meshbesher as co-counsel because they were friends.

Prior to the post conviction investigation for T. Eugene Thompson, Mr. Bailey and Mr. Meshbesher had also represented a chiropractor by the name of Jack Mitchell who was accused of killing his wife. Mr. Bailey's investigator, Andy Tuney and I did the investigation on behalf of Mitchell, and the jury found Mitchell guilty of manslaughter. Mitchell served seven years in prison on that case.

I only met T. Eugene Thompson in person on two occasions, but spoke with him by phone a number of times. I would describe him as a very intelligent individual. He had a successful practice in the City of St. Paul, Minnesota, but was regarded in the community as a bit cocky. I am in no position to state whether or not he was outwardly

Chapter 3 - More homicide: T. Eugene Thompson

cocky, he treated me with respect and appreciation. Mr. Thompson had reddish hair, was a father of children, one of which became a prosecutor in a southern county in Minnesota and is very highly regarded. Mr. Thompson had been married to a respectable woman from a somewhat prominent family in the City of St. Paul. He was known to carry a large sum of money in his pocket, for what reason I do not know.

T. Eugene provided me with some useful information to proceed on his case and vehemently professed his innocence of killing his lovely wife, Carol Thompson.

Attorneys representing T. Eugene hoped to get a new trial and were able to obtain a post conviction hearing in front of Judge Douglas Amdahl. Judge Amdahl was a Hennepin County judge with an excellent reputation, known to be fair and scholarly. The year was 1963. Andy Tuney, who was F. Lee Bailey's investigator, had to return to the east coast to work on active cases so I hit the bricks in an effort to come up with information that would assist the attorneys.

Aside from the principal in this case, T. Eugene Thompson, there were other players. Norman Mastrian, who was the accused middle man, Hank Butler, Donald Sharp, Willard Ingram, and Shelly Morris were witnesses for the prosecution. Norman Mastrian had been convicted in Duluth, Minnesota as a player who set the crime in motion. Mastrian had an excellent defense presented on his behalf by noted attorneys John Cochrane and the late Doug Thomson. These two attorneys were from St. Paul, Minnesota and needless to say were disappointed by the guilty verdict of Mr. Mastrian. There was an appeal on that case and that is when I first met Judge Jack Nordby who went-to work with Doug Thomson in the 60s. He wrote one of his excellent briefs, but was not successful in his appeal of Mr. Mastrian. To this day, Mr. Mastrian professes his innocence and approximately a year-and-a-half ago he phoned me with a desire to get together. He never followed up with a lunch request. I have no idea Mr. Mastrian's age, but am guessing he is close to 80 years old.

The other players involved were in jail prior to the trial and they came forward to state that they had information about T. Eugene Thompson. The authorities jumped at the opportunity and made some deals with these guys. For example, we received information that they were taken out of jail on occasion for dinner, etc. Willard Ingram, who had been a three time loser prior to the charges that put him in jail during the Thompson arrest, after the Thompson case was soon released from jail as was Butler, Sharp, and Morris.

Dick W.C. Anderson had been charged and convicted as being the hit-man of Carol Thompson. Allegedly Mastrian was given a deal by T. Eugene to find someone to kill Carol Thompson. Supposedly he farmed this horrendous task out to Dick W.C. Anderson but it is not known to me how much money was involved for this contract to kill.

The whereabouts of Butler, Sharp, Ingram, and Morris were unknown to me but we were aware that Dick W.C. Anderson had been transferred from Stillwater Prison after it was discovered by the guards that he was carrying around a recantation letter. He was going to send this letter to the prosecutor, Mr. Bill Randall, of Ramsey County in St. Paul, Minnesota. Randall, as many of us know, was described as resembling Abraham Lincoln and he was a very strong presence in the Ramsey County community. Mr. Randall, now deceased, was smart, tenacious, and tough along with having political ambition.

The post conviction issues that were presented by Mr. Meshbesher and Mr. Bailey were as follows: 1) Pretrial publicity; 2) Incompetency of defense counsel; 3) Failure to sequester the jury; 4) Promises and inducements to witnesses that had been in jail and cooperated with the prosecution; and 5) Journalists were allowed to sit inside the railing too close to the defendant and prosecutors.

Working the streets

I began to make inquiries among some known street people, some were former clients of Mr. Meshbesher, others were smart ass guys that claimed to be in the know. Close to the eleventh hour, I was contacted by Tommy Gray and ultimately Lyle Simonson, Donny Larson, and another elderly man whose name I can't recall. The elderly man was a former safe cracker but was working as a locksmith. None of these people were in prison when they contacted me.

Chapter 3 - More homicide: T. Eugene Thompson

We set up a meeting at the Meshbesher law firm at 1616 Park Avenue, Minneapolis, Minnesota and we met in the kitchen/lounge area in the lower level of the building. There was a liquor cabinet and other beverages available for special occasions and certainly I was generous in pouring beverages for this group of men. All of these men stated they knew Dick W. C. Anderson who had been a daytime burglar along with some of the other characters involved. Their M.O. was that of salesmen pushing siding for houses, which in fact, was true. They would call on farmers out in the country and if no one answered at the home, they would burglarize the house. If someone was at home, then of course they would try to sell them siding.

Anderson was described to me by the men I met with as weighing about 125 pounds, an alcoholic, and a guy that also popped some pills. He may have been arrogant and talked like a tough guy, but he was not a tough guy by any means. He was involved in pretty shady activity along with the daytime burglary operation, and he was a frequent patron of sleazy bars. According to the men I met with, Carol Thompson could have knocked Anderson flat on his ass. These guys that I met with were convinced Anderson was not the culprit that committed this brutal murder.

For those who recall the headline coverage of that murder, and for those too young to know the case, Carol Thompson was attacked in her own home. She was hit with a pistol that fell into pieces, the attacker then tried to drown her in a bath tub and ultimately stabbed her. The killer must have left because somehow she made it to a next door neighbor's and died on the back door step of her neighbor's home. This homicide was just horrid and was followed closely in the media. The Twin Cities of Minneapolis and St. Paul had very few homicides and certainly nothing that matched the brutality of this killing.

Donny Larson and Tommy Gray thought this murder had all the ear marks of a guy like Willard Ingram. Ingram was a very violent individual and as previously mentioned, was residing in one of the county jails awaiting trial. His history reflected this man was quite vicious. Donny Larson told me of an incident where Ingram pistol whipped a 65 year old waitress needlessly while he was sticking up a restaurant.

Whatever happened to Lady Justice?

Another incident Donny mentioned was Ingram being in a fist fight with a person much bigger than he was who was beating Ingram almost senseless. Larson said blood was actually running down inside Ingram's pant legs, but he continued to do battle. It was as if Ingram had no fear and a high tolerance of pain. Certainly Ingram had little or no compassion for anybody and as a lay person I am guessing he was a sociopath or psychopath. Seeing as he was a three time loser and having gone to prison, on his last visit the warden probably should have thrown the key away to his cell.

These four guys were helping me out with information and told me they would try to locate the whereabouts of Butler, Sharp, Ingram, and Morris. They also stated they actually liked Anderson and their theory was Anderson may have been along for a daylight burglary of Thompson's house, but so stoned he was left in the car while Ingram went in the house. These guys knew all the players and were certain that even on Anderson's best day, Carol Thompson could have handled him physically. However, not many women, let alone men, could have handled a guy like Ingram.

These guys that helped me out also knew that Thompson carried a lot of cash and had a lot of cash in his home. They described Mr. Thompson as a flamboyant attorney back in those days, smart, but cocky.

Tommy Gray and his friends' theory was this was a daytime burglary, and when the house was entered the person was surprised by Carol Thompson who fought with the intruder and the guy ended up killing her. All along this murder for hire, as it was known, had to do with T. Eugene receiving a large insurance payoff. Thompson had informed me when I visited him in Stillwater that he had planned to take a year off with his family and do post graduate work at Northwestern University. He said he had quite a bit of travel and term insurance which was extremely cheap, to purchase. As I recall, the beneficiary payment would have been around 1 million dollars and back in the 60s that was a huge, amount of money.

Because of the help I received from Tommy Gray and his friends, I was able to interview Hank Butler in a bar on Franklin Avenue. I remember Hank Butler as being a very handsome, blonde, fit-looking

Chapter 3 - More homicide: T. Eugene Thompson

individual who was somewhat soft spoken and quite calm. About all he admitted to me is that there were some special privileges granted to him and others while he was in jail for assisting the prosecution. He really didn't say a great deal to me and my assessment was that Mr. Butler was not acting like a star witness in this case.

I was able to meet Don Sharp at an American Legion hall in a western suburb of Minneapolis. When I met him in a booth, he had a drink in front of him and appeared to be somewhat in his cups and by the time the evening was over, I was half in the bag myself. That was long ago during my drinking days. Sharp also admitted to me he received promises and inducements for his testimony in the T. Eugene Thompson case. I took a handwritten statement which he signed, but this alone was not enough to turn the case around.

The old timers put me on to Shelly Morris and said he had a trucking company and an office behind a gas station up in the Plymouth/New Hope area north of Minneapolis. All I remember is that I drove Highway 169 to his apartment in an attempt to interview him. I had been introduced to a fellow also named Morris who held some type of a grudge against Shelly Morris and he agreed to show me the apartment. We proceeded to this apartment complex one night at about 1:00 A.M. believing that Shelly would be home by that hour. This was a security building, the building had many units and Morris who was helping me, used a credit card to slide back the front door lock. That's the only time I was involved in a breaking and entering incident and I'm sure the statute of limitations has expired.

We went up to Shelly's apartment, I knocked on the door and after a brief period of time a voice responded saying "Who is it?" Through the door I told Shelly Morris who I was, who I worked for, and that I had a subpoena for him which, of course, I did. Shelly became very angry, shouting through the door that he had immunity and protection from Prosecutor Randall and I should get the hell out of there. He was not going to testify at any hearing.

It's improper serve to slide a subpoena under someone's door or leave it in their mailbox, so I had no choice but to leave. However, I had information Morris was taking a trip to Hawaii and leaving quite early that morning. I went home, grabbed a couple hours of rest, and then drove to his office. I parked in a very unobtrusive area where I could view the gas station and his office. Shortly thereafter, a car pulled up and parked. The driver got out and I recognized Morris so I jumped out of my car and shouted to him. Morris took off running so I chased him down in a parking lot and slapped him on the back with the subpoena. One must touch the person being subpoenaed with the document and that is exactly what I did. I can't describe how pissed off Shelly Morris was at that time.

About a year after the post conviction hearing for T. Eugene Thompson, I was having lunch at Danny's Bar & Grill at 15th and Chicago Avenue in Minneapolis. This place is no longer in existence. Shelly Morris came over to my table smiling and in a friendly-way stated "When you came to my apartment that night, I had a .38 pointed at the door and if you would have as much as jiggled the handle, I would have blown your ass away." I am not sure what my reaction was at the time, but I honestly believe he was pulling my chain. I don't believe that Mr. Morris would have done such a stupid thing as shoot through a door at a guy trying to do process service. That's the last time I ever saw Shelly Morris and I am not sure what his story was in connection to the Thompson matter.

Last but not least is Willard Ingram. Donny Larson was able to track down Ingram's wife in some state of this union. Donny knew her and convinced her that he was helping out a guy that may be able to help Willard's old pal, Dick Anderson, get a new trial. Donny said that he wanted to meet Willard and introduce him to me. The woman gave Donny Willard's whereabouts which was attending a classroom session at a Holiday Inn near the airport in Chicago, Illinois. Apparently the class had something to do with farm machinery, a grain dryer as I recall. Willard would have been the front man contacting farmers, co-ops, etc. attempting to interest the prospect about this machinery. Then there would be a follow-up by the salesman, a person who was good at closing a sale.

Donny and I flew to Chicago and checked in the same hotel where the seminar was taking place. We arrived while the seminar was still in session, went to our room and the plan was that Donny would wait outside the class and talk to Willard. Donny took Willard to the bar for some drinks and then the plan was to escort Willard to my room

Chapter 3 - More homicide: T. Eugene Thompson

for an interview. I nervously sat in that room waiting for these two mugs. I had some beer and a small bottle of whiskey available for when these guys returned. Again, those were during my drinking days. I watched a little TV and finally called Ron Meshbesher at his home expressing my concern that Donny and Willard hadn't shown up yet and it was about 10:00 p m. Ron told me to relax and sit tight. Realistically, I had no other options.

A short time after 10:00 p m., there was a loud banging at the door. I opened the door and there stood this wild eyed, wiry guy with big Donny Larson standing behind him. Willard burst into my room yelling "What the fuck is going on?" He started opening drawers, looked in the closet, in the bathroom, under the bed, and obviously I was fearful. Thank God big Donny was there. Donny tried to calm him down. Willard even stripped the covers off my bed.

Donny explained with Willard periodically interjecting that they had gone to the bar and were drinking some beer at a table and talking quietly. Donny explained the bar was practically empty except for a couple guys sitting quite a distance away from them who were also having a drink. Donny said they could not possibly have heard what we were talking about. Either Donny or Willard then said to me "One of these guys got up, came over to our table, introduced himself and said, "Hey, I'm from Minneapolis, too. Why don't we go down to such and such a place and have a drink?" Well naturally, this freaked the hell out of both Donny and Willard. How would these guys know that they were from Minneapolis? Willard expressed to me that he thought he was being set up or something.

At any rate, both Donny and I were very up front with Willard and I showed him my driver's license, calling card, pictures of my kids, anything that would calm him down. I explained to Willard that my boss, Ron Meshbesher, was attempting to get a new trial for T. Eugene Thompson and in the process that there was a strong possibility this would benefit Dick Anderson. I was not making up a story. I had no reason to because if the attorneys were successful at the post conviction hearing, this would open up a can of worms over the entire case.

Whatever happened to Lady Justice?

I did not know what prison Dick Anderson was in. We never had an opportunity to attempt an interview with him. However, he had written a recantation letter which was confiscated when it was discovered in prison, and he was immediately transferred out of Stillwater. I have never lied to a witness for any reason. Often I must testify in court and there is no way in hell I am ever going to perjure myself or convince someone else to lie on the witness stand.

Willard, Donny and I had a drink and he finally calmed down. My questioning of Willard began in a gentle non-accusatory way. From time to time, Willard blurted things out that truly knocked my socks off. At one time, he made the statement, "I can still see that broad with her legs in the air and I wanted to go right for her pussy." How can one ever forget that kind of a comment made by a very scary guy under stressful circumstances? Several times Ingram stated "If I get hurt on this deal, you're going to get hurt." Ingram said enough to me in front of Donny Larson to convince me that he's a very dangerous human being and he damn well may have murdered Carol Thompson.

Ingram would not allow me to take a handwritten or recorded statement and I did not make any notes until he left the room.

Flying back to Minneapolis the next day, Larson and I went over my notes and he made a few after Ingram departed our company. We both heard what we heard and our notes jived. In addition, we both came to the conclusion that we were either followed to Chicago by some Minnesota police officials or detectives, or my phone was monitored because I made airline and hotel reservations. How in God's name would two strangers come up to Willard and Donny and announce that they were from Minneapolis and wanted to take them to some other joint for a drink? That's just incredible.

Ingram's blood type was the same type that was found at Carol Thompson's residence. This testing was prior to the DNA testing. I had found out Ingram's blood type by calling one of the prisons that he had served time in and I'll be damned if they didn't give me his blood type over the phone. When I testified at the post conviction hearing, and Ron Meshbesher questioned me about Ingram's blood type, Prosecutor Randall vehemently objected and made a snide remark. Randall said he wouldn't believe anything that Meshbesher's investigator said. There was a bench conference and the judge consented to let Ron Meshbesher call the Sandstone Prison to confirm Willard Ingram's blood type. Again, the prison gave Mr. Meshbesher the same information they gave me. I was then allowed to state at the hearing what Ingram's blood type happened to be.

Donny Larson also testified at the post conviction hearing and supported what I had testified to concerning meeting Ingram.

People, papers and publicity

When the Thompson murder trial broke, it was headline news all over the State of Minnesota. Publicity was sensational. There were articles with headlines such as Bring in the Big Fish or Reel in the Big Fish referring to T. Eugene Thompson. The trial did not occur outside of the Twin Cities so there was difficulty in selecting a jury that had not read or heard about this sensational case. The failure to sequester a jury was a very strong issue in my opinion. Prior to the post conviction hearing, I had been given a list of those jurors and made efforts to interview them, but with little success. I did meet with a Mrs. Baker who lived in South Minneapolis and traveled to jury duty by bus. She was an elderly dignified woman living in an apartment and the only juror I found who would consent to a face-to-face interview. The reason I remember her so much is because I had stopped smoking during that time and one of the first questions she asked me was whether or not I smoked tobacco. When I told her that I did not smoke, she thought that was a very commendable thing.

Mrs. Baker said that when she used public transportation to go to the trial every day, people would come up to her on occasion and directly ask her about the case! Mrs. Baker said she knew enough not to make any comments, but it was all very disturbing to her. She said the court was absolutely packed all the time with reporters and there were so many that some were sitting on her side of the railing and it was a zoo. One of the things regarding the Thompson case that offended Mrs. Baker deeply was the fact that Mr. Thompson had an illicit affair while he was still married to Carol Thompson. I believed that the jury should have been sequestered because one never knows how many other jurors were badgered or contacted during that trial.

There was only one other person who contacted me about the jury and I don't know how he found out I was making inquiries. I can't remember the man's name but he said his father-in-law was a juror, it was his ex father-in-law. He said he was present when his ex father-in-law would come home from the trial. He would call a lot of his friends, tell them what was going on and blab to his neighbors and family. It was certainly obvious that this guy didn't like his father-in-law and who knows if he was trying to stick it to his ex father-in-law. I made attempts to contact all the jurors and really had not much luck.

This case, <u>State v. T. Eugene Thompson</u>, had some national attention. I was told by someone that the case was going to be written about in Life Magazine and Mr. Thompson was going to be on the cover of the magazine. President John F. Kennedy was assassinated during that time so the Thompson cover story, of course, was replaced with the assassination of President Kennedy.

When I worked on this post conviction hearing, I was very optimistic which I still am concerning the abilities of the attorneys I worked for. I believed that F. Lee Bailey and Ron Meshbesher had a shot of overturning the case and being granted a new trial. My friends tease me relentlessly about my work stating "Vinnie has never worked on behalf of a guilty person." Perhaps it's my nature, but I have always believed it is a jury's duty to determine guilt or innocence. My duty is to gather exculpatory evidence that may assist the defense in proper representation of the attorney's client. If I approached my work being judgmental, then I wouldn't be properly able to complete my tasks. This is not to say that I don't have feelings about a client's innocence or culpability, but those feelings must be set aside. The only cases I have worked on where a client will make admissions are cases involving self defense or making stupid but honest decisions. I have never had the attorney's client tell me they committed an unlawful act, but they want me to do my best to assist them. Naturally I do my best, but the attorney would never put his or her client on the stand and allow them to fabricate a story. In 44 years, I have never seen a defense lawyer suborn perjury. I have seen prosecutors suborn perjury, however.

Chapter 3 - More homicide: T. Eugene Thompson

There is an unfortunate postscript to all of this. Donny Larson, a smiling bear of a man, was later charged as being one of the kidnappers of Virginia Piper. His alleged partner in this was a fellow named Kenny Callahan. These are two old time guys and both had solid alibis when they were originally interviewed by the FBI.

With J. Edgar Hoover in charge of the FBI for many years, there was always an arrogance about this agency. Many of his successors maintain that arrogance and their claim was that a kidnapping case they investigated never went unsolved. I'm deviating from the T. Eugene Thompson case only because of the important witness for the defense, Donny Larson. In the Piper kidnap case, Larson was represented by Bruce Hartigan, a noted criminal defense lawyer who ultimately became a judge and now is retired.

Meshbesher represented Kenny Callahan. Larson and Callahan were convicted at the first trial, but the attorneys appealed, were granted a second trial, and both defendants were acquitted. Judge Jerry Siebel was an in house investigator at that time for Ron Meshbesher and his work on this case was excellent. He was a law school student at the time, but worked long hours gathering evidence that was extremely helpful. My work was done on behalf of attorney Bruce Hartigan, but my results were nothing compared to what Jerry Siebel came up with. There was no money involved because the defendants had no money. This was strictly *pro bono*.

Incidentally, my friend, Lt. Darcy Peterson of the Minneapolis Police Department, had an informant with information regarding the Piper kidnapping. Darcy notified the FBI but told me that they would blow him off so he said "Fuck them, I never want to deal with them again." Darcy said they always want something from you, they never give anything back to the locals as a rule and the FBI always wants to take credit for any success in the criminal justice system.

It is tragic that Donny Larson, having lived through so much strife, charges, and convictions, ended up being convicted for homicide. Donny had a wife and they lived on small acreage north of the Twin Cities. He discovered his wife had been cheating on him. She flaunted it, provoking him, and scorning him. He got a gun and killed her along with some others. He fled the area to a motel near the Minneapolis

Institute of Art where he was going to commit suicide, but he turned himself in to the police. He is an old man now serving the rest of his life in Stillwater Prison. I was sad over this because Donny had some good in him, like the majority of people. He came out of a horrible childhood remaining friendly and often compassionate to his fellow man. I came to like Donny. He must have totally flipped out to commit this violent act because Donny, throughout his life, was never a violent person.

I have no idea what has happened to all of the other characters that were involved in the T. Eugene Thompson case. No doubt most of them are deceased. Wouldn't it be great to know the entire truth about that case, but it's doubtful this will ever occur. The Thompson case was probably the most sensationalized case in the State of Minnesota after the Hamm Brewery kidnap case and up until the Marjorie Congdon matter[1].

---

[1] See chapter 2.

Chapter 4

The Judges: three wise men

Judge Jack Nordby

The Honorable Judge Jack Nordby of Hennepin County, State of Minnesota is considered by lawyers in Minnesota to be one of the great legal minds in this state. He is not only a brilliant individual, he is fair, ethical, knows the state constitution better than anyone I have ever met and has argued in front of the Supreme Court of the United States.

By way of background, Jack was appointed a judge in Hennepin County. He came from a small town in southern Minnesota, Windom, and graduated from that school and went on to Harvard College and Harvard Law School. He had received a scholarship that former Judge Crane Winton helped him get when Crane was on the Admissions Committee at Harvard. Judge Nordby advised me that covers it. There is more to Jack Nordby than just this, however, as the reader will see.

Judge Nordby returned to Minnesota to work on a Ph.D. in English but became bored and also needed some money. He spoke with Judge Winton who advised him to take some part-time legal work and referred Judge Nordby to the late Doug Thomson, an outstanding criminal defense lawyer. He was hired by Doug Thomson. Jack had always wanted to work on criminal cases and ended up practicing law with Thomson for approximately 13 years.

Judge Nordby stated that when he got out of college, he actually wanted to take a particular job in Switzerland, but it fell through. So, he applied to Harvard Law and got a scholarship and the rest is history.

I first met Jack when he was working with Doug Thomson. He was going to write the appeal for Norman Mastrian who had been convicted in state court, along with Eugene Thompson, for the murder of Eugene Thompson's wife. Thompson was a somewhat

Chapter 4 - The Judges: three wise men

flamboyant lawyer in St. Paul and the murder of his wife was a headline story. As a matter of fact, it was scheduled to be on the cover of Life Magazine, but our esteemed President John F. Kennedy was murdered and they took Thompson's story off.

Doug Thomson and John Cochrane represented the alleged middleman, Mastrian.

As mentioned, Eugene Thompson was a prominent St. Paul lawyer. Jack Nordby was not in the community at the time, but the killing took place in 1963. Thompson's wife was killed in March of 1963, it was a brutal attack. She was stabbed many times in their house in the Highland Park area of St. Paul. Somehow, she managed to get out of the house and get to a neighbor, but eventually died. Over a period of weeks or months, it was on the front page of both the Minneapolis and St. Paul papers, some of the papers, really violated journalistic ethics with questions such as, "Why don't they pick up the big fish?" Thompson was ultimately arrested and the claim was that he hired a guy named Dick W.C. Anderson to kill his wife. Mastrian, as mentioned, was also charged and later convicted for being the middleman. Mastrian had been a client of Eugene Thompson. In a nut shell, that is what the case was about.

Pre-trial publicity went on at length according to Judge Nordby, further stating that it was comparable to the Dr. Sam Shepherd case in Cleveland, Ohio. That also was headlined at approximately this same time. Judge Nordby's position on pre-trial publicity is that it has a potential to make it almost impossible to pick a jury because everyone in the State of Minnesota knew about the case. I wrote about this case in the previous chapter chapter to give more details. There is a lengthy record of this case and can be looked up if someone is tenacious enough and anxious enough to satisfy his or her curiosity.

After a lengthy discussion between Judge Nordby and me about the Thompson/Mastrian matter, we went on to other issues in the criminal justice system of serious concern. We talked about the expansion of our prisons in the United States. There has been some documentation that half those incarcerated are because of drugs, either using or selling them. I asked Judge Nordby if there may be a better solution to incarceration.

Judge Nordby said he didn't exactly know what the solution may be, but what we are doing now is not working. He stated people at the bottom of the drug chain are not going to prison as a rule, and, if they do, they have not made a dent in the overall commerce of drugs. The judge then mentioned the drug court in Hennepin County which he does not work-in, but has quite a bit of knowledge of how it is approaching this problem. Judge Nordby states the drug court has been quite effective. They are heavy on treatment and quick disposition of cases, with careful and close repeated supervision of those who are dependent. Judge Nordby commented that "just the other day the Minnesota Supreme Court said you have to start throwing a lot of these people in prison that you haven't been incarcerating." Judge Nordby said he didn't know how that is going to affect things and believes it is only going to make things worse.

Judges Burke, Howard, Summerville and Lynn are the ones that primarily have manned this drug court. Judge Nordby said they understand the mechanics and he believes they are doing excellent work. I know Judge Burke, I do not know the others, but my regard for him is very high. His wife, incidentally, is also a Hennepin County judge, and she also has a very good reputation within the legal circles. It is interesting to note that our Republican Congressman from Minnesota, Jim Ramstad, also supports treatment. Mr. Ramstad is one of the few Republicans supported by numerous Democrats in his district (I, as a bomb-throwing liberal, voted for Jim Ramstad, but that is a side issue).

We know drugs continue to pour into the country in spite of U.S. Government spending $2 billion in Columbia. People may remember our drug czar, retired General McCafferty. Judge Nordby says that they are obviously not stopping shipments coming in but the work they have done and the people they have arrested raises the price of the next shipment. It may be an insoluble problem. Judge Nordby's thought was that we should be dealing with juveniles who are introduced to drugs and using our resources in juvenile court for treatment and education.

Chapter 4 - The Judges: three wise men

Judge Nordby believes that education is only part of it because it is hard to explain logically to juveniles why it is not a good idea to use drugs. Law enforcement must be involved. Merely telling them that it is going to hurt your health, that it is immoral, etc. will not make them stop. There has to be law enforcement along with treatment, and working with the families and the kids themselves. The success ratio is not as high as one would hope.

I went on to enquire with Judge Nordby about sentencing guidelines both on a federal and state level. Judge Nordby stated that he was against the guidelines when they were first adopted because when he started practicing law, the sentencing was completely up to the judge within the maximum. For example, in a robbery case if the sentence was 0 to 20 years, the judge could give a defendant anywhere from 0 to 20. We now have guidelines for sentences for, let's say, between 6 - 8 years, just for the purpose of discussion. It might even be narrower than that. The purpose was to make sentences more uniform, and that they have done. Judge Nordby says that that is both good and bad. For example, when you get a hard-nosed judge who sends a guy away to prison for 20 years, and then another with a virtually identical case who has a softer judge and only sentence the guy to probation, therein lies the problem. So now you get very little flexibility and little opportunity to treat the worst offenders more harshly than the less serious offenders.

In state court, there is more flexibility to wane from the guidelines. Under federal sentencing guidelines, judges have almost no discretion at all. The U.S. Attorneys have to make the initial request to depart from the guidelines or the judge cannot do it. In state· court, there is a good deal more flexibility. Judge Nordby said he is not against the guidelines to the extent he originally was because they have partially accomplished their purpose. He said the guidelines keep a pretty close eye on situations, make adjustments and if they judge is encouraged to do so, he will depart either up or down with a case that may seem to justify a departure.

Judge Nordby feels the guidelines, in his opinion, in drug cases are too high to the extent of being mandatory where they are sending the people we were earlier talking about off to prison for many years when they may have been dealt with more efficiently and economically with strict probation.

I mentioned that this brings up the case of Ralph Chavez, aka "Plookie" Duke[2]. I informed Judge Nordby that some defense lawyers state, on a federal level, that prosecutors are totally running the show. Judge Nordby responded by saying that to some extent that is true because legislation and congress have given power over sentences and, of course, they automatically have power over the charges function. They have the exclusive power to charge anybody with any crime, if they have probable cause.

It is true on a state level, also, and if the statute of limitations has not expired, there is a 100 percent prosecution. What is bad with the federal law now is that they have extended that one-sided *ex-parte* power to the sentencing leaving no flexibility in those cases for anyone. Judge Nordby thinks that is a dangerous thing to have that amount of power in the criminal justice system lodged with one participant.

I then mentioned Judge Rosenbaum (a Federal Judge with a strong reputation for fairness among both prosecutors and defense alike), when I was interviewing Judge Nordby. Rosenbaum was taking a great deal of heat because of his testimony in Washington D.C. over sentencing guidelines. He expressed his honest, intelligent opinion that judges needed more latitude and Senator Sensenbrenner demanded all of Judge Rosenbaum's files be examined. I don't know who examined them, but I expressed to Judge Rosenbaum that as a Republican I could not believe a fellow-Republican treating him so shabbily. Judge Rosenbaum said to me, "I lost my Rabbi," meaning he lost his strong support in Washington, Rudy Boschwitz.

Judge Nordby stated that he did not know a great deal about Judge Rosenbaum's situation but knew Jim Rosenbaum as a tenacious prosecutor and an honorable man. Judge Nordby stated that the frightening part of this scenario is that a hand full of politicians, for political reasons, are trying to intimidate federal judges and they are

---

[2] See chapter 6.

Chapter 4 - The Judges: three wise men

successful in doing so. Judge Nordby said that they are out-and-out scaring some of these judges. Certain politicians are scaring them out of criticizing the guidelines. This is really unconscionable. If anybody should be able to speak knowledgably as a group about what good sentences ought to be, it would be the federal judges because nobody else has seen criminal court in action from a neutral position such as the judges.

However, Judge Nordby said you can talk to federal prosecutors and federal defense lawyers and they may have a different position regarding this.

Judge Nordby stated that in spite of Rosenbaum's position and personal anguish, he does not think it is going to hurt this judge. Judge Nordby said he does not believe that Judge Rosenbaum has ever done anything improper and that he is not going to be removed from the bench or disciplined. Judge Nordby stated, to some extent, he thought Judge Rosenbaum was a heroic figure for a lot of people for having the guts to speak out. I readily agreed with Judge Nordby. We went on to discuss the death penalty, which the State of Minnesota does not have. Judge Nordby stated that he recently attended a debate at the John Adams Society, which some people describe as a right wing society. Judge Nordby feels that is inaccurate because he believes it is more of a libertarian group. It is a debating society and there was a debate regarding the death penalty which was vigorous on both sides. Judge Nordby said he felt it was a cheap shot on the part of Governor Tim Pawlenty to maneuver in this situation; the Governor figuring that if he supports the constitutional amendment for the death penalty, it is a win-win situation. The death penalty is already in the Minnesota Constitution and, according to Nordby, we do not need an amendment to do this. According to Nordby, the Governor could see that by being in favor of the death penalty he would get the votes of the pro-death people regardless of whether or not it passed. He did not think the Governor believed it was going to pass. He doesn't believe the Governor even cared whether it was passed. It was just the idea of picking up some votes.

The judge and I then discussed a number of the murder cases I have worked on over the years and came to the conclusion that the death penalty is not a deterrent to homicide. People do not think of consequences before they commit a murder, they don't think about what state they are in, it is just irrelevant. Judge Nordby stated that there is no significant evidence that the death penalty is a deterrent. Judge Nordby pointed out that we have to recognize that our court system, justice system overall, is quite fallible and it is simply unthinkable that it can always be fairly administered. There are going to be mistakes. Innocent people who are literally factually innocent have often been accused and were looking at execution.

We talked about the University of Northwestern School of Journalism students investigating Cook County and developing ironclad evidence that the person on death row was not the guilty party. There are also people who are not legally responsible because they are insane or children who end up on death row. You cannot undo what happens after an execution. Judge Nordby pointed out that some people were convicted because witnesses and judges were bribed, and all the factors mentioned above makes any offsetting benefit to society other than desired for vengeance and retribution. I reminded Judge Nordby that he seemed to agree with the Pope on this issue, and at that time the Polish Pope John Paul 2nd was still alive. Interestingly enough, Judge Nordby, who has a spiritual side but is not a religious activist, stated that he usually agrees with the Pope. Judge Nordby is not a Catholic.

Judge Nordby did state that the Pope seemed to have it figured out as he is against abortion and he is against the death penalty. Judge Nordby admired him for that position. We did not get into any discussion of the woman's right to choose, but I told Judge Nordby that I do not know anyone who likes abortion, but I know a lot of people that do not wish to impose their view on a young woman who is pondering, an abortion. As some of my strict Lutheran friends have told me, it is between the woman, whomever impregnated her, her family, her pastor and her doctor to assist in making that decision.

Judge Nordby emphasized the importance of DNA. I mentioned the Governor of Illinois at that time. He set forth a moratorium and commuted all the death sentences in Illinois. He was a pretty conservative Governor. Judge Nordby went on to point out that the death penalty always has and always will fall disproportionately on the poor and minorities. Like many cases, it depends on the quality

Chapter 4 - The Judges: three wise men

and skill, along with resources of the defense lawyers. Somebody with a lot of money and with good fortune to have top flight defense lawyers has a better opportunity than the poor and minorities who are given public defenders. This is no slam against the public defenders, but they do not have the financial resources and they are extremely overburdened.

We discussed the famous Lobe-Leopold case in the 1920s where two very wealthy, extremely smart college boys murdered another boy because they wanted to commit the perfect murder. They were defended by the legendary Clarence Darrow and they were convicted, but Darrow, in his brilliance, was successful with keeping them off death row.

Judge Nordby brought up the O.J. Simpson case in reference to excellent defense lawyers, of which Simpson had five. According to Nordby, he believed they did an excellent job. He would not say one way or the other whether Simpson committed the crime, but commented the prosecution's case was so badly damaged that Judge Nordby believed they did not prove beyond a reasonable doubt that Simpson was the murderer. This case went on and on and anyone that followed it closely could see how terrible the prosecutors were at presenting their case.

And speaking of interesting prosecution cases, the following chapter deals with the Duke case, a candidate for mistrial if ever I saw one.

Judge James Gilbert

When I interviewed James Gilbert in April 2004, as stated he was a Supreme Court Justice but he now heads up a Mediation Center in Eden Prairie. A number of former judges work with him such as Robert Schumacher, who was also an Appellate Court judge and r outstanding jurist. The present governor, Tim Pawlenty's wife, who was a Dakota County judge for a period of time works at the Mediation Center. I did not know this woman so I can make no judgment about her, but I do admit that I voted against her husband, Tim Pawlenty, who is Governor of the State of Minnesota.

Judge Gilbert and I talked about sentencing guidelines. He stated guidelines at the state level have to have uniformity because the state has 87 counties and over 1100 different law enforcement agencies. The state had over 300 judges and, according to Gilbert, be consistent and have the same type of sentencing in a crime whether it be committed in a northern community or the metropolitan area. Uniformity of sentencing guidelines was important and that is why it was brought forth.

There is some discretion to depart either upward or downward. The court must put the reasons on the record and those reasons must be compelling. The court will define the reasons, depending on the crime, and define what factors enter in. A major problem Judge Gilbert told me with sentencing is that the legislature is also passing over and above what Judge Gilbert felt the sentencing guidelines are designed to do. In more and more incidents, especially with drug and sex abuse cases, the legislature is establishing some mandatory minimums. The judges have absolutely no discretion regarding mandatory minimums. They have to sentence a person to so many years and months regardless of the facts and the rehabilitative behavior remorse in restitution or anything else. Incidentally, I feel that that is a problem on the federal level and I'll discuss that in a different context.

Concerning the drug court initiated by Judge Kevin Burke, who is also a great judge, that is in a sense an alternative to mandatory minimum sentencing. Judge Gilbert was the liaison to the drug court's initiative throughout the State of Minnesota and he has seen seven different drug courts up and running in Minnesota. Much credit should be given to Judge Kevin Burke. Hennepin County was first, but now Ramsey County, Stearns County, St. Louis County, and Dodge County also have this adult juvenile version of drug court. The priority when Judge Gilbert was a Supreme Court justice was to keep expanding.

I happen to be a liberal and a very strong supporter of the Democratic Party, but I did vote for Republican James Ramstad, who was a Minnesota Congressman, when I lived in his district. He was very strong for alternative methods in dealing with drugs and he and Paul Wellstone often worked on and discussed that issue.

Chapter 4 - The Judges: three wise men

Judge Gilbert felt that there was an absolute need to have these drug courts. If someone had committed a crime while using or selling drugs and carrying a gun, they were not going to get in that system. Gilbert felt that if you treat the underlying chemical issue by getting these drug violators educated and working again and building up their self respect, that they would have a strong chance of not being recycled in the system. I was told that in some counties that there is a 70 percent recidivism rate where dealers and addicts are back in the system after three years. Judge Gilbert agreed with my positive view of Congressman Ramstad, and his efforts to change things.

I did make an inquiry about Federal Judge Rosenbaum who was literally pissed on by Senator Sensenbrenner of Wisconsin. Judge Rosenbaum was being pilloried over his position on sentencing. Judge Rosenbaum is a close personal friend of Judge Gilbert who told him that it would be safer talking to a Rotary Club about these matters of sentencing than it would be to talk to congress.

I mentioned to Judge Gilbert that at his daughter's wedding I sat at the same table with Judge Rosenbaum and told him that I had empathy for what he was going through. I said I can't believe this because it is well-known that you are a Republican and so is Sensenbrenner. Judge Rosenbaum told me that I had to remember that he lost his Rabbi. I asked the judge who his Rabbi was and he said that it was Rudy Boschwitz, who had been in congress and would have come to the defense of Judge Rosenbaum. However, this whole thing will blow over, Sensenbrenner was just trying to snatch a few headlines and it is regrettable that he beat up on a fellow Republican. Everybody I know thinks that Judge Rosenbaum is a terrific judge. He is literally a mentor to hundreds of lawyers and judges in the system, works extremely hard, has had experience trying case. He is well liked by prosecutors and defense lawyers. It is good to know that Judge Rosenbaum had many supporters and, in fact, has supporters in the U.S. Senate on both sides of the aisle.

We discussed overcrowding in prisons, both federal and state, and the fact that it costs more to house a prisoner than it does to send your daughter or son to private school. Judge Gilbert hated that and he believed drug court was going in the right direction He said that the legislature has to realize that they must address more long-term solutions rather than short-term fixes like throwing offenders in the slammer. Needless to say, budgets are increasing and as I write this chapter, the public defenders have been cut drastically. In the meantime, back in 2004, the Governor asked for 900 new prison beds which would add billions of dollars annually to the criminal justice system if they keep going down this path. According to Judge Gilbert, the whole thing is not working.

It is easy to inflame congressmen and senators over drug issues as no one wants to see that activity in their community. Many legislators have personal experience through friends, relatives or neighbors regarding people addicted to drugs. It is a very emotional issue and I agree with Judge Gilbert about that.

I asked Judge Gilbert about paid government informants and jailhouse informants that are trying to lighten their sentences or even make money by being rewarded in that form. Judge Gilbert stated that it is probably going to be part of the criminal justice system, even as we go forward. He has stated that he has seen it lead to problems where the people may not necessarily be as candid or sometimes outright lie to gain a deal for themselves or to gain employment. Defense lawyers harp upon this at trial and cross examine these informants and then the juries generally find out what the underlying relationship of the informant is to the prosecution. If all the information gets out, then a jury is able to judge the credibility of an informant. Judge Gilbert stated that he doesn't think that we ever want to develop a class of professional paid informants that are setting people up or making things up as a way to keep their employment with government or out of government. I mentioned to Judge Gilbert about a couple of cases involving a paid informant named Chambers who received over two-and-a-half million and never paid taxes on that. Judge Gilbert was not familiar with any of those cases because they are on a federal level. He did state that he has been on the Supreme Court for about six-and-a-half years and they have remanded one case back for rehearing because there were concerns about the reliability of one of the informants.

We talked about run-a-way juries such as in civil cases making huge awards. Judge Gilbert stated that we don't have that problem in Minnesota, but we hear stories from other states. We do not have

Chapter 4 - The Judges: three wise men

caps on our personal injury claims and it doesn't seem to be an issue here. It is really a policy for the legislature to decide, not for the courts. In general, Judge Gilbert stated that he thought our court system is designed to align the responsibility with the tortious act and when artificial caps are put in place in some of these damage elements, it tends to distort the balancing effect that the court systems have in adjudicating claims and deciding damages.

There was some tort reform back in the 1980s that set forth that people bringing medical malpractices cases, cases against lawyers, accountants and engineers, would have to have a sworn affidavit from an expert before they could file their case. A lawyer also has to sign an affidavit at the start of the case, but they have to include expert testimony before they can go forward. This decreases frivolous lawsuits. Judge Gilbert did not think we had a significant number for those medical malpractice lawsuits in Minnesota, which is a positive thing. I asked him if getting this expert before filing a lawsuit would tip the hand of the plaintiff lawyer and he didn't believe it would, the party being sued has a right to know what the nature of the claim is and Judge Gilbert said, "We don't play games with that." We have a very liberal discovery and that doesn't impact the quality of justice being delivered.

I asked Judge Gilbert about contingency arrangements for lawyers. John Edwards wrote about this matter. Some lawyers may take up to 45 percent of a settlement which seems rather high. Although my personal feeling is that it would be pretty hard for poor people or less affluent people to hire a lawyer on an injury case or product liability case unless there was a contingency fee arrangement.

Judge Gilbert said that it not only assists the poor, it also assists the middle class and even upper class people. It allows access into the court system. There is risk involved for the lawyer, but too often the only way a person can get into court is to hire a lawyer on a contingency fee basis. Judge Gilbert said he is from the old school and if it works, don't fix it. He thinks that contingency is a fair system.

I also asked why insurance coverage is never mentioned in accident cases and Judge Gilbert stated that someone has to prove the negligence and the damages. He believes it may be prejudicial to allow the jury to know that a major extent of insurance would cover any award. Most jurors understand that there is insurance, it is a white elephant not talked about in the courtroom.

We talked about when a judge should recuse himself. If a judge had a case in front of him that he had to be part of the decision and a relative was involved in the case, he would naturally have to recuse himself Judge Gilbert recused himself if any member of the Meshbesher law firm would appear before the Supreme Court even if he didn't know that person. I reminded him that Judge Scalia, on the United States Supreme Court who went on a hunting trip with Cheney, yet did not recuse himself when Cheney's secret energy commission case came before them. The argument, of course, is that we are supposed to have an open government and we should have known who was on that energy commission. I was personally outraged that Scalia did not remove himself because he was a pal of Cheney.

We also discussed the death penalty, which Minnesota does not have and has not since approximately 1912 when there were several hangings that were botched. The media rose up and the legislature decided to rescind the death sentence. We have not had it since. I personally hope we never have the death sentence but that is an argument for another day. Judge Gilbert knows a justice in California who has 100 death sentence cases on his desk and he, of course, reads every page, every word before he makes a decision. That California judge says that it is excruciating for him.

DNA has been a terrific tool, of course, and Judge Gilbert talked about how much it has helped the prosecution and the defense. It has exonerated a number of people. Sometimes there is a question about how samples were handled or if there was contamination, but the science itself is extremely accurate. You never say something is fool proof, but it is very strong and we both agreed that we are happy it is available.

We discussed the public defender system such as reporting of fees and confiscation of fees, which was all the doing of the feds. Some active criminals would not hire a private lawyer even though they have the money stashed somewhere because in the final analysis,

Chapter 4 - The Judges: three wise men

the attorney will not get the money. The feds now even state that prosecutors will claim the funds were ill begotten gains, the feds can now confiscate cars, homes, jewelry or whatever. One of the problems is that if your son got arrested and you had loaned him your car and drugs were found in the car without your knowledge, the car could be confiscated and then you have to jump through hoops to get the car back. That is not exactly right. Judge Gilbert said he felt the feds should take another look at their policy on forfeiture to see exactly what has occurred in both the federal and state system.

In 2004, it was pointed out to me that only about two percent of criminal cases were tried in front of a jury, the public defenders had such heavy case loads that they would plead out many of their clients. It must be noted, however, that the defendant has a right to reject a plea and can go to trial, but nevertheless a small percentage reached the trial stage. I pointed out that when I first started as an investigator for Meshbesher and then later other lawyers, often public defender cases were ~spun out to young lawyers who wished to be involved in the criminal court system. Judge Gilbert thought it was good to have young lawyers try some of these cases for experience, but he mentioned it is not happening now-a-days. He said the private defense bar in Minnesota has shrunk to a hand full, maybe two handfuls of lawyers that handle most of the private defense criminal cases, with the exception of drunk driving and some minor assaults.

I asked Judge Gilbert about the white collar crime we see, the various scandals on Wall Street, etc. I was informed that there are a hand full of lawyers in the private sector that handle those cases. On a state level, there are not very many white collar cases, most are in the federal system.

I asked Judge Gilbert if he thought the day of the private criminal defense lawyer was passing. He said he thought it had already passed. He believes this is an evolutionary process, that it is not over and there may be a point in time when we see the system change. I was reminded by Judge Gilbert that tax payers are paying part of the public defender system and there may be up to 400 public defenders in the state.

Whatever happened to Lady Justice?

I asked Judge Gilbert what he thought about electing judges, campaigning and money coming in, etc. and he stated that there are two extremes. The federal system has the appointment by the President, confirmed by the U.S. Senate and then they have a lifetime appointment. The state system has some sort of modified electoral process. In Minnesota, when we have a vacancy, the Governor initially appoints the person, but we have a merit selection commission now made up of lawyers and non-lawyers, Democrats, Republicans, Independents that make recommendations. That has increased the quality of candidates coming into the judiciary in Justice Gilbert's opinion, but we have over 300 judges in the state that are elected. The work a judge does is complex and most people do not necessarily want to know all the details. They want to know that they have good people in place to make complex decisions. There are over 65 judges in Hennepin County and about one-third of them are on the ballot every election. There are too many names for people to recognize and make decisions about and, as I pointed out to Judge Gilbert, during the election period I even have friends call to ask me about what judge to vote for.

Judge Gilbert stated that the bottom line is that he will never support removing elections from Minnesota judges because he believes that it can be used to remove judges without impeaching or indictment. When judges get into trouble and make huge mistakes, Judge Gilbert said the electors usually figure that out and decide who should be removed. We have a very populace state in Minnesota; people do not necessarily like the electoral process, but they don't want to eliminate it either. Judge Gilbert stated that for the time being, it seems to be okay. He did point out that he ran statewide four years ago and· it was a grueling experience. The judge has to spend hundreds of hours campaigning. There were some positives in the experience. The whole campaigning process in the United States, in my opinion, is nuts.

I mentioned to Judge Gilbert that he tried cases before he was a judge and knew his way in and out of court as did people such as Judge Hartigan, Judge Nordby, Judge Mabley, and Judge Wernick and I appreciated that trial experience in a judge. Judge Gilbert agreed. He shared a judicial commission for seven years for Governor Arne Carlson who happened to be a Republican that I voted for. Judge

Chapter 4 - The Judges: three wise men

Gilbert was involved in appointing close to 100 district court judges with the Governor. The one requirement they wanted was not only that the individual be well educated and experienced in all areas of law, but they had to have trial experience. If they did not have trial court experience, Judge Gilbert said they had very little chance of being appointed to the bench. They also looked for people that had been involved in the community and were giving back to their communities in some sort of volunteer work. A well rounded combination of positives makes for a good judge.

Regarding corruption in the court system, Minnesota seems to be squeaky clean. Perhaps now and then there is a political favor done, but certainly I have never heard of a bribery case nor had Judge Gilbert. Judge Gilbert said that is true of the legislature, too. We seem to have elected good people to do their best even though there are differences of opinion.

My last question to Judge Gilbert was whether he thought there were too many law schools in the State of Minnesota. He stated that we swear in over one thousand new lawyers a year. There are over 25,000 lawyers in Minnesota and that Minnesota has a vast over supply of lawyers. Judge Gilbert is concerned that many of these young lawyers coming through law school have incurred enormous debt; some of them $80,000 or more. They are hitting the working world and nobody is hiring because we have an over-supply and a decrease in legal services. There is a decrease in the demand for attorney's time and lawyers are more efficient now with technology. In Judge Gilbert's opinion, all of this has created a problem that he is concerned about. He stated that we have seen too many young lawyers go into depression or become chemically dependent because they come out of law school with high expectations that are not being met, along with these huge debt obligations. Judge Gilbert felt that law schools must be more careful about who they let in and what they tell them about job prospects.

Judge Gilbert went on to mention that in 1972 there were approximately 6,000 lawyers in the State of Minnesota and he felt positive about women entering the profession. We then concluded our interview and, at that point, I asked him if there was anything he wanted to ask me. I do not feel comfortable stating what he said to me because it was far too flattering.

Judge Paul Anderson

When I interviewed Judge James Gilbert, Associate Justice Minnesota Supreme Court, he had graciously made arrangements for me to interview Judge Paul Anderson. Judge Anderson, as expected, was very gracious and cooperative regarding my book project. There was one problem on that day, he was awaiting a special meeting and did not wish to start a tape recording and then be interrupted and then try to reschedule matters. However, he did answer questions and I was able to take some notes. He also presented me with information that I was able to review, specifically Chapter II of his Appellate Advocacy book pertaining to ethical issues for prosecutors on appeal. I will touch on some important points, but his Chapter 11 covers 10 pages plus 32 references citing cases and rules of professional conduct.

As one can see, Judge Anderson's Curriculum Vitae is quite impressive. This is a man with a broad life experience. I was impressed that he served as a neighborhood attorney for New Haven Legal Assistance, New Haven, Connecticut.

My first question to Judge Anderson was whether or not state and federal judges were truly able to exercise their power concerning sentencing. Judge Anderson stated that, in his opinion, there was not enough latitude for judges, particularly in federal court. My next comment was that I recalled Thomas Jefferson making a statement about every ten years we need a revolution (non-violent). The judge stated that we did need change in the 1980s, all of it was well conceived, that during the 1980s it became very tough on crime. The judge stated further that it is true that rehabilitation of criminals has not been as effective as everyone desired. The judge mentioned Judge Rosenbaum's situation that I touched on with Judge Gilbert, and he also mentioned Judge Magnuson, both who have taken the political criticism, but Judge Anderson believes that these gentlemen would weather the storm.

Chapter 4 - The Judges: three wise men

Judge Anderson mentioned that Judge Magnuson felt that some sentencing played harshly on females and that the judge's comments can be found on the internet on Google. I inquired with Judge Anderson about some of the common errors in court that resulted in appeals. His response was misconduct by a prosecutor or defense attorney, or police agents. He stated that this does not occur a great deal in the State of Minnesota, but it must be closely monitored. The judge was then gracious enough to give me a syllabus of <u>Alonzo Ferguson v. State of Minnesota</u> filed on June 13, 2002 along with a copy of the syllabus filed July 9, 1998, same case.

In a nut shell, Mr. Ferguson was convicted in the homicide of Alan Wheatley, Jr. In the appeal, there were claims that Johnny Edwards, a witness that perjured himself, was a habitual criminal and that he was paid monies for his testimony by the government in their efforts to convict Ferguson. The court concluded that there was more than sufficient evidence to support the jury's findings that Ferguson was guilty of the murder of Alan Wheatley, Jr., and the case was affirmed. Judge Paige stated the most damaging evidence against Ferguson came in testimony from Johnny Edwards, a police informant, who more than 12 months after Mr. Wheatley was shot, offered to testify against Ferguson as part of a plea agreement related to crimes Edwards was charged with, but had nothing to do with the Ferguson case.

Edwards had testified that he saw Ferguson and other buds (gang members) prior to the murder in the early morning of September 24th, and Ferguson, who had an argument with Wheatley, allegedly told Edwards he planned to kill Wheatley.

In June 2002, the same case was affirmed in part and reversed in part. Ferguson had raised another petition for post conviction relief and the Supreme Court remanded to the post conviction court for further proceedings in accordance with this opinion. I did not bring up the Ralph Duke case because that was a federal court case, but it has some similarities to the Ferguson case in that a paid informant was involved, and it was shown in Duke's case that the man perjured himself. There was another case the judge cited to me and gave me a copy of the syllabus. The case that came before the Court of Appeals was the State of Minnesota v. Katherine Streiff. The opinion was 14

Whatever happened to Lady Justice?

pages long with additional writing whereby Judge Paul Anderson wrote a concurrence. He starts out with a profound quote from Robert Morton concerning the Winslow boy that says, "It is easy to do justice, but it is much harder to do right."

The following is the opening paragraph of Judge Anderson's concurrence:

> I join in the court's opinion. Under the laws of the State of Minnesota, our rules and the separation of powers doctrine, it is not a manifest injustice for the state to have charged Katherine Streiff with a felony for her alleged misconduct. Nevertheless, I write separately to add some comments on the concepts of justice, injustice and punishment. This case demonstrates how difficult it is to establish the lines separating the executive branch's power to charge a criminal offense from the judiciaries' authority to supersede that power. Moreover, our holdings illustrate that the executive branch's power to charge a criminal offense is awesome and sometimes may be difficult to exercise in a just manner. The facts of this case and our holding provide the opportunity for me to explore the issue of whether it is sufficient for the state to see that justice shall be done,[3] or whether the state also has an additional obligation to ascertain that the right thing is done.

It must be noted here that Ms. Streiff had filed a motion under Minn. R. Crim. P. 15.07 requesting she be allowed to plead to a lesser offense. Under the rule, a district court may accept a plea of guilty to a lesser offense if 1) the court is satisfied following a hearing that the prosecutor cannot introduce evidence sufficient to justify the submission of the offense charged to the jury, or 2) it would be a manifest injustice not to accept the plea. The district court granted

---

[3] It is noted that the U.S. Supreme Court has stated that a government lawyer is a representative not of an ordinary party to a controversy but of a sovereignty whose obligation to govern impartially is as compelling as its obligation to govern at all; and whose interest, therefore, in a criminal prosecution is not that it shall win a case, but that justice shall be done.

Chapter 4 - The Judges: three wise men

the motion over the state's objection and accepted a guilty plea from the defendant to two lesser gross misdemeanor violations. My personal opinion is that the prosecutor, who appealed this, was also interested in justice but more interested in crime and punishment and a conviction. I completely agree with Judge Anderson that we are looking for justice in court and that is what it is supposed to be about. My personal conviction is that we really don't see much of what we believe to be justice.

We went on to discuss the death penalty, and people in this state realized that Governor Pawlenty favors this and, once again, the judge's opinion was that Pawlenty's position was strictly political to gain a vote of law and order guys.

We also discussed whether or not judges should be appointed or elected. Basically, Judge Anderson feels that qualifications are the main thing. We do elect judges in this state on every level, and Judge Anderson did agree with me that when the judiciary is on the ballot, about 95% of the people have not taken the time to find out about these folks. This is bothersome. Another point I brought up is that I hate to see judges campaigning because they must raise funds, and here we may have special interests contributing heavily to a particular candidate. I think Grisham did a novel on the election of a Supreme Court judge, I cannot recall the title but it was an excellent piece of work.

I inquired of Judge Anderson what his thoughts were regarding the McNaughton rule. "The McNaughton rule, in the State of Minnesota, has to do with an insanity plea, it is a 19th century rule, most people I know feel that it is totally dated." The author's simplistic definition of the McNaughton rule, without looking it up, is that it means if you can't tell an apple from an orange, then you are a wacko. If you can tell the difference, then you can't be insane. I think if you talk to psychiatrists, you will be told that is not necessarily true.

Judge Anderson pointed out to me that "Europe and South America have no insanity defense. If you have murdered someone, and it is proven that you have murdered someone, then you must face the consequences."

The United States, however, is one of the few countries in the western world that have the death penalty, which I (the author) discussed with Joe Margolis, an expert in that area, who handled death penalty cases in Texas and now teaches at the University of Chicago.

I was able to squeeze in one more question to Judge Anderson pertaining to law schools. He agreed with my position that, at least in the State of Minnesota, we have too many law schools. We have the University of Minnesota, William Mitchell, Hamline and St. Thomas. The judge agreed with me and stated that he had told the University of St. Thomas people when they were planning a law school, that we did not need another law school. He did say, however, the school has been put together quite well.

In Judge Anderson's book, <u>Appellate Advocacy: Ethical Issues for Prosecutors on Appeal,</u> he was kind enough to give me a copy of Chapter 11. In the first paragraph of this chapter, Judge Anderson wrote that, "in the course of a discussion with a friend pertaining to the standard of ethical conduct for lawyers, his friend pulled out a text from his book shelf and read to Judge Anderson the following: It is a prosecutor's primary responsibility to see that justice is accomplished. He then said if a prosecutor keeps this principle in mind, the prosecutor will likely behave in an ethical manner."

In paragraph three, Judge Anderson writes that the chapter reviews the principle of accomplishing justice, which is basic to how a prosecutor performs his or her duties. The other principle is sustaining ethical conduct. The responsibility to see justices accomplished, and what it means to a member of a profession is paramount.

Judge Anderson goes on to write that "when publicly professing a commitment to a high standard of conduct as lawyers must do, lawyers take an oath that binds them to a specific code of ethical conduct." The judge goes on to speak of what Robert Bolt articulated, what it means to be bound by an oath. "In the place where Thomas Moore's daughter pleaded with her father to swear an oath to King Henry VIII, even though he did not believe the oath in his heart. Sir Thomas Moore, who ultimately was canonized by Rome and became

Chapter 4 - The Judges: three wise men

a Saint responded to his daughter saying, 'When a man takes an oath, Meg, he's holding his own self in his own hands, like water, and if he opens his fingers, then he needn't hope to find himself again. Some men aren't capable of this, but I be loathe to think your father one of them.' "

In my opinion, it is obvious that prosecutors and all lawyers are held to a high standard. Prosecutors have dual roles as advocates and ministers of justice. Unfortunately, these standards have too often been violated.

It is blatantly clear that Judge Anderson is very concerned with conduct of attorneys and the duties that lie with these people who take an oath.

The judge then had to leave for his conference. He was most generous and encouraging, stating that he wanted very much to see my book published. It is nice to have a little nudge from a man of stature.

Chapter 5

Ralph Chavez Duke

In 1989, Ralph Chavez Duke was convicted in federal court on numerous counts stemming from a drug case that he was not involved in.

This was Duke's first criminal case in either federal or state court and this particular case was in federal court. This means he was a first time offender, yet ultimately his sentence was life plus 40 years. My son facetiously inquired of me, "Does this mean if Duke croaks in prison they mummify him and keep him around for another 40 years?" This is all indicative of how convoluted an inconsistent sentencing is between federal and state court. I have worked on cases where the attorney's client was convicted or took a plea bargain on a murder case and went to the gray stone hotel for no more than 17 years. Some got out in a fair quick amount of time. So what is the message here? Once again, justice is a vagrant thing and obviously life is not fair.

I'll start from the beginning regarding Mr. Duke.

In 1989 and 1990, my wife and I were on a volunteer program at St. Vincent Island in the Grenadines. I knew nothing about the Duke matter.

I learned about his case upon our return and then ultimately went to work on his appeal. Howard Bass agreed to also work on the matter and it was strictly *pro bono*. We worked on this case for approximately three years. I had met Mr. Duke on a few occasions; the first time had to do with a homicide case, State v. Jay Box. I will refer to this man as J.B. In brief: this is a sketch of J.B.'s case. He was in a bar on University Avenue in St. Paul and he had an altercation with a man known as Sweet Man Harris. They argued at the bar and ultimately went outside. This was not a racial confrontation, although J.B. was one of the few Caucasians in the bar except for the bartender, John Locketz. Outside the bar on the sidewalk on University Avenue, a large crowd surrounded the men and J.B. was

Chapter 5 - Ralph Chavez Duke

banging Sweet Man around pretty good. Sweet Man then pulled a knife on J.B. According to testimony, J.B. backed up and in the process was handed a pistol by John Locketz. J.B. took the gun, spun around and said his intent was to shoot Sweet Man in the leg. However, at the same time Sweet Man seeing J.B. with a gun in his hand, pivoted and began to flee. At the exact same time, J.B. pulled the trigger and hit Sweet Man in the ass. Everybody fled but Sweet Man was taken to Ramsey County Hospital. Sweet Man's wound to the buttock was not considered fatal, but unbeknown to the hospital staff, Sweet Man was a diabetic. He was fed intravenously and apparently given glucose which caused a diabetic reaction and he died.

A few months went by, but a detective in Minneapolis who had an intense dislike for J.B. took it upon himself to work up an investigation. The detective, now deceased, was known as Red Presley, a fair skinned black man, and a good guy but he had a dislike for J.B. A friend of mine, Lieutenant Darcy Peterson also deceased, was a partner with Presley and spoke highly of him.

Ultimately, because of Presley's work up, J.B. was tried on a murder two case, the trial took place in Ramsey County. J.B. was represented by Ron Meshbesher. I was an employee at that time and given the assignment. Ron introduced me to Ralph Duke a/k/a Plookie Duke who was known in the black community. Ron figured that Duke could introduce me to the witnesses· who were all African American.

I met with Plookie Duke and over a period of time we made the rounds to the witnesses and I was introduced to these people as being a stand up guy. They cooperated and I took signed statements and they told the story exactly as I have laid it out. There was one witness that was hostile, but that often happens. J.B. was acquitted and it was a rather dramatic trial.

The next time I met Duke was because he had a motorcycle accident and retained Ken Meshbesher as his personal injury attorney. I interviewed some witnesses on that particular case.

I really didn't know Duke, did not socialize with him and what I knew about him pertained to him being a very tough individual. Physically he looked like a black Marlon Brando. I knew that he did some collections for people in Las Vegas and that he repossessed cars for a friend of his that had a used car dealership in St. Paul. I forget that man's name, but he also was black.

I never heard anything regarding Duke or his activities from any of the criminal defense lawyers that I worked for over the years. As I said, he had a reputation of being a very tough guy but I later found out that several police agencies had been looking at him over the years. His phone had been monitored, there was many government snitches in the Minneapolis/St. Paul area, but once again for many years Duke was never charged with a crime. Obviously he had a reputation with the various police agencies of being a bad ass and he was blamed for all sorts of criminal activity that took place in the community. They had been watching him for so long that if he had done something I am amazed with their resources and their snitches that he wasn't charged with something if he was engaging in all sorts of criminal activity.

I was home approximately a year or so when I got a call from a prison from Ralph Duke. At that time, he did not have a lawyer. Judge Jack Nordby, before being appointed to the bench, represented Duke on some very important issues. Jack won the battle but lost the war. So Duke was in the slammer and he wanted me to take up his cause, and interview some of the witnesses that gave statements or testimony against him. I had empathy for his plight, talked to Meshbesher who gave permission for Howard Bass and me to go forward.

I then visited Ralph at Oxford Prison in Wisconsin. He gave me a list of everyone that he thought I should interview. I also learned that he had his throat slashed in federal prison in Ohio. He told me some people there wanted him to get some drugs smuggled in, they knew through the prison grapevine that he had been convicted on an alleged big drug deal in Minnesota, but Ralph turned them down. He insisted to them that he was not a big time drug operator. In retribution, he had his throat slit and I am surprised he survived.

Chapter 5 - Ralph Chavez Duke

Interviews

I interviewed numerous people during the appeal of Ralph Duke and all of this was newly discovered evidence because at the trial of Ralph Duke and others, all these witnesses had lawyers. If you have a lawyer then an investigator is not allowed to speak with the attorney's client so none of this would have been available during the trial of Duke because everyone had lawyers.

On July 22, 1998, I interviewed a young man by the name of Theryl Dugas. I tape recorded this interview and actually I have a copy of the seven page statement. I am presenting the basics of this statement. Mr. Dugas was charged with aiding and abetting and maintaining a stash house for drugs in 1989 on the same Ralph Duke indictment. Mr. Dugas is a relative of Ralph Duke's older brother, Claude Duke.

Mr. Dugas informed me that he was introduced to Marcel Duke by a guy named Scott Treadwell. Mr. Dugas said it turned out that he was a relative with Marcel. Mr. Dugas stated he did not meet Ralph Duke until approximately 1987, stating he was an older guy, always out of town, you never saw him around much, but when we were kids he was always driving a fancy car and we were crazy over that. Mr. Dugas met Loren Duke and they would hang out. He also knew Monte, Lamont Nunn; Ralph Dukes youngest son; along with Larry Hutchinson from high school. He also met Ramone Hutchinson sometime in early 1989.

Mr. Dugas stated that they were all doing drugs on the street, buying and selling, and he stated that he was at Lake Calhoun one time and a guy he didn't know came up to him and knew his name. The guy who had later turned out to be the undercover informant, Andrew Chambers, he asked Mr. Dugas if he knew what was coming down on Wednesday. Mr. Dugas said he didn't know what he was talking about, but a few days later, seeing this guy, he brought him to Ralph Nunn who said this guy is good, it's all okay. Mr. Dugas said he never hung around with Ralph Nunn and he was suspicious of this guy who had come up to him (Chambers). He said that the guy drove a Mustang and he saw him a few times around town. Mr. Dugas said he asked a few of his relatives about this guy and they said that Monte and some others were anteing up some money for the purchase of some drugs. Mr. Dugas said he was broke at the time and he didn't even bother asking to get in on the deal. Mr. Dugas said he didn't know about any of the planning or any specifics, but he did know something was coming down. He said Ralph Duke's name never came up at any time. These were all young guys that knew each other and hung around with each other.

A guy named Virgil Kirkwood, Ralph Nunn, Loren Duke, Ramone Hutchinson, Monte, Marcel Duke and Scott Treadwell put up money. Mr. Dugas said that there may have been some other guys that put up some cash.

Mr. Dugas then went on to talk about Scott Treadwell. He said Marcel and Treadwell were partners; that Marcel and Treadwell had some money together stashed from other deals. Marcel went to Las Vegas to see a fight; Mr. Dugas thought it was a Tyson fight. Treadwell then decided to take the money which was approximately $13,000, go out of town, buy some drugs and be back to the Twin Cities before Marcel returned from the boxing match. Mr. Dugas said that wasn't a good idea, but Treadwell did it anyway. Mr. Dugas said Treadwell didn't come back for approximately eight months. Upon his return, he was apologetic and said he had the money. He didn't explain anything, but Mr. Dugas said they didn't trust him anymore. Mr. Dugas said that it was interesting that Treadwell's mother and sister moved away and he and others thought that Treadwell may have gotten busted and came back to try to set them up. He said they were taking a ride one time and he wanted to stop and make a phone call. He said they wouldn't stop as we figured maybe he was going to call the Feds. Mr. Dugas said he broke down and cried. He said he thought they were going to hurt him. Mr. Dugas said we were never going to hurt the guy, we were not that way, and he never saw Treadwell again until he testified in Ralph Duke's trial.

Mr. Dugas said that Ralph Duke never associated with Treadwell and when Treadwell testified, he lied about Ralph Duke. He said Treadwell did some business with Terry Glass and Loren Duke and this business about picking drugs up at Ralph Duke's house is just bullshit.

Chapter 5 - Ralph Chavez Duke

Mr. Dugas said that he wasn't on trial at the same time as Ralph Duke, but he was sitting in the back of the court room when Treadwell was on the witness stand. He remembered the prosecutor's name as Hopeman. He said the prosecutor, "seen me in the back of the court room and asked Scott, while he was on the stand, which was wrong because I wasn't even on trial yet, tell me about Mr. Dugas and your involvement." Scott told them that he knew me and he was sorry for what he was about to do, but he introduced me to drugs and how to sell it and that I was a very minor player, just out making $20 bills and if I got lucky I would make $100 in a day. Treadwell testified that Mr. Dugas was a happy camper. Mr. Dugas said Hopeman didn't like to hear that. He said he wanted Scott to elaborate on something bigger, but there really never was anything bigger. Mr. Dugas said that it was all petty.

Mr. Dugas said that they then put me out of the court room because I started calling Treadwell a liar.

The Feds really wanted to know what I knew about all this stuff. They asked a lot about Ralph Duke. I told them that Ralph Duke had nothing to do with this sting operation they ran and their reaction was to laugh. I asked who he talked to and he said Hopeman and a guy named Michael Kiery, a DEA agent. Mr. Dugas said he was about 19 years old at the time and he didn't know anything about sentencing guidelines and procedures, but he told him several times that Ralph Duke was not involved in this thing. They even drew up a chart to show who the players were and how much time they were going to get in prison. He said it was like a triangle on a piece of paper.

Ralph Duke's name was on the top of this triangle or diamond they drew and they told Mr. Dugas that it was like a domino effect, they were going to knock on everybody hard and they were going to do this much time so everybody would turn. By turn, they meant they are going to testify against Ralph Duke and Mr. Dugas. Mr. Dugas said they showed him a piece of paper that had Loren Duke's name on it and a signature of Marcel Duke. Mr. Dugas said that this was kind of a shock because Marcel was never on the original indictment. Mr. Dugas said this took place before the trial and they said Loren was going to testify against his uncle, Ralph Duke. They wanted Mr. Dugas to testify and they told him this was the only way he could save his butt from going on trial himself. Mr. Dugas said to them that the only guy he got his drugs from was Scott Treadwell. He said the Feds didn't like to hear that. Mr. Dugas said that it was the truth and that he didn't get his drugs from Marcel. He said Treadwell was his man.

Shortly after that, his lawyer came to him and said he was getting 18 months. He said· I went from 15 years to 10 years to 18 months so quick because they finally figured out that I had nothing to do with this and I was useless to them.

All of this was a lengthy process for Mr. Theryl Dugas. There were many conversations with his lawyer and with federal representatives, and he said they tried to point out to him that they wanted everybody to testify against the next shelf on their diagram right on down the line.

There was no higher ranking or anything according to Mr. Dugas. He said their goal was to bring down Ralph Duke and they just came up out of the air with him. I asked Mr. Dugas if he was convinced that all along they knew that Ralph Duke did not put in any money and was not masterminding any type of a buy which resulted in the sting. Mr. Dugas said that he had nothing to do with it at all and they knew it. They had other statements, gave deals away, people would come back into the pod, meaning the holding tank, and they would talk about being coerced. Mr. Dugas said that they would throw bait out and try to do anything to nail Ralph Duke, and ultimately it worked.

Mr. Dugas said that all of the guys involved that he knew admitted to him that Ralph Duke had nothing to do with that deal. Mr. Dugas mentioned Lamont Nunn talking to him about it on several occasions while they were in Stillwater holding. They were in separate cells but they were together a lot. Lamont would come down to see him and he also talked to Ramone Hutchinson and a few other people. Mr. Dugas said they tried to split everybody that knew each other and succeeded. They made a lot of enemies among everybody, there were a lot of lies told, and the stories were never the same. Mr. Dugas said the truth is the truth and they finally made a case against Ralph Duke.

Chapter 5 - Ralph Chavez Duke

Mr. Dugas also knew a guy named David Yoman. He was a friend of Mr. Dugas and a three time felon way back in 1989. They were telling Yoman that he was going to do life if he didn't say something that was going to be good enough to the jurors and the judge against Ralph Duke. Mr. Dugas said he spoke to Yoman before he testified, it was a phone call through a mutual friend, he said we had clicking over the lines and I asked him what was going on. Yoman said, "Theryl, I got to do it, they're making me do it." This was right before the trial. Mr. Dugas was out on bond at that time.

Mr. Dugas said that when Yoman took the witness stand, while they were reading him his oath, they told him to sit down and he said no. Mr. Dugas said that Yoman said that he wanted to apologize to his family and in front of the judge, Hopeman and everyone in the court room, he said "They are making me do this, you know my history, you know my past and you know this is not me, this is something I would never do and this is something I have no control over." I asked Mr. Dugas if he thought the jury was present and he said he thinks so, but he's not quite sure. He said they had to be there because Yoman was sworn in. Mr. Dugas was in the court room. Mr. Dugas said that Yoman said on the witness stand that he made a purchase from Ralph Duke, and that was the end of it. Mr. Dugas said that he believes Yoman was coerced into saying that, particularly after he made his announcement before he took the witness stand.

Mr. Dugas said that Yoman did that otherwise he would have gotten life in prison since he was a three time felon. He said they threatened the whole bunch of them with outrageous time. He said, "I mean for me to be 19 years old, one day I'm free, just had my first kid and I got indicted and they said I'm going to do 15 years and that's a lot of time." He said a lot of people said that they didn't want to do that kind of time; that they didn't even know Ralph Duke, but they would say what they had to say, follow the prosecutors and let the prosecutors do whatever they wanted to do. Mr. Dugas said they wrote a script and all the dialogue.

Mr. Dugas said that Yoman may have known Ralph Duke but didn't hang out with him. He said a lot of guys knew Ralph Duke, but Duke was older, out of town a lot and none of these young guys were hanging out with him.

Monte never went to trial, but had people testifying against him. He said Monte told him that they wanted Monte to give information about some murder and Monte didn't know what they were talking about, but he was curious. Monte had a lot of hearsay that he told the Feds about.

He said that one time they were over night at the adult detention center in Ramsey County and the Feds were talking to all of these guys and Monte thought he had some kind of a deal for eight years. He said the conditions were that he had to talk about Ralph Duke. He said Monte came back to the cell after talking to the Feds and he was crying and he said they wouldn't give him the deal. They told him he had to do something else because they reneged on his deal. Monte said the prosecutor stabbed him in the back. Monte was 19 years old at the time and he said that they used him to say something for nothing, they got him to tell something that didn't have anything to do with Ralph Duke for a deal and if he did this they would probably kick him loose for no time or minimum time. He said he did that and they came back and said no deal, you are still on trial, no bail and Monte was distraught. Mr. Dugas said they held a lot of people and wouldn't give them any breaks and the judge wouldn't give any breaks and Monte kept saying that he had to do something. He said he had to buy time to talk to his lawyer and get his lawyer to talk to his father. Mr. Dugas said Monte faked suicide so he could go to the hospital and buy some time before his trial. Monte ended up never testifying about anything.

I asked Mr. Dugas if he ever knew the name Kevin Walker. Mr. Dugas said that he was with a family that did their own thing, he was a hard dude, a big dude and Mr. Dugas thought he was already in jail in Florida. He said they wanted him to testify to get time off so they shot a deal down to him and he testified against Ralph Duke and he got the offer of some time off. Mr. Dugas doesn't know if he testified because Mr. Dugas wasn't present in court if Walker did testify. He thinks Walker did testify because he was relocated somewhere; he may have even been released. Walker wasn't involved in that sting because he was already incarcerated. Mr. Dugas said Walker was a young guy and he was never involved with Ralph Duke.

Chapter 5 - Ralph Chavez Duke

I mentioned a guy named Kim Willis. Mr. Dugas said he was a close friend with Willis, they went to school together and Willis and Monte were good friends, too. He doesn't know if Willis put up money in that sting deal, but he never had involvement with Ralph Duke. Willis never testified.

There was another guy named Andre Billips, but Mr. Dugas wasn't sure about him. I asked about Joe Ballard and Mr. Dugas had never met him. I asked about Danny Givens and Mr. Dugas said he was a snake and if he talked about Ralph Duke, it wasn't the first time he turned on someone to save his own skin. Mr. Dugas said he had a feeling that Givens may have put up some money in that sting deal.

The name Sandra Jefferson was familiar to him. Mr. Dugas said he thinks Sandra Jefferson, who got busted in Iowa on an unrelated matter never testified in the case, but she got some kind of a deal.

He said there was a guy that sat with them when he was able to attend part of the trial, he never was indicted, and he may have put up some money in the sting thing. He said Virgil Kirkwood never got indicted on their case.

I proposed the following to Mr. Dugas. Why would Ralph Duke, an alleged kingpin with incredible amounts of money, houses and fancy cars need about 30 people to kick in $100,000 to buy 100 kilos of cocaine? Mr. Dugas said that was a good question. Mr. Dugas said it is just bullshit and it is also bullshit that there was some kind of a Duke organization or a Duke gang.

Mr. Dugas said Ralph Duke was actually like a true uncle. Once in awhile when he would come around, he would say that he heard about him and I don't want to hear about this anymore. Then he'd be gone. He said Ralph Duke didn't even want to really deal with this, but he didn't want to see any of the young guys he knew getting into trouble. Mr. Dugas said Ralph Duke loved to be out of town. He loved his cars. We were in awe of him. Mr. Dugas said he was buying and selling cars, some were collector cars, they were all exotic cars.

I then took Mr. Dugas back to this guy, Chambers, who used the name Randy and set up this whole thing with Monte. Mr. Dugas said he found out that was the guy who he met at the lake about two years previous to all of this. He said I remember his face and one day at a club he popped up out of nowhere wearing all this jewelry. He said that is the second time he popped up in my presence. He said he could get me 10 ounces for $5,000. Back then I was shocked so I talked to a friend and my friend said we don't know this guy so leave him alone. This guy disappeared. Mr. Dugas said that was too good of a buy. He said that's not somebody from Minnesota that offers you that deal. He had dropped names with me, dropped the Duke name stating he knew my cousins, the Dukes. I told him that I was not a Duke that I was a relative, distant relative, only through marriage. We hung out some.

This Randy guy (Chambers) was a wrong guy. He wanted to be too friendly, wanted to know where everybody lived, but he never told anybody where he lived. He said he never on any occasion mentioned Ralph Duke's name. He only mentioned Lamont and some younger guys.

In summary, Theryl Dugas said that Ralph Duke was not involved in this purchase of narcotics that turned out to be a sting. He never had anything to do with it. Mr. Dugas said he did his time, not for what they convicted me of, but regardless he said he knew damn well Ralph Duke was not involved in that sting deal. He said he never had a stash house on 4th Avenue in Minneapolis; no one ever stashed any drugs there, but I took a fall on that. Everybody involved, everyone who testified, the prosecutors, they all know Ralph Duke had nothing to do with the deal that ended up as a sting. Mr., Dugas said he talked to Scott Treadwell, as he called me up and told me that he wanted me to forgive him for doing what he did. Treadwell was a guy that my family took in, he slept in my bed, I introduced him to my friends, he was like a brother to me and he said everybody else had more access to money and could get lawyers and so forth, but he was just a peddler. I told Treadwell that he needed to tell the others he was sorry, not me and I told him never to call me again. He promised he wouldn't, but he asked if he came back to Minnesota would he get hurt. I told him he probably would. I asked if he was still working for the government and he said he wasn't working for the government, he was driving a truck. Mr. Dugas said he thinks he is still in Minnesota and he knows he got a new name as I'm sure they set him up; meaning the Feds. Mr. Dugas told Treadwell that he hurt about 30 people just to save his own ass.

I have other statements similar in context to what Mr. Dugas told me on tape on July 22, 1998. The fact is the Feds would have done anything to take down a guy with a bad reputation such as Ralph Duke. It was irrelevant to the Feds that Ralph Duke had never been charged or convicted of anything and this was the way they got him. They had been looking at him for years — and it is shameful that anyone regardless of their reputation should be convicted on lying testimony, especially when there was a paid government informant such as Chambers who the Feds knew about and allowed to take the witness stand stating lies and stating he had no criminal history.

As previously stated in this section, Jack Nordby wrote an outstanding brief when he was with the Meshbesher & Spence firm, and was counsel for the appellant, Ralph Duke. He was appointed by the court. With permission, I am going to quote the appellant's petition for rehearing and suggestion for rehearing on En Banc. Mr. Nordby's legal issues presented are as follows:

Whether a defendant was sentenced to life in prison on a first conviction in a drug case is entitled to dismissal, a new trial, or at minimum, an evidentiary hearing, where there is unrebutted new evidence showing that a key government witness committed blatant perjury concerning his criminal record, the perjury was specifically elicited by the government, the witness' trustworthiness was vouched for by both the assistant U.S. Attorney and the case agent, and the defendant alleges the government intentionally used the perjurer's testimony to convict him and sentence him to life in prison.

The district court denied a hearing to indigent *pro se* defendant who alleged the government knowingly used perjured testimony, both to convict him and sentence him to life in prison. The panel did not order a hearing, stating such conduct was harmless error! Mr. Nordby goes on to say that "I express a belief that the above question, based on reason and studied professional judgment is a question of exceptional importance."

Whatever happened to Lady Justice?

Statement of the Case: Duke began this number 2255 action as an indigent *pro se* defendant who has been sentenced to life in prison in a drug case. Andrew Chambers, a paid government witness, set up a so-called reverse sting with Ralph Duke's son and nephew, for 20 kilos of cocaine. The 20 kilo transaction led to Duke's life sentence. During Chambers' set up, Chambers testified that the young men bragged they were getting the cocaine for Ralph Duke. In the opinion affirming Duke's conviction on direct appeal, this Court mentioned his name some 29 times.

Duke's Demand for Informant's Record: The government vouches for Chambers' credibility.

Before trial, Ralph Duke's lawyer specifically demanded Chambers, the informant's record. The assistant county attorneys told Ralph Duke's defense that Chambers had no record and stated in their opening statement that Andrew Chambers is a young man who works as a confidential informant. He's never been arrested, he's never been convicted of a crime, he doesn't use drugs, he doesn't even drink.

Trial transcript

(T. 25, A. 193-194) The same assistant asked Chambers the following leading questions:

Q:	Have you ever been convicted of any crime in your whole life, sir?
A:	No, I haven't.
Q:	Have you ever been arrested?
A:	No.
Q:	Have you ever used illegal drugs?
A:	No, I haven't.
Q:	When did you first come to Minnesota?
A:	In February.
Q:	And at whose request did you come up here?
A:	Bob Bushman.
Q:	And Mr. Bushman works for the BCA, is that correct?

Chapter 5 - Ralph Chavez Duke

A: Yes, it is.

T. II, 117-118, A:195-196.

Robert Bushman was Chambers' "controlling agent." Chambers said he had worked on some 40 cases for the government (T. ill, 28-34, AI91-197). Robert Bushman of the Minnesota Bureau of Criminal Apprehension who was assigned to a federal drug enforcement administration task force, testified as to Chambers:

Q: Why did you select him?

A: We selected Mr. Chambers because he has proven reliable, he is very trustworthy. Mr. Friedberg

(Duke's trial counsel): Objection, your honor, that is nonresponsive and we ask it be stricken, it is a matter of question whether he's trustworthy. The court: I'm going to overrule the objection. The witness can go ahead as to why he chose him.

A: (By Bushman) As I said, we chose Chambers because he was very reliable and trustworthy.

Friedberg objects and the court overrules.

A: (By Bushman) Chambers was trustworthy, he does not have a criminal record, doesn't use drugs and is willing to work many long hours under dangerous circumstances.

Duke discovers the perjury and makes a *pro se* request for a hearing. While in prison, Duke indigent acquired documentary evidence proving this was a blatant perjury and prepared a *pro se* motion under 28 U.S.C. 2255 (A.I6FF). Although done by a non-lawyer and not entirely articulate, the motion is in the proper form and clearly alleges the known use of false testimony, it's exploitation in opening by the government and nondisclosure of exculpatory and impeaching material. Specifically, Duke demonstrated with exhibits of authenticity and accuracy, which have not been challenged, the following:

Chambers had an FBI rap sheet which listed charged being a fugitive in St. Louis, Missouri in 1978, second degree forgery in Paducah, Kentucky in 1985, charged with second degree forgery using a false name and issuing false financial statements in Kentucky in 1985.

The government had intervened on his behalf in the 1985 case. Chambers had been arrested and released on bond in University City, Missouri in 1988 (A.207, 172, 174) apparently for assaulting his fiancée.

Chambers had been arrested and convicted in Bell Ridge, Missouri in 1978. Chambers admitted in a Federal criminal trial in California in February of 1989 that he had lied about his criminal record and other things in other Federal trials and he sometimes had lied in court.

Chambers admitted in another Federal trial in 1992 that he lied under oath about his criminal record. He admitted in a different trial that he lied under oath whether or not he paid taxes on a $143,000 that he received from the government for acting as an informant.

Mr. Nordby goes forward in his document stating, "Therefore the motion established at A) Chambers committed perjury at Duke's trial; B) the prosecutor elicited this perjury and held it out as true, and as evidence of Chambers credibility, to the jury; C) the primary law enforcement officer testified to Chambers trustworthiness and reliability; D) in fact Chambers had a record of arrests for offense among other things involving fraud and false statements; E) Chambers had admittedly committed perjury about these and other things in other Federal criminal trials; F) various other federal prosecutors and agents were aware of Chambers' record and perjury; and G) the prosecutor in Duke's case told defense counsel that Chambers had no record. [4]

In Howard Bass' 93 page appeal to the 8th Circuit Court, Howard's introduction is as follows:

> Few things are more repugnant to the constitutional expectations of our criminal justice system than covert perjury, especially perjury that flows from a concerted

---

[4] Jack Nordby is now a State Judge. My interview with him is included in this book. His excellent brief signed March 8, 1994 was rejected by the 8th Circuit Court of Appeals. Pages 1114 of his brief are included at the end of this chapter.

Chapter 5 - Ralph Chavez Duke

effort by rewarded criminals to frame a defendant. The ultimate mission of the system upon which we rely to protect the liberty of the accused as well as the welfare of society is to ascertain the factual truth, and to do so in a manner that comports with due process of law is defined by our constitution. This important mission is utterly derailed by unchecked lying witnesses, and by any law enforcement officer or prosecutor who finds it tactically advantageous to turn a blind eye to the manifest potential for malevolent disinformation.

Howard then goes on to cite various cases supporting Duke's position. On page five of Howard's brief, he states:

Mr. Duke's main contention in his previous section 2255 __was that newly discovered evidence that Chambers committed perjury is and always will be significant.

Later in the brief, Howard Bass submitted my November 2001 affidavit that included the accompanying appendix, statements I had taken that was newly discovered evidence. Howard Bass' appeal was denied by the 8th Circuit Court and they made no comment. I was shocked by this in that I naively believed as Bass pointed out on page 74, the newly discovered evidence of perjury by government witnesses at Duke's trial reflects a campaign of deception and perjury by government agents and prosecutors aimed at securing Mr. Duke's conviction at any cost.

By the time I got to the witnesses, most of them had served their time and I assured them it was extremely improbable they would get in any trouble by giving me statements. They had paid their debt and I just could not imagine some government agents finding out they had cooperated with the appeal and coming down hard on any of these witnesses.

On several occasions in Howard's brief, he went into talking about various witnesses and referred to my affidavits For example, Ralph Lamont (Monte Nunn) confirms that he orchestrated the 20 kilo transaction with Andrew Chambers and that his father had absolutely no involvement in that deal. Also, Anthony Turner and Loren Duke corroborate that affidavit. A copy of Danny Givens' interview was included in the brief and in the course and scope of my investigation it was substantiated that neither Scott Treadwell, Andre Phillips, Kevin Walker, David Yoman, Loren Duke and Marcel Duke ever bought drugs from Ralph Duke.

Previously I mentioned Theryl Dugas confirmed that no Duke gang ever existed. The fact of the matter is through the investigation and throughout Bass' brief, it was noted all these young people chipped in money, Monte set up the deal for the buy and Ralph Duke had nothing to do with any of this.

All along, the government had put it out that Ralph Duke was running some kind of a gang similar to the Crips, the Bloods, the mafia or one of the Asian gangs and it just wasn't so. Joseph Ballard ;a nephew of Ralph Duke; was a witness in the case and Arcel Magee confirmed no Duke gang. On approximately five occasions, Joseph Ballard transported cars for Ralph Duke from California to Minnesota for resale or new sale. Contrary to his testimony at trial, Ballard never transported drugs in any of these cars. In fact, on April 27, 1989, three weeks before Duke's arrest, the police stopped Ballard and his brother, Jeffrey, in Faribault, Minnesota, and seized their vehicles. Although the police thoroughly searched the vehicles, they found no drugs and released the Ballard brothers the following day.[5]

According to Ballard, in a statement to me, before he was released from custody DE Agent Kerry put a gun to his head and accused him of transporting drugs for his uncle, Ralph Duke. Approximately two months later, Joseph Ballard was arrested and told by Agent Kerry that he would do 30 years for big time transportation of drugs. Ballard ultimately agreed to falsify his testimony against his uncle to avoid a lengthy prison sentence. This was the pattern of conduct of the government. It goes on and on. Incidentally, Ballard's father, who was a deputy sheriff, one of the few black deputy sheriffs, gave me a statement that his son falsely testified in Ralph Duke's case for fear of going to prison for 30 years. A brother, Jeffrey Ballard, also gave a

---

[5] Joseph Ballard was released barefoot.

Chapter 5 - Ralph Chavez Duke

statement that no Duke gang existed. Jacqueline Ballard, Joseph Ballard's sister, also confirmed to me that no Duke gang existed. She corroborated Jeffrey Ballard's claim that Ralph Duke was trying to straighten out their brother, Joseph Ballard. As previously mentioned by Mr. Dugas, Duke was actually like a *bona fide* uncle to a lot of these cousins and nephews wanting them to remain on the straight and narrow.

The pressure the government agents and prosecutors put on all these young people in an effort to convict Ralph Duke was simply enormous. For example, David Yoman was threatened with 10 years in prison and the indictment and imprisonment of his mother and pregnant girlfriend if he refused to testify against Ralph Duke. Yoman falsely testified to avoid all this misery. All of these people recanted and it is incredible to me with all these recantations that were consistent, that the appellate court totally disregarded the numerous statements that I had taken, Bass' support by precedent of rules and regulations governing perjury testimony. All of this bugs me.

It is absolutely unconscionable that prosecutor Denise Riley and John Hopeman would have suborned perjury. Denise Riley is now a judge and Hopeman is in private practice. Nothing happened to those people by way of a reprimand even though allowed Chambers to lie and they represented him as a straight guy. Everyone was so hell bent on convicting Ralph Duke that they just didn't give a damn how they did it. Every snitch on the government's payroll has a handler. The knowledge of Chambers, whose activity went on for a long period of time as a snitch, who testified in many cases and who ultimately was paid millions of dollars had to be known among agents and prosecutors throughout the country. I don't know how they can put spin on this bullshit, but of course they will. It amazes me that Riley and Hopeman can sleep at night.

Regardless of one's reputation, whether it is horrible, honorable or just average, reputation is basically hearsay. Our actions, conduct, demeanor and the people with associate with are indicative of who we are. If somehow an individual has developed a bad reputation in certain circles, that is not enough to make an attempt to charge and convict that individual. If, indeed, the police, drug enforcement agency, Bureau of Criminal Apprehension, FBI and whomever had been looking at Ralph Duke for such a lengthy period of time with all those resources why wasn't he ever charged? The government had to falsify evidence to convict Ralph Duke. I have no idea what Duke had been up to over the years and there is no reason for me to know what he was involved in. You should prosecute Hitler for his crimes, not for the crimes of Joseph Stalin,. There are numerous cases of the government suborning perjury, manipulating evidence, and the recent dismissal of former Senator Stevens' case is a classic example. I am writing this in April of 2009 and the Attorney General of the United States threw Stevens' case out the window. The prosecutor's conduct by withholding evidence from the defense was absolutely outrageous and there is a possibility that the prosecutors in that case may be charged. At a minimum, they should be fined and disbarred. Now Stevens was a republican senator in Alaska, I personally did not like him, but he got screwed without getting kissed and I find that reprehensible.

I enclosed four pages of Honorable Jack Nordby's argument from 1994 brief. The entire document is a matter is of public record. The same pertains to attorney Howard Bass' brief that was absolutely brilliant. I did not enclose excerpts from Bass' brief in that my intent was to do a chapter on Duke, not an entire book.

I did not include an interview with my good friend Howard Bass but I should have. He is an honorable man, intelligent, tough as a cob. I have worked with him on numerous cases and he has high standards, expecting his support staff to complete their tasks in a timely fashion. I like this. I do not like loose ends or unfinished business hanging over my head. Howard is great strategist and I will give you an example.

In the Hold That Tiger chapter, the passenger in the truck that Mary Hartman was allegedly chasing was on the witness stand. His name is Court Garloff. The prosecutor, for good reason, did not call the truck driver, a shady character as we know because of my background investigation of him in the State of Iowa. Howard Bass would have stripped him naked in front of the jury.

Regarding Garloff, when the prosecutor was questioning him, Howard Bass was not objecting to some of the bullshit trickling off the tongue of this creep. I quickly figured Howard was giving the guy

Chapter 5 - Ralph Chavez Duke

enough rope to hang himself upon cross-examination, Howard also gave t his guy plenty of room. Garloff even came out of the witness box to physically demonstrate a point he wanted to make. He was dramatic and ultimately pissed the jury off. Howard nailed this creep on cross but the hammer really came down on Garloff during Howard's final argument. As you know from that chapter, Howard got a not guilty verdict. Howard Bass is one of the great criminal defense attorneys in the state of Minnesota. Ask one of his colleagues if you doubt my word. To conclude this chapter on Ralph "Plookie" Duke, it is true when the Feds searched a locker he owned, they found a silencer for gun. I do not know his explanation for possessing this object, nor do I have an explanation of any other evidence that was used against Duke. My concern and entire focus regarding the post conviction investigation for Duke was his arrest and conviction based on lies. That of course was the essence of Bass' outstanding brief. Duke has paid dearly for his transgressions whatever they may be. The asshole agents who orchestrated Duke's false charges on his case even paid for a bill board in St. Paul, Minnesota. It showed a guy in front of a car, the caption was bye-bye, Plookie. I wonder if prosecutors Riley and Hopeman chipped in some cash for the billboard.

I am quite certain no prosecutor, D.E.A. agent, F.B.I. sleuth, judge or politician gives a rat's ass about my opinions. However, because we have freedom of speech still in this country, I offer the following: on a Federal level, those in power constantly abuse their authority and strive for convictions using any means they can. The end justifies the means. I further believe in the Duke case that 8th Circuit Court of Appeals just didn't give a damn about a black man with a bad reputation. Even though the prosecutors suborned perjury and numerous witnesses recanted their testimony, there were other charges against Duke that held up in court. Never mind those charges were the fruit of the poisoned tree. Regarding the trial judge Doty, his sentence of Duke could not have been more brutal, sending this first time offender to life plus 40.

State Court, city police, sheriff's department and Minnesota B.C.A. are superior to the Feds in every respect. I have great respect for the many Minneapolis Police officers I have known over the years. Also, I have had the pleasure of knowing great judges such as the late Stan

Kane, Crane Winton, Mark Wernick, Kevin Burke, Lucy Wieland, and of course Jack Nordby. I must say, Honorable Judges Mike Davis, Richard Kyle, and James Rosenbaum are men of integrity, fair and impartial. These judges are highly regarded federal jurists. Remember, federal judges are politically appointed of course the same is often true on a state level but then they must run for reelection. My final thoughts about prosecutors Riley and Hopeman and those nasty agents who did the dirty work, things that go around, come around.

Argument

The appellant who is serving concurrent life sentences based upon circumstantial evidence in a government reverse sting operation in which a paid undercover informer was the central and most important figure, is obviously entitled to a new trial (or at the very least an evidentiary hearing on his motion) where:

> The prosecutor in his opening statement vouched for the informer's reliability, credibility and good character and emphasized he had never been arrested or convicted; the primary law enforcement agent, who was the informer's controller, forcefully vouched for his good character, reliability and trustworthiness;

> The informer committed blatant and intentional perjury by specifically denying that he had ever been arrested in his "whole life";

> In fact, as appellant discovered after trial, the informer had been arrested on multiple occasions and convicted, and had in previous federal criminal trials admitted committing perjury as a government witness;

> This information was readily available to the prosecution, in standard FBI records and other judicial records, and well-known to other federal prosecutors and law enforcement agents; the prosecution did not disclose this information to defense counsel, though clearly required to do so, and told defense counsel the witness had no record;

> The district court denied appellant's *pro se* post-conviction motion within a week of the government's response, without even holding a hearing or awaiting the filing of a response, in an order that is clearly mistaken as to the applicable law and the evidence.
>
> The absence of the evidence denied the defendant his rights to due process and confrontation.

This record contains absolutely conclusive evidence of a serious federal felony crime, brazenly committed in the presence of a cloud of unimpeachable eyewitnesses, including a federal judge, federal prosecutors, twelve jurors and their alternates, a clerk, a court reporter, bailiffs, the defendants and their lawyers, and whatever spectators were on hand that day.

Letter from Duke

Mr. Duke on his own continues to send me information supporting his innocence in the case that led to his conviction. The following data is what he has sent to me from prison. He is serving life without parole in a Federal Supermax prison. Damn interesting I must say.

> Vinnie,
>
> After talking to you Sunday I just wanted to conclude these facts in the story of Marvin McCaleb, if you could talk to Mark Kallenbach, and find out if he would be of help in this matter, as far as contacting Dennis Gauthier, his investigator who went to interview Mr. Virgil Kirkwood in the Anoka County Jail and having Dennis give you a sworn statement of what he was told. Vinnie, if you would mention to Mark about him getting a copy of the statement that McCaleb first gave, to prosecutor Hopeman, and Michael Carey, when they went to Los Angeles and seen him.
>
> Government Witness, Marvin McCaleb had been convicted of Manslaughter at 18 in 1978, of rape by force in 1979 and possessing 25,000 grams of cocaine Dec 28, 1988, with intent to distribute, but what the prosecution left out was these facts.
>
> Marvin McCaleb was being investigated by the DEA in 1988. McCaleb was busted Dec 28, 1988 with 25,000 grams of cocaine, Los Angeles, California along with his partner Dwayne Davis, at this time McCaleb was given a $1,000,000 bond, where he remained locked up from Dec

Whatever happened to Lady Justice?

28, 1988 until sometime in March of 1989. After his release he was found to have violated the terms of his bail. He did not pass his drug test, and was found in possession of two grams of cocaine. During this whole time, never once was the name Ralph Duke mentioned in the McCaleb Investigation). The arrest of Ralph "Plookie" Duke was May 17, 1989 in a government sting operation. Prosecutor Jon Hopeman and Agent Michael Carey flew to Los Angeles, California in July to interview Marvin McCaleb. Marvin McCaleb gave Jon Hopeman and Michael Carey a signed statement to the effect that Ralph Duke sold him a new Jaguar in the state of Minnesota, Dec 23, 1988, that Ralph Duke lived one block from where he lived in Baldwin Hills, California. That Ralph Duke was not a drug dealer and that he believed that Duke's girlfriend was a prostitute.

The second time prosecutor Jon Hopeman, and Michael Carey confronted Marvin McCaleb they threatened to indict his Mother Dorothy McCaleb on money laundering charges, because the auto McCaleb bought from Duke was put in his Mother's name. Marvin McCaleb testified for the government against Ralph Duke to protect his Mother from being charged for his signing her name on the contract of the 1989 Jaguar Dec 23, 1988 at Simpson Leasing, Roseville, Minnesota. None of Duke's co-defendant's had ever even heard of Marvin McCaleb, until he showed up to testify against Duke. Marvin McCaleb was never indicted in the Duke indictment. McCaleb had charges pending in Los Angeles, California, for possession with the intent to distribute 25,000 grams of cocaine. McCaleb was sentenced to 7 years, and Duke who had never been convicted of any crimes period, state or federal was a first time offender, but was sentenced to life plus 40 years. McCale completed his sentence of 7 years, and continued on selling drugs, where he was busted again, and after 20 years from falsely testifying against Ralph "Plookie" Duke, McCaleb on his 6th or 7th bust has been sentenced to life plus 242 months as of 2009.

Dated Dec 7, 2009

Well Vinnie, I really do think that makes for some very good reading, anyone who will read this will wonder What's Going On! Thank you for everything.

Thank You

Ralph "Plookie" Duke 12.8.09

Chapter 6

'Broadway' Joe Friedberg, Attorney

I first met attorney Joe Friedberg in the 1970s when he had an office in a charming building that was across from the Hennepin County Courthouse. The building has been demolished and in its place stands the Lutheran Brotherhood located on Fourth Avenue South in Minneapolis. Joe Friedberg is one of the most delightful attorneys in the Twin Cities. He is quick-witted, obviously very smart, free of pretenses and respected by everyone who has contact with him. He is also a very grateful individual; not only to his staff, but for the many good things that have come his way in life. He and his wife had a child that died and, of course, nothing could be more traumatic than that. Joe also had a serious operation that disabled him for a period of time, but he bounced back to continue his successful career. He is also a person that has shown genuine concern for everyone's rights.

Mr. Friedberg, as I write this, is one of Norm Coleman's lawyers in the horrible senate election controversy that is before the Supreme Court of Minnesota. It is my guess that this will go on to the Supreme Court of the United States. The whole thing has been a burden on the citizens of Minnesota and also Amy Klobuchar, our other senator. Some of my friends have wondered how and why Mr. Friedberg, being a criminal defense attorney, thus a liberal, would assist in the defense of a George Bush supporter. My answer to this may not be totally thorough, but I believe most defense attorneys will represent anyone regardless of the person's politics. If a case is challenging and interesting to a defense lawyer, he or she will go forward and do the utmost to give proper representation to their client. I also tell people that every citizen has a right to counsel, particularly good representation. If you can hire one of the best attorneys in town, then you should do so. Politics does not play a part concerning your client.

On March 20, 2006 I interviewed Joe Friedberg at his office. This was a recorded interview, but I am reducing the transcript to more of a narrative which may make it more comfortable for the reader. So

Chapter 6 - 'Broadway' Joe Friedberg, Attorney

everything I say regarding Mr. Friedberg remains on a tape and I have copies of the transcript.

Joe Friedberg went to the University of North Carolina Law School and his first year out of school, he taught at Stanford Law School. From there, he went back to New York City and clerked with a Wall Street law firm for awhile prior to coming to Minnesota.

Joe came out to Minnesota to sell encyclopedias because he needed to make some quick money in that his expenses were rising in New York. He told me he borrowed $250 from a buddy, left his wife and child in New York, came to Minnesota and ultimately stayed.-He tells people he ran out of money half way on the way to the west coast and had to stick around Minneapolis.

Joe was born in Brooklyn, New York and raised on Long Island in what he described as a little village. He claims he was lucky to live there because you knew everybody and-he knew everybody in his high school class. In Minnesota, he was admitted to the bar in 1966, but didn't actually set up a practice, but volunteered with a couple organizations to take some criminal cases for free. The first couple of years he never got a fee and never asked for one. He represented indigents or those that may not have trusted the public defender. Joe said around 1968 or 1969 when dope had effectively moved to the suburbs, some people came to him and were able to pay a fee so that is how his practice began.

Joe said that he has been fortunate to work with great lawyers such as Ron Meshbesher and Doug Thomson, claiming they were mentors to him and he learned a great deal in that process. He has also worked with William Mauzy, Peter Thompson, and a host of others and Joe has been very gracious with his praise of all these lawyers.

I informed Joe that it was always a delight for me to work with him. Many of his cases were not high profile, but damn important felony matters. Joe reminded me that every case is important to the defendant and every case deserves attention and good representation. I asked Joe if he recalled a particular case that he was appointed by the court, whereby two black individuals were accused of raping a physically and mentally challenged young female. Joe said he remembered that quite well.

Joe stated that when he got appointed to that case and he read the complaint and police reports, he went up and talked to the defendant in jail. He said he recalled asking me to also talk to the defendant and to go forward with an investigation. Joe said I really didn't want to deal with this guy because the allegations made the guy look so loathsome that he preferred to have me visit the man in jail. Joe said "I'll try the case, Vinnie, you do the investigation." He said about two weeks later I came to him and said that this guy is innocent. Joe said later on he became a little embarrassed because it turned out to be true that the guy was innocent.

Joe said that the co-defendant, who had been represented by a public defender who essentially had thrown in the towel, had already been convicted and got 20 years at Stillwater. The prosecutor, after the acquittal of Joe's client, went to the judge with Joe and informed him that an innocent guy was in prison for 20 years and they got the other guy out of the slammer in about a week. Rob Lynn, at the time, was the prosecutor and now he is a Hennepin County Judge. Lynn was always an honorable guy and, of course, I agree with Joe on that. Joe was pretty hard on the public defender in this matter and gave me a great deal of credit for his success in gaining an acquittal.

I reminded Joe that there was a great deal of luck involved and reminded him of what happened. I had been looking unsuccessfully for witnesses who lived in an apartment by the old Minneapolis auditorium on Grant Street. I had banged on doors at various times of the day and was getting absolutely nowhere when one tenant told me that she knew something about this matter and it was a guy named Chicago Jackson who might have been a witness to Joe's client and others partying out front of the apartment. Apparently there were quite a few people out in front of the apartment drinking wine and smoking weed. This person told me that Chicago Jackson hung out at a particular saloon on Nicollet Avenue and that he drove a little convertible that was green in color. Jackson also ran around in a brightly colored jumpsuit.

Chapter 6 - 'Broadway' Joe Friedberg, Attorney

I went to this bar and the front part was patronized by blacks, and strangely enough, on the other side of the building it was all country western kind of redneck. I went in the bar holding up my card and stating that I was looking for Chicago Jackson, and that I wasn't with the police. Jackson then appeared, listened to my pitch, lined up all these witnesses for us, and the witnesses testified in the case. The evidence revealed that the accuser, when walking back to her group home was violating her curfew. Joe's client had walked her home and she made up a story about being raped that was all bullshit. She thought she was going to be punished for violating the curfew.

We then discussed a case that was absolutely wild and involved a number of defendants and lawyers and tried in federal court. Ron Meshbesher's client was an attorney named Norm Perl and it had to do with Norm and other employees at Norm's firm that was then called the DeParq Law Firm. They did a great deal of railroad work along with the personal injury cases that came in. Rich Vosepka was the prosecutor for the government; Bill Mauzy, Phil Resnik attorney Mile and Ron Meshbesher represented various defendants. A civil investigator by the name of Bob Olson was Joe's client and he was a very likeable teddy bear-type guy, outgoing and friendly. He had a lot of contacts on the Iron Range having come from that territory.

Joe remembered that Perl's firm was accused of having an insurance adjuster from the Aetna Insurance Company on their payroll when they were settling Dalkon Shield cases for women that were injured by that product. It was an emotionally charged federal trial. All the local federal judges disqualified themselves and Joe said that after the first week, the prosecutors and defense lawyers didn't even speak to each other. The trial lasted 16 weeks and everybody was acquitted of every charge which in retrospect made it all worthwhile. Joe said it was the most acrimonious trial he had ever been in.

Jacqueline Stone and I worked on that case dividing up witnesses, but certainly we will never forget what took place. Jacqueline, who is now an investigator for public defenders in three counties, did a marvelous job. She interviewed quite a number of women who may have been more comfortable speaking to her rather than me.

The prosecutor, for about a week, out of earshot of the jury, wanted me named an unindicted co-conspirator. Ron Meshbesher finally lost it and the judge, in essence, told the prosecutor that there will be no more of that crap. Joe said that the first day of trial, Ron Meshbesher's client, Norm Perl, was really in a state of high anxiety. He would pace behind counsel table when the jury had been on a break, and one time while at counsel table, he yelled out an objection. All the lawyers in the case went to Ron Meshbesher and said that he needs to tranq him or they would all cop out and testify against him. Ron Meshbesher calmed Mr. Perl down and Joe said he believed Ron Meshbesher took him to a doctor and got him a prescription for medication to help him relax.

Friedberg went on to say that his client, Bob Olson, was an absolute wreck during the trial which went on for 16 weeks. I told Joe that part way through the trial, Bob called me and said that Ron Meshbesher's client owed him money. He was very upset about this and said he was thinking about going to the prosecutor and cutting a deal. I immediately went to Ron Meshbesher and told him that his client has to somehow calm Olson down.

. After the case was over, Bob Olson contacted a well-known professor of law by the name of David Graven and something was worked out concerning the money that Olson claimed was owed to him.

Joe said that the defense lawyers worked extremely well together in that case. He said that he repressed quite a bit about the entire experience. He had been friendly with Prosecutor Vosepka going into that trial, but after the trial they were never reunited as friends. Joe said there were terrible hard feelings and he thinks that trial was the downfall of Rich Vosepka. Shortly thereafter, Vosepka left the Feds and went into private practice. My understanding is that he is doing fine right now.

I brought up the expert witness aspect of the case. The defense had hired a former CIA document expert, one of the last guys to leave Viet Nam. This expert came in ready to do battle, but had expressed to me that after picking him up from the airport, he was not a hired gun, he called things as he saw them.

Chapter 6 - 'Broadway' Joe Friedberg, Attorney

Joe said he thought the expert deliberately tried to piss off the prosecutors, Tom Heffelfinger and Rich Vosepka. Joe felt that the expert deliberately refused to pronounce their names and would refer to them as Vavaka and Hellifunker, which just annoyed the hell out of the prosecutors. It turns out that the expert was an excellent witness, but neither Joe nor I could remember exactly what he testified to. Joe said that what he thought happened in the case is that the jury hated everybody. They hated the prosecutors, the judge, the defense lawyers, the defendants, the witnesses, and they were determined not to take any action and get the hell out of town.

The judge had come up from Iowa and lost control of the whole courtroom. At one point in time, Joe could not remember who made the comment, but someone said to Miley "That judge is Catholic, why don't when we take a break you go talk to him because you speak Catholic." It was just absolutely nuts.

I turned the recording machine off at one point to ask Joe if it would be inappropriate to speak about a very sensitive case I had worked on for Peter Thompson and him. Joe assured me that it would be appropriate to chat about former Judge Crane Winton's case because Winton has come out of the closet and has a partner and is doing very well. Joe gave some background.

Joe stated that Crane Winton was one of the most prestigious, well thought of judges who has ever been on the Hennepin County bench and he had presided for a number of years. Ironically, prior to the judge's legal dilemma, he had been kind of glorified in one of the local magazines who also made him the most eligible bachelor in town. Judge Winton had the admiration of everyone including prosecutors, defenses lawyers, civil lawyers, other judges, and he was a well-known bachelor who lived in the prestigious Kenwood area of Minneapolis. Joe said that in those days there were some folks who suspected he was gay, it wasn't openly talked about and nobody cared. Joe was extremely friendly with the judge and the gay issue just was not an issue between either one of them.

What happened in the case is that WCCO TV Eye Team in conjunction with the Bureau of Criminal Apprehension were looking into juvenile male prostitutes that hung out in Loring Park in Minneapolis,

Minnesota. Loring Park is a downtown Minneapolis park surrounded by some small restaurants, newly built townhomes and renovated apartments. It has a small pond, tennis courts, basketball courts, etc. In the course of the investigation by the BCA, Crane Winton's name surfaced as a customer of some of these male prostitutes, and he was charged with using under aged male hookers.

Peter Thompson and Joe were friends with Judge Winton who asked both of them if they could work together on his case. At the time, Joe and Peter had never worked a case together but knew each other and had a great deal of respect for one another. In addition, attorney John McNulty and Marcy Wallace contributed to the case, both of these individuals are first rate lawyers and John McNulty was a one time sitting judge.

The first order in the case was the criminal aspect and that worked out okay. Joe said it was one of the toughest things he had to do in court, but he and Peter pled Judge Winton to a misdemeanor charge. The Honorable Judge Charlie Kennedy presided because they couldn't have a local judge hear the case, and Winton was fined $200 or $300. At the time of Judge Winton's plea, he had written out what Joe and Peter would call a coming out statement which Joe read in court, and it was an admission of being gay. That was the end of the criminal issue. It was a very emotional experience and after that, the Board of Judicial Standards came after Crane Winton for stuff that arose out of the criminal matter.

I brought up to Joe during my interview with him the role that the WCCO Eye Team played in this matter. Some of the witnesses that were picked up by a BCA agent who was accompanied by Don Shelby of the Eye Team, ended up going to the TV station when they thought they were going over to the BCA. The station put them in disguise and disguised their voice and put them on TV. I interviewed these witnesses who were male hookers, all 18 or over. When I interviewed, they were very angry with the fact that they were put on television. A couple of them said that they were going to sue because they thought they were going to the police station. My question dealt with the ethics of an investigative journalist going out on matters with a BCA agent. Frankly, I thought it was pretty damn tacky.

Chapter 6 - 'Broadway' Joe Friedberg, Attorney

Joe said that he and I got in trouble because of that case. During the time of the investigation, the criminal case went so well that Joe remembered that he and I went looking for a couple of witnesses that had gone missing. We decided to go down to Loring Park, along with a friend of Joe's by the name of Freddy Brunshun who drove a Corvette convertible. Joe said that we would attract these hookers easier with a Corvette and the top down. Maybe they will think we are johns and approach us.

We started out at a gay bar called Ya'll Come Back Saloon, which in itself was an experience and we were told by the owner that we would find these guys down at Loring Park. We were specifically looking for a guy named John John. We had just arrived when we heard some screaming and yelling. We went over to the area and there was a young fellow that we talked to who stated he had just been assaulted with a knife by this John John. Lo and behold, this guy turned out to be a witness in Crane Winton's case and John John had not only assaulted him, but robbed him. We alerted the police even though cell phones hadn't been invented, we were able to do this and a warrant was issued for John John. I had interviewed John John previous to all of this, and he had turned on me later on because I also interviewed his young boyfriend who John John abused. The boyfriend had called me about it. As I said, John John turned on me because I interviewed his boyfriend.

I have to add a little story here. My wife and I, on a Friday night, went out; our children were old enough to leave home by themselves. We returned home at about 11:00 P.M. and found our daughter had locked herself in the bathroom. I knocked on the door and she came out and put her arms around me. She told me that she got this terrible phone call from a guy. She was frightened. I asked her who the guy was and what did he say. My daughter said that the guy who called asked her if Vince the cocksucker was there. She said that it scared her and that is why she had locked all the doors and barricaded herself in the bathroom.

About an hour later, at midnight or so, the phone rang and I was still awake and answered it. The person at the other end said, "Is this Vince, the cocksucker?" I said, "Who's this?" He said, "John John." I said, "You're a little mixed up, I'm the investigator and you're the cocksucker." That shocked the hell out of him and he made some goofy threats and hung up.

After Friedberg, Freddy and I talked to this guy at the park who was assaulted by John John, I met the guy the following morning and took his statement in a little restaurant by Loring Park. We had a very inexpensive breakfast. However, at a later date, I was ambushed by Al Austin of the WCCO Eye Team while I was painting screens in my garage. I informed him that that there was a gag order on this case and nobody is supposed to talk to anyone about it. But his response was, "Well, Vinnie, you gave that guy I had interviewed 10 or 20 bucks for his statement." My response was, "Mr. Austin, that is absolutely absurd, can you imagine bribing someone with $10-20?" This is just bull shit.

Mr. Friedberg went on to say that they defended Judge Winton in front of the Board of Judicial Standards and that there was some amazing testimony in that case. The Board defrocked him as a judge, but he wasn't disbarred as a lawyer. The Supreme Court affirmed that. Mr. Friedberg said he got in more trouble because he was so mad about the Supreme Court de-judging him that at the press conference, he called their opinion sub-intellectual and he got in some more hot water over that. But to him, it was all for the best cause in the world as the man should still be a judge to this day!

I responded to Mr. Friedberg's comment by stating that we have a dual standard; one for homosexuals and one for heterosexuals. Mr. Friedberg said that is exactly right. He said that he was putting witnesses on the stand left and right in an effort to determine whether this tryst of Judge Winton brought the bench into disrepute. He was calling witnesses to testify whether or not the state's law against consensual sodomy was often violated. Mr. Friedberg said he called one witness after another, a number of judges and lawyers. The prosecutor, whose name was Kelly Gauge, got to the point where he wasn't paying too much attention. Mr. Friedberg said he had Doug Thomson on the stand and he said to him, "Mr. Thomson, based on your training and experience, your observations over the years, what percentage of sitting judges violate the state's proscription against consensual sodomy?" Mr. Thomson said, "95 percent." Mr. Friedberg said at that point and time people started to laugh in the gallery,

Chapter 6 - 'Broadway' Joe Friedberg, Attorney

which was packed, and Kelly Gauge had missed the question completely so Mr. Friedberg then asked Mr. Thomson, "Based on your training, experience, your observations over the years, what percentage of the practicing bar violates the state's proscription against consensual sodomy?" Thomson's response was, "99 percent." Mr. Friedberg said, "So that leaves one percent that don't engage in consensual sodomy." Mr. Thomson's reply on the witness stand was, "And that's me."

Mr. Friedberg said people were in hysterics and the judges were extremely angry because they were making light of the whole thing, which is what the defense intended to do in the first place. Mr. Friedberg said one of the judges asked Mr. Thomson, "What authority do you have for your testimony?" Mr. Thomson's reply was, "Other than my personal observations, I have Playboy Magazine and the Kinsey Report." Mr. Friedberg said when Mr. Thomson went out in the hallway, the press just mobbed him. Mr. Friedberg said that this was the fun of practicing law. The reporters said to Mr. Thomson, "Are you claiming that you are the only lawyer in this state that doesn't violate the law against consensual sodomy?" Mr. Thomson said, "Yes, I am, but I'm constantly the victim of it." It was the quintessential Doug Thomson. What a great story.

I mentioned to Mr. Friedberg that I just finished reading a book authored by a man named Carr on the Bulger Brothers out of Boston. Whitey Bulger is the most wanted guy on the FBI list and his brother, Billy, had been President of the State of Massachusetts Senate and then Chancellor of Boston University where he ultimately resigned. Mr. Friedberg suggested that I read the <u>Black Mass</u>. It is the same story about Whitey and the corrupt FBI agent, Connolly, one of Bulger's friends. We talked about informants and I mentioned Chambers in the Duke Case and Red Adams. Mr. Friedberg mentioned a guy named Chuck Stevenson who invaded Ron Meshbesher's office through, his girlfriend, who worked for the Meshbesher, Singer & Spence law firm some time back. Stevenson had been a client of Mr. Friedberg and something really strange took place with Stevenson, but Mr. Friedberg said he never looked into it because he didn't care. Stevenson was convicted of forgery. Mr. Friedberg lost the appeal, but strangely enough Stevenson never went to jail; he vanished and never did his time, but he turns up as

Whatever happened to Lady Justice?

the guy who maneuvered the burglary of Ron Meshbesher's office at the request of a narcotics agent by the name of Ron Johnson. Johnson was on loan to the DEA, which back in those days was known as the BNDD (Bureau of Narcotics and Dangerous Drugs). Mr. Friedberg said there was some very bad narcotics agents back in those days who would do anything to get a conviction.

Mr. Friedberg went on to say that the whole snitching thing is really deplorable. He stated that when he first started in practice that he wouldn't represent anybody that was going to cooperate with the government and make up stories to save his own buns. Mr. Friedberg said he believed turning on friends is more immoral than the selling of the drugs. Mr. Friedberg said he stated that he thinks the whole system is directed toward turning people into stool pigeons and other birds of prey. He said that nowadays in order to make a living, you are compelled to represent some of these snitches. When the government sends out a missile that says we want your client's cooperation, you have to deliver the message to your client. Mr. Friedberg said they pay in different ways, meaning ordinarily they pay by reducing the snitch's time which technically violates the bribery statute, but good luck on getting anybody to rule that way. To Mr. Friedberg, it increases the immorality of the whole milieu that we are dealing in and it is a very troublesome thing, but all the criminal lawyers in this town will participate in it. There are lawyers around the country who have taken a position that they will have nothing to do with anybody that cooperates and will withdraw from a case if they do. These lawyers are from bigger cities with higher crime.

Again, I mentioned Chambers who was paid huge sums of money for testimony. Mr. Friedberg said that those are the ones who essentially keep working with the government, are encouraged to keep working, and the government doesn't care what these guys do.

I expressed my anger over the Duke case pertaining to the prosecutors, Denise Riley and Jon Hopeman, knowingly and wittingly allowing Chambers to perjure himself on the witness stand. I reminded Mr. Friedberg that if he or any other lawyer did such a thing, they would really be hammered. I asked him what his sense was of this in that the prosecutors were never chastised for any misconduct. Mr. Friedberg said that he didn't know the answer to

Chapter 6 - 'Broadway' Joe Friedberg, Attorney

that question. He said that Ralph Duke fired him prior to the sentencing, and he wasn't around when I turned up the newly discovered evidence.

Mr. Friedberg recalled how he got involved in this case. He said Ken Meshbesher called and said that Duke had been a client of the Meshbesher firm going way back and Ken did not think he was a drug dealer, he was running cars. Mr. Friedberg said when he looked at the Complaint which was strictly the deal of the purchase of 20 kilos that Chambers was involved in, he said, "If this is what the case is about, it's a bit skinny and I might be able to win the damn thing." It's not easy to win Federal cases. The indictment swallowed that all up. The indictment went back years and with the evidence that came out pursuant to the other parts of the case, Mr. Friedberg said that they were overwhelmed with evidence. But in relation to that discreet transaction, it didn't seem like Duke's deal. It never did seem like it was Duke's deal, but that became somewhat irrelevant in the trial of the case because there was so much other evidence against him about other deals. I think that is why the appellate courts won't reverse claiming it was harmless error in the trial. My position was that of fruit from the poisonous tree; meaning that all the other stuff that came out about Duke was a result of him being busted on this 20 kilo deal. Obviously, my poison tree theory does not hold water.

Mr. Friedberg went on to say that it never mattered that Duke was a first offender. Mr. Friedberg talked about this guy that came in from Hollywood, California to testify against Duke, a good-looking black guy with a prior for manslaughter and a prior for rape. Mr. Friedberg said he would never forget him walking through the door as he looked like he stepped out of Gentleman's Quarterly and testified that he had been Duke's partner for a couple of years. Mr. Friedberg said he couldn't move him on cross-examination and he said the guy buried them: He said he turned to Duke and said, "It's over." He had corroboration for what he was saying. He talked about people running dope east to west for Duke. Mr. Friedberg said that it appeared that the car business that Duke was in was really phony, but if he had been tried on just the 20 kilo transaction, which Mr. Friedberg believed he was innocent of, all would have been fine.[6]

Again, I brought up the point of these young guys that testified, his own son, nephew, and the others who were threatened and intimidated and subsequently said what needed to be said to convict Duke. I wondered why all the other stuff wasn't pulled together and Duke charged on these other crimes instead of being charged on the 20 kilo deal. Mr. Friedberg said that they had those people ready to testify for some period of time and they had wire taps that were incriminating.

I informed Mr. Friedberg that I don't know why the sentence by the judge was so harsh. Mr. Friedberg felt that it was because the judge was convinced that Duke was running a drug dealing operation that was very big time, and they discovered in the search that he had two silencers. Mr. Friedberg thought he got 20 years for each silencer. Nevertheless, Mr. Friedberg felt that the sentence was incredibly unfair.

Mr. Friedberg mentioned a case I did for him in Detroit that was pretty out of this world where a body popped up in a trunk. That was the brother of Leland Carriger, now deceased, who was known as the King of Wings in Minneapolis. His brother was a hardnosed gangster in Detroit. He convinced Mr. Friedberg's client, Leland, to invest in an apartment building. Unbeknown to Leland, in a room in the basement there was a safe and it was busted by the Feds illegally and they found drugs and approximately $100,000 cash. This had really nothing to do with Leland, but he was charged and ultimately Mr. Friedberg won the case. I am sure now all the players are dead as this was a long time ago. But the brother's name was Buddy.

---

[6] Friedberg represented Ralph Duke, was informed by the prosecutors that Chambers was never charged or convicted with a crime. Also, the young witnesses were all represented and it was way after the trial they recanted to the author. Friedberg tried the best case on behalf of Duke that was possible.

Chapter 6 - 'Broadway' Joe Friedberg, Attorney

Buddy was taking me around to see witnesses. We went into one residence and briefly interviewed a woman. When we came out, Buddy's Cadillac had been stolen and all my luggage was in it., but thank God I had the file in my hand. I ended up staying all night at Buddy's house. In my follow-up investigation, I had all the witnesses come to my hotel.

The body that showed up in a trunk in front of Buddy's residence was a younger ex-girlfriend of his. Buddy was much older than I was, but I saw a picture of this woman in his family room and she was absolutely gorgeous. Buddy told me that he once said to her that if she was going to leave him, step up, don't step down. But he said obviously she stepped down and she got wacked by some scumbag who left her in the trunk of a car in front of Buddy's house. What a world.

I wasn't in attendance at the trial that Mr. Friedberg won on behalf of Leland, but he told me one night that he decided to go for a walk and had gone about a block toward the Joe Lewis Arena and was stopped by two cops. He said they patrolled in pairs and they came up to him and asked where he was going. He said he didn't give a smartass response, just told him that he was out for a walk. He said the cops told him to go back to your hotel, chances are if you continue walking you won't return. Detroit, in those days, was one hell of a rough area.

I asked Mr. Friedberg if he had recently heard from Candy Brown who did some work for Leland in L.A. She was the Queen of Wings. Mr. Friedberg said that the last time that he saw her was in Las Vegas, she was dressed to the nines wearing a white mink coat and he bumped into her at Caesar's Palace. He said in the little lobby there she said, "Mr. Friedberg, how are you?" His response was, "Candy, you seem to have come along quite well."

Doug Thomson had represented Candy on some occasions and Mr. Friedberg remembered that she had shot her boyfriend and it was kind of a famous St. Paul case and she shot the guy in front of a lot of people. She went down on second degree, it's a long story but she was tried as an adult and she was really a juvenile at the time. Judge Sid Abrams, a school mate of mine, reviewed her appeal and released her. Sid liked her and, of course, she adored the judge.

Mr. Friedberg said she would always call him when Doug wouldn't represent her on something, but I would never take her case because she was known in the legal business as one that would stiff you for the fee. She was very smart.

I informed Mr. Friedberg that when her brother's body was found in a dumpster out in Wayzata, I tried to help her out and we made some rounds up on the north side of Minneapolis, in the black community. I swear to God within a half-hour everybody knew some white guy was up there with Candy Brown asking questions. I never got anywhere and then ultimately Candy thought Duke was responsible for her brother's death.

Mr. Friedberg said the first time he ever came in contact with Ralph Duke was when he represented a guy for shooting at Duke with a sawed-off shotgun because Duke had hit on his lady. It took place at a bar and Duke was too far away outside when the guy blasted at him and missed. The guy got prosecuted, but Mr. Friedberg won the case at the preliminary hearing probably because Duke didn't show up.

I asked Mr. Friedberg what he thought about the attitude, mindset, and the general approach of prosecutors nowadays, both federal and state. Mr. Friedberg felt that the entire world has become a lot more mean-spirited and the legislators keep raising the sentences of those convicted. He said that we talk about 15 years now like it is 15 months as it used to be. There is a great deal of mean-spirited folks out there and he said that it applies to prosecutors and judges.

We talked about Judge Rosenbaum's situation and that asshole Senator, Sensenbrenner, who got on the judge's case concerning sentencing. Mr. Friedberg said that there was no reason to make Judge Rosenbaum's life miserable because he's a conservative judge, a registered Republican, respected by defense lawyers and prosecutors. Mr. Friedberg felt that Judge Rosenbaum is not an easy judge, he certainly is not a liberal but he was served up on a platter to this jerk-off Sensenbrenner who will probably stay in congress until his last breath.

Chapter 6 - 'Broadway' Joe Friedberg, Attorney

We talked about doing pro bono work which Mr. Friedberg does quite often and, of course, his position is that every lawyer should do some-free work for the poor and the disenfranchised.

I thanked Mr. Friedberg for his time and he said that if I get the book published, that he wants an autographed copy. I told him that since he was such a dynamite encyclopedia salesman, I would give him the downtown Minneapolis territory and pay him the biggest commission he ever saw for moving this book. That gave him a big laugh.

Chapter 7

Sex Crimes & False Accusations

There is an old saying that "Hell hath no fury as a woman scorned."

Unfortunately this can be all too true in sex crime cases. Several years ago I investigated a case for Dan Guerrero of the Meshbesher firm in which this notion appeared to be the underpinning of the case. Dan represented a University of Minnesota student from Mexico, Juan Adame, who had been charged with 1st degree criminal sexual assault.

Adame came from an affluent Mexican family. At the time of the incident he was living in a coed dorm, studying to obtain his bachelor's degree. Adame had a reputation as a bit of a flirt, who fancied himself as a ladies' man. Adame had sexual relations with numerous fellow female students on campus.

One evening Adame visited a woman who lived in his dorm. On at least one previous occasion, he had had consensual sexual relations with this woman. On this occasion, the woman invited Adame in, and they proceeded to have sexual intercourse. When Adame got up to leave, she became upset. When he informed her that "I have told you that I have made no commitment to one particular person," and informed her he was headed off to see another woman, she became outraged.

When Adame returned to his dorm room some time later, he learned the police were looking for him. The woman had called the police and accused him of rape. During the course of the investigation I interviewed a woman who lived in a room adjacent to the alleged victim's room. She indicated that she often heard voices next door, and recalled the night of the alleged rape. She did not recall any sounds of a struggle, anyone calling out, anyone banging on a wall, etc., although these details were alleged in the police report. Ultimately, in great part based on the testimony of this witness, Adame was acquitted at trial.

Chapter 7 - Sex Crimes & False Accusations

My opinion in this case is that the investigating officer rushed to judgment based solely on what the alleged victim told her. Unfortunately, this is not uncommon. Many prosecutors and police investigators appear-to have little interest in exculpatory evidence.

Sex Crimes

I think that everyone would agree that a sexual offense or sexual crime is one of the worst possible offenses we could imagine. The recent case in Minnesota and North Dakota involving the murder of Dru Sjodin was one of the most despicable acts imaginable. Also child sexual abuse cases are shocking and needless to say traumatic for family, friends and the public in, general. It is impossible to understand how and why an individual would be sexually attracted to a child and go forward and abuse an innocent little human being. As equally impossible to understand how anyone could rape a woman and beyond that, kill the victim. Perhaps someday medical science will discover what triggers these horrid impulses in pedophiles and rapists.

A normal reaction within the community after such a horrendous sex crime is to seek revenge against the perpetrator. Whenever I see on the news or read in the newspaper about someone charged with a sex crime, my initial reaction is one of sadness and anger. I have heard people comment that such a perpetrator should have his genitals cut off and be paraded around the community in an open cart so people can throw rotten fruit and spit upon the individual. However, after the initial angry thoughts have passed, my thoughts are only about having justice served and hoping due process of the accused takes place.

In a recent editorial in the Minneapolis Star Tribune dated January 6, 2005, there was commentary about sex offenders and change for its own sake. I quote the opening paragraph of this article which states "Not every tragedy can be prevented by legislation. Not every crime is reason to revamp the criminal code. These are lessons Minnesota leaders should take to heart as they think about how to handle Minnesota's sex offenders." It is not at all clear that any of the various reforms so far proposed would actually enhance the public safety.

Whatever happened to Lady Justice?

What to do with sex offenders is the question. My personal opinion is that those who have been convicted of an offense more than once are unlikely to ever be rehabilitated. Consider the Catholic priests who repeatedly abused young altar boys, even — after the church sent them on retreats and administered counseling. These priests continued the same vile activity when assigned to a different parish thus compounding the tragedy. Even though the church has paid out millions of dollars in civil lawsuits and claims, in my opinion those in the hierarchy of the church, bishops and archbishops, should have been charged criminally for aiding and abetting these despicable crimes.

If one reads Jimmy Breslin's book about this subject entitled "The Church That Left Christ Behind", they will understand how the behavior of these priests and the cover up by the hierarchy broke his heart. I'll venture to say it broke the heart of many Roman Catholics, and for that matter, people of all faith. Breslin was reporting on this despicable activity for one of the newspapers he writes for in New York City and it deeply affected his relationship with the Church. My impression of Jimmy Breslin is he was a devote Catholic, one who attended mass every Sunday, gave assistance to the homeless on the street with the thought in mind — what would Jesus do under these circumstances. It is not any easy book to read by any means, but Breslin, who is a Pulitzer Prize winner, gave an excellent account of what happened in the area where he resides and how these crimes against children has affected him and others. Breslin does, however, write about a priest working a very poor area serving the homeless' and the struggling working poor, so Jimmy Breslin does acknowledge and gives praise to the many priests, nuns, those in religious orders and lay people who truly practice their faith and are conscious of the teachings of Jesus Christ. It is my understanding that the Catholic Church is now handling the situation in a more honest, forthright manner when dealing with those accused of pedophilia or other sexual improprieties. Let us hope so.

Based upon my experience as a criminal defense investigator, I do keep in mind that there have often been false allegations against the clergy. Two cases that stand out for me are cases that I did not work on, but the claims against two rather prominent bishops were false. The Bishop in the Arch Diocese of Chicago, who was actually a

Chapter 7 - Sex Crimes & False Accusations

Cardinal, and is now deceased, had a claim made against him by a person who ultimately recanted and apologized. I am not sure if the recantation took place before or after Cardinal Bernardini passed away.

In Minnesota, there was a truly screwed up guy who made a claim against a retired bishop by the name of Dudley. This claim went absolutely nowhere and no one who was in the same class with the claimant even recalled who he was. He was not an altar boy, and after Bishop Dudley retired, this person went back to his old parish and grade school where Bishop Dudley had been the parish priest and put information under the windshield wipers of parishioners making allegations against the Bishop.

The individual who made these false allegations which were damaging in many respects was not exactly the Catholic Man-of-the-Year. He openly admitted he had engaged in drugs in the past and led a very marginal life so I suspect his motive was money. I am not going to name this individual and my only comment about him is to say I resent his false accusation. I was not a friend of Bishop Dudley, but had met him on occasion, however, I have many friends that attended the school where Father Dudley had been assigned and everyone I know spoke very highly of this man and stated on no occasion would Father Dudley ever have done anything that would raise a question of impropriety.

Concerning cases where it has been proven in a court of law that a certain individual is indeed a sex offender, how should government deal with these offenders? Again, my position is that I doubt these people today can be rehabilitated and I think medical science which includes psychiatry, is the proper approach to understanding these offenders. Being in the general population in a prison does not appear to be the answer. They should be segregated from society but treated in some fashion. Perhaps someday medical science will discover why these individuals behave in such an impulsive and despicable way. That may be a long time coming. Perhaps when the sex offenders die and an autopsy is conducted, the brain should be examined and studied to determine if there is some type of a defect causing this terrible behavior.

In the course of my modest career, I have had the occasion to work on more sex cases than I would have liked. I have investigated a number of cases where false accusations were made and what is disturbing is too often when a claim is made, there is a rush to judgment, the individual suspected of the offense is investigated and often charged wrongly. Unfortunately, I have had cases where the accuser has been immediately believed by the authorities, which is very unfortunate. Let me present a couple of examples. I don't wish to mention names, but these are actual cases and to the best of my knowledge those involved are still alive.

One very disturbing case that I investigated on behalf of attorney Howard Bass who was in the criminal department at the Meshbesher & Spence law firm, was a grandfather accused by a granddaughter of molesting her. The granddaughter's mother was a single parent, she was a good person and doing her best to raise her child. However, this child was constantly in trouble and had been jailed in juvenile detention, had been through various programs, etc. Once again, I would like to emphasize the mother was doing the best she could as a single parent, worked very hard. On Saturdays, the mother of this child who was the accuser of her grandfather, would take the child to the grandparents home and the mother would do laundry at their residence. There would be cousins that also would visit their grandparents and other adults present. This would always be a Saturday morning and Saturday afternoon event. The grandfather was a football fan, and he would watch college football games in the den always with the door open. The grandchildren and children of this man would freely roam the residence, walk by the den, pop in on gramps and chat with him.

The female grandchild, in this case, had numerous problems. She was being interviewed or counseled by someone in social services and accused her grandfather of molesting her. Now I can't prove this, but my thought was it may have been suggested to her in counseling that she was a victim and was acting out in a hostile and rebellious way. I think the grandchild was hip to the juvenile system, counseling and treatment techniques. She was clever enough to pick up on how to play the victim role, drop the dime on gramps and that would excuse her past nasty behavior. Unfortunately, the grandfather was charged with a crime and retained Mr. Howard Bass to represent him.

Chapter 7 - Sex Crimes & False Accusations

I interviewed family members who vehemently denied that the grandfather had engaged in any type of inappropriate behavior with anyone he ever came in contact with. I learned in the course of my investigation that the mother of the accuser had a male co-worker who would sometimes take care of this child or young adult. This particular man was a bachelor who owned a farm down in Iowa and sometimes the mother of the accuser would let the young girl go down to this guys farm over a weekend. The mother trusted this man. He was a co-worker and it's understandable that the mother would need a break on occasion from her busy schedule of being a working, single mother. I learned who this man was and obtained his phone number and called him no less than nine times at various hours of the day and night. I left messages on his machine, but never received a response. On three occasions, I drove to this individuals residence at different times of the day, rang the bell, but no one responded. I also left calling cards in his door. It upset me that this individual would not respond. The question came to mind, why because she now considered herself a victimwouldn't he respond, did he have something to hide? If he had evidence that the young lady shared with him, why wouldn't he want to bring that forward or just what the hell was going on. I get very passionate about many cases when I think there has been a bogus claim and it pissed me off that this elderly client whose wife had cancer would be experiencing the trauma of a false allegation. Why didn't the cops follow up with this man and why would they ignore what other family members have said and furthermore, why did they fail to consider the source of the accusation, a screwed up teen. To be sure, the young accuser had serious problems but I suspected, and once again cannot prove, that a light bulb might have gone off in her head when she had talked to a social worker or counselor which led her to think she could blame all of her problems on some one because she was now a victim.

To make a long story short, the situation was resolved without a court trial, and the grandfather, his wife and other family members made the difficult effort to get on with life. The prosecutor still wanted the grandfather to go through some type of counseling and he vehemently opposed that stating that he has never done anything wrong and therefore did not need any counseling. I do not know the final resolution of this matter, but my conclusion was and still is, the investigators for the State did a piss poor job and the case should have been knocked out of the box based on our investigation. This is not the only case of a false accusation and I will illustrate another one that I was involved in with attorney Richard Kyle, another outstanding criminal defense lawyer on par with Howard Bass.

If a prosecutor wanted me to have counseling for something I was falsely accused of, I would tell him or her to kiss my American Irish ass on the steps of Bull Shit Palace, a.k.a. Hennepin County Government Center. This is a matter of personal integrity and honesty.

Kyle was retained by a family whose son attended a private school in a community that I won't mention. The school happened to be a Christian school, but I don't know if that is a factor in this case or not except for the fact that the claimant fabricated her story. Very un Christian, we know that the ninth commandment is "Thou shalt not bear false witness against thy neighbor." Of course, we know many so called Christians routinely lie.

The young student, who Kyle represented was accused of sexual impropriety at the school under a stairwell that was in a rather public place. The stairwell connected to a hallway that led to the gymnasium and the stairway led up to classrooms where there were lockers out front, etc. The young lady involved was caught up in a situation whereby she told her boyfriend, who coincidently wasn't the client, that she had made out with a guy at school under the stairwell. We have no idea specifically what she said to her boyfriend, but the boyfriend told his young girlfriend's mother.

The mother, who at one time worked at the school in some type of administrative capacity, notified the school and set up a meeting with the principal. The school then did their own investigation to determine what may have taken place. They interviewed a number of students. The school authorities reached a conclusion that this was a he said-she said situation and they did not take any specific action. The result of the school investigation highly pissed off the mother, who some witnesses characterized as a pain in the ass, so the mother went to the police. As a result, the family retained Mr. Kyle.

Chapter 7 - Sex Crimes & False Accusations

Mr. Kyle is an excellent criminal defense attorney and a very hands-on person who often likes to go with me when witnesses are interviewed. Under those circumstances, he asks most of the questions and I am the prover, so to speak, because the attorney could not take the witness stand if a witness changed his or her story and I could take the witness stand as they prove to impeach the witness. We interviewed the principal and three teachers, who were, very neutral, not taking an adversarial position one way or another and they were quite forthright. We were also able to obtain notes and reports of their investigation which was quite helpful.

There were a number of witnesses that I interviewed without Mr. Kyle being present, but some that were interviewed by him and me together. In essence, this is what we learned upon interviewing numerous female witnesses that were friends of the accuser.

First of all, in my inquiry concerning the conduct and demeanor of the accuser, I learned that she was a pretty young woman, but that she needed a lot of attention and there was one female witness who stated that she felt intimidated by this accuser. This led me to believe that the young lady probably had a strong personality and high opinion of herself. We also learned that the young lady who had a boyfriend at the time she made the accusation, was sexually active with this boyfriend. We were also told by the female witnesses that the mother of the accuser would not believe that her wonderful daughter would engage in any sexual activity with a male.

The client and this young female had flirted at school and agreed to go under the stairwell together. The client and this young lady had been flirting on and off for over a week and on the day in question, he walked down the hallway where she was chatting up a couple of her girlfriends and then they walked off together. This was right around the lunch hour. The young female witnesses who went to the lunchroom and were at the lunch table stated that after a certain period of time, this young accuser joined the group and made the statement that "I've just had my high school fling." She was by no means upset, made no complaints, did not appear disheveled nor did she state the client stepped over the line so to speak. Everything was hunky-dory. We took photographs and measurements of the particular area and had someone been under the stairwell engaging in some type of activity, they would have been noticed by a student passing by and no student came forward to say they saw these two people fooling around.

Unfortunately the young lad was charged with fourth degree sexual assault and if convicted, he would have had to register as a sex offender for the rest of his life. Mr. Kyle was able to work out a settlement in this case, the client transferred schools and I have no idea what happened to the female accuser. There is more detail about this matter, but the fact remains this young female willingly went with the client to the stairwell, and engaged in some form of petting. He denied touching her in a certain manner, but did admit brushing his hand over her fully covered breast. This is a situation where a young female was put between a rock and a hard place when her soon to be ex-boyfriend ratted her off to her mother. The mother then goes crazy and pushes for the prosecution of Mr. Kyle's client. The case never should have been charged out by the assistant county attorney, but obviously he didn't have the balls to stand up to the mean spirited mother of the accuser.

Scott County

There are three recent books that can be found in bookstores in the Twin Cities pertaining to cases that I have worked on. One book is entitled *Dial M* by William Swanson, the murder of Carol Thompson. The publisher is Borealis Minnesota Historical Society. The next book is entitled *Will to Murder* by Gail Feichtinger with prosecutor John DeSanto and his investigator sidekick Gary Waller and they are out of Duluth, Minnesota. The third is *Secrets and Nightmares,* author Tom Dubee of Jordan, Minnesota. Mr. Dubee writes about the Scott County sex cases that took place in the 1980s. He worked on this book for approximately 11 years. It's an excellent account of what took place in that County, as many will remember the prosecutor Kathleen Morris was politically motivated, accused and charged many innocent people resulting in the entire town being traumatized and ridiculed. After working on that case with investigator Jackie Stone, I thought to myself - "Never again do I want to work on an alleged sex case, it was devastating to everybody." However, I have since taken on a number of investigations where allegations of sex crimes have been made by the State.

Chapter 7 - Sex Crimes & False Accusations

Mr. Dubee did an enormous amount of research in pulling together facts and information about the Scott County allegations. He interviewed as many people as possible. He went through newspaper accounts and court documents. Needless to say, a number of employees and former employees at Scott County would not speak with him, but he did interview one of the key players by the name of James Rudd, who is presently incarcerated in Minnesota. I too, had interviewed Rudd on three occasions after the acquittal of Mr. and Mrs. Bob Bentz. My interviews with Mr. Rudd were very enlightening concerning the conduct, demeanor and tactics of attorney Kathleen Morris.

The Bentz couple was represented by two lawyers of distinction, Earl Gray of St. Paul, Minnesota and Barry Voss of Minneapolis, Minnesota. These two individuals are seasoned criminal defense lawyers and are both tenacious advocates for their clients. My friend and colleague Jackie Stone worked on behalf of the Bentz's. At the time, I was working on behalf of former police officer in Jordan, Minnesota, Greg Myers. I was also working on behalf of retired Scott County Deputy Sheriff Buchan,and Jackie had some assistance from a law student by the name of Ellen Briskman who I am sad to say, is now deceased. Some time after the Bentz case was over, Bob and his wife divorced and he then, married Ellen. Ellen was an excellent student, very attractive, smart woman, but when she was preparing to take the bar exam, she had purchased some type of a health food supplement that was contaminated. She almost died and ended up confined to a wheelchair. Earl Gray represented her against the manufacturer and settled the case for well over one million dollars. Ironically, Ellen did die, and six months later Bob Bentz died. It was a very sad situation for people who survived, their children and friends that cared deeply about them.

What I was doing was totally compatible with what Jackie and Ellen were doing, and at a point in time, Jackie, a tall, attractive, very personable woman, developed a contact within the Scott County Deputy Sheriffs Office. Jackie had her deep throat just like Woodward and Bernstein had in the Watergate matter. I am not at liberty, at this moment, to divulge the individual's name, but he has long been retired. This person detested Kathleen Morris, stating she was unethical, committed unlawful acts, and was a thoroughly disgusting person. He told Jackie about a particular case whereby he wrote a report, and he was called to the witness stand by Morris, Morris read the report, and while on the witness stand, she asked him if this was his report. The deputy responded, "No! This is YOUR report, Ms. Morris, you edited and reconstructed what I had reported to the file." I would have loved to have been there for that moment, this honest, ethical police officer really stuck it to that woman, and rightfully so.

The Bentzes had three children. Marlin was the oldest child and the parents were accused of being involved in a sex ring abusing children. This was unadulterated bullshit, which the defense had to prove even though the burden of proof lies with the State. Rudd was a perpetrator, and that's the only one I can honestly say was guilty of an offense. Bentz worked at the Ford plant in St. Paul, which is quite a commute from Jordan, and his wife worked in Chaska, I believe, at a printing company. I do not have my file on this particular matter, unfortunately and I do not want to step on Mr. Dubee's shoestrings, but there were some incidents that I wish to point out here that Dubee was not privy to. There does remain a court transcript of the Benz trial.

Bob and Lois Bentz's oldest son, Marlin was put in a foster home, as were the other children involved in this case. There was never any consideration of putting these children with a grandparent or an aunt. Morris was closely aligned with the social service people in Scott County, and she made sure they were placed with foster parents, who indeed, would report information back to Morris. Not only were they being paid as foster parents by the County, they were snitching off all these little children. Marlin Bentz, on occasion, was able to leave the foster house on his own, I don't know how he did it, but he would call Jackie and give her information concerning the interrogations by Morris and the conduct and demeanor of the foster parents. This was very valuable information. We learned that Morris and her minions had interviewed some of these children forty and fifty times, had given one child a bicycle, had taken the kids out for hamburgers and it certainly showed there were promises and inducements for cooperation by the children.

Chapter 7 - Sex Crimes & False Accusations

Any expert in the area of interviewing or interrogating children will tell you that after two interviews, if you don't have the information, then forget about it. I personally heard the Honorable Judge Kathleen Guerin of Ramsey County state this at a seminar in Mankato, Minnesota some years back. At this seminar, Kathleen Morris was on the speaking panel, but she cancelled out so I decided to attend anyway and it was quite informative. Attorney Guerin is the one that stated, if you don't have it from a child after two interviews, do not continue.

Contrary to what many of the experts used to say, children will lie, children have imaginations, and certainly they can be easily manipulated. Many children just want to please. Marlin Bentz never caved in, he was a darn tough kid. Some of the other children were interviewed countless times and told conflicting stories and were totally manipulated by Morris and her thugs. They had power and early on public support. They abused the system from the beginning.

Mr. Myers' son was allegedly molested, by his parents and perhaps others, I can't quite remember, but he was interviewed on numerous occasions. On one occasion, there were accusations that some of this sexual behavior took place at a park/campground near the Minnesota River outside of Jordan. The prosecutor and her crew took young Andy Myers to that park to reconstruct, up to a point, what allegedly had happened and for him to answer questions. They videotaped this. When the defense requested a copy of the video and audio tapes, they were told by the prosecution that it didn't come out, something to do with high winds and it couldn't be heard and bad video. I personally think that was absolute horseshit because at a later date, Andy Myers recanted.

Attorney Carol Grant, prior to the trial of the Bentz's worked at the Meshbesher, Singer and Spence law firm in the criminal department. She worked very closely with Ron Meshbesher and Myers hired the Meshbesher firm to represent he and his wife who was also charged. Ron gave the assignment to Carol. I am guessing that if it had gone to trial, Ron would have involved himself, but I will point out, Carol was very capable, an extremely smart and attractive attorney.

Whatever happened to Lady Justice?

I do not know the details, but Carol left the firm and went to work with her husband, attorney Mark Kurzman. I traveled, along with the file, and continued to work on Carol's behalf. Mr. Kurzman also got involved.

I made the suggestion one day to Carol that perhaps she could get her own expert and interview Andy Myers, Greg and Cindy's child. She agreed to make the attempt and I had recommended a Minneapolis police official, James O'Meara, who at that particular time was in charge of the Sex, and Family Violence Division with the Minneapolis Police Department. Jim O'Meara was a very experienced, highly professional, police official, he had been Deputy Chief at one time and early on in his career he ran the morals squad in Minneapolis. Jim is now retired and living in Texas.

Court permission was granted for an interview with Andy Myers and Detective O'Meara conducted this one on one interview. Andy Myers recanted everything he had told Kathleen Morris and her lap dog investigators. O'Meara, God bless him, was able to get to the truth. Andy Myers was never abused.

This case escalated to the point of utter ridiculousness, but the trauma was still present among the defendants and those on Morris' shit list. Many people in Jordan didn't wish to speak to me, those that did, were potential targets of Morris and were quite fearful. The reputation of this pretty little town was absolutely tainted. It got to the point where there were accusations of murder, bestiality, bodies thrown in the Minnesota River, talk of a black limousine appearing in town on a couple of occasions occupied by mafia members. The BCA and FBI finally got involved. At great expense, they dragged the river and came up with nothing. I have no idea how much money was spent on this case by Scott County, but needless to say, Morris was voted out of office after she had been censored by the State of Minnesota.

One bizarre little incident I was involved in concerned one of these people allegedly having sexual intercourse with a horse on the property of a Jordan individual, whose family kept horses on several acres. I was able to obtain the name of the owners, I phoned them and told them about this allegation and the man said to me, "Are you

Chapter 7 - Sex Crimes & False Accusations

absolutely crazy?" The allegation was about one of the young boys involved in the case. The man stated it would be virtually impossible for a kid to hump a horse. I informed this person that I was embarrassed to even call him about this, but the allegation had been made and I had to check it out.

Another individual I had to call was a veterinarian about alleged sexual relations with a dog. He laughed and explained to me that with the facts I gave to him, this was extremely unlikely. This was a veterinarian that had treated this particular animal and he further stated that at no time was there any evidence of something occurring of that nature.

Jackie's deep throat informed her about an incident whereby Kathleen Morris was having discussion or minor argument with one of her social worker people concerning the best route to the courthouse in Minneapolis, At any rate, it turned out that Morris' route was the best and she actually spit in the face of her colleague, in a sense celebrating the fact she was right.

One of the most egregious offenses that were discovered had to do with not sequestering a number of children prior to the Bentz trial. Jackie again, received a tip from her contact to check out the Radisson Hotel on Highway 494 in Edina, Minnesota immediately because Morris was there with a number of children. I wasn't home at the time Jackie got that call, but she phoned me while I was eating dinner with my family and I immediately got my buns out to the Radisson where I met Jackie and her mother in the parking lot. This is what the scene was like.

Morris had taken these children out to the Radisson, had fed them, housed in nice rooms and they were swimming at the indoor pool. Jackie and her mother, the beautiful Lois Taylor, took a camera with them and they were sitting in chairs alongside the pool taking photographs of the children. They had every right to be there, they were verifying a violation of the court order to sequester witnesses prior to trial. In the process of Lois taking pictures of these kids, a detective by the name of Pint approached them and told Jackie and her mother, they could not be taking pictures. Well, I must say, neither Jackie nor Lois can be intimated by anybody and Lois got right in this asshole's face and told him she was out having a drink with her daughter and they were taking some pictures at the hotel and that was none of his damn business so he could take a hike.

When I arrived and we met in the parking lot, as luck would have it, Kathleen Morris and one of her people came out into the parking lot, but they did not approach us. However, if looks had been arrows, we would have all been dead.

Ultimately, there was a hearing regarding Morris. Neither Jackie, Ellen nor I were called as witnesses even though we had a great deal to say. Morris was censured, she should have been disbarred, but she caught a lucky break. As mentioned earlier in this piece, she was voted out of office and it my understanding that she is practicing law somewhere in the city of Shakopee, Minnesota. I believe her area of law is family law. This really is disturbing to me and many others who are familiar with the Scott County witch-hunt. This woman was responsible for destroying families in the city of Jordan, because of ambition, selfishness and in general, abusing her power as County Attorney.

David Brooks, moderate conservative columnist for the N.Y. Times wrote a terrific piece published in the Minneapolis paper March 25, 2006. His political column - The Greeks had a word for it "Thymos." He states Plato famously divided the soul into three parts: reason, desire and thymos (the hunger for recognition). Morris, in my opinion, was devoid of reason but possessed an overabundance of thymos and desire.

Summary

We live in a climate of political correctness. Often overreaction by police and social workers, if they truly did what they were supposed to do regarding some of these cases, commonsense would dictate. It's a waste of time and money to go forward with the prosecution of two teenage kids making out on school grounds. Commonsense would tell you that perhaps 50% of the teenagers at one time or another have played a little grab ass at school. Having gone to a boys' school myself, we didn't engage in that type of activity, we had to wait for our weekend date if we were lucky enough to get a date who would do some minor necking with us. There is no comparing my life and times in high school to those of teenagers nowadays. Ours was a different culture completely. I will refrain from pontificating about the good old days.

The question of what to do with sexual offenders is a complicated one. I do not believe repeat offenders can be rehabilitated. Consider Catholic priests who have repeatedly abused young boys, even after their church sent them on retreats and counseled them. As we have become all too aware, many of these priests continued their abuse when moved to different parishes, thus compounding the tragedy. The Catholic Church is now paying large sums as a result of numerous civil lawsuits and claims, however highly placed individuals in the church hierarchy who had knowledge of the actions of the priests have not been criminally charged with aiding and abetting these actions.

The question of how to deal with sex offenders is a difficult one. I don't believe many of these people can be rehabilitated. Medical science, which includes psychiatry, may hold out the most hope for addressing repeat sexual offenders. Putting offenders in the general prison population does not appear to be the answer. Although they clearly need to be segregated from society, they also need to receive some type of treatment to address their underlying pathology.

In the course of my career I have investigated more sexual offenses than I would have liked. What strikes me is how often there is a rush to judgment when an individual is alleged to have committed a sexual offense, and how quick law enforcement and the prosecution are to investigate and charge out such offenses. Perhaps more so than in other cases, it appears the authorities are quick to believe the accuser, even without supporting evidence.

Chapter 9

Unsportsman-like conduct

I have not worked on many cases involving athletes in trouble either on a professional or college level. Perhaps I have received seven or eight assignments over a 44-year period. Like so many people in the community, I have been a baseball aficionado and am interested in primarily smaller college sporting teams. My friends and I particularly like the women and men's teams at places such as St. John's, Concordia, St. Thomas, and Gustavus Adolphus. The students seem more prone to academics than the big-time athletes. It is a fact that the women athletes on the major college level always have a higher GPA than the men and certainly are far better behaved than the men. At the University of Minnesota it was recently published that men rate last in-the Big Ten for graduation rates, the rate being 54 percent.

This is not to say there are not good students on a big time college level. I personally met some of these men and women and these people are family orientated and contribute to their community. Yet what seems to intrigue the average sports fan are the scandalous behaviors of male players in the professional league and the college league. There is also criticism of the greedy team owners who want cities and states to build stadiums for them, daggers thrown at college coaches who cheat when recruiting or cheating in other areas.

Numerous books have been written about all aspects of sports, both positive and negative. You could fill up the Minneapolis main library with such books. What I have to say on the subject is nothing new, but yet interesting to myself. I have interviewed some people in the community that were involved at one time or another in big-time sports and they basically supported what I thought all along. It's all about the money.

Every season on a yearly basis there seems to be some type of scandal in the pros or on a college level. There is just no end to it. On November 5, 2009, the Minneapolis newspaper reported that

Chapter 9 - Unsportsman-like conduct

basketball player Royce White who had been expelled from De La Salle High School in 2007, has been charged with shoplifting and assault at the Mall of America in Bloomington, Minnesota. One of his comrades, another basketball player named Devron Bostic, has been suspended from the team for rules violation. A third player, Trevor Mbakwe, is awaiting trial for an assault in Miami, Florida. He denies assaulting a woman physically, and thus it is a he said-she said situation unless there is a witness. We must remember that in this country; you are innocent until proven guilty and convicted by a jury. No one should jump to conclusions.

Back in 2008, a trio of University of Minnesota ball players were investigated over a sexual incident involving a woman who passed out from drinking too much alcohol. One of the not too intelligent ball players filmed this on his cell phone. The story goes that she consented to engage in sexual activity with these young men but was passed out when one of the guys masturbated while being on top of her. That ungentlemanly person was convicted of a crime.

Since the year of 1971, with the arrival of former basketball coach, Bill Musselman, now deceased, there has been trouble in River City concerning the basketball and football athletic programs. Mr. Musselman had over 100 NCAA violations in a four-year period. In 1972, the University of Minnesota was involved in an on court brawl. A Minnesota player stomped on the head of an Ohio State player who was sprawled on the floor.

The 1986 incident that took place in Madison, Wisconsin and involved charges of sexual assault against three Minnesota basketball players at a hotel. This was another negative headline news items that received television and print coverage in Wisconsin and Minnesota. I was asked by the then University of Minnesota President Dr. Kenneth Keller, to make some discrete inquiries about this incident. Kenneth Keller was a personal friend of my wife and I from the time he arrived in Minnesota as an associate professor at the University. Our friendship continues to this day. I agreed to attempt to find out what I could about the charges against the basketball players and I went to a friend of mine who was very active in the black community in the Twin Cities of Minneapolis and Saint Paul. He agreed to assist, as long as I did not divulge his name. In addition, I asked the same favor of a life-long friend who was a high official in law enforcement and he also wished to be anonymous and his request to me was acknowledged.

Both of these friends gave me similar information concerning what happened to the woman in Wisconsin who claimed she was raped by three basketball players who attended the University of Minnesota. One of the players invited the young woman after the ball game to come to his room. She may have been an athletic groupie or just a naive person. However, the young lady went to the ball player's room at the hotel. According to the information passed on to me from two sources, she had voluntary sex with two of the ballplayers, but did not want to engage in sexual intercourse with the third player. The information that was brought to me said that player number three forced her to have sex while the other two men watched. Therefore, one person at least was guilty of sexual assault in the first degree since there was penetration of this woman. The two observers were accomplices and therefore were also guilty of a crime. The three players were suspended from the team until the trial began. One must remember they had broken team rules by staying up all night and having someone in their room. There was much talk about where were the coaches, the supervision, etc., whether or not there was a bed check and in general criticism of violation team rules. Ultimately, these three basketball players were tried together in State Court in Madison, Wisconsin. Often times, they would have been severed, meaning there would have been one trial for each individual, but for whatever reason, the prosecutor chose to try them together. Personally I thought this was a mistake on the part of the prosecutor because when, prosecutors separate people, they often elicit information from the three defendants and play on off against the other.

These young men were all acquitted and there was a very distasteful incident involving one of the players who was allowed to rejoin the team. He showed up for a game with a champagne glass shaved in his head. In another words, he is making the statement that we should celebrate his acquittal.

Some of the sports writers, specifically the self-promoting Sid Hartman-alleged dean of sportswriters for the Minneapolis Star

Chapter 9 - Unsportsman-like conduct

Tribune-were highly critical of Dr. Keller. The criticism first centered around his cancellation of two basketball games that were scheduled after the Wisconsin game and he had cause to do so because training rules were broken, a criminal case was pending. The same criticism came from the Boosters, a jock club as I call them. There had been much animosity by many in the community jock club toward Dr. Keller because he wanted to streamline the University and had implemented a program entitled, "Commitment to Focus." This was not Dr. Keller's plan alone. There was input, from other experts who contributed and it is doubtful the jock crowd even glanced at the paper. Dr. Keller was called an East Coast Ivy League Elitist among other names. The underlying major factor of the criticism is that it was President Keller's desire, along with others, to do away with a duplication of many programs which would have saved money, time, and made the University of Minnesota more competitive.

The University of Minnesota had a college called General College which offered a two-year AA Degree. There were many other two-year programs throughout the state, some very close to the university, and these of course, were excellent programs. Basically they catered to young people who were really undecided which direction they wanted to go in higher education. The programs were less expensive and they attracted adults who were out of the main stream for a while. The credits accumulated at the general college could be transferred into the university system.

It was common knowledge that many athletes attended general college and remain in that program up to three years or even longer. Basically, it was a hide-out for non academic athletes.

I wish to make it perfectly clear that many athletes are serious students and I know personally a number of these people that have gone on to graduate school. Mike Wright, who was an All-American football player, attended the University of Minnesota School of Law and commuted to Canada to play professional football. He also retired as a successful CEO at SuperValu. Jud Dixon, Carl Eller, Paul Moliter, and many others, completed their degrees. George Thomas, while playing in major league baseball, ultimately obtained his degree. These people are to be commended and many of them gave large sums of money to the University of Minnesota. Richard (Pinkie)

Whatever happened to Lady Justice?

McNamara has been an enormous influence at the university and has contributed millions of dollars.

Most people are supportive of a young, minority athlete having opportunities because of exceptional athletic talents to receive a scholarship and obtain a university degree. I am totally in favor of any qualified minority person or a highly academic non-minority person to be given an opportunity to attend the University of Minnesota. Nevertheless those that receive this opportunity have an obligation to accept the responsibility of doing the necessary work to complete their degree. Unfortunately throughout the country, there are many athletes that are recruited who do not have a foundation to take on college-level work. Too many young people from elementary school through high school are passed along because they are exceptional athletes. Too many people come from poverty-stricken homes or from a single parent household which cannot devote the time to assist the child in school. Anyone in education or in real life knows that it all starts at home.

On a big-time athletic level, the recruiting of many people is a disservice to the person who may never obtain a degree and never reach their goal of making large amounts of money on a professional level. It is also a disservice to the university and non-athletic minority students who are highly intelligent and would die for a full scholarship at a place like the University of Minnesota.

The whole situation is a dilemma, but it needs to be addressed. Perhaps one of worst scandals we had at the university prior the present coach Tubby Smith coming on campus was the scandal of former coach Clem Haskins. President Keller was the one that hired Haskins and he thought highly of this man. Haskins is a good man and Mr. Ronald Meshbesher was one of the attorneys who assisted him after he left the University of Minnesota. The scandal involved academic cheating. There was a woman who was actually writing papers for some of the ball players. This woman is now deceased. To make a long story short, all sorts of folks got in trouble. Whether Haskins was asked to resign or if he left on his own makes no difference. There was a dispute about his contract, therefore lawyers became involved. In the final analysis, all one can think is how tragic this situation was and matters of this nature should never occur.

Chapter 9 - Unsportsman-like conduct

Interview with Jerry Thomas

Vinnie: What I want to talk to you about is athletics on a university level I know you have experience there, and then you have experience in professional baseball. Now you were recruited by the University of Minnesota in the 50's, correct?

Jerry: Yes.

Vinnie: For baseball or both baseball and football?

Jerry: Just baseball.

Vinnie: Okay.

Jerry: Dick Seibert recruited me.

Vinnie: He was a nationally known coach, right?

Jerry: Yep.

Vinnie: Former major leaguer himself?

Jerry: Exactly.

Vinnie: Now in those days, they offered you a scholarship. Would that be a full scholarship?

Jerry: Actually, at that time Vince, the recruiting was just to be a walk-on, because as far as I know, they had not given a baseball scholarship to anybody prior to me coming to the university. There were some guys that played baseball that were on scholarships, an example would be Paul Giel. Giel was there but he was on a football scholarship. Jerry Kindall came at the same time that I came to the university but he was on a basketball scholarship. Jack McCartan was on hockey scholarship. But they had not given any baseball scholarships. It wasn't until my — I can't remember if it was my sophomore or junior year that I did wind up getting a scholarship.

Vinnie: How did guys support themselves back then?

Jerry: Back then you could have a job, unlike today, an athlete cannot have a job while they're in school. Back then you could work in whatever you wanted to do. In my case, I wound up — I worked for Art Hayes who owned about 10 parking lots in downtown Minneapolis and was also a family friend. All the way through school I worked in the parking lots downtown.

Vinnie: That's where the famous Lefty Brick worked.

Jerry: Lefty Brick and Dick McKenna worked there. Doug Gillen, who also played baseball at the university, worked in the parking lots too.

Vinnie: Were there a lot of companies or businesses that would assist athletes that way?

Jerry: Yes. Most of the athletes had a job of one type or another. How much they worked was another question.

Vinnie: Well, we've heard of phantom type jobs, and I remember talk about John Horan, the all-American basketball who went to Dayton, and he had some kind of...

Jerry: What I heard is John's job there was - he actually worked for the school. He would go into the gymnasium in the morning at around 7:00 or 7:30 or whatever it was, turn the lights on, and then he would come back at like 10:00 at night and turn them off, and he was paid for the time in between. I heard — I can't swear to it — but I heard there were a number of those jobs at the University of Minnesota, and specifically for football players, where they really didn't work, but they got paid.

Vinnie: There's a question of ethics there. Now at the present time, I know you have a lot of awareness because you're involved in the M Club and what not, but at the present time you said that an athlete is not allowed to work. Does that mean all year round?

Jerry: No, they can work during the summer. They can get a job during the summer but they cannot have a job during the

Chapter 9 - Unsportsman-like conduct

school year. I don't know when the rule came into effect, but I'm assuming it's probably been in effect for some time and it probably was put into effect to cut out this make work type stuff that had been going on in the past.

Vinnie: A lot of young guys, especially poor guys coming out of tough environments, how do they support themselves?

JERRY: They get essentially a free ride. They get books, tuition, room and board, you know, all of that stuff. Then it's up to them as far as getting extra. I don't think they get any spending money at all, but it's up to them then during the summer to get a job or hopefully their parents can help them out. I don't know if sometimes they're skirting the rules a little bit and they have maybe alumni that are slipping them money. That very well could be. That's the case at Michigan with the Fab Five. Weber and Jalon Rose, those guys that played basketball at Michigan, there was some booster that was...

Vinnie: Yeah, he died. Allegedly he gave Weber $250,000, which is a lot of money, and Weber did give a deposition or something. I don't know if that's a closed deposition or whatever.

Jerry: It's more of a probability that that kind of stuff is going on. I don't know. I wouldn't say that it's rampant, but it's probably happening.

Vinnie: I worked a couple of cases at the university investigating. Only one involved an athlete, and that was Mick Tinglehoff. It was a bullshit case. There's no question about it.

Jerry: He was your client, right?

Vinnie: He was a client. Naturally, all my clients are innocent. When I was over there and I was interviewing the coach and some other people, there were a number of nice vehicles in the parking lot and I asked about one in particular and it belonged to a quarterback at that time, Fogge. I'm wondering how in the world can these guys buy a car like that or do car dealers let them use a car?

Whatever happened to Lady Justice?

Jerry: That's kind of like the LeBron James deal. He was still in high school and all of a sudden he's driving a Hummer.

Vinnie: That does not project a very good image for a Catholic high school.

Jerry: No, and supposedly it was his mother that provided it for him, but it was pretty obvious that she really didn't have the wherewithal to buy him the car, so somebody was fronting the dough. There's probably some of that that's going on right now too.

Vinnie: It's real corruption.

Jerry: I don't know if I ever mentioned to you but I can remember back in 1955 or 1956 when Bobby Cox transferred to the University of Minnesota from the University of Washington. He wasn't on campus very long and all of a sudden I see him driving a brand new Chevrolet convertible. I don't know exactly where that came from.

Vinnie: He was a friend of mine. I never asked him about too much. He did tell me after a good spring game against the alumni he went in to Murray Warmath, the famous coach, and said he needed more money, otherwise he was going to Hawaii. He stayed. My sense of it all, and I'm no expert, is that it wasn't as bad in those days as today, particularly in the area of violence and crime. In your day, I don't recall reading about guys getting in trouble. All the ballplayers you knew, were they pretty well behaved?

Jerry: Back then, as you know, drugs were almost nonexistent. A big deal from an athlete was maybe he smoked or drank beer. That was about as bad as it got. So there wasn't the drug thing that really escalates.

Vinnie: I picked up the paper, and you may have seen this, but three Viking players assaulted this guy. It sounded vicious. They kicked him when he was unconscious.

Jerry: Supposedly there were a couple of cops that saw them doing it.

Chapter 9 - Unsportsman-like conduct

Vinnie: I find it hard to truly understand. These guys come from a different culture and background, but I think even from a rough background you know right from wrong.

Jerry: There has been no information about the guy that got his butt kicked, but unless he was really stupid or really drunk, why would he want to get into any kind of any altercation with three professional football players. It's beyond my imagination.

Vinnie: But you would think ballplayers, who could lose their livelihood over this, would have the sense to walk away from a bad situation. They had just gone through some conferences a couple weeks ago about behavior. We've also seen some criminal activity on a big time level. There was that case down at Baylor where the ballplayer shot his pal, and prior to that in Oklahoma where they had those great teams under Schweitzer there was drugs and shootings.

Jerry: Recently, and it's been fairly prevalent, it seems like every couple weeks or so in the newspaper you read some football players or basketball players from the University of Kentucky or North Carolina or whatever, they committed a robbery or something, they stole something, or they got caught for shoplifting. It seems to be really prevalent now.

Vinnie: If you criticize the fact that most of these are black kids you're going to be accused of being a racist, but this brings to mind screening when they offer scholarships and bring guys in to play ball. Do you have any idea how well they screen these people?

Jerry: I don't have any idea, but I would guess that the screening is very, very minimal as far as background and stuff, unless a kid has some kind of a record. Then they might be a little careful. The bottom line, can the kid run, can he tackle, can he shoot a basketball, can he hit a baseball, that's the key? Sports in colleges nowadays has gotten so big time, and it's such a big, big money thing. These coaches are making big time money, and in order to keep their jobs they're got to win. A lot of times they're cutting corners in order to win.

Vinnie: The Shark, Jerry Tarkanian, he had quite a reputation.

Jerry: Look at Clem Haskins.

Vinnie: Ken Keller, former president of the university, he thought very highly of Haskins. He liked him as a person. It really disturbed him when all of this happened, even though he wasn't president anymore. Keller also told me that most of these young fellows coming in are not academically qualified and they have to carry a certain amount of credits. He said it's tough on them and not fair in many ways, so they will design some programs to try to help them along.

Jerry: What's interesting is they always talk about it's got to be the same for the regular students, the athletes have got to perform the same way, but really in truth that doesn't happen because the athletes I think are held to a higher standard. They have to be showing more progress towards a degree. A normal student can figure it will take him seven years to get their degree because they'll be working and what not, and they don't blink an eye over that. But with an athlete it's a completely different story year don't they?

Jerry: They can red shirt. A lot of these kids though are good students and they red shirt them and a lot of them have graduated before they even get to their last season and what they wind up doing is registering for grad school and start taking some graduate courses. They're not all bad. In fact, it's probably a real small minority.

Vinnie: There are two sides to the coin. Keller told me that he's met what Sid Hartman has said, that really supported athletics. In fact, when he was an undergrad at Columbia he played some sports, I forget what, but he liked athletics. He said a lot of these guys have come back to him and said, "Geez, I was promised I would get a degree and here I am working as a laborer, etc." Do you think there are some false promises made maybe by alumni?

Jerry: There might be. I don't know how much the athletic departments help kids once they've used up their eligibility or if they've lost their scholarship for one reason or another,

Chapter 9 - Unsportsman-like conduct

          whether they continue to assist them in any way. To me, it's all up to the individual.

Vinnie: You're right about that. We're responsible for ourselves. You can't blame society for everything.

Jerry: That's very true.

Vinnie: How do you think we arrived at this point? We've got all these bowl games now and all this hype.

Jerry: It all boils down to one thing, Vince, and that's the dollars. The bucks.

Vinnie: Did that start when TV came in and offered to show games?

Jerry: It's just kind of mushroomed over the years. You remember when we were kids, Vince, what was there, like in football there was maybe six or seven bowl games. Now there are 25 or 26 or something like that, and it's all based on the money that can be made by participating in these bowl games. On the other side of the coin, it gives the schools that wind up playing in these bowl games, it gives them extra practice time. They're limited as to how many days of practice they can have and when they can start the fall practice and what they can do during the winter, which is not very much, but if you're going to a bowl game, you just keep right on going after the regular season stops. It's a time when kids that didn't get much playing time or somebody that's a real prospect, they get to work with them more and get them tuned into the system.

Vinnie: I suppose it helps with recruiting too.

Jerry: Definitely, especially if you're going to major bowl games that are on TV. It's TV that drives all this money. The kids say yeah, you go to a bowl game just about every year, I like that.

Vinnie: That kid from Ohio, that running back.

Jerry: Maurice Clarett.

Whatever happened to Lady Justice?

Vinnie: I think he was showcased. He got in trouble. He did a criminal act - insurance fraud or some damn thing.

Jerry: He made false statements to the police about a robbery that had happened to him. A burglary. And then he fessed up and said no, it wasn't really that.

Vinnie: I remember my days as an adjuster, and 95 % of the people that had a burglary loss said the hat was new, I just bought that hat. They all embellished, hoping ...but at any rate, he wanted to become a professional and he has not been able to do so.

Jerry: I forget what the rule is in the NFL. I think you have to be in school at least three years before you're eligible for the draft. That would include a red shirt. You can use a red shirt year as one of those four years, but Clarett is one who played as a true freshman. I think last year was his sophomore year, so he's a year short. That's why they would not allow him to go into the draft. Of course that's up to the courts to decide whether that's discrimination or what.

Vinnie: Back to recruiting, what do you think of these guys that come in for one or two years and then leave for the pros? Basically, they're just using the university to expose themselves or mature a little bit.

Jerry: Exactly. I don't think it's right, but it's gotten to be so prevalent that the college coaches and stuff realize when they're recruiting, especially if they got a real blue chipper, you know, they've got to figure that I'm probably only going to have this kid for maybe two years.

Vinnie: Some of these kids make a mistake. I think Richert, this kid from Duluth, they're good guys. But leave too early

Jerry: Humphries. He's probably closer to being a real potential for the pros. Richert should have stayed at least another year I think.

Chapter 9 - Unsportsman-like conduct

Vinnie: I'm sure a lot of guys, you know, they go to college and they think they're going to go into the pros, but what's the percentage?

Jerry: It's real, real small. Some of these guys, too, they make - the NCAA does leave them a little wiggle room. As long as they don't hire an agent, they can announce for the draft, and if they don't hire an agent they can always come back. Rashaun Leonard did that. He did that. He didn't hire an agent and I think he got drafted late in the second round or something and then he said I'm going to go back to school for another year. So he was able to do that, but too many of these kids they hire an agent and then they're dead. Once you hire an agent, whether you get drafted or not, you're ineligible.

Vinnie: Back in your day there were no agents.

Jerry: No.

Vinnie: You signed with Detroit and who assisted you? Your father?

Jerry: Yeah, essentially, and that was it. Of course back then there was no draft. It was just you went wherever the best money was and, of course, then you were an indentured slave for life almost. But you would look for the best deal and go with that team.

Vinnie: Now your brother George, who is an outstanding athlete, he also signed after two years at the U?

Jerry: Actually, he was at the U for two years. If you remember back then, freshmen were not eligible, and so he only played one year. Like I said, there was no draft or anything so you could do whatever you wanted to do.

Vinnie: They had funny rules about bonuses though, didn't they?

Jerry: Any bonus over $6,000 or something like that, you had to go to the major league ball club. You had to be on the roster and be kept on the 25-man roster for two years.

Vinnie: That's what happened with Harmon Killebrew?

Whatever happened to Lady Justice?

Jerry: Yes. That happened to my brother. They changed the rule after his first year. Then they made some changes and they didn't require that the person who was signed be on the big league roster.

Vinnie: I remember John Blanchard. He must have been a little bit before because it was published he received $50,000, and that would have been in 1951, which was a hell of a lot of money. Paul Pettit, I think was the first guy with $100,000. Yeah, he never made it. Do you think it's reasonable now with the draft and they're still giving these - it looks like Joe Mauer is worth it.

Jerry: The salaries are so much better nowadays then they were back then.

Vinnie: Say a AAA ballplayer, what would he be making?

Jerry: It would all depend on whether the guy is on the major league 40-man roster or if he's just like a free agent type When you're on the 40-man roster, you work out your contract with the club whether you play in the big leagues or the minor leagues. That's what you get paid.

Vinnie: When you signed, did you get a bonus?

Jerry: What I did, and this was illegal, but everybody was doing it at the time, what I got was the major league minimum salary at that time was $6,000. They guaranteed me that they would pay me that amount for three years.

Vinnie: So you got the minimum $6,000. Yeah, I remember reading — I am a baseball aficionado. I have a lot of baseball books. I remember Jerry Coleman going back to San Diego to his winter job in a haberdashery. Guys had jobs.

Jerry: When I was playing professional baseball, I don't know if there were — I don't think there were 10 guys in the major leagues that were making $100,000 or over. Those guys were all hall of famers. It would be guys like Ted Williams who was still playing, Mickey Mantle, Warren Spawn was still around. Those kind of people. At the time when I was playing, the

Chapter 9 - Unsportsman-like conduct

average major league salary would have been under $20,000, probably about $18,000. But that was not bad money back then.

Vinnie: The average working American was maybe making $5,000 or something. But, if you compare it to today, it's unbelievable. Howard Cosell wrote a book called "What Wrong With Sports." I researched that but - and nothing seems to change. Bob Costas, after that horrible baseball strike, wrote a book and he had some great suggestions. But all of that's ignored. Costas would make a good commissioner. Maybe even George Will.

Jerry: I don't think there will ever be another strong commissioner unless some of the rules are changed, because the league is still run essentially by the owners.

Vinnie: There should be salary caps. Steinbrenner - it ruins things.

Jerry: Most of these owners in all major sports, they're their own worst enemy. They bitch and moan about the salaries and stuff that they're paying but who the hell is paying them? They don't have to.

Vinnie: Rodriges, he signed for how much?

Jerry: Multi-millions.

Vinnie: Of course, he had signed with Texas. Unbelievable. I mean nobody objects to somebody making an honest living, but there's got to be some parity.

Jerry: It's just like, you know, Kevin Garnett with the Timberwolves. What does he make? He makes $13 or $15 or $20 million or something a year. Now who is worth that kind of money?

Vinnie: It's the same in the movies. The most blatant are people like the Enron people and who is that Kowalski? There's a local guy, that healthcare guy, McGuire, who has taken a lot of criticism. He pulled out $92 million. My son's mother-in-law works there. She's a mid-level person, well educated, but she said that they get three percent raises. They don't get those stock options.

Jerry: That's where those big numbers you see from these guys, a lot of it will come from the stock options. Granted, some of them their actual base salary is pretty damn high, but where they really make those big numbers is in the stock options. Of course, they've got to exercise those options.

Vinnie: They get an option hypothetically $25 a share and then they sell it at $60. But at any rate, that's another area. Now there's been talk about maybe paying college athletes and just kind of like hiring them.

Jerry: I think that is a good idea. I've got one big reason for it, and that is that again, sports at the college level, especially at the Division I schools, is a big huge money deal, and the schools are making millions of dollars off the athletes. Granted they're giving them an education and stuff, but they're not paying them anything. They're the ones that really bring that money in.

Vinnie: Does the money go just to the athletic department, or is there a share that goes to the general fund?

Jerry: I would guess that that probably may vary between schools, but as far as I know, the majority of the schools that money goes right to the athletic department.

Vinnie: And that creates kind of a vicious circle.

Jerry: Yeah, it starts pitting the athletic department against the other departments and stuff. The other departments are saying, "Hey, they get all this money and we're laying assistant professors off."

Vinnie: There's got to be something better. What do you think about an athlete having an alternative. If he wants to be a student then he can be a student and get this. If he just wants to represent the university then he gets something else and maybe take reading.

Chapter 9 - Unsportsman-like conduct

Jerry: There's been talk, and I don't think it will ever go any place, but actually turning college almost into the professional level where they just hire guys to come in, whether they're students or not. It doesn't make any difference. They'll pay then and they really don't have to go to class or anything like that.

Vinnie: It's already a free farm system. The pros should be supporting these.

Jerry: _____ subsidizing a lot of this _____.

Vinnie: Lefty Brick attended some thing at St. Thomas College where the sports reporter, Reusse and he talked about how much he enjoyed interviewing these small college kids and following their sports. He writes about small town. You know him, don't you?

Jerry: Slightly. Not real well. What's he's talking about, of course, is the small colleges and stuff where there are no scholarships. I mean the kids, they pay their way.

Vinnie: And there's very little crime and corruption. He enjoys that. I suppose he gets tired of dealing with big egos or something.

Jerry: Yeah, that, and Pat Reusse to start with is a small town boy He grew up in Fulda, Minnesota. I played baseball there one summer. He was a real young kid. I don't know that I knew his dad.

Vinnie: He has a reputation of being a very good guy. When you played out there - when you played ball in the summer in college, were you allowed to get some money expenses?

Jerry: I could never figure, and I never asked questions, but you were able to make money for playing baseball, and I don't know if the way they got around it was they considered it was expense money for you, because hell, I was making $500- $600 a month.

Vinnie: That was big money in those days. That was terrific.

Whatever happened to Lady Justice?

Jerry: It was real good money.

Vinnie: It was good baseball though. That was before the Twins came to Minneapolis

Jerry: Almost every town in the state of Minnesota had a ball club and most of them had lights on their fields and stuff. There were, I don't know how many different town teams throughout the state, and then as the Twins came in it started to kind of fade away.

Vinnie: I recall Jim Pollard pitching down in Jordan. They still have that nice park with the lights.

Jerry: Jim Pollard was down there, and do you remember Jimmy Holstein?

Vinnie: Sure.

Jerry: Holstein played down there too.

Vinnie: Skowran was down at Austin.

Jerry: Yep. Toothpick Sam Jones was at Rochester.

Vinnie: Was he?

Jerry: Yea.

Vinnie: And the great Paul Scanlon was up at Morris.

Jerry: A lot of people don't remember this, but Herb Score pitched up in Brainerd.

Vinnie: I remember Orlando Zapeda playing class C ball at St. Cloud, and then Hank Aaron was over at Eau Claire. Are we old, or are we old?

Jerry: We're old. You know how old Joe Torre is, well I played one year against him.

Vinnie: Did you? What was the name of that league?

Chapter 9 - Unsportsman-like conduct

Jerry: The last year that I played pro ball I hurt my rotator cuff and they put me on the disabled list and finally they just said we've got to move you someplace in the system. I said well, if you can move me someplace — I was in Knoxville, Tennessee at the time, I said if you can move me someplace that's between Knoxville and Minnesota I'll go, otherwise just give me my release. They were going to send me to Duluth. Duluth had a team in the northern league. It was a Tiger affiliate. They were going to send me there and then all of a sudden they found out at that time you could only have X number of what they call veteran players. For that league, a veteran player was someone that had three years or more in professional baseball, and I had three plus years. So they would have had to have sent somebody else out from up there. So I said just give me my release. I was ready to come home and I got a call from a guy by the name of Harry Dalton who was the general manager for the Orioles. He said I just saw it come over the wire that you got your release, are you interested in playing? I said if you've got something between Knoxville and Minnesota. He said we need someone that's been around for a while to go to Aberdeen. I said I'm your man. I played like the last month of the season in Aberdeen and Joe Torre played Eau Claire.

Vinnie: Now they didn't have that sports medicine back in those days. Now they would have done surgery on that arm. Dave Thies who was in Kansas City, he had a couple operations.

Jerry: I don't know what his problem was, but it was not rotator cuff.

Vinnie: A lot of guys have come back from that. Is there anything else you can add concerning crime and corruption?

Jerry: Not really. I think a lot of these owners are corrupted nowadays.

Vinnie: What about universities? Ken Keller told me, he said, "You know these universities, they don't trust each other."

Jerry: They don't.

Vinnie: They have a hard time getting together.

Jerry: Any chance they get they'll blow the whistle on another school if they think they've got the goods on them. It's all one-upmanship.

Vinnie: Do you remember that alleged rape case? I use the word allege because the guys were acquitted over in Wisconsin.

Jerry: Mitch Lee?

Vinnie: Yeah. Well I got some inside information on that. Even though they were acquitted, they broke training rules and so forth. Aren't there consequences for that?

Jerry: You would think so.

Vinnie: I know Sid Hartman was pissed off at Keller for canceling a couple of games and still can't resist bad mouthing him.

Jerry: You've got to consider the source.

Vinnie: Well this has been very helpful. I was very interested in how it was in the old days compared to today. But society has also changed in general.

Jerry: I hope it helps you out somewhat.

Vinnie: It will. I appreciate it. When are you going to retire?

Jerry: As long as I enjoy coming to work, I'm going to keep going.

Big Time Athletics

Over my 74 years on this earth, from a very young age, I participated in some sports and have thoroughly enjoyed following sports. I have friends that were outstanding athletes and am proud of them. I did have a great opportunity in the U.S. Army in Germany to play on a championship team where most of the players played on a college level. Our center, Merle Evak, a graduate of Alfred University in upstate New York was drafted by the Minneapolis Lakers. My pal, Fran Connors, played at St. Joseph in Philadelphia.

Chapter 9 - Unsportsman-like conduct

However, over the years, I, like any other sports fan, have seen overemphasis in sports and too much pressure on children. Everything is totally organized. Today, kid's spontaneity has been stifled. If a child doesn't get involved in sports at an early level, then he will never have a chance once he reaches high school to play on the high school team. You have to keep pushing forward. During my youth, kids played two or three different sports in their season. There were no summer camps and very little parental involvement, yet, from my generation, a number of people went on to professional sports and some had careers in major league baseball, football and basketball. None of these folks such as John Blanchard of the Yankees and Jerry Thomas of the Twins made big time money, but at least they get a decent pension, it seems today, that on a college level and a professional level, everything is about money, and how to get a handle on this is beyond me. So I called upon some people that have some expertise and were involved in big time athletics.

I interviewed my beautiful niece, Patti Smith, who resides in Houston, Texas and is a producer/reporter for Fox Sports Network. She has interviewed countless athletes on a professional and college level. Patti has a degree of insight concerning sports as does her husband, David Smith, who has been involved in athletics all his life. He is an athletic director and coached on some big time levels. He is now an A.D. and football coach in the Houston area on a high school level. He was sick and tired of moving onward and upward and the constant travel, so he and Patti settled in Texas.

I know my lovely niece's background, so I'll include some of it here. She, herself, was an outstanding softball player and I thought that maybe she would play ball in college on a scholarship. However, Patti, who is smart as a whip, chose another career and in Atlanta went to work in the print media. Patti worked for a magazine or paper called "The Sporting Times" and began interviewing ballplayers, coaches, managers, etc. I got a great kick regarding her first interview, and that was with the late Paul Newman. I asked her how she was able to pull that one off as he really didn't grant too many interviews. Patti said she was at a media party promoting something, which she can't even remember, but it did have something to do with those Malibu race tracks and pro race stuff.

They have these little cars that you can drive and Newman wasn't familiar with any of that.

So Patti went on to say that it was at this event, at the Atlanta Motor Speedway, that she saw Paul Newman walk by. He actually walked up to her and asked her how the batting cage worked. There was a batting cage at this event, so she told him how to do it and informed Mr. Newman that she was going to be out at the speedway the following day and asked if she could sit down and do an interview with him. Patti said he agreed and told her to call his agent. So she called his agent, who was not very happy about this interview. She told Patti that she didn't know how she pulled this one off, but since he agreed she granted the interview.

I found this to be rather exciting as anyone who attends movies is a fan of a guy like Paul Newman. He does a lot of charity work, and the proceeds from his salad dressings all go to charity. He was a very remarkable person. I asked what Patti's impression of him was and she said a very decent guy, a little bit quiet. She had difficulty hearing him when he was responding to questions. She also said he was very generous. I must say I was probably more thrilled over this than she was.

Since then, Patti has progressed in her profession. I asked her if she felt many athletes felt a sense of entitlement, or a feeling that they were bullet proof from critics and the law. I was interested in her opinion on this. Patti felt that some of these athletes were of that mindset. She did not wish to stereotype these men, but she stated she found it more prevalent in basketball players first, football players second and baseball players third. Certainly this is not true of all athletes, she wanted to make this point, but she felt she saw it more in the NBA than other sports.

I inquired why these NBA players' behavior is so objectionable and asked Patti if she had any knowledge regarding that. I asked her if it was because they have been coddled as athletes and/or that many of them grew up in tough environments and in only one parent families. Pattie said that she thought that was exactly it. Patti went on to talk about the lack of family structure with these young kids coming out of the inner cities and going from virtually having nothing to having

Chapter 9 - Unsportsman-like conduct

everything at such an early age. They do not have the tools to know how to handle this sudden success.

Patti went on to say that in basketball, a person can come right out of high school and enter the professional league. A baseball player must go through the minor leagues whether he comes out of high school or college and there is an opportunity for them to learn how to be on their own, they have to follow certain rules and regulations, and they have older ball players around them.

With basketball, a young kid who comes from a family with no money, if they are good enough, they could be offered a large sum of money immediately if they sign the basketball contract. What is a young kid to do? He can immediately go out, make a living and take care of his family. Patti said these kids are getting there too soon and it is too much. Many end up sitting on the bench and not developing properly with a college experience, or they end up like Kobe Bryant.

As it is today, the colleges with basketball are the NBA's minor league. According to Patti, NBA should strengthen their requirements for athletes coming into the league.

I mentioned to Patti that there are those who believe that we should be blatantly honest and if the universities want big time teams, they should pay these athletes and not represent them as students. Patti's response was that their schedules and responsibilities to the practices and the games make it difficult for them to truly lead an academic life. Most of these athletes have very little loose change in their pocket to go to a movie or get pizza, and that, in turn, may put them in a position where alumni are granting them favors under the table. The whole system, according to Patti, is totally screwed up. She felt they should at least have a stipend to avoid some corruption but then that opens a can of worms regarding where to draw the line. Apparently they are not allowed to work, which I'm not so sure about but in my day, big time athletes had a job out of season and many of them actually worked. The whole system is out of balance.

Patti said that the bottom line is that it is all about money and it is a vicious circle. There are television contracts which can control the time of the games, there are huge bowls at the end of the year, complicated ratings and everybody wants to be in the top ten. Patti stated that a coach may have some bad characters on a college level playing for him and if there is a young man bursting with talent, the coach may turn his head to a lot of unsavory behavior.

I interjected by stating that it is interesting that the women in sports, and there are some big time basketball and volleyball programs, do not seem to get in trouble. Some of them may have some academic problems, but you never see them in bar fights, sexually harassing or raping anybody; they are just a higher quality citizen. Patti agreed and, of course, I told her that I am a feminist and I am not bullshitting about that. But that is a discussion for another time.

I inquired of Patti what she thought about coaches at major schools and their million dollar contracts whereas some professors will never make that kind of money. Patti's response was that she would rather see the coaches getting the big contracts than the players. I asked her why and she said that she is married to a coach, he doesn't make even close to a million dollars and most coaches do not. Patti said she doesn't believe that athletes don't work hard, but this coaching business is 24/7, they eat, sleep, breathe the sport and sacrifice their personal life with their families. She states that there is not a coach that steps out of high school and gets handed a big time job at a college. Your million dollar coaches are the ones that have been breaking their hump year-after-year and finally some of them make the big time. Patti went on to say that as far as she is concerned, the coaches are more entitled to a large salary than any player.

Patti stated that out of 500 nationally known teams, how many are able to pay $200,000 a year and how many of these coaches are making $1,000,000 per year? She stated maybe the top ten percent at best and if you take the top ten percent of any profession, they are going to make the top dollar. I mentioned to Patti that two of my friends, Marty Dworkin, an internationally known microbiologist, and Ken Keller, former President of the University of Minnesota and international biochemical engineer, never came close to being paid $1,000,000 a year. Patti said, "How much money did they bring into the university?" My response was, "They bring in quite a bit of money from corporations because they do a tremendous amount of research for companies such as Medtronic, Honeywell, etc." I told her

Chapter 9 - Unsportsman-like conduct

that money was shared with other departments at the university, all of it did not go to the department that raised the money. There are also inventions coming out of the university, but the individual who consults on the project with others is not the one that gets the patent. Patti said that she has not studied this issue, but said that she cannot disagree, life is not fair all over the world.

I suggested to Patti that what if all the university presidents who have big time football programs got together and made a serious effort to clean up their act? I told Patti, even before my time, the University of Chicago discontinued football because they didn't feel that it had a positive influence. Patti stated that she really didn't know what kind of solution there may be or what would be a common sense approach. Again, there is so much money involved, it becomes a Catch-22.

I brought up the subject of steroids, which seems to be more prevalent on a professional level than a school level, but Patti reminded me that there have been young athletes that want to be bigger, stronger, and faster and they will experiment and take steroids. Patti said that you can try to educate them about the dangers to health and lecture them, but often they are still going to do it. She stated that, with the Players Association on a professional level, they are all getting a slap on the hand and it takes three to five times being caught for a suspension. Patti said it is laughable. She did say that things are starting to change on the professional level and ball players may have to sit out for a year and if it is extreme, they could blow their whole career.

Patti stated that she believes the disciplinary action after the fact is what is going to prevent the next generations from engaging in enhancement drugs. Patti said she recently did an entire story about those athletes who do not use drugs being upset with those that use these drugs. It was basically about steroid use. Patti did say people in sports often use legal supplements such as vitamins and other products that may help energize them. Those may be deemed illegal some day, also. Another factor in this equation that Patti mentioned was that the manufacturers of steroids and enhancements are always one step ahead of those that are trying to track this and catch any illegal manufacturing.

Patti gave me an example of a great ball player who is outspoken on this position, Lance Berkman, who is totally against anybody that juices up. He would be against a teammate who did this. He wants everyone to be equal, and succeed because of their own ability. Berkman told Patti that he would love to be tested. He said he wished they would test everybody so he could prove he doesn't do it and maybe it would help everyone be on a level playing field. He said these guys are cheating and he is very much offended by that.

I reminded Patti about Barry Bonds and Mark McGuire when they were in that terrific home run competition and it is sad to believe they cheated. I mentioned that there were guys in the 1930s, 1940s and 1950s that did not rely on enhancers. I said a lot of them drank alcohol; a classic example is Mickey Mantle, but Ted Williams did not even do that, he was a health fanatic. They broke all sorts of records.

Patti's response was that we don't know if they were cooking their bats or what they were doing. She said she's not calling everybody a cheater, but she said it is easy to say in the olden days that it was better. My feeling is that ball players, in the old days, didn't juice. If anything, many of those guys abused their bodies by boozing it up far too often and keeping late hours. Patti said sports have never been totally pure and that we shouldn't kid ourselves. She mentioned guys that would put Vaseline on the ball when they were pitching, etc.

Patti said that as far as cheating, corruption and crime on campus is concerned, she believes her husband, David, would be more qualified to enlighten me. Ultimately, I did interview David Smith for part of this chapter. Patti thinks, in her opinion, things have improved because there is such a microscope on big time college athletics. However, there is a caveat that goes with this, may be just in society in general things may be improving and, after all, athletes are part of society and behavior may be improving.

Patti said that based on her experience and having some knowledge of the history of sports, she states the pendulum swings back and forth. They are all now under the microscope and there are so many people against cheating. There is no clear answer to the question of cheating and corruption and efforts have to continue and rules must be abided by.

Chapter 9 - Unsportsman-like conduct

I asked Patti how she is treated by players when she schedules interviews. Patti said that they are really great about this and that she has had two people in 12 years that she considers total jerks. She stated that she thinks they are complete assholes, but only two out of all the interviews she had. Patti said that she could not give me their names.

I asked Patti about "Neon" Deion Sanders who grew up in Patti's home town, Fort Myers, Florida. I told her that my opinion was that he had this huge ego and may be difficult to deal with. Patti's response was that Deion was always fine with her. She said she has seen him be a jerk to other people, but Patti said her advantage has always been that she is a female. Patti did not acknowledge that she is a gorgeous female, she is not that kind of person, but I could see that. Patti went on to say that women can complain all they want about the fact that there is a lot of chauvinistic behavior in this world, but she said that she just never had a problem. She said that she would go up to a ball player either outside or in the locker room and they would always ask her what she needed. She said it is a respect thing and she said she has been around these ball players and teams for so long that professional relationships developed.

I asked Patti if a lot of ball players hit on her and she said that earlier on, but not any more. She said she is old enough to be their older sister. She said that she made a rule early on to never ever date a ball player. She said now, of course, they all know I'm married with children. Patti said if a female reporter has just one date with a ball player, the word will get out and you won't get any respect from the other ball players. She said she certainly never wanted to be locker room talk.

Patti said it could happen easily to some female reporters and it happened with Deion Sanders. She said that was when Sanders was in Atlanta, Georgia and Patti was a single woman and Sanders was married. Deion called her and asked her to have dinner with him. She told him she would not have dinner with him because he was a married man. She said he responded by saying that he was a big boy and he could do whatever he wanted. Patti told him she was sorry but that there was no way she would go out with a married man, let alone a ball player. She said Deion avoided her for a couple of months, but got over it. She said from that point on, she has seen Deion many times after he left Atlanta and he has shown me respect.

The Academic World

I hope that no one thinks I am a name dropper. The fact of the matter is over 70 plus years through my profession, neighborhood and childhood friends, I have had the pleasure of meeting people in-different trades and professions. Many of these people remain close friends which is a blessing to me.

I happened to meet Kenneth Keller in one of my south side neighborhoods. Our homes were back to back and our son and his two boys would crawl under the fence and play with each other. My wife and I were invited to their home one evening for cocktails and I was somewhat apprehensive because I knew he was a university professor. I didn't hang out with university or college professors. We met, liked each other, had some things in common and have remained friends since the early the 1960's. Kenneth Keller is now the director of John's Hopkins School of International Studies in Bologna, Italy. Previous to this he was a member of the Council on Foreign Relations in New York City and had an outstanding career as a bio-chemical engineer at the University of Minnesota. He did not seek the job of the presidency, but accepted that position and throughout this period our families remained close. We see him when he is in the States and when have visited him in Italy.

I interviewed Dr. Keller when he returned to the university and was offered a chair at the Humphrey Institute. I was seeking his insights into corruption in big-time college athletics.

First, I will give a little of his background. Ken Keller was born in Brooklyn. He grew up in a section called Borough Park which was a mixture of Italians, Irish, and Jewish people. He attended one of New York City's science high schools by the name of Stuyvesant which is located on Manhattan Island. He informed me that he was motivated toward the sciences mostly because of peer pressure. His parents were not educated people, but of course they wanted something better for their children. The parents always pushed the children to

Chapter 9 - Unsportsman-like conduct

do well in school. To attend Stuyvesant, one had to take a special entrance exam.

Dr. Keller was also involved in athletics and was a great Brooklyn Dodger fan and being a baseball fan myself, we had that in common. Dr. Keller attended Columbia University as an undergraduate. The Korean War was on so he took a NROTC scholarship to pay his way through college. That is the Navy Reserve Officer Training Core.

Naturally, he had a commitment to the Navy, took an extra year and applied for the Nuclear Submarine Program. This of course would be good engineering work and he was personally interviewed by Admiral Rickover. He was selected by the Admiral who I am informed was an extraordinarily disciplined tough man to work for. Most of their work was in Washington, D.C. where they were designing and building submarines, but everyone was required to spend time on submarines and time in the location where the ships were being built. Dr. Keller's background has been extremely interesting.

We spoke how athletics has become important in this country. Dr. Keller believes that over time, it has become a major form of entertainment and it kept growing. From an entertainment point of view with television, money, etc., it became successful. Early on it was primarily for students and student spectators. As more money became involved, it became more professionalized. This was true particularly in football and encouraged by the professional teams who draft players from the college level. In a sense, it is the farm team system for the pros and I doubt if they give a damn if an outstanding player is a decent student. The same is true for basketball and in many schools-hockey. They become part of the farm system for the professionals. Baseball, tennis, track, volleyball, and golf are in a separate category. The same can be said for women athletes. According to Dr. Keller, football, basketball, and hockey in this part of the country were the three sports that developed a highly professionalized money making part of the enterprise. Only three sports make money at the university. To make money, you have to produce better teams.

Dr. Keller stated big-time athletics can lead to corruption. He felt there was less criminal activity involved than corruption. The corruption has come about in an interesting couple of ways that go beyond the cycle of which we are speaking.

Dr. Keller stated NCAA has an objective of keeping the playing field level, resulting in many silly kinds of rigidities in the system. There are rigidities which make it even less accommodating and flexible so that the things you might do to make the system less corrupt you are prevented from doing are the very rules the NCAA puts in place. As an example that Dr. Keller stated may be we are stuck with having to produce really good teams and good athletics and get athletes in and they don't start out being very interested in academics. So what's the choice for the university? It does not have the choice of getting out of the game. People like Sid Hartman who is a sports writer with the Star Tribune would ask, "What you are doing?" They will claim you are doing something which is embarrassing them. The criticism is you can't diminish the importance of major college athletic teams; that would bring shame on the university. When things aren't going well, the first thing some of these fanatical boosters call for is firing the coach and if that does not improve things, fire the president. Unfortunately, the answer is if all Big Ten schools for example, as a group, decided to do away with recruiting those students who have no academic interest, they could avoid corruption, but the quality of the teams would diminish. This is not going to happen of course because the pressures are too great for every university to put forth winning teams.

Dr. Keller gave an example of one of the NCAA obstacles to doing what an institution of higher learning must do. The example he gave is, if I have a student coming in who just scrapped by in high school and he says to me I want to go to school, I don't have any money so I am going to have to work 30 hours a weeks, so what courses should I take? I say, "You had better start slow. You don't start with four courses for twelve credits that wouldn't make sense. Start with two. Let's get you through some stuff." That is against NCAA rules. The NCAA rules would say that student is not in good standing because he is not taking twelve credits so the NCAA forces the athlete to take an academic load that they would never recommend to a non-athlete student. Dr. Keller said the only way we can do that is create easier courses. Then, they can register the students for twelve credits.

Chapter 9 - Unsportsman-like conduct

Keller said this not something we would do-create easier courses just for athletes. We give the student extra help.

Some of the poor kids are put in a position where they are barely scraping by, but they cannot receive any more aid than a kid who comes from a middle class or affluent family. Coaches are getting extra cars from the car dealers around town. Sometimes their own radio program and if a coach wins a bowl game, he gets a bonus-maybe around $25,000. The kids in this system don't get these perks. So there is an exploitation of the kids.

I enquired of Dr. Keller what about young athletes who showcase themselves for a year or two and were on scholarships and then sign a pro contract. Dr. Keller said he thought they were making a mistake even though the outcome may not be the worst scenario. The worst outcome from Dr. Keller's point of view is remembering kids that came to him after they played for four years at the university and not getting a degree, that are now working day labor jobs. Some have come back to see Dr. Keller when he was president and these kids stated to him, "I don't understand it, I played my heart out. I did everything everyone asked for four years and now I don't have a degree and I don't have a job. What happened?" Dr; Keller said he didn't have a sufficient answer for these young people. What has happened is that some recruiters and boosters made false promises and in turn, the athletes expectations were too high. That is the human tragedy. That in many ways is worse than the corruption. It is destroying a person's life for not having done what we should have done.

At the University of Minnesota when Dr. Keller was president, they would take back a student when their eligibility was over and find the money to support them if the student had the motivation.

Dr. Keller informed me that there are perhaps 95 scholarships for football, 15-20 for basketball and number of scholarships for hockey. You may end up with at least 150 students on athletic scholarships. You try the most perfect screening possible, but if you come out at 90 percent on your screening, you would be doing very, very well. He stated that most of these kids are really good kids even though some are rough and come from difficult backgrounds-they are basically good. He said even some of the good kids can get in trouble, there are a lot of temptations.

I inquired how the NCAA became so powerful. Dr. Keller said there are two things. It got powerful because it controls the competition which makes the whole system work and it developed those rules because every school is suspicious of every other school. The NCAA wanted to make sure that no school got ahead of the other so they kept putting more and more rigid rules to what they called a level playing field, but it was a rotten playing field. In the final analysis, Dr. Keller stated if you had losing athletic teams every year, the alumni, faculty, students, and sportswriters would be up in arms.

I asked Dr. Keller about boosters, clubs, and the media. He stated boosters sometimes can be a problem because they get out of hand, but they are not always a problem. The newspaper, Star and Tribune, invests quite a bit of money in the size of the sports section so they have an interest in university sports and professional teams being prominent and competitive. If we went the way the University of Chicago did back in the 30's and discontinued athletics, every columnist in the state would be on our back.

When I interviewed Dr. Keller, he gave me a great deal of leeway and time. I am sure only because we are friends. We went into areas covering expert testimony, going back to the days when he was a bio-chemical engineer, selection of people on juries based on his experience, acting as an expert and becoming familiar with court procedure. He made a comment to me, "I remember an incident on an elevator with you after I testified on behalf of Michael Robins' clients." This was a civil case. A woman on the elevator asked, "How did you get so smart?" Dr. Keller stated to me, "I make a good presentation and somebody a lot smarter may not make a good presentation." It would be nice to think the woman on the elevator made the comment because the facts I presented in the case were good and I was also good at presenting these facts. This is where the expert witness aspect of court trials becomes a problem. Some people may not be able to make a clear and articulate presentation in a way juries can understand what they are saying and it may result justice not truly being served.

In summation regarding Dr. Ken Keller, it has always been a great pleasure for me to be around people that are smarter and who are gracious, tolerant, and base their friendships not on wealth or level of intelligence.

Marvelous Marty

I had an interview with Dr. Martin Dworkin in 2003 at the University of Minnesota. Dr. Dworkin is now retired from an outstanding career at the University of Minnesota as one of the nation's leading microbiologists. He is a close friend of the former President of the University of Minnesota, Ken Keller, who approximately 35 years ago introduced my wife and I to Marty and his brilliant wife, Noni. The purpose of the interview was to gather his thoughts as a university professor on big time athletics, ethics within higher education, his views on legal issues, specifically expert witness testimony in court. I reduced the question answer session to a narrative and will quote all of Marty's answers.

Marty grew up in New York City. He is the son of immigrants, neither of whom went to high school. They were working parents. He was an only child growing up during the depression. His parents had a tailor shop in a rough area in New York City. He attended Brooklyn Technical High School because he felt he wanted to be an engineer and New York, at that time, had a series of high schools for high ability students and these schools were city schools. Marty was required to take an exam to qualify for the school and our mutual friend, Ken Keller, went through the same process but attended Stuyvesant.

After high school, Marty attended CCNY which he stated was a great university at that time and a vehicle for getting out of the ghetto. He grew up in a slum neighborhood across from the Hotel St. George. It was a rough neighborhood. In high school, Marty was the only Jew in his class and stated "It's something we really didn't pay attention to."

Marty then attended Indiana University, this is before the GI Bill kicked in and tuition was low. He said he had no idea where the university was but seeing their catalog it looked like an attractive place for a college student. This was toward the end of World War II and he was the last batch of draftees. When he got out of the army, he used the GI Bill for his education and commented that Bill changed the life of hundreds of thousands of people and changed America.

It was at the University of Indiana that he discovered microbiology. He read a book by a professor who had written on the chemical activities of fungi that captivated him. That professor was in Texas so Marty applied there, was accepted and that is where he got his Ph. D. He did a post doctorate at Berkley where he met his wife, and then got a job offer from the University of Minnesota in 1962.

Before I got into my questioning session with Marty, we had a little bantering back and forth trying to remember when we met. We met through Ken Keller and it would have been approximately 30 years ago. Marty said "That's about right Vinnie, and I've admired you ever since." My response was "Flattery will get you whatever you desire."

My first question to Marty was his thoughts on the major problems causing a great deal of bad behavior in big time athletics and what could be done about it. Marty's initial response was "I don't know how to respond to that other than usual clichés that it is inappropriate, scandalous, and not what universities should be doing, but I don't know what the solution to the problem may be." He went on to say the whole thing has gotten so immense and so penetrated in our culture that it is difficult to know how it could be put back in its proper place. Any kind of proposal would almost be unrealistic. On the other hand, he said he becomes impatient with people who categorically deny the roll of athletics at universities, intercollegiate and intramural programs. Marty said he thinks both have an important role to play at universities and that's part of the mood and spirit of a university.

I inquired why regents, faculty, presidents of all the big ten universities can't sit down and make an attempt to overhaul the athletic system. I asked if that would be a fantasy on my part to even suggest this. Marty said it would be a fantasy because there are certainly enough leaders in higher education who have wanted to do that for a long time, but have had no success. He had no specifics concerning efforts to clean up any corruption in big time athletics,

Chapter 9 - Unsportsman-like conduct

but stated "It's a problem that has social implications in terms of its racial implications, obviously because so many of the athletes are black. It has financial implications in terms of the amounts of money that are donated to universities." Marty stated that Ken Keller, former President at the University of Minnesota, did not believe there was a clear relationship between winning and donations to the school. Keller felt that argument is not that strong. Nevertheless, there have been many minority students who have obtained their university degrees who were on athletic scholarships, however, there have been many Caucasians and minority athletes who have not completed their university programs, have turned professional or left school even though they had scholarships.

I mentioned to Marty that the University of Chicago, an excellent educational institution, had once been a member of the Big Ten, had a famous coach, yet they chose to focus on the academic and discontinued the football program. Marty was very aware of that and stated the University of Chicago survived without big time athletics. He stated for a public university, athletics certainly enhances the loyalty alumni have. He said "Other than that I don't know where to go with this problem." He stated he never had a personal interaction of the sort where he was approached by a coach or anyone else to upgrade a failing student. He stated that athletes just don't take his courses.

I mentioned plagiarism specifically because we had a scandal at the University when Clem Haskins was the coach. There was a woman, now deceased, who was writing papers for some of the basketball players and the situation exploded. Mr. Haskins, who Ken Keller hired and thought of highly, resigned. I am not familiar with the legal aspect of his contract being bought out even though Ron Meshbesher was one of the lawyers representing Mr. Haskins. He may not have known what was going on, but he was the boss and it all fell on his shoulders. I also mentioned to Marty the recent scandal at the New York Times whereby a reporter was fired for plagiarizing and offered my opinion that this, in essence, is cheating, unethical, and may be even theft for not giving credit to the owner or the writer of books, articles, etc.

Marty's response was "In order for plagiarism to be a crime, you have to be able to define what it is and that seems to be fundamental." He has never really seen a definition of plagiarism. How many words have to be duplicated before it becomes plagiarism? It's difficult to determine, yet in the case of the woman writing entire papers for student athletes that is out and out cheating. Calling plagiarism a crime seems to Marty would only occur in the most egregious case, or large segments of something were stolen word for word. The fact remains you don't steal anybody's ideas or words, it's just not supposed to be done at a University.

Marty has come across incidents of plagiarism, caused primarily by cultural differences. He said the first offense is free, the second you get an F and the third suggests the plagiarist might be incorrigible. He doesn't know if such people are expelled but he thinks they should be.

The cultural reasons with foreign students start with them not being familiar with our customs. Among many foreign cultures, learning is memorizing and repeating. You memorize what somebody else did and then you regurgitate it back. Secondly, many foreign students are uncomfortable with our language and are eager and desperate to express an idea but don't feel they can do it properly in their own words so they use someone else's words. That strikes Marty as being an innocent kind of mistake so he tends to be lenient with foreign students who do that.

We then went on to talk about science in the courtroom. I asked Marty if he had ever been called as an expert to testify in court. He stated that I had contacted him one time to interview somebody who was a principal in a case that I was working on with the Thompson Lundquist firm. He stated that he was requested to write an opinion in an effort to make a judgment about the validity of the scientific plan in the case. His other experience dealing with a lawyer and science pertained to an eye injury on a farm where the person developed an infection.

I requested whether or not Marty could offer an opinion concerning the battle of experts in the criminal arena. The defense often brings in their experts, as does the plaintiff on injury cases and, in criminal

Chapter 9 - Unsportsman-like conduct

cases, pathologists and other experts may be brought in. It ends up in a battle, and it makes it difficult for juries.

Marty stated that he agrees that there are kinds of scientific information that are beyond the ability of a lay jury to evaluate. For example, one of the things that he has read about finger prints is the extent to which finger prints are or are not a categorical indication of identity. This depends, to a large extent, on a very sophisticated analysis and to some extent a jury may not be able to deal with that. DNA analysis, for example, is very complicated. However, it seems to Marty that for those sorts of things, it should be possible to arrive at settled guidelines that one would ask the defense or the prosecution to adhere to in terms of evaluating this data. These guidelines could be formulated by a scientific group and with those guidelines in mind, it should be possible to present data to a jury and say to a jury this analysis fulfills the requirements and on the basis of that, we can say yes indeed the DNA has a 99.9% probability of coming from the individual, and a jury can understand that. I would imagine, however, that there are certain things that are so indeterminate that they require a kind of judgment that a jury is not able to understand that may require a scientific panel rather than a jury to adjudicate and present the recommendation to a judge. Marty said he thinks there is room for improvement, but it should be possible to make much of the scientific evidence that is used in law understandable to a jury. Marty incidentally supports the jury system.

Marty further stated "I think it's like many other things in society, there is a dialectic that goes on, a pendulum that swings back and forth. We over shoot the mark in one direction and then over shoot it in the opposite direction and the pendulum should come to rest some place in between." His opinion has to do with the notion of entitlement. The notion that we should all be risk free and this has manifested itself in the most extraordinary kinds of decisions all of us have heard about. It's an attitude that people often have that they are entitled to zero risk.

We shifted to the subject of lawyers and the fact that there may be too many lawyers in our society. I brought up the example of Japan, who has very few lawyers per citizen and we seem to have an excess of attorneys. We both agreed that a law degree is an excellent degree that can be used in other areas such as business, finance, and even science. Marty stated that it affects him as a professor. I suggested that too many people in a certain profession may breed some unethical chasing of business or excessive lawsuits. I mentioned the Rajender cases at the University of Minnesota.

The Rajender cases blossomed out of a claim that a woman made that was absolutely valid concerning tenure. She had been screwed over. She won her case. Out of the woodwork came hundreds of other claims, most of them frivolous but the University went forward and settled those cases because it would have cost too much to try every case in a court of law.

Marty's comments about the case were that much of this had to do with a mood that immerged in society regarding entitlement and self-esteem. He stated that this can affect him, as a professor, when you have to worry more about the student's self-esteem than worry about whether you are accurate in reflecting how well the student has done. He said it has gotten crazy. Marty stated the University has a tremendous battery of lawyers and stated that this upset Ken Keller when he was President. Ken was upset when he talked about substituting legal settlements for academic judgments.

Marty also stated he didn't want to fall in the trap of some sentimental nostalgic view of the past. He did say "Nevertheless, there was a time at the University where there was a set of shared values where one could adjudicate disputes on the basis of those shared values. That has gradually been displaced; shared values no longer work to adjudicate disputes. One has to have a contract, one has to have it stipulated, and one has to have everything down in black and white and in incredible detail. When that happens, you need a lawyer so the need for lawyers has immerged, in part, as a result of this shift in society from a dependence on shared values and trust to a dependence on contract stipulations."

We talked about the Dr. John Najarian case which was handled by attorney Peter Thompson and John Lundquist of the Thompson, Lundquist & Siccoli law firm. I mentioned this case in this book and Najarian was acquitted of all charges. Marty stated he thought the Najarian case was a massive mistake. He said that Najarian was

Chapter 9 - Unsportsman-like conduct

pilloried on the basis of an issue that was out of proportion. The issue Marty was speaking to was the anti-rejection drug called ALG. Marty stated not only was it a good product, it saves lives and after it went off the market, there was a period of time until replacement could be found and that presented a problem. Marty said the whole affair was screwed up from the start.

Once again, I mentioned this case in this book and remind the reader that Najarian was charged on numerous counts, some pertained to travel charges.

We discussed the period of time Ken Keller was President of the University of Minnesota. For a lengthy period of time, every day Keller was pilloried in the press. It started with the University of Minnesota Daily who discovered some impropriety in the plant management department at the University. They came across a desk that Keller, as President, purchased for his office. It should have been emphasized, but wasn't, when a professor, faculty or President requests a piece of furniture, it must go through plant management. Often bids are involved, but I don't know in this instance if it was an outright purchase. The fact remains that when the President leaves office he does not take the desk with him.

From the desk matter, he was then attacked about the renovation of the President's mansion. Keller did not wish to move in the mansion, it was a white elephant. It needed extensive repair. There were gaps between the walls and the floor where you could even see down into the basement. There was lead paint on site. He already had a home that he and his wife were very happy in, but the mansion is used for entertaining dignitaries at dinner. The kitchen was small, the dining room small, and some guests had to be seated in the basement for God's sakes. To make a long story short, Ken took so much crap about this that he resigned.

The very sad and disgusting aspect of Ken's situation is the fact that the regents and even the governor should have stepped up, offered a response, and said enough is enough. That didn't happen.

Marty Dworkin stepped up to the plate on behalf of Ken and related to me the situation that he was involved in. Marty had written a letter to the Minneapolis Star Tribune that took the regents to task for failing to defend Ken Keller. Marty took the position that one of the functions of the Board of Regents was to stand as a buffer, in a sense, between the University and the legislature to represent the University to the legislature and protect the University from political pressure as much as possible. He got a call from WCCO one day asking if he'd be willing to appear on a panel discussing the Keller case. He accepted and asked who was going to be there. They mentioned David Roe, who was a regent at the time. Marty showed up at WCCO, was greeted by the person who organized this, and David Roe walked in and was introduced to Marty. Marty said he turned red and Roe said something to the effect of "Are you the son of a bitch who wrote that letter about the regents in the Tribune?" Marty said "Yes." Roe then said "I'll be God damned if I'm going to appear on any panel with this guy" and he stomped out. So here they had this thing already programmed and scheduled and were supposed to go on in five minutes, and Roe stomped off. To make a long story short, finally what the station negotiated was that Roe and Marty would not appear together because Roe refused to appear with Marty. It was the only basis Roe agreed upon.

Marty then commented that this gives you the sense of the caliber and quality of some of the regents at the University during that period of time. He said "Fortunately the quality has improved."

Marty pointed out that the media is concerned as much with image and personality and style as it is with substance. Many Minnesotans were not comfortable with Ken Keller's style as President of the University. In my opinion, an entire book could be written about that period leading up to an honorable man's resignation. It is interesting to note that Dr. Keller returned to the University, was given a chair at the Humphrey Institute, and is now the Director of John's Hopkins International Studies in Bologna, Italy. Marty and I know him to be a man of immense compassion, understanding, extremely high intellect, and one that wanted to put the University on the course of striving for excellence.

Dr. Martin Dworkin and I went on to discuss other matters and all I can say is that my wife and I are fortunate to have he and his family as friends. I must add this, Marty is an outstanding musician, his

Chapter 9 - Unsportsman-like conduct

instrument is the clarinet and for a long time he played in a band. Marty was also an outstanding fast pitch softball player. He could no longer adequately play the clarinet because he has two fingers that were broken and he is unable to properly play the instrument,

If one evaluates good athletes, good baseball, football, basketball and hockey players, generally speaking they start out playing with the older guys. They usually played a level above their age and this made them better in their field. My mom used to tell me to have good quality friends and I always did think the same concept in athletics pertains to life, that is keeping good companions, and if possible, companions that are smarter than you. Most of my friends are smarter than me and this truly lifts me up. I am proud of these people, sometime in awe of them, and have always appreciated our friendships.

Chapter 10

King of the Sex Cases

Time to let you good folks listen to some of the other people I've rubbed shoulders with during my career. Here an attorney I love like a son.

Robert Sicoli

I interviewed Attorney Robert Sicoli on a cold March day at his office, and this took place when the title of the firm he was with was Thompson, Sicoli & Aho. John Lundquist, who is now with the law firm of Fredrickson & Byron, had been a partner with Peter when they started the firm, but decided to leave and went with an excellent large firm doing criminal and civil cases. Lundquist is a very smart individual and he and Thompson had a successful career together. Mr. Sicoli joined them shortly after Peter and John purchased a building on 25th and Park Avenue, one of the old Piper mansions, right next door to the Shriner Building.

Robert Sicoli, like all the attorneys I worked for, is very outstanding to say the least. It is a real joy to be still working with him. Bob's wife, Becky, helps him in his legal practice by keeping the books and transcribing reports. His oldest daughter is a sophomore in college at Knox. She is a very good student, has a partial basketball scholarship, and she looks like she just came over from Italy. She is absolutely gorgeous, tall and a wonderful young woman. Bob's son, Anthony, who is an athlete, enjoys hanging around with his dad. We have been to many ball games together and he is also very Italian looking. Bob and I have a great time working together, laughing, and discussing all sorts of topics.

My first question to Bob was what motivated him to become a lawyer. His response was that he always wanted to be a lawyer, even when he was a kid, and probably since the fifth or sixth grade. Part of that was due to his father being a lawyer in Italy. However, he unfortunately died when Bob was eight years old. Bob said that being a lawyer is probably the only thing he is good at. I disagreed with him

Chapter 10 - King of the Sex Cases

on that. Bob went on to say that he was always good at arguing and maybe that is a factor, also.

I asked Bob about his father and he said that his father was born and raised in Figline Vegliaturo. This was a small village which grew to be a city, but the closest big city was Cosenza. He went to law school in the southern part of Italy and Bob has his diploma on the wall. His dad practiced criminal defense law. He came to the states in 1948, shortly after the war. Politically, his father was a socialist and was the right-hand man of the socialist party leader in Italy. It caused his father some problems when he gave speeches, he would be in some danger, and he had to avoid coming in contact with anybody in Mussolini's government. I told Bob that back in the 70s in Brazil, their criminal code was based on Mussolini's code. Brazil has changed and is now a democratic country.

Bob said his father basically came to the United States following his mother. His mother had come over in the 30s, perhaps around 1934, prior to World War II and she was just a child. His mother and father knew each other in Italy and really cared for each other, but they were separated for 11 years prior to them reconnecting. Bob said that his father used to aggravate his grandparents because he was the kind of guy that was a true socialist and he would give everything away. Bob said he would have given away the kitchen table if he could. Bob's mother's father, his grandfather, was working in the United States in the 30s and sending money home to the family in Italy. His grandfather had called the family home stating Hitler is doing crazy things, so they came to the United States, too.

They went to Chicago, Illinois where there was a large Italian community and where Bob's grandfather was working. His father never practiced law in the United States. Ultimately, they moved to St. Paul around 1959 or so.

I asked Bob if it was a factor, his family history, his dad being a socialist, seeing many poor people in Italy, that this gave him an attitude that he wanted to represent people that had problems. Bob said, "I think so. First of all we have to remember that the immigrants that came over back in those days felt that way, also. Just as a general rule the immigrants were pretty supportive of the lower class because all of them came with very little money and perhaps they were all lower class. Even if they became successful, they remembered the type of life that they came from." Bob said his mother used to tell him stories about how his dad would represent people and be paid for his services with chickens or eggs. He just had a strong sense of helping people out. Bob said maybe it is in their genes because he not only wanted to be a lawyer, but he wanted to help out the less fortunate.

Bob attended the University of Minnesota and his undergraduate degree was in Political Science & Economics. His first job was clerking for a white collar firm, Briggs & Morgan, and then he was hired as a summer associate. He wanted to do litigation, but was working in a business capacity. He said he weaseled his way into court with a bankruptcy attorney who did not like to go to court, and that is what Bob liked to do.

Bob met Peter Thompson about six months before he was hired by Thompson & Lundquist. He and Peter met at a seminar dealing with evidence, and six months later Lundquist phone Bob. Lundquist had talked to a friend of Bob's, Pete Cahill, a defense lawyer, subsequently, and John interviewed Bob and they hired him. He has now been a lawyer for approximately 21 years.

I reminded Bob that when my wife and I went away on a sabbatical in a volunteer program, my friend Bill Carberry took over my duties. Mr. Carberry is now deceased and his wife, Carol, always asks, "How is that young man, Bob?"

I told Bob that it was always a delight working with him because he never procrastinated. He would get a case and immediately give me the assignment. He wanted to be thoroughly-prepared when going to trial. I appreciated that because I hated scampering around the community at the last moment. Our theme is leave no stone unturned.

I brought up a sex case that he had in a rural community and asked if he could talk about it without mentioning names. We could mention names because there is a court record made and it is available if one wanted to review the transcript. It was a criminal sex one involving a

Chapter 10 - King of the Sex Cases

teacher and a very attractive female student. Bob said that he certainly would never forget that case because his teacher/client was found not guilty. He stated the female was 17 years old at the time of the incident, but technically speaking, if a 17 year old consents to sexual activity with a person over 21, it is legal. The age of consent in Minnesota is 16.

Under most circumstances, it is usually two people who do not work together and do not have a business supervision type of relationship. Legally, a 55 year old man could have sex with a 16 year old girl, or a 16 year old young man could have sex with a 40 year old woman and it would be legal.

I then asked him how this applies to a teacher/student situation in that the teacher may be in a position of authority. Bob responded that would be a crime with a 16 year old if something sexually occurred. Bob said that they have actually changed the law since his case, which was in about 1995 or so.

Bob went on to talk about the 17 year old student who had sex with a teacher. The sex was consensual. However, the teacher was charged. Bob said that under our system of law, which is something he doesn't necessarily agree with, if a therapist is told about a sexual situation that may possibly involve abuse, even though the one who committed the act is consulting with the therapist, the therapist is mandated to report to the authorities. Generally, with a therapist, psychologist, doctor, psychiatrist, and priest, there is a relationship that protects whatever the person has said. So what happened in this particular case, where it was consensual, the psychologist called the police. The psychologist informed the police that he had a situation where a person has admitted having sex with a student. The teacher obviously felt guilty and went to see the psychologist, but the psychologist was mandated to inform the police.

Close to the same time, the student was in the process of reporting this act she had engaged in voluntarily, so that is how the case began.

I believe what this means is that if you feel remorse, you want to repent, and you are trying to get help from an expert, they must call the authorities which then messes with the effort to heal and learn how to control your sexual desires. Bob stated what they were faced with in this case, and the defense lawyer must be creative, in that no way are you going to gain an acquittal by denying to the jury that your client had sex with a student. There was a report made by the psychologist and, of course, the psychologist would have to testify in court. Bob said they have to decide on whether to take a plea or do they argue that he was in a position of authority but did not use that position of authority to get the young woman to submit. That is what he did, that was the argument, and the jury acquitted the client.

I'll give the background, but I won't divulge any names because all of these people are still in the State of Minnesota and it doesn't serve any purpose to be passing out names. The young lady, who lived on a small farm, was extremely attractive. According to some fellow students who did not like her, she literally was chasing the teacher around, flirted with him heavily, and according to these students that I interviewed, he really did his best to avoid her. In fact, on one occasion, he gently chastised her but she continued with her seductive ways. I had interviewed a number of these young students, found that most of them were quite bright, and according to these young witnesses, they felt the young lady was in the wrong for literally trying to seduce a teacher. Evidently, the teacher was very young, too, as he was in his mid 20s. The teacher had a wife, but no children and, as stated earlier, went to a psychologist because he felt terrible about what happened.

It was a holiday and the young lady drove over to the teacher's residence. The teacher's wife was gone for the day and he made the mistake of letting her in his home. At a point in time, she asked where the bathroom was, but she didn't return to the living room where they were talking. He hoped that she wasn't sick so he walked down the hallway and found her lying naked on his bed. He made the mistake in engaging in sexual intercourse with her.

Bob's theory of why she went to the authorities after his client is that the teacher told her that he went to see a psychologist and that he was going to go to the authorities because he thought what he did was wrong. Bob believes at that point, she made a report and said that she was going to say that he forced her to do it. That was her quote on the witness stand.

Chapter 10 - King of the Sex Cases

I interviewed this young lady fully expecting that I would be rejected by her parents or her, but I was not rejected. The young lady's mother let me come-into their nice home, and the young lady was in bed as I was told, at approximately 11:00 in the morning. Her mother summoned her and she said she would talk to me but did not want her mother present. This was in the summer, so we went out in the front yard area where I spoke with her. She told me her version, immediately stating that she was a victim, that she did nothing wrong, etc. She had all the technical language down which obviously she heard from counselors or social workers. She cried at the picnic table and I must say that always tugs at me, I gave her a handkerchief and went on and conducted the interview.

I am always a gentleman, I don't accuse people, I merely try to elicit information in a civilized way. She did not say she was upset at me for coming to her home. Bob was very grateful and complementary about my work in that the students had provided information of value.

I regret that I was not able to attend the trial. Bob stated that when she appeared on the witness stand, she really did look rather sexy. He said this was a mistake on the prosecutor's part. He should have had her dressed as an innocent teenage girl. Bob said that when she was being asked questions by the prosecutor, she was sort of weepy and sad as she was with me. Bob said that once he started cross-examining her, he saw that she wasn't a weak person. In fact, she snapped at Bob several times. You don't want a jury to ever see your client with that kind of behavior. Bob said that this was a tough, young woman, not a little girl with a ponytail. He said that she was a very attractive young woman and that she was wearing a very tight sweater on the witness stand.

Bob said that he did not think that her rather sexy attire hurt him, and of course, the snappiness helped him. Bob said, to the judge's credit, he allowed Bob to make some comments that the young lady had said to his client regarding her past sexual conduct. She made comments about going to motel rooms with guys and other powerful sexual comments.

According to Mr. Sicoli, normally prior sexual experience and conduct is not admissible, but it is admissible if it is used for other purposes than showing that the female is a tramp. Bob said he was trying to show that she was making comments to his client about these things for a specific reason, to get him to realize that she wanted to have sex with him. Because she had made those comments to the client, the judge allowed it. If she had just had sex with other guys, and hadn't said anything to the client about that, the judge appropriately would have kept this evidence out.

I interjected by saying that I learned from the witnesses that she had some problems at home, that there was some alcohol abuse in the family and other problems. Bob followed-up by saying that the judge would not allow that in, although he made the effort to get in into evidence. There was also a past allegation of sexual abuse that she made against some other officials at the school. Bob asked that those records be submitted for the judge for *in camera* review. The judge reviewed those records and allowed Bob to get some of that material into evidence. *In camera* review means that the judge will read and evaluate the information and then make a decision on whether the records can be admitted into evidence. Sometimes a judge will redact part of the information out of a document then allow the rest of the document into evidence. The young woman had gone through some counseling and the judge allowed some of those records in as well, but not all of them. In Bob's opinion, the judge's rulings were probably appropriate, deleting some, but allowing other portions to stand.

Bob stated that he didn't want to make too much of the fact that his client was an innocent-type guy from a moral standpoint, he should have not engaged in sexual intercourse no matter what. Bob argued that it was not a criminal offense, he was weak, did what he should not have done, and it is understandable that a young man, being confronted by a naked woman who had been talking to him about her sexual activities, would cave in.

In the old days, 60s, 70s and 80s, I gave no thought to interviewing a beautiful young woman on a one-on-one basis. Even though I am an old dog, a broken down 75 year old grandpa, I do not wish to interview young, attractive, sexy women unless someone else is in

Chapter 10 - King of the Sex Cases

the room. It would be devastating to be falsely accused by someone of acting inappropriately.

Bob said that it was a quick verdict, but you never know if that is to your advantage or disadvantage because he has had quick guilty verdicts as well as quick not guilty verdicts. Bob said he felt pretty good about the jury coming back after approximately 2-1/2 to 3 hours, but a little nervous. It meant that the jury had enough to think about and if they came back quickly, they were probably not going to find his client guilty.

I stated to Bob that it was a hometown jury. Bob said that was true, but he got the case moved to a smaller town, yet many people knew the teacher because he was well-liked and somewhat prominent. I said that in rural areas word does get around about unusual events. The judge, however, came from a neighboring county and there were enough grounds to move it to the judge's county. The jurors knew the judge well, many called him by his first name, but not knowing the prosecutor may have been to some benefit. The county attorneys usually do not try many cases and they are elected. However, in this case, the county attorney handled the case.

The witnesses that I rounded up were pretty factual and we didn't have to get into issues concerning any lack of respect and popularity of the accuser. These witnesses gave examples such as on one occasion, a group of students, along with the accuser, happened to be on a bus with the teacher and she kept trying to sit next to the teacher. There were other examples pointed out showing that the young lady was on the make.

Bob said that he put his client on the stand and he made no excuses, admitted that what he did was wrong, and that he went to a psychologist before the case even came to light. There was no dancing around, he was honest and the jury saw that.

Bob said that it helped when picking the jury that the judge gave a little bit of latitude. Bob said to the first juror during *voir dire*, "We are not going to deny that the young lady and my client had sex, but that is not what the law says." I said to Bob that he was able to get a great-deal of information from the jury and, obviously, they must have thought you were an honest guy because you were telling them what the case was about, and the proper application of the law to such a case.

Bob emphasized that you have to do your best to communicate with the jury. Often he gets help from the National Jury Project, headed by Diane Wiley. Jurors sometimes totally dislike the client. If the attorney can get the jury to like and respect the attorney, and you can demonstrate that you are being honest, that can rub off a little bit for the client.

I asked Bob if people came up to him and sometimes say things like how can you possibly represent some guy that has committed a terrible offense? Bob said, "I don't really have any problems with it." Generally speaking, we have a system that has been set up whereby we do not want to convict people unless they can be proven guilty beyond a reasonable doubt. I am part of this system, I fight against the government, but my rule is basically to make sure the system is not steamrolling over somebody. Even the guilty have a right to be represented and if the government cannot prove guilty beyond a reasonable doubt, then a jury should not find the defendant guilty. Again, we don't want to send innocent people to prison. Bob states that there have been many mistakes with capital punishment in the past. Now we have DNA and other more sophisticated ways, but there are still some that slip through the cracks.

I reminded Sicoli that in Illinois, it was a conservative Republican Governor that halted the executions because he came to realize too many mistakes had been made. The Governor certainly wasn't a radical liberal, but the consensus is that he did the right thing.

We then talked about a case Bob had in Brainerd, Minnesota where even the prosecutor thought that Bob would win his case. In a nutshell, it was on a holiday and Bob's client, who was in his late 50s, had a party. His son and many others attended the party at the lake home and his son was serious about a young lady who was present. There was far too much drinking, and eventually they went into the town of Brainerd, drank at a few bars and all these young people were really intoxicated.

Chapter 10 - King of the Sex Cases

The client's son was so drunk that he rode with his brother and the son's fiancée rode in the client's truck. She regurgitated in the truck, so he pulled into a resort and she ran into the lake to clean herself up. He admitted to his lawyer that he was helping her clean off, she had vomit all over herself, and there was vomit inside the front passenger seat of the truck. Naturally, while helping her clean up, he had to be holding her in certain ways and later she said that he groped her in a sexual way, but there was no intercourse. She claimed that the client and future father-in-law made her touch his penis, she got upset, and they went back to the cabin where she told her fiancé, the client's son. Ultimately, they reported this to the police.

The young woman had run into the lake in a very dangerous area. A short time before this incident, there was a drowning at that location, and the client was aware of that and didn't want her, in an intoxicated state, being in that lake by herself, so that is why he retrieved her and help clean her up. Bob stated that this is a classic example of showing why an accused should not talk to the police without a lawyer present. Bob's client, when the police requested, gave a statement and made no admissions, but damaged his own position. Bob stated that the client always denied having any sexual contact with this young lady, but obviously the jury had a hard time believing that he was not guilty and he was convicted.

The police did not actually go out and interview the young lady, the officer assigned to the case took a type-written statement that her fiancé brought to the police station. He never followed-up on an interview. She was never asked pertinent questions. It is really unbelievable to accept such shoddy police work. Bob cross-examined the police officer, criticizing the work that the officer did and because he was in the home town of the accuser, it must have pissed the jury off. Bob said that it seemed like obvious criticism to him. In Minneapolis, it would have been obvious criticism, faulty police work.

Sicoli said that to show you how grossly incompetent the investigation by the police was, the original beat patrol officer was called to take the statement of this girl when they first reported. The accuser and the client's son met the officer at a gas station about two in the morning. That police officer expressed some doubts in his report that the woman was telling the truth, and the police officer said she seems to not really have a good recollection of what was going on. She seems not to be answering my questions and evading my questions. Bob said that what he did was he said to the jury the police officer did his job, he was looking at it with a skeptical eye and he gave it to the detective to follow-up. The detective did nothing. He didn't do his job and we probably would not be here if the detective had done his job correctly. One other family member, a brother, was present and also that brother's friend. Those witnesses oppose the accuser. Bob said that he held one officer up as the man who did the right thing, and the other detective as the guy that screwed up, so it wasn't complete criticism of the entire police department.

When a detective gets the kind of information he did from the beat cop, who was skeptical, that should raise the eyebrow of the detective and yet he never went out to talk to the person. He just accepted a typed statement from her.

I had to take the witness stand because I took photographs and measurements of the client's truck and lake area where — the young woman washed up. I got a little feisty with the prosecutor who was pushing at me and trying to elicit a contradiction. I had apologized after my testimony to Sicoli and I was back on the witness stand after the lunch break. Bob said that he didn't think it meant anything in the final analysis, but I should have let Bob rehabilitate the situation on his re-direct.

In the prosecutor's final argument, he stated, "I don't know about you people, but I am sick and tired of people criticizing the police department." I talked to the prosecutor after the case when I saw him at a seminar and he said he went back to the office after closing argument and told his staff that he had about a five percent chance of winning. He said he thought Sicoli was going to win the case.

I thought the young lady was a complete phony. She walked to the witness stand with this very pained look. She immediately started to weep and I thought she was acting. She had thrown up all over this man in the car, on the floor and all over herself. She claimed they had kissed but how would someone kiss in such a repugnant situation? I

Chapter 10 - King of the Sex Cases

also felt there was an enormous amount of reasonable doubt, but we were all wrong.

Another thought I had was that everyone was intoxicated. The client had too much to drink also. The whole night was, in my eyes, bizarre. I don't think the average healthy father would go out and get drunk with his kids. It is just kind of tacky.

Mr. Sicoli's client took the witness stand, obviously the jury didn't care for him, but it was his decision to testify. Bob said he told his client that since he desired to testify, he, as the lawyer, must allow this, but he cautioned his client to never lie. The defense attorney cannot support a client lying on a witness stand and allowing the person to testify to lies. If someone the attorney is representing takes the stand against the attorney's advice, it is the attorney's duty to ask him only questions that will avoid any lies. My comment was in my 40 plus years as an investigator, I have never seen a defense attorney suborn perjury, but I have seen prosecutors allow snitches to get on the stand and lie. Bob's comment was that he has seen the same.

I mentioned to Bob that there was a highly publicized case that he had involving an owner of a steel fabricating company who hit a Latino man in the head with a board. The facts of this case were somewhat contradictory, but the client of Sicoli had gone from his office to the fabricating building and a young man was there that did not work there. Bob's client requested that he leave the area and quit bothering the employees. All the employees were Latino and Bob's client hired them through an agency in St. Paul, Minnesota, paid them higher wages than competitors, and, in some cases, offered to send them to school so they would be able to learn English and be able to understand the math involved with their particular duties. Unfortunately, Bob's client returned at the noon hour and found this same young man sitting at a table with his workers who were taking their lunch. Bob's client, again, told the guy to leave. The young man became quite sassy. The client's story is that the young man had picked up a board and the client thought he was going to be attacked. The client also picked up a board and hit the young man over the head. The blow to the young man was quite severe and the young man almost died in the hospital. He did make a full recovery, however.

The client exacerbated the problem by fleeing the scene and the client was not found until approximately three days later when he turned himself in to the authorities. He had phoned his sister to tell her where he was and to have the police come to his location. The defense was that of self-defense and, of course, the argument the prosecutor presented was that Bob's client was the aggressor.

I asked Bob what his sense of the entire trial was. His client had been found guilty of this serious assault and Bob said that the whole trial was sort of a nightmare with regard to the rulings the judge made. Bob stated the judge, who I don't care to name, made rulings that Bob felt were totally wrong, and he did not allow an expert to testify for the defense. Bob stated the most important error the judge made concerned a juror who happened to be an African-American woman who was trained as a police officer. Her father was also a police officer. Bob felt that she should not have been on that jury and should have been stricken for cause.

Bob stated that under our system of law, it states that you are not allowed to strike jurors who are black or of a different race unless you can give a race neutral reason for the person to be stricken from the jury. The judge did not allow Sicoli to strike this person so she served on the jury. In addition, the judge did not allow my photographs of the scene to be entered as evidence giving the reason that they were not turned over to the prosecutor in a timely fashion. That ruling was absolute nonsense and the judge later reversed himself and my photographs were allowed in.

Bob filed an appeal and went all the way to the Minnesota Supreme Court. On a four to three decision, the court granted Bob's client a new trial based on the fact that he should have been allowed to exercise his strike concerning the juror that had police training, and her father also being a policeman. Bob's client had gotten 91 months in prison for a sentence and he was actually serving time while the appeal was pending. Bob believes his client served approximately 26 months in jail. They were set for a retrial and his client decided he wanted to plead guilty straight out in front of the same judge. Sicoli

Chapter 10 - King of the Sex Cases

entered a plea of guilty and then filed a motion asking the judge not to send his client to prison again for multiple reasons. Sicoli said, "To my surprise, the judge actually granted our motion at the sentencing hearing and did not put him back in jail so he served 26 months out of a 91 month sentence."

I investigated the case and interviewed a, few Latinos, with an interpreter, that had been on the premises. They had changed their story. Their original story, after the incident and after the police and ambulance had arrived, supported the client. They told their story to a female office employee. We thought there was some undue influence by relatives of the injured party, as the relatives had come out at a later date, to the fabricating location and spoke with two young Latinos. I told Bob that I think a factor involved in this case was the fact that the client informed me that he was an alcoholic and he had fallen off the wagon. Alcoholism is not a defense, but in this instance, it certainly had affected the judgment of Bob's client. When he got sobered up, he turned himself in.

Sicoli felt the disservice in the whole case was not anything the prosecutor did but the way the office of the prosecutor framed the case from the beginning. They wanted this case charged out as an ethnic hate crime. Fortunately, that did not happen because it was not a hate crime. The information I was able to gain from the labor broker was that Bob's client had a good relationship with Hispanic people and, as stated earlier, paid them a higher wage than his competitors and wanted them to learn math and the English language.

It was quite troubling for Bob that his expert, former Ramsey County Coroner, who examined the photographs and measurements, would have been able to reconstruct, to a degree, by looking at the location of the blood. It would, have confirmed Bob's theory that the Latino guy was up out of the chair, going after Bob's client. There was a blood trail going toward Bob's client and Bob was perplexed that the judge would not allow the forensic pathologist to testify. Nevertheless, this is part of the appeal and the District Court Judge did not send Bob's client back to prison.

The judge on this case is now retired. He is a decent human being, but his rulings were wrong. Coroners always testify about the cause of death or injury, and the fact that they do this is not invading the province of the jury.

Maybe it would not have made any difference at all what the coroner said, but the fact remains that sometimes judges make the wrong rulings and it often results in an appellate court overturning the case.

We continued to discuss various areas of the criminal justice system. We both agreed that the public defenders are extremely overburdened. They are also somewhat limited in the funds they can devote to hire experts. Bob also felt that the forfeiture laws in place are very political and can hinder the hiring of private attorneys by clients. Bob's position is that the ultra-conservatives would like it if private lawyers were totally out of the picture. I had heard that attorney Barry Voss, who is an outstanding criminal defense lawyer, is challenging the system by means of a lawsuit concerning people being able to hire private — lawyers, and the forfeiture-laws in many cases are highly suspect.

Bob Sicoli is a one man gang now. The Thompson, Lundquist & Sicoli firm split up shortly after Peter Thompson retired. Bob has an excellent reputation among lawyers of the Minneapolis/St. Paul community and they refer cases to him. Bob's wife, Becky, assists him when needed and I do his investigation along with Gary Thorvig. Gary is a CPA, former IRS agent, and he is outstanding in the field of white collar crime. I imagine Gary is quite busy these days with all the scandals going on in the economic arena.

Chapter 11

The Police (part one)

Anthony Bouza

On March 10, 2004, I interviewed Anthony Bouza, former Chief of Police of Minneapolis Police Department. Mr. Bouza was born in Bilboa, Spain, immigrated with his family to New York City and began his history in the criminal justice system prior to 1953. His lovely wife, Erica, was born in London, England after World War II, but has memories of the difficult times people in England had recovering from that horrible war. Both Bouzas are well-known in the State of Minnesota and probably considered two of the most interesting individuals in the Minneapolis community.

After he retired, Mr. Bouza was convinced by others he should run for Governor of the State of Minnesota. At that time, the eccentric Jessie Ventura was running against slippery Norm Coleman and Skippy Boy Humphrey. Mr. Bouza was very close to garnering the Democratic nomination, but he came out with a statement concerning gun control. He was much in favor of hand gun control which inflamed all the gun toters in the state. The NRA put out letters against him and he did not get the endorsement from the Democratic Party. Many of us were greatly disappointed.

Both the Bouzas are sophisticated people in a very positive way. By this, I mean that they are well-traveled, realistic, and intelligent and have supported causes in the community, such as fundraisers for diabetes, programs that uplift the poor and disenfranchised members of society, education, and basically anything that supports fairness and justice. Anthony Bouza's history as a New York City Police Officer reflects that he was promoted often, and at one point in time was the number two man in the Transit Division. Prior to that, he had been in charge of what was called Fort Apache Bronx and Paul Newman made a movie about that particular precinct.

Mr. Bouza's history goes back shortly before 1953 and, to him, the criminal justice system is not only the legal system, but includes

Chapter 11 - The Police (part one)

corrections, prosecution and police. He believes that crime levels in the United States began to rise in the 1960s and there have been dramatic changes in the system since that time. In the 1960s, there were riots, increase in drugs, etc. and it was driving everybody crazy according to Mr. Bouza. Mr. Bouza states that the system did respond to that and the Supreme Court had issued decisions that were changing the law or the interpretation of the law. He pointed out Miranda v. Arizona was one big decision and it required police to give poor defendants the same rights as rich ones. He said the rich ones would come in with their lawyers and all their rights and the poor defendants were usually pretty helpless. But now we are required to warn them that anything they say could be used against them, which preserves the right against self-incrimination or the Fifth Amendment. Mr. Bouza states that most of this was sparked by Justice William O. Douglas and the rest of the court went along. Gideon v. Wainright, the right to counsel; Escobedo v Illinois, the right to counsel; Matt v. Ohio, pertaining to the Fourth Amendment, the right to be protected against unreasonable search and seizures and that, according to Mr. Bouza, is critical. He stated that he didn't think anything has given the Supreme Court more trouble than searches and seizures or pornography. The definition of indecency is interpreted by many people in many ways.

My comment to Mr. Bouza was the search and seizure issue is paramount right now because of the Patriot Act. Mr. Bouza responded that even without the Patriot Act, the search and seizure issue will always be a difficult one to evaluate. The reason search and seizure will always be with us deal with the issues, what can the police search. Can they search your person, your surroundings, etc.? With or without probable cause? When can they arrest you? So the reasonableness of search and seizure is critical. Mr. Bouza thinks we have come closer to protecting and preserving the constitution over the last 50 years than in the not so distant past. At one time we had the Alien Act, Alma Raids, Red Squads searching for communists under the bed and many of these searches and seizures were a violation of the constitution. So, the reality is that the police were remarkably more observant of the United States Constitution in 2004 than they were in 1954. Mr. Bouza states that he remains active in the justice system by means of giving expert testimony, therefore, he must be kept abreast of what is happening with the Supreme Court and other courts.

He states there have been some interesting initiatives and some foolish ones. The laws relating to mandatory sentencing almost without exception are nonsense. Legislators are caving into the pressure tactics, unthinkingly filling our prisons with non-violent offenders and leaving no room for many violent offenders. No one wants to stand up in the state house and ever hear himself accused of being soft on drugs, regardless of whether or not there are many non-violent drug offenders incarcerated.

I reminded Mr. Bouza about Judge James Rosenbaum and he was quite familiar with this distinguished judge's situation of being attacked by Congressman Sensenbrenner of Wisconsin. Mr. Bouza went on to say that what the legislators are doing is building an "Iron Bed of Procrustes." If you are too short, they stretch you until you die, and if you are too tall, they lop off your legs and head to make you fit. It is a symbol of enforced conformity. They want it to fit the circumstances of the sentencing guidelines or to be just that, guidelines. We hire judges to judge, to bring their insights, wisdom and experience to each individual case. In Judge Rosenbaum's case, it is really ironic, first of all the man is a Republican and was a U.S. Attorney prosecuting in a tough way, many, many cases. Now the people like Sensenbrenner are trying to tell the public that Judge Rosenbaum was soft on crime. "Give me a break!" That demonstrates the raw headedness and stupidity of the system.

Mr. Bouza went on to say that this type of behavior among legislators is not just offensive, it is bad public policy and unwise. He stated the reality of the system needs discretion and flexibility, and that should be considered for all judges. The police officer on the street has enormous discretion. Mr. Bouza noted that each defendant brought before a judge is a different person and there is a different history, etc. You need to tailor the response to the defendants as individuals and it is madness to try to create uniform standards that apply universally. I agreed with Mr. Bouza, adding my two cents, that if prosecutors found that a certain judge was too soft on crime; in their opinion, before they went in front of that particular judge they had

Chapter 11 - The Police (part one)

the opportunity to file against such a judge and request someone else to hear the case.

We then moved on to the Second Amendment, the right to bear arms. Mr. Bouza believes it is indisputable and well-established that the Second Amendment allows for well-trained militia to bear arms. According to Mr. Bouza, it is not a complicated question to him. In 1939, or about that time, in <u>Miller v. United States</u>, the Supreme Court held that the Second Amendment, which roughly says that a well-regulated militia being essential to the defense of the state or the right of the people to keep and bear arms shall not be infringed upon.

According to Mr. Bouza, in the Miller case, which has never been touched or overturned, said that a well regulated militia speaks to a militia. But even assuming that it didn't and it was thrown out, shows that there isn't a single right that is not circumscribed. Freedom of speech does not give the right to pre-sedation or incite riot or to create panic in a theatre. The right to practice religion does not permit us to have cults that practice human sacrifice, for example. The same with the press, they are not allowed to print slander. So the reality is that every freedom is circumscribed. What we do in this country, in terms of guns, is scandalous and crazy and we kill enough children and adults to prove it. The American Medical Association has statistics showing how many of our youth die from gunshots and it is outrageous.

I then asked Mr. Bouza why the National Rifle Association fights gun control so vigorously and why do they have such enormous power since they do not have millions and millions of members. He responded by saying that because of the National Rifle Association's middle name. They always forget their middle name; that it is rifle that they are trying to protect. Mr. Bouza pointed out that nobody in the United States seriously wants to restrict long guns. That means shot guns, rifles, and hunting sticks. Who cares about that? What we worry about are concealable weapons and machine guns, which have been banned since 1934, but yet people are able to somehow acquire automatic firing guns. We worry about assault weapons which have been banned for approximately ten years now such as pistols, automatics that create havoc. Now the NRA has a powerful lobby, a lot of money, and two to three million members. They spent all their energies really trying to defend murderous weapons that no respectable hunter would ever be associated with. I interjected at this point stating that I have some friends that hunt and they are also conservationists. I agree with the culling of the overpopulated herd of deer or birds, but I don't know any of my hunting friends that carry pistols with them. Mr. Bouza stated that is one of the points that he tries to make.

Mr. Bouza stated that one of the arguments with the NRA is that they feel it is a slippery slope, if you outlaw the guns made for the purpose of killing humans and not the hunting guns. He says it is like the camel's nose in the tent, eventually the camel gets in the tent. My interjection was that I think that is a fallacious argument. The NRA argument is that if we can keep a criminal from buying a handgun today, tomorrow the — government will be taking away the hunter's rifle, and most hunters in Minnesota, Wisconsin and the Dakotas are passionate about hunting. It is an old argument according to Mr. Bouza, the slippery slope. Where does it end?

Where it begins is with the handguns. The cowboys, of course, had handguns to kill the rattle snakes and varmints. Unfortunately, Mr. Bouza states that this country has a long and violent tradition and I could not agree more. He went on to say that we, alone, amongst the advanced industrialized nations of the world, permit a huge proliferation of concealable weapons. Japan, Australia, Canada and all of Europe do not do this and they have the homicide rates to prove it. Their rates are negligible considered to those in the United States. And, again, there are those that are accidentally killed by anything but the hunting stick, there are suicides, accidents where children somehow get a hold of a loaded pistol in the house or take it out of the house and shoot someone else.

Mr. Bouza and I were of one mind concerning pistols and machine guns. I have been a criminal defense investigator for 44 years now and have never felt that I should go down and get a gun permit and start packing a .45 caliber pistol.

We then proceeded to what is always a hot issue that keeps coming up –that being abortion. At one time, this was a criminal offense, but

Chapter 11 - The Police (part one)

of course the rich would fly to Switzerland or South America and the other poor females would have a back alley abortion, many died. I related to Mr. Bouza regarding one of my earliest cases of a back alley abortion that went bad; the woman died and our client went to prison. My feeling then, as it is now, is that this woman may have lived had she been in a proper clinic or hospital. I also pointed out that nobody is a cheerleader for abortion, it is really not a good thing. But what if a 13 year old female was impregnated by a diseased adult and there is a possibility that the baby would be born disabled or with some type of mental disease? A 13 year old can by no means raise a child, let alone a disabled child, and does any good come out of an evil act?

Mr. Bouza put forth a very interesting study and it runs as follows: He stated that a University of Chicago professor along with a professor from Stanford and one from Minnesota just produced a study within the last three years. The study demonstrated that Rowe v. Wade, going back to 1973, has been up and running for 31 years and provides abortions to impoverished teenage females who are on welfare, ignorant, or unable to care for children. The professors, and this sounds a bit cold, stated that under the circumstances of abortion, it actually reduces the number of at risk males in the population who normally go on to becoming the street criminals of our society. So they ascribed the declining crime rate, street crime in America in the late 1990s and early 21st century to Rowe v. Wade in their study. Mr. Bouza pointed out that this is the one and only definitive study of Rowe v. Wade as it applies to criminal experience.

Mr. Bouza stated that strange as it may seem, the only person who has written on this subject is he, former Chief Bouza. Mr. Bouza informed me that, in one of his books ten years ago, he said the most important undertaking in the criminal justice field to reduce street crime in America was Rowe v. Wade and then he went on to describe why. He also pointed out that teenage pregnancies have been reduced in what has been called the underclass, meaning the people below the poverty level, who are generally screwed over but are the ones that provide street criminals to America. According to Mr. Bouza, "The pregnancy rate, and even the rate of sexual intercourse, has been reduced dramatically. As a consequence, we have received an unexpected kind of peace dividend in Rowe v. Wade. There is no doubt in America that the upper middle class, or the over class, has always had abortion available to them as I previously pointed out."

Mr. Bouza informed me of a case in Scarsdale, New York when friends of his, who are Japanese, became aware that their daughter was pregnant with an unwanted pregnancy. They flew her to Japan for an abortion. He knows of other cases and mentioned a woman who had a psychiatrist certify that another child would induce severe mental strain and really unbalance her life. But, in the days Mr. Bouza was working as a Peace Officer in New York and I was working as a defense investigator in Minneapolis, abortion was a crime. Bouza stated, "Yes, it is terrible to kill a fetus, but sometimes the alternative is worse."

I then brought up the position with the Holy Roman Catholic Church which I believe to be Roman and Catholic, but not always holy, and Bouza stated fortunately the church does not make our laws in the United States.

Mr. Bouza and I discussed the present situation and stated that naturally we need to control criminals in America; he believes that we should even execute some. I disagree with that because I do not support capital punishment, but we are all entitled to our opinions. Of course, he emphasized that "proof, beyond a shadow of a doubt, must be the key component and it should be very discriminative." He said these hotels we call prisons have a limited capacity. We need to sequester those that are most dangerous to society. I added that, in ancient times, one who was detrimental to the tribe was banished from the tribe which, in a sense, is a death penalty. Mr. Bouza was for better education, treatment, parole, probation and supervision as opposed to throwing everyone in the slammer. He pointed out that it is "cheaper to send someone to Harvard than to send them to the Gray Stone Hotel."

We went on to talk about narcotics and I mentioned William F. Buckley, the intellectual conservative who some years back suggested that many drugs should be legalized and taxed. I have mixed feelings about this, but do remember reading about the 1920s and early teens where laudanum and liquid cocaine was purchased in

Chapter 11 - The Police (part one)

the drug store. Coca Cola originally contained some cocaine and, in my opinion, America was not a country of raging drug addicts.

Mr. Bouza said that some time around 1914 an old law kicked in pertaining to the possession of narcotics. Mr. Bouza felt that some measure of decriminalization of marijuana and lesser drugs should come into play, but the hard drugs should not be decriminalized.

We did not get into the history of prohibition, but did talk a little bit about gambling. Mr. Bouza stated that, in Minnesota, gambling quintupled in volume when it became legal to do so. Of course he recognized people were gambling when it was illegal, but not at the rate they are currently gambling.

Our next topic of discussion was the jury system. I pointed out that, indeed, we have some bizarre verdicts, but the most outstanding one is the O. J. Simpson case. It is the one that had international publicity. I also mentioned about a guy in Texas who chopped up his neighbor and was acquitted. Mr. Bouza said he wasn't exactly acquitted, he was found guilty of something less. He thinks Texas always comes up with some bizarre verdicts, but Mr. Bouza tends to support juries. He says that you are being judged by your peers and he thinks most juries work hard and struggle to find the truth. It is a flat instrument, but it is the best system we have in place. He felt that with jury experts and extensive questionnaires that it is easier to assess a group as to how they might feel toward any given type of defendant.

Mr. Bouza commented about O.J. Simpson stating that it was really a special case and it was destroyed by a police officer, Fuhrman, who said that if he had lied about using the "N" word, he would have lied about everything else. It was proven that Fuhrman used the "N" word by tapes he was on and it undermined his whole testimony. Mr. Bouza felt the jury worked very hard and effectively on the Martha Stewart case. This was a difficult case and they came up with a verdict. Mr. Bouza thinks there are many other examples of jury's that have done their job and he considers the O.J. case an aberration of the jury system. He thought the prosecution was weak, and that the defense was clever and strong, and there was something to the racial payback. All you have to do is look at how the black community in America responded whether it was at a University, a restaurant or school. Anyway you look at it, the blacks applauded the verdict. It had nothing to do with the minorities thinking Simpson was innocent. I commented that Simpson did not have a history of being a friend to the average black person, but Bouza said they identified with him anyway.

This interview with Mr. Bouza was prior to the election of Barack Obama and one can see today the progress that blacks in America have made in this country. My feeling is that it is about time. The color of one's skin, nationality, etc. has absolutely nothing to do with integrity or honor.

Concerning the notion of informers, Mr. Bouza generally supports the use of these individuals, but said he doesn't expect them to be solid citizens and the government needs to develop intelligence and information any way it can. He stated that he resents the notion that the government is breaking the law in order to enforce it. Mr. Bouza stated that you are going to be dealing with disreputable types who are informers, therefore, one must be aggressive and secure the information that is gathered that is within the bounds of the United States Constitution.

I brought up the U.S. v. Ralph Duke case, which is mentioned in this book. Mr. Bouza reminded me that the system is ripe with imperfections, but we can't throw out the baby with the bath water. He stated he worries about when the police overstep the bounds for no probable cause when someone is arrested. There are abuses in every area of society, banking, manufacturing, etc. But the idea is to keep them to a minimum.

I inquired of Mr. Bouza if any incoming chiefs or deputy chiefs contact him for direction in certain areas or for advice. Mr. Bouza responded, "Never!" He said it is really interesting who contacts him; it is lawyers who call him all the time for his expertise. He said he charges them $200 an hour; they sit down and take careful notes about everything he says. He states they will give me a case with all the evidence and ask for a constructive theory, which witnesses are important and which are not, which evidence matters and which does not, and how he feels about testifying in the case if they hire him. Mr. Bouza says he only takes the cases he likes. He gets calls

Chapter 11 - The Police (part one)

from lawyers all over the U.S. and said there isn't a single police chief, not even people he trained, who has ever called him on a single issue seeking his advice. He said I am a virgin in this experience.

My response to this was almost incredulous. I commented that I could not imagine not seeking some wisdom and direction from a woman or man who has a wealth of experience. Maybe it has something to do with ego. Mr. Bouza said it really doesn't affect him that some police agencies do not contact him. He has his life to lead and has to keep moving forward.

I commented that it is obvious that he is going forward since he has written about eight books. I asked him if he ever considered teaching as another career. Mr. Bouza stated that he has taught in the past. I mentioned to him that I am thinking on a level of a university on a full-time basis.

Mr. Bouza said that he felt that it would be too draining in that he is still writing, doing expert witness work and consulting. He said he taught on two occasions; once at Hamline University and once at the John Jay College of Law in New York City. He didn't feel it was, quite as rewarding as he expected and, frankly, was shocked by the students' lack of preparation. John Jay is a criminal justice school. Mr. Bouza said he was shocked by the lack of enthusiasm of students. He said at Hamline, the students were graduate students and they were there to work. If he gave them an assignment, they did the work. Nevertheless, it was very draining. The essence of teaching is basically to get students to write. Then, of course, you have to read their writing and it is long process and the pay is appalling.

I brought up the subject of corruption in big time athletics and the mischief that takes place. Mr. Bouza acknowledged that he was an avid fan of many sports, but he has never had experience with corruption in sports and hasn't studied or analyzed it. He said that it is difficult to understand America if you don't understand sports. He stated that he felt the stakes have risen in the importance, particularly in college athletics. This all involves money and the ability of college athletes going into the professional ranks. Millions of dollars are at stake, stadiums must be filled, there is always some city that wants to build a new stadium and the corruption becomes shocking.

Mr. Bouza mentioned that his son went to Amhurst College and the contrast is that they are strictly student athletes, true amateurs. I commented that it is the same in Minnesota with excellent colleges such as Carlton, St. John's, Gustavus Adolphus and St. Thomas. Mr. Bouza commented how it stunned him about St. John's and what happens when playing away from home. They win!

Mr. Bouza suggested that an excellent person to talk to would be Supreme Court Justice Allen Paige who played for the Minnesota Vikings and attended law school at the University of Minnesota. I was advised by Justice Gilbert that Judge Paige does not wish to discuss his athletic history. I did not mention that to Mr. Bouza, but I shied away from contacting Judge Paige.

Mr. Bouza stated there are many people leaving college after four years who can barely read or write, so the exploitation of the student athlete is already an oxymoron and it makes for corruption. He pointed out Coach Clem Haskins' dilemma, whose reputation was highly regarded and who was hired by then President Ken Keller. It is a damn shame that Coach Haskins ended up resigning because of this scandal. It is extremely difficult for a coach to put a winning product on the field when you have players who have no interest in academics. I mentioned to Mr. Bouza that I was doing a chapter on corruption in athletics.

In concluding my interview with Mr. Bouza, which was tape recorded, I asked him if I could quote him from some of his books He was very generous giving me formal permission to use any material from his book "Police Unbound" and left me with an autographed copy.

It should be noted that Mr. Bouza's family immigrated from Spain, arrived in New York and this is another wonderful example of immigrants taking advantage of opportunities in this country — educating themselves and overcoming obstacles that were challenging and difficult. Mr. Bouza's wife, Erica, actively protested the war and is a member of Women Against Military Madness, WAMM. She had been arrested several times for trespassing non-

Chapter 11 - The Police (part one)

violently at some Honeywell manufacturing sites. Honeywell manufactured fragment bombs that have a wicked effect on the recipient. My wife was arrested a few times, also, but was not incarcerated as was Erica Bouza and our dear friend, Karen Hansen. These are women that always wanted to make changes in society. Whether or not these women believe this, they do have had an impact on society.

Chapter 12

The Police (part two)

Within the ranks of police and prosecutors, both state and federal, there are some who think that defense lawyers and their investigators have contempt for authority. This is absolutely wrong. It is obviously based on the fact that some very good criminal defense lawyers have gotten acquittals on highly publicized cases. Certainly everyone wants a great police force to protect and serve the public from violence, burglaries, thefts, armed robbery, white collar crime, and vandalism. It's obvious the millionaires and billionaires, the corporate thieves, have always wanted their mansions, offices, and private jets protected. They, on the other hand, have committed their offenses in this capitalistic society by means of manipulation, lies, and cleverness. Fortunately, many of these people have been investigated, tried and convicted.

I have noted in this chapter on law enforcement that have, over the years, a number of police, investigators, and patrolmen who are personal friends. These were high quality people, well educated, well trained and to them it was all business and nothing personal.

After my interview a few years back with Sgt. Mike Young, we both agreed there certainly didn't appear to be any corruption with the Minneapolis/St. Paul Police Departments. However, it turns out that during the year of 2009 some very negative publicity arose out of the Metro Gang Strike Force's behavior. Throughout the year, there were reports that some of these officers had raided homes of alleged suspects, confiscated property, sold some of it, and seized about 18 vehicles. Their record keeping was abysmal and it was learned that they shredded reports and documents, and fail to even report on certain matters. The Metro Gang Force was comprised of officers from Minneapolis/St. Paul· and suburbs. There was a special unit to crack, down on the gangs in the area.

In addition, there was a scandal about two informants. The FBI and the Minneapolis Police Department had been working with a male informant and-a female informant. The male informant was in some

Chapter 12 - The Police (part two)

serious trouble and was giving information to law enforcement in an attempt to lessen his personal charges. The female informant was a paid snitch and wanted to remain on the payroll of the City of Minneapolis: she had accused a policeman of impropriety. All of this business with these snitches fell apart and there were never any charges brought against anybody. There was a very intelligent and courageous Minneapolis police officer that came to the conclusion that the male snitch was playing games with his handlers.

About February 6, 2009, a Minneapolis police officer was arrested and charged with robbing some banks and other establishments. That, of course, is a very unlikely act for a policeman to commit. The reports were that he was in debt and it appears very desperate.

In final analysis, it is doubtful that there is any more mischief in law enforcement than any other trade or profession. Based on my experience in life, reading, and cases I have worked on, it is my opinion that there is really as much crime in the suites as there is on the streets. In the late 60s and 70s, it always disturbed me when certain people referred to the police as pigs. Those were the days when I played ball and would drink a few beers with a number of my law enforcement friends, and we had a lot of respect for each other.

Michael Young

On January 13, 2005, I interviewed my good friend, Michael Young, who was 39 years old at the time and resided in Waverly, Minnesota. Mike is currently a Minneapolis Police Officer, but prior to that, he worked in the Wright County Sheriff Department in the Patrol Division. Mike worked for the county for approximately six-and-a-half years and, in 2005, celebrated 13 years on the Minneapolis Police Force.

Mike's father, Harvey Young, and I were close friends since first grade. Unfortunately, Harvey passed away in October of 2007. It is interesting that Mike has seven sisters so I asked him if he had a feminine side. As he was stifling a laugh, he said he didn't think so.

I asked Mike what his official title with the Minneapolis Police Department was and to describe his job duties. Mike is a Sergeant currently assigned to the SWAT team as a team leader and executive officer for the unit. He stated that there are approximately 74 people on his team, including tactical and non-tactical making it a rather large group for the City of Minneapolis.

I asked Mike to explain what kind of assignments that he received and he said that each city has their own flavor, so-to-speak, of what they do. In Minneapolis, Mike stated that they handle all the high risk entries to residences and buildings. That ranges in numbers between 300 and 600 per year, but he said that they also handle what they call Operation 100. Operation 100 is where they have a full unit call-out due to either a hostage situation or a barricaded suspect or a shooter. The Minneapolis SWAT team handles approximately six or seven of those per year.

I mentioned to Mike that the duties that he and his colleagues are involved in appear to be quite dangerous. I asked him how he would characterize these duties. Mike said that there is a certain amount of danger, but statistically he believed construction work and farming proved to be more dangerous than in what he was involved.

I inquired of Mike what motivated him to enter law enforcement. I reminded him that his sisters went through college for various training. Some had Master's degrees and some were teaching and some were involved in nursing. Mike said that there were a couple of things that encouraged him toward his career choice. Mike's father, Harvey, had a good friend working for the Wright County Sheriff Department and that had some influence. He stated that he was looking for a career that challenged him mentally and physically and the military or law enforcement seemed to fit his needs. Mike was interested in construction, his father was a master electrician, but there were too many layoffs in the trades which did not seem to offer much security. He also considered the military.

My interview with Mike was in 2005 and it is delightful to know that his son, Jake, is now a plebe at West Point. Mike's other children are in college, but getting an appointment to West Point was a unique and special event. Mike, through his son, is experiencing a fantasy of a military career. He could have gone that way, but law enforcement won out for him.

Chapter 12 - The Police (part two)

I inquired of Mike if he could discuss some of the politics within the Minneapolis Police Department, reminding him that practically all my life I lived in the city. Specifically, I inquired why Minneapolis does not seem to appoint a chief from within the department as they do in the City of St. Paul.

Mike explained that the political climate is a little different between the two cities and some of the issues the two cities deal with are different. Mike felt that politics in the Minneapolis Police Department was not a large driving force. However, Mike stated that there seems to be a verbal force that believes there is wide spread corruption in other issues surrounding the department, and this particular group looks to the outside for people to come in and head up the department that have never had previous ties to Minneapolis. Mike emphasized that in his service with the Minneapolis Police Department, he has never seen corruption.

I mentioned to Mike that I have gotten to know retired Chief Anthony Bouza fairly well and recall when he came here from New York City and was appointed Chief of Police. I told Mike that Chief Bouza stated to me that he united the police force; they all came to hate him! But when Anthony Bouza was appointed, there were different factions supporting different people.

At the time I interviewed Sergeant Young, Chief Robert Olson had just left the department. I informed Mike that in the late 50s and early 60s, there were a lot of young men I knew who went on the police department and ultimately people such as Jim O'Meara and Darcy Peterson, would have made excellent police chiefs.

Mike said that from where he was sitting, "which is definitely not high up in the department," I perceive the reason they hire and push for outside chiefs as to what I said earlier. There are some people in the community that feel it is safer to bring a person in from another community. Mike said he wasn't a huge fan of the former Chief of Police, he didn't think that some of these guys were totally committed to a long-term of service. Mike said there are people he likes to call professional police chiefs that bounce from city to city like carpet baggers and finally get a big city to satisfy their ego and their lifestyle. He said, "I think they come in and they are not concerned about the long-term issues within the community or the department." I reminded Mike that Chief Bouza was a horse of a different color because he still lives in this community and has been retired for quite a lengthy time. Mike said that is very positive as far as he is concerned. Mike did not serve under Chief Bouza.

There has been a recent book written by a retired police officer by the name of Mike Quinn that has the theme of corruption. Mike has not read that book, but stated that one of his colleagues has read it and he believes that some colleges that offer criminal-justice programs make it a required reading. Mike stated that the corruption described in the book took place in the 40s, 50s and early 60s. Personally, I have heard talk and read articles that go back to the 30s and 40s, but I have no firsthand knowledge of corruption.

I asked Mike what would constitute corruption. Would receiving a bottle of whiskey at Christmas time by the beat cop be considered corruption? Would accepting a hamburger at a cafe where the police officer patrolled the neighborhood be corruption? Mike said that it would be tough to consider that as corruption. He said he believed his definition would be a concerted effort by a group or a few people toward one final goal of illegal gain. Independently, a police officer should use their own judgment concerning receiving a minor gift or a lunch from a citizen. Mike said that if such a thing was blatant, the individual officer could be dealt with through some disciplinary measure. Mike said as far as he is concerned, and as long as he has been around, he has seen zero corruption in the Minneapolis Police Department.

I asked Mike what the general attitude is of his colleagues and him concerning criminal defense lawyers. Mike stated that depends on a lot of different things and his own attitude has changed over the years depending on what unit he was in and how often he was dealing with criminal defense lawyers. Mike said you don't deal directly with a defense lawyer, but you may have dealt with his client in, the past. Mike went on to say that attitudes change, much has to do with the person's general maturity. He said he could remember being very angry at defense attorneys early on in his career for raking him over the coals. But he said after 10 to 12 years of experience, you can often come out of that with a new sense of appreciation and

Chapter 12 - The Police (part two)

you may even tell your partner that was one sharp guy, meaning the defense attorney. You don't necessarily have to like him, but you appreciate that he is good at what he does.

Mike stated that because of the type of work he does in the community within the city he is assigned to, the majority of the defense attorneys were public defenders. He described that most people in the areas he works are economically challenged so it would be rare for him to come in contact with a private lawyer. Mike and his team work in the Fourth Precinct which is located in North Minneapolis roughly between the north side of Cedar Lake to 53rd Street North and from Theodore Wirth Parkway to the river. This is considered a rough part of town, but I would like to say that there are many lovely homes within that area. The area is comprised of African Americans, Asians, Caucasians and recent immigrant, therefore making it quite diverse.

I told Mike that racial profiling can be somewhat confusing or difficult to define. I gave the example of police looking for a bank robber who was described as having bright red hair naturally the police may be stopping red-headed people in some areas of the city. Therefore, concerning terrorists, for example, most of them seem to come from the Mideast. Mideastern people do not look like people from Norway, Finland or Holland so wouldn't it be appropriate if you were looking for a terrorist who was suspected of coming from Afghanistan, you would not be stopping people from northern climes such as Norway, Finland and Holland.

I asked Mike how he avoids being accused of racial profiling. Mike said he thinks it is a difficult issue, but also one of the hot button issues that come and go over the years. Mike stated that he has seen it go from the department having to teach the entire department about sexual harassment since the Clarence Thomas situation. In fact, it was state mandated. Mike said that died out after about 18 months and the next issue was vehicle pursuit at high speeds and that went on for approximately a year-and-a-half. Every department in the country had to redo their vehicle pursuits.

Then, of course, it was racial profiling and now that has begun to fade away. Mike said there doesn't seem to be any real study brought forward. There was a lot of money thrown at the racial profiling issue, but Mike stated that there was a small group of people that were doing most of the complaining. He said that they were very vocal, but they were very convincing. Mike said he believes that these vocal people seem to go through phases depending upon their rewards and their own political agenda. He said that just because these people are not elected officials doesn't mean they are not politicians.

I suggested to Mike that discrimination still exists and that it is not just those in the African American community that are discriminated against. It can often be women, Asians, Jews and whomever else. Mike agreed with this comment and stated that it was damaging to everyone in the community at large when false accusations are made. An example that I brought up about false accusations dealt with a police informant who, unfortunately, was in a home that was busted by the police and he was caught up in an illegal drug, arrest. Later on he claimed that he was sodomized with a broom by a police officer and this was headline news. I asked Mike about that case.

Mike stated that it was a completely fabricated story but it took some time to discredit this guy. Mike said it was easy to discredit him, but to get the word out that he was a career criminal merely took some time. It was an out-and-out false accusation. A careful investigation was done; there was no physical evidence that the man had been sodomized. The people that originally backed him, fled from him like rats off a sinking ship. We both agreed that this is not what creates racism, false accusations, but it does enforce certain people's beliefs about a specific group of people.

Mike Young stated that with his job you come across people who believe the police are inherently evil based upon a negative news story about the police. Many of these people have not had contact with police officers, but have a tendency to believe everything they read. I made a point that people should stop to think that police are dealing with horrible situations sometimes, and often have to report to a parent that their child was injured or their husband was accidentally hit by a car, etc. The police are the ones that are dealing with criminals and negative situations. Along that line, I asked Mike if he knew anything about Lieutenant Mike Sauro's case.

Chapter 12 - The Police (part two)

Mike informed me that he knew Lieutenant Sauro personally and he did recall a little bit about Lieutenant Sauro's case. Mike recalled that the guy that sued Sauro, the Minneapolis Police Department and the bar was not exactly the citizen of the year.

Apparently he had been a student at one of our local colleges and he had been in this bar and was 86'd, which means thrown out of the bar. The guy came back and jumped on the back of Sauro, who was working that night as a bouncer. Mike explained that is technically assaulting a police officer and it is a felony crime. In the end, I think this guy got about $600,000 to $700,000 but concerning Sauro's employment, this went to arbitration. The arbitrator, Mr. Jack Flagler, a retired University of Minnesota labor law professor, ruled in favor of Sauro and so he was able to keep his employment with the police department. It also came out that the guy that got the huge award had, in the past, forged a check. Once again, it may have been a case that was settled too quickly. I don't know as I did not work on the case, but perhaps a jury should have made the decision.

Mike Young stated that he had nothing but good things to say about juries. He is partial to federal juries and I can understand why because they are more inclined to convict. As Mike stated, federal juries draw from a larger, more conservative area. Mike stated that he has testified in federal criminal cases and also civil cases and felt that he has had good luck concerning jurors.

Mike did state that often the truth is difficult to bring out in front of a jury. He stated that sometimes one lawyer is far better than the other lawyer in a particular case meaning plaintiff and defendant, and the lawyer who is the best and most convincing wins for his client. Mike felt that in a highly technical scientific case that it would be better off to be tried in front of a judge, who is generally better educated than a jury. Mike felt that most judges would comprehend things that the average layman could not.

I suggested to Mike that too often the best people are stricken during *voir dire* and not for the right reasons. For example, the prosecution or the defense may not want a highly educated individual on the jury because that person may not respond to the magic and illusions that the attorneys may create. My position has always been to try to get smart people on the jury if you can determine that they truly do not have bias and prejudice, but it is impossible to read a person's mind.

Regarding sentencing, Mike Young, based on his experience, said, "It isn't very often the court uses a maximum on the sentencing guidelines, at least in district court." He felt that in federal court that they did not deviate as much toward the low end, but Mike felt that state court sentences were more lenient. I told Mike that I certainly agreed and asked him if he knew who Plookie Duke was. Mike said that he did. I then explained that Attorney Howard Bass and I worked on Duke's appeal. He got life plus 40 on a first offense. Duke had such a terrible reputation that everybody in law enforcement celebrated it when he was convicted. I told Mike that my position was that sentencing was excessive, there was perjury involved and Duke should have received a new trial. Mike was not familiar with that case and said he really shouldn't make any comments.

I did ask him what his relationship might be with the FBI, DEA and alcohol, tobacco and firearms. I informed him that my late friend, Darcy Peterson had information on the Piper kidnap case through an informant of his, but the FBI just blew him off. Darcy wanted nothing to do with those people after that.

Mike said that he did not have much dealing with the federal agencies, but he has seen some incompetency on the part of the Feds. Mike Young said that their crime lab handled fingerprinting, photographing, videotaping, crime scene, and stuff like that, but the very technical stuff goes to the BCA and stated that they seem to do a good job for them. He stated that he has not been involved in sending stuff out to the FBI labs. Mike pointed out that like any profession such as doctors, lawyers, scientists and police officers, there is going to be a few that are not competent and that is the way it is in life.

We went on to talk about guns, such as hand guns, and Mike is a proponent of the right of an individual to carry a firearm if they are a law abiding citizen. My position is that there are too many guns out there in the community and it is too easy for the gangster to get a hold of a gun. Mike said that there is nothing we can do about this. There is capitalism involved, there are gun manufacturers, and the

Chapter 12 - The Police (part two)

NRA is a strong lot. Mike stated that he is not exactly a fan of the NRA, but nevertheless he feels that individuals, for protection, who are law abiding citizens, should be allowed to carry a firearm. One of my arguments with Mike is that in my 40 plus years as a criminal defense investigator, I never had a case where a homeowner was required to use a handgun, but I have had civil cases where there were accidental shootings in the home due to a child finding a loaded gun and shooting someone. Mike stated that it wasn't the home owner that should have the gun to protect the house or protect members of the family; it is more when a home owner is out in public. It is a protection issue on the outside.

We went on to argue this point and talked about mass shootings in schools and some of the post office shootings, but Mike Young felt that guns are so ingrained in our culture that it would be literally impossible to correct it at this point. My argument is that we should start somewhere.

Because I have known Mike from the day he was born and have been a dear friend of his father and mother, I hold Mike and his family in very high regard. He has a wonderful wife, who is an excellent mother and Mike's mother, Bonnie, who was legally blind, had always been a pillar of strength and a very calm individual. I reminded Mike that I went out with his mom one time to a Sadie Hawkins dance. He asked me if I was a gentleman and I told Mike that I was offended by that question, they don't call me, Vinnie the Pure for the hell of it!

Our interview ended with laughter.

Roger Concannon

I first met Roger Concannon, a retired Boston police detective, on the Island of St. Vincent in 1989. I had started an AA group at which I had been the only attendee for a few weeks. One night Roger came in, accompanied by two women, Laura and Susan. Laura, Roger's lady friend was helping him to renovate a small hotel. Susan taught diving to some of the serious yachtsmen in the area. She accompanied Roger to the meeting because she had been involved In a relationship with an alcoholic, and hoped that the meeting would be helpful to her.

Roger is about 5' 11", extremely well built, and he has a great voice. He can often be found singing with some of his Irish friends in various pubs. He was also an athlete. I've seen him play racquetball, and was impressed with his athletic ability, as well as his power and endurance.

Roger described his background as similar to the one portrayed in Frank McCourt's Angela's Ashes. He was raised in a government housing project which he described as a "blacktop jungle." He indicated his neighborhood was comprised of saints and sinners, and lots of alcohol was consumed. It wasn't until recently, when heroin rose in popularity, that drugs became an issue in the neighborhood. According to Roger, it was Whitey Bulger who originally introduced heroin to the neighborhood.

Roger came from a law enforcement family, and this motivated him to join the police force. Roger's father was a cop, reaching the rank of detective back in 1941. His grandfather was a lieutenant of detectives back in 1905. Following in these footsteps, Roger reached the rank of detective in 1966. Roger took part in establishing the Boston Police Patrolmans' Association, and was on its executive board. This group worked in some capacity with the Massachusetts House of Representatives. Roger, and others from the Association, negotiated with then Mayor of Boston, Kevin White, on what Roger called the best police contract ever negotiated in the United States.

Roger had numerous stories about interesting cases he and his family had worked on, and contacts he had made with the wise guys in Boston, both the Irish, and the Italians from the North End. One of the cases Roger discussed involved his Grandfather James F. Concannon. Concannon had a partner on the force named Benjamin Alexander. On July 4, 1925, Concannon and Alexander were tailing a notorious jewel thief when the thief ducked into the Pickwick Club. This club had been in a serious fire several weeks earlier. The club was allowed to reopen, despite only cursory repairs. According to Roger, this was part of the corruption which was rampant in Boston at the time, and indicated that the city inspectors were likely paid off.

Chapter 12 - The Police (part two)

Following standard procedure, when their suspect entered the building, one officer followed him, and the other remained outside to make sure the suspect did not leave by another exit. Concannon was outside the club when the building suddenly collapsed, killing numerous people, including Alexander. When Alexander's body was first found, people assumed Concannon had also been killed, since the two men were inseparable. Roger still feels Alexander's death was mysterious, and he does not know whether the suspect was among those killed. He hopes to go back through the police files on this case some day to see if he can find any more answers.

Roger spoke about a case involving his father and Officer Dan Somilisky. The two officers were in pursuit of a known murderer who had just shot a local pawnbroker in the stomach. When pursued, the suspect fled toward a housing project. When Somilisky looked up toward the roof door, the suspect fired a round which went through Somilisky's hat and out the back of his hat band. The other officers were able to drag Somilisky out of the line of fire, and shot the suspect. According to Roger, it was one of his father's rounds that struck the suspect in the head. The suspect turned out to be a notorious New York City killer who was wanted nationally for numerous murders in 1954.

According to Roger his cases were more mundane than some of those of his father and grandfather, but involved effective police, work. He discussed the riots of the 1960's and indicated that while they were shocking and terrifying in their violent suddenness; it was also frightening for the police who raided Black Panther headquarters on Blue Hill. Included in the documents seized in that raid were documents which listed Roger's name, his address, and the name of his wife and children. The police believed, based on the documents they seized, that the Panthers planned to go to the homes of police officers and kill their families. (Although I do not personally have proof of this, I trust Roger's comments, and know from experience that many documents with a police department are not made available to the public.)

At my request, Roger discussed the relationship between the Italian wise guys, and the Irish gangsters in Boston. I had previously heard from Andy Tuney, a former state police investigator during the Albert

De Salvo case, that the Italians considered the Irish to be crazy, and did not want to have anything to do with them, so I was curious to hear Roger's opinion. Roger indicated that during the Prohibition years, there were numerous killings between the Irish and the Italians which resulted from territory disputes. During Prohibition, alcohol was illegal, but readily available across the country. A strong argument can be made that Prohibition brought about the birth of organized crime in the United States.

When the city of Boston ordered mandatory bussing in 1974, the Irish and the Italians united, marching together in an effort to prevent their children from being bussed into neighborhoods they believed were dangerous. The united groups called themselves R.O.A.R, which stood for Return our Alienated Rights. According to Roger bussing was a failure because many neighborhoods were not integrated, students still tend to hang out with their cultural groups, and bussing did not lead to greater integration. As support for his position, Roger points out that in 1970 the Boston schools were 80% white. Today the Boston schools are 80% black. This may have more to do with white flight to private schools or population shifts than a failure of integration. In the 1970's most children lived in small ethnic neighborhoods and were able to walk to school. Although I am not a sociologist, and have not researched any studies concerning bussing, I will bring up the late Gwen Jones Davis, past director of Antioch College. Jones Davis would not allow her children to be bussed because she wanted to be able to eat lunch with her children at home, which was within walking distance of the school.

Roger grew up in South Boston, and knew the notorious Whitey Bulger and his family. James "Whitey" Bulger is a well-known gangster whose brother, a former Massachusetts Senate President, recently resigned as Chancellor of the University of Massachusetts amid controversy over the federal probe into the disappearance of Whitey Bulger. A third brother, John "Jackie" Bulger, a former juvenile court clerk magistrate, lost his job after being convicted of perjury for lying to a federal grand jury about the whereabouts of his brother Whitey. Roger spoke to me about the Bulger family, and how one son became a renowned politician, and the other a gangster. According to Roger, the Bulgers lived next door to his family in the old Harbor Project housing development. Roger and the Bulgers were

Chapter 12 - The Police (part two)

born on the south side, brought up together, attended school together, played sports together and shared an interest in politics. This was in the days where the Democratic party was the party of the blue collar working man. Roger and the Bulgers were all baptized democrats. Roger believes the current Democratic Party is a party of special interests, but we have not argued this point. I believe the Republican Party is the party of rich special interests (Enron, Tyco, etc.), whereas the Democratic party supports the "special interests" of the environment, health and education, and it is currently considered the anti-war party based on the debacle in Iraq. This, however, is my analysis, and Roger would likely disagree with some of it. Nonetheless, he supported and worked for William Bulger from the beginning, and William went on to become a well know Senator from Massachusetts. William stepped down from his post as Chancellor of Boston College.

Whitey's life, on the other, hand, took a different path. Roger described him as the feds' worst nightmare, and as a Frankenstein monster created by the feds. According to Roger, Whitey has been doing so much work for the feds as a double agent going back to the 1960's that he deserves a pension from the government. After his "partnership" with the government unraveled in approximately 1993, Whitey disappeared, and the government has not been able to locate him.

Roger and I discussed his frustration with the legal system. Roger believes it is essentially a revolving door, and that the rate of recidivism is extremely high. This is a view shared by Ramsey Clark, the liberal former Attorney General of the United States, who has stated that the rehabilitation model has been a failure. As an example of this revolving door, Roger mentioned a suspect who had 252 defaults (presumably failures to appear in court). After searching for this suspect for six weeks, she was located in a boarding house, brought to court and placed in a secure lock down hospital ward for four days. She subsequently defaulted again at her arraignment and at last count was approaching. 300 defaults and had not been heard from.

Based on his experience as a police officer, Roger felt juries should be professional and should be structured more along the lines of a grand jury, where jurors would serve for a longer period of time. Roger believed that perhaps jurors should be elected, and that certainly they should be better educated in their responsibilities. His opinion was that most juries seemed ignorant.

My personal experiences have made me leery of the both the grand jury and petit jury system. Grand juries originate from the British system, as do many of our laws. In Great Britain, Parliament originally created the grand jury system to ensure that people were not indiscriminately charged with a crime. Unfortunately this goal has been perverted in the U.S. legal system. Our grand juries are orchestrated by the prosecution. The target of the grand jury has no rights in the process, including the rights to call his or her own witnesses.

With regard to the petit jury system I have personally seen acquittals in cases where the evidence seemed to strongly weigh in favor of conviction. I have also seen cases where I was thoroughly convinced of the innocence of a client who was found guilty by a jury. From my point of view it does not matter whether a client is guilty or innocent. This is a jury question, and my job is to assist the defense by finding and interviewing witnesses and assisting in general in the search for exculpatory evidence. Several prominent cases have raised concerns about the effectiveness of the jury system, most notably the OJ. Simpson acquittal, and the case of real estate heir Robert Durst who admitted to killing and dismembering an elderly neighbor but was acquitted by the jury after putting forth an argument for self-defense. Cases like these cause many to doubt the fairness of the jury system.

Roger indicated that corruption on St. Vincent was endemic. Bribes and kickbacks are commonplace, and are an understood cost of doing business. I experienced this myself when we got shipments of donated supplies for the school. When I went to pick up the items the post office would stall, open boxes, and inspect them at great length until I learned that I could speed this process up by offering the clerks various small items.

For anyone interested in black intellectual writers and their analysis and opinions about their culture, I suggest reading John McWhorter,

Chapter 12 - The Police (part two)

Stanley Crouch, and Steven Carter. McWhorter, a Professor of Linguistics at the University of California Berkeley, is a highly regarded intellectual in the United States. In his book "Losing the Race", he discusses the themes of the cult of victimization, separatism, and anti-intellectualism. McWhorter believes there is a strong sense of separatism within the black culture. If this is true, Roger's beliefs about the old neighborhoods working better may be accurate. I have no expertise in these matters, but continue to make an effort to understand the factors that lead to the prejudice, racism and intolerance in our culture. It is for this reason that I read the books by the authors listed above, although I believe many of these authors are viewed by some in their communities as traitors to those same communities.

Stanley Crouch considers himself an American Negro rather that an African American or black. Crouch has written numerous essays, including "Notes of a Hanging Judge." Crouch emphasizes personal responsibility in his writing, and does not stop short of singling out various people within his community. Crouch, a noted jazz critic, contributed to Ken Burns's History of Jazz documentary, which was aired on PBS. Crouch has also written many pieces for the Village Voice.

Steven Carter, another noted black intellectual, has published a book of civility among his other works. Carter's views on history, sociology and the law are worth noting, and he is one of the black intellectuals who are willing to disagree with the opinions of other noted blacks such as Jesse Jackson, Louis Farrakhan and Al Sharpton.

Chapter 13

Snitches

There are a number of different names given to a person who informs such as *fink*, which is German and means, stool-pigeon, snitch, tattletale, and turn coat. Turn coat was a term used during the Korean War for American prisoners captured in North Korea who gave information about their fellow soldiers thus turning their American coat in for a North Korean coat.

To my knowledge, the most well-known of all informants was Judas Iscariot who informed on Jesus Christ to the Romans as to the whereabouts of Christ. Little is known about Judas and for that matter we have little or no information about the family background and professions or trades of the other followers of Christ with the exception of Peter, who was a fisherman, and perhaps some other fisherman. It would be interesting to know what Judas did prior to meeting Christ, was he, married, did he have a family and children, etc. Unfortunately, for many inquisitive Christians, particularly those that do not have "the gift of faith", much of the history of Christ and the original followers may have been lost in translation or because the gospels were not immediately written down. My understanding is that there were originally eighty gospels; why only four were selected is a good question. Originally I am told the gospels were written in Latin and Greek, ultimately translated to other languages and who knows for certain what was added, left out, misinterpreted, for example, when translated to German, and, finally put to print for all to read with the invention of the Gutenberg Press.

One theory concerning the motivation of Judas to inform on Christ was related to me by a good friend, retired University of Minnesota Professor Jack Hershbell who is also an Episcopal priest. Mr. Hershbell has an outstanding academic background, graduated from Lafayette College at age 16 and went on to Harvard, ultimately graduating from Harvard Divinity School. He taught the classics at the University of Minnesota, speaks fluent German, Latin and Greek along with his native language. Jack has always been an excellent source for those of us who had questions pertaining to the classics and the Bible along with theological questions.

Dr. Hersbell states that there is a school of thought that Judas may have had a plan to have Christ arrested, brought to trial whereby Christ would call down a host of heavenly legions to wreck havoc on his enemies. As we know, this did not occur, the plan having backfired on Judas, he went out and hung himself. If one stops to think about the motivation for informing on Christ, it's hard to imagine it had to do with the 30 pieces of silver, that wasn't exactly a fortune.

Informants

Never in life would I want anyone to think that just because I detest professional snitches that I do not believe that crime should not be reported by witnesses. If I was a guy strolling down the street and witnessed a vicious mugging, certainly I would report such an act and be a witness for the victim. Regarding any crime that someone happens to see, it should be reported and the person should be prepared to be a witness against the wrong-doer. Unfortunately, among certain gang-bangers, they have had t-shirts printed that say "Don't Be a Snitch." These are given out or sold in the ghetto areas. There is a particular situation in Philadelphia where witnesses were totally intimidated. This, of course, is an obstruction of justice but if you are threatened by a gangster or your family is threatened, it is a very, frightening situation.

When I speak of informants, I am talking about those who have worked for the government for pay or for the promise of lessening their own sentence. Unfortunately, I think on too many occasions informants have been handled in a careless fashion. The objective, by certain government agencies, is to get a conviction and they don't give a rat's ass about how they get this conviction. Using informants is a delicate matter and much has been written by experts. I have included an article by Mr. Ron Meshbesher who quotes a judge on this subject.

In the course and scope of my career as a defense investigator, I naturally came across a number of snitches who were paid by the government to make cases for the DEA or FBI. I would like to quote some information published in Mr. Jim Redden's excellent book entitled "Snitch Culture, How Citizens Are Turned Into the Eyes and Ears of the State." Mr. Redden has probably written the most definitive book on the corruptness and complexities of prosecutors using paid informants on their cases. Mr. Redden is not the only one who has written on this subject, there is a paper published by a judge in California, attorney Ron Meshbesher has written about this, so within the criminal justice system, much is known about informants, but the general public has little knowledge of the disgusting and sometimes harmful use of paid informants happens to be.

Snitch Culture - by Jim Redden

On page 55 of Mr. Redden's book, he points out that paying for incriminating information is a time honored tradition. Law enforcement agencies have shelled out billions of dollars over the years for tips, Wanted Posters, long offered awards for information leading to the arrests and conviction of criminal suspects. But the sheer number of government agencies paying for dirt would surprise most people. They include virtually every agency with any law enforcement or regulatory authority including the, U.S. Customs Service, the U.S. Fish and Wildlife, Secret Service, Immigration and Naturalization and many more.

The rewards vary tremendously depending on the agency. For example, U.S. Customs Service once paid Fred Mendoza a former Columbian emerald dealer nearly $2 million for his help in Operation Casablanca, the Department's largest money laundering investigation. The payment to Mendoza included $1.7 million in commissions.

Some of the most heavily rewarded snitches in American history provided crucial testimony when the federal government was preparing its racketeering case against former Panamanian President Manual Noriega. According to the May 1996 article in the Pittsburgh Post Gazette, at least 20 members of drug cartels around the world received drastically reduced prison, sentences and were allowed to keep their drug money. One was Max Mermelstein, a Miami dealer, who testified Noriega had taken profits from the Medellin Cartel in

Chapter 13 - Snitches

exchange for allowing smugglers to use his country as a refueling and transfer station for drug shipments. Despite admitting to 56 tons of cocaine with $1.25 billion brought into this country, Mermelstein was released after serving only 2 years in a special protected witness unit and allowed to keep whatever drug money he had left.

Three of the most unsavory, lying, manipulative, psychopathic informants I came across over the years happen to be a guy by the name of Mike Montana, which was his alias, Harrison McCoy, a/k/a Red Adams, and perhaps the richest of all, a man that testified on numerous cases throughout the country by the name of Andrew Chambers. I am going to briefly summarize my encounters with these people, starting with Red Adams.

Red Adams

Attorney Peter Thompson, now retired, was representing a local Minneapolis man of Greek descent who was charged on a narcotics case. My assignment on this case was to make an attempt to interview the government informant who was involved only to rule out that attorney Thompson's client made any purchases or sales of narcotics in Chicago, Illinois.

I can't recall how Peter Thompson came by the name of Red Adams as the snitch in this case, perhaps it was in the discovery process. The discovery process simply means the government must turn over all their information, statements, documents, photos, etc. to the defense and the defense, in turn, must provide the government with names, statements, documents, or photos that they may use in a trial. Thus, I had to locate Red Adams who, of course, was an elusive individual who made cases in St. Paul and Minneapolis. I learned that he originally came from Chicago, that he had a murder conviction and served time for that offense, but how and when he became a paid informant I did not know.

I contacted various people in the black community that I knew who could maybe point me to the whereabouts of Adams and ultimately I located him residing in an apartment on South Hennepin Avenue between Franklin and 26th Street. There are a number of older apartments in that particular neighborhood which has changed considerably in the last decade, now there exist many restaurants and older apartments that have been renovated.

I had no telephone number for Red, he wasn't listed in the book and I did come up with the address and had to make several short trips to his apartment building, hoping to catch him at home. On my fourth or fifth attempt, I got lucky, Adams answered the buzzer to his apartment which was a security building, and after an introduction I told him that I had a simple question to ask him, he buzzed me in. I entered his apartment which was rather small, but did have a tiny kitchen area with a table. Adams had a couple of chairs, one of which had a jacket lying on the chair, he removed the jacket and a pistol fell to the floor. How could I ever forget that moment? He immediately picked up the pistol, wrapped it in the jacket and put it in the sitting room. We then sat, down at the table and I explained that my only reason for calling on him was to rule out the fact that Mr. Thompson's client had any Chicago connection and did not do drug transactions out of that city. I requested of Red Adams that he allow me to write up a brief statement confirming what I related to him. Adams agreed, but stated he had to go over to St. Paul for an appointment and asked if I would drive him to his destination. I agreed to do that if he would agree to stop on the way back at the Meshbesher office where I was sub-letting space from Ron Meshbesher's firm.

I drove Adams to St. Paul. En route, there was irrelevant conversation that did not pertain to the case I was working on or any other matter. I can't exactly recall where I took Adams in St. Paul, but it was in the Selby/Dale area. I parked, he went in a building and was gone for perhaps 15 minutes, exited the building, got in my car and we preceded to 1616 Park Avenue where I took his statement. The statement was exactly what Peter Thompson was looking for. Adams then left the office, I had offered to drive him back to his apartment on Hennepin Avenue, which was not much more than a mile and a half to two miles from 16th and Park, but he rejected the offer. I did not believe that he was high on any type of drug, he didn't carry any packages out of the St. Paul building he had gone into, and he was articulate and agreed to sign the statement. I thought that would be the end of the matter.

Chapter 13 - Snitches

Some months later, Thompson went to trial on this particular case, but I was not needed to serve subpoenas or to assist in organizing the witnesses or prepping them for testimony. I learned from Peter Thompson, after his final argument, that Red Adams did testify, changed his story and so Peter impeached him with the signed statement that he gave to me. Peter then told me that Adams claimed on the witness stand that I had given him a sum of money which was rather small to drive him to St. Paul and that is why he agreed to give the statement. He went on to say that back at 1616 Park, he snorted some cocaine in my office and then left.

Such blatant bullshit I could hardly believe and I had wished Peter would have called me as a witness, but the fact of the matter, he didn't need me. Apparently, the jury did not believe anything Red Adams testified to and Peter's client was acquitted on a number of counts, including the one in Chicago, so the jury basically ignored this paid informant. Later on, I heard from attorney Jack Wylde, who had a case in St. Paul where Adams testified for the government that a witness in the hallway made a derogatory remark to Adams and Adams then punched the guy. God knows what kind of a melee took place. Another piece of information that I learned, which happens to be accurate, is that Adams, while in the office of the DEA, stole $1,000.00 out of a drawer. There was talk about prosecuting Adams, but federal attorney Joe Walbrand came to Adams support and nothing happened to this scurrilous pathological liar. My involvement with Red Adams was over 25 years ago and he is probably deceased by now or as some say, "in box city". I further learned that he took down his own step-daughter who had been cashing checks using some type of a check verifying apparatus, but it was a phony payroll check. This is the type of person that would have taken down his own mother if he were paid. God only knows how much he was paid over the years.

It's rather disconcerting to know that, the government uses people like Adams to make cases. Rumor had it that in the black community, that Adams was, brought in to Minnesota to make cases, that DEA funding may not have been increased because their numbers for arrests and convictions had been rather flat so they wanted to increase their arrest and convictions, thus keeping the money flowing to the local agencies. I can't verify that, but this was the word on the street. Whatever the use for a guy like Adams is absolutely shameful, but that was the name of the game in the 70's and it hasn't changed to date.

Mike Montana

The next notorious creep I had the opportunity of meeting was a tall, blonde, handsome, well built innocent looking Caucasian residing in the town of Two Harbors, Minnesota. This was Mike Montana. I've searched for his given name, but can't seem to come up with it at the present time. He was an electrician by trade, I learned that he scored a fair reward for turning in a somewhat affluent guy who kept a plane up at the Crystal airport in the suburb of Crystal, Minnesota. This suburb is a short distance north of Minneapolis, it has a small airport used by pilots flying Cessnas and Pipers, etc. It came to be known that he ratted this guy off on a drug deal, the guy owned a plane and had other assets which the government confiscated and good old, electrician Mike Montana was presented with over $100,000.00.

The handsome snitch then moved to Two Harbors where he began setting up very minor cases whereby he would sell or get someone to sell marijuana to the locals. Then he had an arrangement with the sheriff's department of Two Harbors to have these guys busted. This is basically Mickey Mouse shit, I don't think Montana was paid too much on these cases, but nevertheless, he continued to be player. Two Harbors is a lovely little city on Lake Superior, a short distance north of Duluth, Minnesota, which is charming city. I was working a case for attorney Howard Bass who was a partner at the time with Ron Meshbesher of the Meshbesher & Spence law firm. Ron the rainmaker, I call him, among other things. Howard was representing a fellow by the name of Bellene who was indicted for attempted sale of cocaine, money laundering and I forget the other changes. It's really irrelevant, in that, Mr. Bellene was in some serious trouble.

Bellene was married to a very lovely Canadian woman at the time, I spent a considerable amount of time gathering information from he and his wife. They had a fishing boat and Bellene had a pretty good business taking fishermen out to Isle Royale, which is quite a distance north of Two Harbors. There is a very small motel in the small town he sailed out of and the operator has one of those ship to shore type

Chapter 13 - Snitches

radio, communication apparatus and fishermen will call in getting weather reports and other data. On one occasion I had to go up there to meet with Bellene and he came in with a very nice salmon catch and gave me some fresh salmon to take home. What a treat.

Bellene absolutely denied any dealing with Mr. Mike Montana. Mike Montana did in fact, approach Bellene, went on Bellene's boat and Montana was wired up at the time. He claims that a cocaine transaction took place, but poor Mike's recorder wasn't functioning so he never got the, deal on tape. It's all bullshit I'm convinced because I learned Montana had zero credibility with anyone in the community and as a matter of fact, it got to the point where he was despised by all the citizens.

When I first met Montana, I had gone to his residence which was in a wooded area outside of Two Harbors. He was not home at the time, but his wife happened to be home and she did allow me to come in the residence. I remember her being a very attractive woman, not unfriendly by any means and we did have a conversation. She hinted to me that there were problems in the marriage, and that they were in the process of getting a divorce. She was very hesitant to answer any questions, I was quite polite as I always am and did not put pressure on her, but nevertheless, remained persistent. I had been in the residence perhaps 15 to 20 minutes when Mike Montana came home. As stated, he was a very good looking Scandinavian appearing person and really had the look of an altar boy. He was polite to me but stated that he didn't want to talk about Bellene or anybody else and that was the ends of any dialogue with him. In doing a background on Montana, I proceeded to the courthouse in an attempt to gather some information. I heard that he had been receiving some welfare benefits so I went to the welfare office where I was informed that that information was privileged. A man in the back room heard my conversation with the desk person and called out, "Vinnie. Hang on a minute." He then appeared and I'll be damned if it wasn't Bruce Meyers who is an attorney and who I worked with on occasion when we were representing Marjorie Caldwell after she was charged with orchestrating a murder of her mother and the night nurse. Talk about a small world.

Bruce is a very interesting person and I gave a bit of a sketch of him in the Congdon case included in this book. Bruce suggested that I go to the civil court records clerk and go through the divorce file of Mike Montana and that might be helpful to me. It was a great suggestion; normally I do take that course of action looking for any civil suits on people like Montana for the purpose o f discrediting these animals.

I went over to the courthouse, the clerk located the file and in his testimony in the divorce case, he talked about getting welfare and food stamps. Now this was important because he recently, as I mentioned, was given over $100,000 and if you have those type of assets, you sure as hell don't qualify for welfare. Besides that, he supposedly was working as an electrician. So, this was a nice bit of information regarding this professional snitch but that's not the end of it. In banging around town, I located a car dealer that Montana had ripped off, and he actually stole from a hardware store. I interviewed people both at the car dealership and the hardware store. Why he wasn't charged on the theft at the hardware store is beyond me but obviously the sheriff was protecting his ass.

I also was able to locate a few of Mike Montana's victims, as I describe them, he had set a number of guys up that had even done work for him and they were busted for small amounts of marijuana. At the American Legion Hall, I interviewed the woman who was the evening manager and bartender who told me that Montana was definitely snorting cocaine, he admitted it at the bar, he went in the men's room to snort and she described him as a piece of work.

Obviously it wasn't too difficult to gather information to discredit Montana if indeed he was called to the witness stand. I went back to see his wife after being in the community for a couple of days, his car was not on the premises and so I figured maybe he was now living elsewhere because of the divorce. She answered the door and to my shock and surprise, she had a black eye and a red cheek. She did not want to talk about anything and she seemed very fearful, it was apparent she was also suffering from anxiety. She would not tell me how she was injured, but my guess is that Mike Montana banged her around after I had talked to her and contacted their friends and reigned them in a few days earlier. She had been working at a hotel resort, I knew that if we needed to subpoena her there was a good

Chapter 13 - Snitches

chance I could track her down. Her employer at the resort motel was a male and a friend of Mike Montana. I called upon him but he absolutely stonewalled me, he refused to even give his name or give me any information whatsoever about big Mike. I thought, what the hell, if Howard wanted to subpoena him that also wouldn't be much of a problem. I did take a run at the sheriff up in the Two Harbors area, but of course, he had nothing to say to me either.

Howard's client, Mr. Bellene, had told me about a guy in Florida, in the Homestead area, which is where the air force base happened to be located, south of Miami, but a little bit north of the Keys. Bellene told me that he did in fact buy a couple of small bales of marijuana from this guy but the guy was a standup guy, he wasn't in trouble and it wasn't worth the effort to go and see him. Well this still bothered me, who knew that if in the future the guy was somehow confronted by the DEA or local authorities, he may just flip on Bellene. I informed Howard's client that my daughter resided in Homestead and if he worried about expense that was unnecessary, because if I went down to interview this guy I would be staying with my daughter and taking my meals there also. Bellene said however there was nothing to worry about so it wasn't my call to independently go down to Florida, the attorney runs the case and I just take directions on these matters.

The trial was commencing, *voir dire* was taking place and bingo, the Florida jerk-off shows up on the witness list for the prosecution. To make a long story shorter, Howard negotiated a deal on behalf of Bellene, one that Bellene readily accepted, he was given a short prison sentence. To this day, I thought maybe we could neutralize the Florida guy and I felt Bellene's position was one of penny-wise and pound foolish.

The final scene concerning this case was rather humorous. Bellene wrote a letter to the judge and stated they charged him on the wrong thing, that he wasn't dealing cocaine and the marijuana he brought back was rotten and he couldn't give it away. Bellene stated that the stuff that he bought from that guy had been thrown overboard by a smuggler, the stuff is supposed to float to shore, then a dealers colleague would pick it up. Apparently this grass was really soaked with salt water and just had no value. But Bellene in his letter told the judge that his real crime was skimming money from his previous coin-operated machine business, it was money that he and bar owners took out of the machines, but hid from the IRS.

I liked Bellene and I liked his wife, but he was kind of on the edge so to speak but yet his personality was pleasing and he was-a good fishing guy. Some years later I learned that his wife divorced him which often happens when someone is incarcerated.

Regarding Mike Montana, I have no idea where he would be, whether or not he is still snitching, but in my book, he's certainly a criminal and a disgusting human being who will probably end up in deep ca-ca and may even cross the wrong guy who will blow his head off.

Angel face Mike and silver tongue Red Adams are birds of a feather. Whatever makes these slime balls do what they do is difficult to figure out. My guess is that they are amoral, which is a form of psychopathic behavior, and they live this way and absolutely nothing bothers them. What is truly sad is that the government knows about these psychopaths and yet they continue to use them on cases, condone their lying, thieving, disgusting behavior and often put them on the witness stand and allow them to lie through their teeth. Suborning perjury is supposed to be a crime. If the defense ever did such a thing, paying witnesses for example to testify, then the defense would be prosecuted, the lawyers would be disbarred, their investigators charged and that would be the end of it. Never in life have I ever been asked by any lawyer to commit an unethical act, an immoral act, suborn perjury, deceive a witness or lie on the witness stand. Isn't it interesting that Martha Stewart was charged with lying to government agent or prosecutor, run through the mill, beat up by the press, sentenced to prison, yet the government can lie to everybody and there are no repercussions? What a great fucking country.

Scoundrels

George Seldes, author of a book entitled," Witness to a Century," which he wrote at age 90, in the 1980's had three scoundrels that he mentioned in his book. Seldes has written approximately 10 books, was an independent journalist, covered the Civil War in Spain which

Chapter 13 - Snitches

actually wasn't a Civil War, but a military takeover by Franco, and Mr. Seldes was highly regarded in his profession.

George Seldes first scoundrel is Errol Flynn, the Australian film actor, who some may remember doing action movies. He was a very mediocre thespian, and immigrated to the United States, living primarily in Hollywood. After the conclusion of World War II, there were some rumors that he may have been a low level spy for the Nazis. It was common knowledge Flynn was somewhat of a sexual predator, at one point in time, he was charged with statutory rape, which means he was with a female under age and I'm not quite sure how that case came out. Flynn was famous for his drinking and publicity seeking, Seldes saw him in Spain during that conflict. Flynn apparently arrived in Spain, was driven to the front lines with a photographer, has his picture taken and then immediately left the Country. He did the same thing in Cuba during the Castro revolution. Suffice to say that Errol Flynn did not live a very honorable life.

The second scoundrel that Seldes mentioned was the poet D' Annunzio who was actually, very good at his craft and was well known early on in the 20th Century. Seldes states that D'Annunzio actually founded the fascist party in Italy and had been a friend and ally of Benito Mussolini. The story as told by Mr. Seldes, money had been sent to the party from Italian immigrants in the United States that totaled over one million which was quite a sum back in those days. Somehow or other, Mussolini got a hold of the money and aced out D'Annunzio and of course took over the party. I'm certain there is more to it than that, there was much intrigue dealing and double crossing that took place, but I'm sure it was a contributing factor to the rise of dear Benito. Seldes names D'Annunzio as a scoundrel because of this less than honorable person double crossed and ripped off a famous Italian actress of the day. D' Annunzio was going to publish a book or a play about her life listing certain affairs she had. The woman came to D' Annunzio, pleaded with him not to ruin her reputation and offered him a large sum of money. D' Annunzio agreed to accept this money and not publish so she traveled and acted in plays in England and the United States, raised the necessary amount and gave it to the poet. However, D' Annunzio kept the money and published the story of her life anyway.

Seldes last scoundrel he pretty much leaves it up in the air naming three people that the reader could pick. Now I can't name just three scoundrels that I've come across in my career, after all that wouldn't be fair to the other 123. Needless to say, one of my scoundrels would be George Bush, Jr. in that he is a man of no accomplishment having failed in business and having been bailed out with family money that gave him other opportunities. He started a war based on false information and what could be worse than that ill-fated deed.

Andrew Chambers

My next scoundrel would be a government undercover informant, one Andrew Chambers who has testified in perhaps 60 to 70 drug cases on behalf of the DEA and the FBI. He is a liar and had been convicted of crimes yet in the case of U.S. v. Ralph Chavez Duke, the prosecutors knowingly and willingly represented Chambers as "a young man who works as a confidential informer, who has never been arrested, who has never been convicted of a crime, he doesn't use drugs, he doesn't even drink." That was the opening statement by the Assistant United States Attorney on that case. There were two U.S. attorneys representing the government, John Hopeman and the other was Denise Riley. Riley is now a judge and Hopeman is in private practice.

Chambers who testified at great length stated the following. This information, by the way, has been taken from the magnificent brief written by attorney Jack Nordby, who is now a Hennepin County judge and former criminal defense lawyer at attorney Ron Meshbesher's firm and prior to that, a partner with attorney Doug Thomson.

At the outset of Chambers testimony, the exchange went like this:

Q: Have you ever been convicted of any crime in your whole life, sir?
A: No, I haven't.
Q: Have you ever been arrested?
A: No.
Q: Have you ever used illegal drugs?
A: No, I haven't.

Chapter 13 - Snitches

Q: When did you first come to Minnesota?
A: In February.
Q: And at whose request did you come up here?
A: Bob Bushman.
Q: And Mr. Bushman works at the BCA? Is that correct?
A: Yes.

Bushman was his controlling agent and obviously knew Chambers background and the fact that he had been doing extensive undercover work all over the Country on behalf of the government. Bushman also obviously knew Chambers had committed various crimes and had convictions and it's impossible to believe that the prosecution team was not privy to this information yet they knowingly allowed Chambers to perjure himself.

Unfortunately Judge Nordby appeal to the 8th Circuit was denied, he won the battle but lost the war.

Chambers testified in another case in St. Paul, Minnesota entitled <u>United States v. Long Cadillac</u>. I did not work on that case for Meshbesher or Peter Thompson in that my wife and I were at the time on the island of St. Vincent in the Caribbean teaching school at St. Martin's Secondary School. That's a story and a half by itself.

I did arrive home to Minneapolis as the trial started and attorney Mark Wernick who is also now a judge was representing one of the parties involved. I did a minimum amount of work on Judge Wernick's case and listened to some of the testimony.

Peter Thompson, who represented one of the members of the Long family — a very good family incidentally with an excellent name in the St. Paul community - did a scathing cross examination of Chambers. This case took place well after the Ralph Duke case and so the defense attorneys had book on Andrew Chambers. Peter had documented information that Chambers was paid over 2 million dollars for his testimony and on the witness stand, asked Chambers if he ever paid taxes on that money. Needless to say he hadn't and Chambers response was the DEA was going to take care of that for him. Incidentally there was only one conviction, minor as it was, in the Long Cadillac case and one of the Long boys was given house arrest for a period of time.

The three major snitch cases that I was involved in happened to be a drop in a bucket. As author Redden writes in his excellent book, the use of informants is really corrupt. It's one thing to play defendants off against each other, he who talks first walks, but to pay people to set others up for a crime is unconscionable. Entrapment is rarely a defense because most of these people being busted are minorities and may have a propensity to buy, sell or use drugs.

In Chapter 17 of Mr. Reddens book titled "Stop the Snitch Abuse", he states it looks impossible given how many government agencies employers and non-profit advocacy groups are currently gathering and swapping information. Who can slow its growth on the international level since the United Nations is not even a democratically elected body. But over the years, according to Mr. Redden, populations have repeatedly woken up to the harm caused by the misuse of paid informants.

A favored kingpin

The Phillippi and Pebbles cases serve as dramatic examples of how the government sometimes harshly punishes uncooperative underlings and favors cooperative kingpins, who are supposed to be the drug war's primary targets.

Jan Phillippi — mother of two, onetime office manager and sometime cleaning woman in St. Paul — saw a chance to make $1,000 a trip carrying packages from a high-living lawyer she had met in a bar, according to her trial testimony. The packages contained cocaine, and she was caught in a government trap. She also had been buying cocaine on her own.

St. Paul lawyer Larry Pebbles was the leader of a $25 million cocaine ring. The longtime drug dealer drove Rolls-Royces, traveled the world and distributed cocaine in five states, using female couriers to avoid detection. But one of them — a mother of two — turned on him and brought about his arrest.

Chapter 13 - Snitches

The difference between Phillippi and Pebbles is that she would not cooperate with the government and thus received a 10-year sentence. She recently was released after serving almost nine years.

Pebbles, on the other hand, quickly agreed to help the government. For four years, while living in county jails, he was available for government duty: He testified in a Kentucky case, assisted in gathering wiretap evidence and testified against one of his own major distributors, a stockbroker.

His cooperation won favor from federal prosecutors and enabled him to escape a mandatory minimum sentence.

As a drug felon who already had spent four years in prison and then gone back into the drug business, Pebbles faced a sentence of 20 years to life. But he put in only five more years and is back in the Twin Cities. He declined to comment.

Phillippi, in contrast, was lectured at her sentencing. The prosecutor told her she had to be punished for doing a tremendous amount of damage to society, to the people, to the youth.

Although she declined to be interviewed, she said in a letter that she made the honorable choice in refusing to cooperate. "I have done my time, compromised no one in doing so and can honestly say from my heart, 'If it were tomorrow, I wouldn't waver in making the same decision.' "

Chapter 14

More Attorneys: Peter Thompson

Peter Thompson, an attorney who is now retired, is a native of Minneapolis, Minnesota and he is in his early 60s. Peter attended Washburn High School in South Minneapolis, was an excellent hockey player and received a scholarship to Rensselaer Polytechnic Institution where he played in a big time college hockey program. He got a degree in Business Management and Engineering and then went on to the University of Minnesota Law School in which he graduated in 1968. Since retirement, he went back to a prestigious seminary and now has a theological degree. He works on a volunteer level for a religious organization.

Peter started his law career as a federal prosecutor, then he did state and federal public defense work prior to forming his own law firm, Thompson, Delaney & O'Rourke. Peter has also done a great deal of pro bono work, has represented war protesters and American Indians who have protested for their civil rights. Peter is truly a compassionate, anti-war, anti-violence figure in this community and is highly respected by his peers. He has been a dear friend to me since the early 70s and he has also been one of my mentors.

We first met during the Kronholm kidnap case that was being tried in Anoka, Minnesota. A very nice woman by the name of Eunice Kronholm was kidnapped by Jim Johnson, who was represented by Ron Meshbesher. Peter represented the accomplice and monitored Johnson's trial in Anoka County. Amazingly enough, Ron Meshbesher put forth a duress defense for Johnson. I did the investigation and was in Chicago on the Saturday that the not guilty verdict came in. Ron Meshbesher left a message at my hotel, and trust me, I damn near fainted because there was no question that Johnson initiated this kidnapping and held Mrs. Kronholm in a hotel in Lakeville, Minnesota for a rather long period of time.

Ron Meshbesher argued that "Mike's boys forced Johnson to kidnap Kronholm in order to pay back a debt to Mike." Johnson was shot in the head in Lakeville, maneuvered his car to a restaurant parking lot

Chapter 14 - More Attorneys: Peter Thompson

at County Road 50 and 35W where he crashed the car. The police arrived and he was partially out of the car and bleeding from the eye, According to the investigating police officer, it appeared that he was dying. Johnson gave a dying declaration that Mike's boys shot him. The Friday night before the jury was to deliberate, I was in the Lakeville area in the wee hours in the morning looking for this police officer. At approximately 1:30 a.m., I was able to connect with him and he consented to meet with me and give me a statement that Johnson made what he considered a dying declaration. I left a subpoena with this officer and he testified and told the truth. This, of course, contributed to the defense of duress.

Peter mentioned the head FBI investigator describing him as kind of a classic FBI guy. Peter said that the agent went drinking with Ron Meshbesher and Peter when they were waiting for the verdict and he had testified for Ron under compulsion in the Kronholm kidnap case. Ron asked him about how the mafia worked. He asked him if they had a strong center in Chicago and brought up the fact that they were very dangerous to deal with. Peter said he was quite impressed because the FBI agent told the absolute truth and Peter pointed out that knowing police officials, they rarely give you any information that is beneficial to the defense and often they stretch the truth.

Peter then reminded me that Johnson was re-charged in federal court. The allegation was that he had extorted money in the kidnap case from the bank that Mr. Kronholm was president of in South St. Paul. Naturally, Ron Meshbesher challenged this, but his challenge was unsuccessful and Johnson was convicted in the federal trial. Ron's position was that the demand was being made from an individual who just happened to be president of the bank, but apparently some instructions were phoned into Mr. Kronholm when he was at work and that must have been enough for the feds to try him in federal court.

Incidentally, word came back to me that I was the one that set up the whole shooting, shot at Johnson and the bullet ricocheted off his side view mirror and hit him in the eye. I don't know who the agent was that made this ridiculous allegation, but I'm very unfamiliar with guns, do not own a gun, and have not shot a pistol since Army basic training in 1954.

Of further note, Peter Thompson's client, who I choose not to name, never served a day in prison, demonstrating to me that Mr. Thompson was one hell of a defense lawyer.

Mrs. Kronholm, after being kidnapped, was kept in a motel. The motel rooms had phones and the office was not attached to the motel unit, it was almost like a house up on a hill. In those days, this was way out in the country. Often she was left alone in her room while Johnson went off somewhere and his partner in crime wasn't present. I wondered why she didn't pick up a phone and call someone. People have informed me that she must have been suffering from the Stockholm syndrome. In essence identifying with her captors and she was in such a state that she couldn't act.

Regarding the defense duress and coercion that Ron Meshbesher put forth, during the trial I was in the witness room with Johnson. Johnson never would talk about Mike's boys. I brought the subject up and reminded him that anything he said to me fell under attorney/client privilege and it would be important to identify these guys that threatened him and coerced him into committing this kidnapping. Johnson literally turned white in the face, looked away from me and would not make a comment. That, plus the fact that he was shot led me to believe that he owed these guys a lot of money and when he borrowed money for his construction company, he was dealing with some very mean organized crime figures.

As mentioned, Johnson did some time on the federal conviction, got out of prison and was again building houses by himself and he seemed to be doing quite well. I lost touch with him, not that I socialized with any clients, but I later heard he was charged on another offense involving a homicide and a body buried on a little island in the middle of the Mississippi. I don't know, I can't confirm that and he may have turned state's evidence against some people. It is really a shame as he had a nice wife and he was a good builder.

We went on to discuss the evolution of the criminal justice system and I suggested that it has become more difficult for the defense than it was 40 years ago. Peter stated that he agreed with that. Peter went on to say that in the practice of law generally, there has been much criticism and allegations against defense lawyers of accusations

Chapter 14 - More Attorneys: Peter Thompson

of ethical violations coming from prosecutors. Peter said that it is almost like in a civil litigation where there are motions to disqualify opposing counsel as one of the standard motions that get filed just to have an advantage. Peter described it as "sharks swimming in the water together."

He stated that regarding the constitution of the United States and the interpretation by the Supreme Court, things are much less favorable now for defendants. Please note that Peter is a constitutional lawyer which means he has appeared before the Supreme Court and, unlike Ann Coulter, one cannot make this claim of being a constitutional lawyer unless one has appeared before a Supreme Court. Peter said there are two huge factors nationally that make defense work much more difficult. One is that a lot of constitutional protections are being eroded by various cases. He said it is a classic case of bad facts making bad law. He pointed out an example of serial killers or child molesters whereby bad law has been made making it more difficult to defend when the facts and law appears on the side of the defendant. Peter, who is a liberal and extremely pragmatic, not a politically correct screwball, pointed out the judiciary right now in the Supreme Court and appellate courts along with federal courts are Bush/Reagan appointees.

He also talked about sentencing and this was discussed in other chapters in this book with highly knowledgeable judges. Peter stated that if you have a defendant with no prior criminal convictions who have ties to the community and throughout life have been a decent citizen, often the judge would put the person on probation. Now, however, under the Federal Sentencing Guidelines, these people just get clobbered.

I also mentioned Judge Rosenbaum's situation which also has been touched on in this book. Peter said that they should review the cases of federal judges that give too much time. He stated that no one wants to review that. He said that attitude is that everyone should get put away; give them a fair trial and hang them. We have more people in jail in this country than any other so-called civilized nation. He said we have more black males in jail than there were blacks in South Africa at the height of apartheid. Peter stated that it is costing in excess of $30,000 per year to house an inmate and it is absolutely crazy. You can go to the best universities in the county for that kind of money. Peter said that there are many people in prison that are minor drug sellers and users. Treatment would be a far less expensive and more effective way of dealing with those kind of folks that are incarcerated.

Peter knew that I had worked on the Ralph Duke case and that Howard Bass was writing the brief. I reminded Peter that Duke got life plus 40 for his first offense by Judge Dody.[7]

Peter was aware of the paid government informant in the Duke case because Peter had cross-examined this disgusting person in the Long Cadillac case. Peter stated that Judge Dody is very tough at sentencing. Peter said that there was not a lot he could do if the conviction was valid because they have him charged as a career criminal even though he was never charged and convicted previously. Peter pointed out that it doesn't make much difference that he was a first offender in federal court. Peter said that he is assuming Duke did something wrong in his life, but stated there are more tragic cases and he knew the ones Judge Rosenbaum struggled with because he has talked about those cases often.

Peter stated that there are 19 year old black kids who have no priors and they get caught with a little too much crack cocaine so it is a ten year minimum mandatory. He said many of these kids are screwing around with drugs because it looks exciting and they can make some money pedaling some, but when they are caught they are really slammed and have to do two-thirds of the ten year minimum mandatory. He said these kids come out of the brick house at age 26 or 27 and it's as if they went off to college, they learn a lot from their peers in prison and they become hardened.

I mentioned to Mr. Thompson Judge Pamela Alexander. She took the position that crack and pure cocaine were one in the same and these black kids were getting a higher sentencing for possession of crack. Peter said that financially these young people in the black community can afford crack, but not pure cocaine. Peter said that it was a denial

---

[7] See Chapter 6 on Duke.

Chapter 14 - More Attorneys: Peter Thompson

of equal protection under the law and the Minnesota Supreme Court upheld that.

I asked Peter what he thought the right wing philosophy and mindset was, and where he thought these ultra conservative people were going with this approach within the justice system. Peter responded by saying that he does have some inclination as to what is going on. He stated that he thinks the whole idea of bias against welfare recipients and race raises its ugly head. The neo-cons would deny it and say that they are maintaining objectivity. Peter went on to say that based on his life experience as a prosecutor and defense lawyer, he doesn't see it that way. He stated that he thinks they see things through the prism of George Bush, John Ashcroft and Gonzales and other Bush friends and look at it politically and ideologically believe it must be the right thing to do. And they believe that the majority of people are in favor of it. My comment was that there has been so much propaganda from certain media such as Nancy Grace, Bill O'Reilly and Rush Limbaugh who play loose and fast with the facts that the average citizen often buys into the approach of neocon ideologies.

I then asked Peter about former Attorney John Ashcroft. My feeling is that he must be insecure since he had to cover a naked statue considered a piece of art. I thought there was something wrong with a man like that.

Peter said that he thinks Ashcroft is a very dangerous guy. He went on to say that he thinks he is more dangerous than an armed robber. He said the armed robber has a mask over his head and you try to stay out of his way. Ashcroft had a three piece suit and his weapons are far more dangerous. He said all their political power and the fear that has filled this country since 9/11 is a result of that entire group of people, Cheney, Ashcroft, Bush, etc. emasculate our constitutional protections.

Concerning the mideasterners in this country who are citizens being immediate suspects means they don't have the protections that we have. Peter said that it may take longer and it may be tougher to go after someone like us, but remembers they went after Ron

Meshbesher on a couple of cases where it never went anywhere. My comment was I will never forget!

I brought up a paid government informant by the name of Red Adams that Peter dealt with in a case. I also mentioned paid informant Chambers who Peter had for lunch in the Long Cadillac case. Peter really gave this guy a new orifice.

I'll quote Peter verbatim on the following as I don't want anyone to think I am blowing my own horn. Peter brought this up and told me it should stay in the book. Peter said "Vinnie, there was no one in the business of investigation who could have done a better job than you concerning Red Adams." Peter said "You relate to people and are able to talk to them and were able to interview Adams who freely spoke to you. As a result, I was able to cross-examine Adams effectively. "

Peter went on to say that there is an interesting story regarding Adams who was a former convicted murderer out of Chicago. Peter said that the client he had at the time, John Lambross, was convicted. Peter went on to say that every buy that Red Adams had anything to do with the jury acquitted Lambross because they totally disregarded Red Adams. Peter said that he remembers that in the trial of Lambross, Red Adams claimed that you bought his testimony.[8] That, of course, was completely false. Peter went on to say "You know the government had paid Adams thousands of dollars and he needed a ride somewhere and you gave him a ride." Peter said there was nothing wrong with that and giving a guy a ride surely isn't a payoff. Peter said that after the trail of Lambross concluded, Red Adams, whose real name is Harrison McCoy, was down in the DEA's office and he saw $1,100 in cash and stole it from the DEA. He did this after he had been paid thousands of dollars for his work. He confessed to stealing the money and prosecutor Thor Anderson wanted to string the man up. Joe Walbran had been working all these cases that Adams had testified in. So Walbran went to bat for Red Adams.

---

[8] I gave him a ride to St. Paul.

Chapter 14 - More Attorneys: Peter Thompson

Peter felt that Adams should have been prosecuted. I told Peter that I normally I don't have any frightening experiences, often I am rejected, but when I went over to see Adams in his apartment on Hennepin Avenue, it was a bit spooky. I reminded Peter that all he wanted to do was rule out that his client, Lambross, had gotten drugs out of Chicago. When I finally got in Red Adams' building, he buzzed me up. He lived in a small apartment and he removed a jacket off the kitchen table and a gun fell out. I knew he had been convicted of murder and all of this made me very uncomfortable.

I next asked Peter about the informant in the Long Cadillac case who was the same informant in the Ralph Duke case. Peter said that he thought the previous cases Chambers testified in, the government had obtained convictions. Peter said that in the Long Cadillac case, where there were several lawyers involved, we won almost the entire case. It must be noted that in federal court it is difficult to get severance when there are a number of defendants involved and are tried as a group.

Peter said that some of the other defense attorneys had asked Chambers about money he made and Chambers was paid $50,000 in cash. At one of his earlier trials, he admitted he hadn't filed tax returns for the year and, of course, there is no legitimate reason for Chambers to be paid by the government in cash, therefore, encouraging him not to pay taxes. I asked Peter why they paid him in cash. Peter said he wondered the same thing. He also wondered if he filled out a CTR when he got the cash.

Peter stated that he found in another transcript on a different case when he was asked the same question and at that point the government was savvy to this line of questioning. When Chambers was asked by Peter about receiving cash, he said he was in the process of filling out his tax returns and the DEA is helping him do it., Peter said that the government didn't realize that I had looked up the old transcripts and so I led Chambers down the garden path and soon found out he hadn't filed any returns over the years. Peter then said he pulled out the transcripts and said, "If a year ago the DEA was working on your tax returns, who was the agent?" At the end of the cross-examination Peter said Judge McLaughlin called the government to the bench and asked if they were still using this guy,

Chambers. The judge then said that it was disgusting. Peter said that for a federal judge to say it is disgusting is pretty amazing. They usually are pretty pro prosecution.

Peter had a horrendous case some years ago where he was appointed by the public defender's office because there were other defendants involved. I did some work on this particular case and Nancy Berg helped me when she was a law student. Peter represented a guy by the name of Dale Olson who had been in jail and came under the influence of a guy named James Black. This is just too horrible a thing to happen, but Black somehow convinced Olson when he got out of jail to set fire to Black's girlfriend's duplex apartment. The woman and her child burned to death in the fire.

This case involved a great deal of error that entered the trial. Peter had numerous legal arguments based on evidence. To make a long story short, some illegal evidence came in. Peter appealed and there were a number of constitutional issues. In final analysis, the 8th Circuit Appellate Court stated they were not going to review the case. Peter said they refused to grant certiorari. Peter said that we put everybody in a perfect box legally but since it is a one-way street you always have a way out and they just refused to reach the issue. It was a long tortured proceeding and the reason it came out the way it did was because it was one of the most heinous crimes ever committed in the State of Minnesota, and nobody was going to let a guy out after that. As Judge Anderson of the Supreme Court of Minnesota told me in his interview, sometimes there is law and sometimes there is doing what is right.

The late Judge Stan Cane, a wonderful man, had tried the case and took Peter aside after the trial and told Peter that he had a very difficult time with his evidentiary ruling and he was in a terrible spot. He said that he would have to let one of the worst crimes ever go unpunished or he would have to rule as a matter of law that the evidence was going to come in that shouldn't have come in. That was the way of Judge Cane telling Peter that he was in a terrible position and that Peter was right, but the judge could not exclude the evidence.

Chapter 14 - More Attorneys: Peter Thompson

I mentioned to Peter that people have often asked me how I could assist in the defense of some rotten SOB when it appeared this degenerate person was guilty. Peter said that he was glad that he could defend some of these people because they had constitutional rights and we are bound to protect everyone's rights in a court of law. Peter further said that he is happy that there are gutsy young defense lawyers and public defenders who can also defend the alleged criminals. Peter said that he could not do the Olson case today as it would be too difficult. He said he can't even stand reading about physical abuse or the murder of children.

I told Peter that I completely understood and that the pressure of being a defense lawyer takes a tremendous toll on one. Peter said that when you get to a certain age, you just can't take it any more, but he is happy there are young and aggressive attorneys in the field with the same mindset he once had.

Peter went on to say that we must have a system set up as ours and now we have the help of DNA. We have to continue following the system the way it was originally intended to be, meaning it is better that a hundred guilty guys go free than one innocent go to prison. He went on to say that there is even an easier way to say it. He said if some hot shot had come to him and asked the question about how you can defend scumbags, his answer would be "Mr. hot shot what if your daughter got busted for possession of cocaine and you brought her in to see me? Would you want me to try to defend her adequately or would you want me to give her a big lecture and send her off to prison?" Who can argue with that!

I made a point to Peter that I thought the real lawyers were the litigators fighting for someone's life, not the Washington lobbyists and the slick corporate guys charging $600~800 an hour. Peter said that he agreed. "It is the lawyers that are in front of juries all the time that expose lies by others through cross-examination. Peter said those are the real trial lawyers. Peter then illustrated by stating that he remembers during the Crane Winton case he and Joe Friedberg were sitting next to each other while Judge Winton was being cross-examined by Kelly Gage. Peter and Joe Friedberg are criminal defense lawyers and Kelly Gage apparently was not. Peter stated that it would have been easy for he or Joe to do an effective cross-examination

Whatever happened to Lady Justice?

had they been in Gage's shoes and Peter wished to emphasize that Mr. Gage was well respected and a well qualified lawyer, but he didn't touch Crane Winton. Peter said a criminal defense lawyer with experience would have carved Crane Winton into little pieces based on the record, the depositions and everything else. Peter said most lawyers don't know how to cross examine in a criminal case because they haven't been in the battlefield and they don't go for the jugular. Peter said you must be able to take your opponent apart.

I worked on the Crane Winton case and I learned that former Congressman Don Fraser had very strong positive opinions about Judge Crane Winton. Peter and Joe Friedberg contacted Don Fraser and Peter stated his testimony was absolutely brilliant. Fraser incidentally is a lawyer himself and a very decent human being as is his wife.

Peter Thompson went on to say that Don Fraser is probably one of the most decent politicians this country has ever seen. The overview of Judge Winton's case is as follows:

This judge, since his legal dilemma, has come out of the closet so-to speak and is living a quiet life and has a partner. One of the tragedies concerning Crane Winton is that he was an extremely well regarded jurist, helped many people during his lifetime such as Judge Nordby. What we know about homosexuality in the past is that the majority kept their sexual orientation quiet and that is exactly what Crane Winton did. He, unfortunately, did solicit male prostitutes, he had gone to Loring Park where a number of these male prostitutes hook up with their johns. A local television station, WCCO, conducted an investigation and Judge Winton's name surfaced. This, of course, became big news.

Judge Winton retained Attorney Peter Thompson and Joe Friedberg to represent him. I was assigned to do the investigation. The judge, of course, was familiar with all the outstanding defenses lawyers and naturally he picked Thompson and Friedberg, wanting someone of that caliber. One of the important prostitutes that the judge was charged with visiting was a guy named John John Shriver. He was a month or so away from his 18th birthday. What happened is that Shriver and a couple other male prostitutes were picked up by a BCA

Chapter 14 - More Attorneys: Peter Thompson

agent. The investigative reporter, Don Shelby, was riding with this agent and they took these witnesses to the WCCO studio. These witnesses thought they were going to the BCA office (Bureau of Criminal Apprehension) to give an interview. These people were given disguises and went on camera and told their story. At a later date, I interviewed John John Shriver and a couple of these young men and they were highly irate and feeling they had been deceived. A couple of them said they were going to hire attorneys and sue WCCO.

Incidentally, I had met with Shriver on approximately three occasions, but he turned on me when I interviewed his boyfriend who he had beat up on more than one occasion. The boyfriend phoned me at my residence; John John had my card, and wanted to meet with me. I did meet with him and John John found out and called my house one night when my wife and I were out, my daughter answered the phone and he said "Is Vince, the cocksucker, there?" When my wife and I returned home, we found our daughter had locked herself in the bathroom. She was frightened and told me what happened. A short time later, John John called again and said "Is this Vince the cocksucker?" My reply to John John was "I think you have things mixed up, John John, I'm the investigator and you're the cocksucker." That comment resulted in a long pause and then a complete verbal explosion on his part. Nothing ever came of it.

Peter said that the tragic part about Crane Winton's case is that the judge did not believe John John was a juvenile. Thus, the felony charge was dropped and the judge pled to a misdemeanor. People plead all the time to simple prostitution; sometime getting a fine or diverted into a treatment program. In the program, you learn about the effects of prostitution, how to control urges, etc.

Peter said that they ended up on something similar to a Scopes trial.[9] The trial lasted for three weeks and was on the front page of the newspaper every day. Peter said it was clear that the reason this went on for so long was that Judge Winton was gay.

---

[9] The famous evolution case tried in the south where the great Clarence Daron defended Scopes who, in a school, taught evolution.

I interjected by mentioning the hypocrisy in this case because there had been a number of prominent people who had been found keeping company with female prostitutes. Peter said that with the help of one of these people who was very courageous, that they were able to put some files into evidence so the judge knew similar conduct had resulted in reprimands. That is exactly what Peter and Joe said should have happened in the Winton case. The difference was that Winton's transgressions were homosexual acts rather than heterosexual acts.

I asked Peter about the role of the media. Peter pointed out that there is a lot of yellow journalism. He said it gets people to watch television. The media naturally was very interested in the court proceedings, so after court Joe and Peter would meet with the media and give a press conference, but would exclude WCCO, the people that had initiated the investigation of male prostitution.

I mentioned to Peter three incidents I had involving WCCO and their eye team investigators where I was accused of impropriety. It is infuriating because if you have never done anything unethical or illegal in your career and what they are saying has virtually no basis, it can really piss you off. On one of their tacky reports, Dave Nimmer was sitting dramatically behind a typewriter and whipped the page out of the machine, looked at the camera and announced, "Isn't it ironic that Vincent Carraher has been involved in three cases where he allegedly bribed witnesses."

The following day of this report, Mr. Bob Shaw, whose wife had been an office manager at the Meshbesher law firm, phoned me. He had been the president or director of the news council and said I should take this matter to the council and complain about the WCCO report. I told Mr. Shaw that at that particular time, I had a lawsuit against the Minneapolis Star and just had too much going in my life to bother. Ultimately, the Star settled with me, but the condition was I could not divulge the dollar amount. The dollar amount is not important; the fact that they gave me money means my position was correct. Of course, they would say they settled because the lawsuit was a nuisance, but that's bullshit as they screwed up.

Chapter 14 - More Attorneys: Peter Thompson

I asked Peter if he would be comfortable talking about the Dr. John Najarian case that was tried in federal court in St. Paul, Minnesota. Dr. John Najarian was a prominent transplant surgeon, Chief of Staff at the University of Minnesota Hospital, and a remarkable surgeon. Dr. Najarian did the first infant transplant in the world. He had developed an anti-rejection drug called ALG. The FDA had not finally approved the drug, but allowed the drug to be sold to various university hospitals and other hospitals throughout the country. The money went back into the program.

Peter said that he didn't think I had enough tape to discuss the whole case so I am going to briefly illustrate the facts. Dr. Najarian had a man running the lab along with other assistants that worked in the lab. The FDA was very slow in approving this for the overall medical market and the guy in the lab, Mr. Condi, did very little to follow through with the necessary paperwork. Condi enjoyed being called Dr. Condi, but he did not have a Ph.D, he had a masters. That did not mean he was "lesser than" in his lab work. However, Condi, a strange individual based on my investigation, had been conducting a little, side business. There were byproducts from this drug and his underground business involved selling the byproduct overseas and maybe "even locally.

A routine audit had been conducted and Condi was discovered to be crooked. He immediately blamed the whole thing on Dr. Najarian and cut a deal for his testimony. But the poetic justice in this case is that Dr. Najarian was acquitted in a very lengthy trial and Condi was stuck with his deal.

One would think that the University administration would rally around Dr. Najarian, who incidentally is still working at the University, but they more or less hung him out to dry. The University attorney, whose name is Rottenberg, actually involved his former law firm, the Dorsey firm in Minneapolis, assisting and cooperating with the government. Rumor has it that the Dorsey firm was paid one million dollars. A woman at the Dorsey firm conducted some rather mean-spirited, dirty-minded interviews of female staff members that worked with Dr. Najarian.

There were numerous counts, including Dr. Najarian fudging on his expense account. My good friend, Gary Throvig, did the intricate and major part of the investigation as far as I am concerned. Gary is a CPA, had been an IRS investigator, but decided to start his own business. He crunched all of the numbers for Peter and Peter's partner, John Lundquist. Peter and John tried this case together. They had volunteers that worked in different areas of the case that were very important: Dr. Najarian's wife and sister-in-law, and a young intern that helped Peter and John during the trial, and I was the interviewer of approximately 60 to 80 witnesses. My job was to contact witnesses that had transplants, verify they had been given sufficient information concerning the risks and that they absolutely were well informed. The government claimed that these people were not well informed. We showed the government was wrong.

I only had two rejections by witnesses. These were from people whose spouse or relative had died after the operation. It must be noted that this was an extremely radical procedure and much depended on the anti-rejection drug. Medical experts in the field have told me that at that time, Najarian's drug was the best anti-rejection drug available. I also interviewed surgeons who had worked with or trained under Dr. Najarian and, of course, one of the outstanding surgeons who is still at the University and is keenly involved in the diabetes disease is Dr. Sutherland. To make a long story very short, 14 counts against Dr. Najarian were thrown out during trial by Judge Kyle. Also, during the trial, but out of earshot of the jurors, Judge Kyle made the comment openly to the prosecution and defense, "What are we doing here? This should have been handled in house." If ever there was a case of select prosecution, this was the classic example. I found Dr. Najarian, his staff and 99 percent of the people to be extremely good at their profession. My impression was that these folks were ethical and devoted to what they were doing. One very lovely woman that worked closely with Dr. Najarian had been truly upset when she was asked if she ever had an affair with a doctor. My response when she told me this was that the interrogator had a dirty mind.

It was a great victory for Dr. Najarian, perhaps he did not keep the best records when he traveled to conferences, etc. pertaining to his expenses, but Gary showed that the University ended up owing him

Chapter 14 - More Attorneys: Peter Thompson

money! His wife helped him a great deal at these conferences, and she was not paid, she did this out of the goodness of her heart.

There was a celebration at Dr. Najarian's residence after he was acquitted and many of the jurors attended along with some of the parents whose children had transplants. Peter asked me to bring some of my affidavits so these jurors could read them because the counts I had worked on were dismissed and Peter wanted to reinforce with the jurors their not guilty verdict.

I met a woman I interviewed from Texas who had witnessed the assassination of JFK. She wrote a book titled She was on the Grassy Knoll and swore to God all the shots did not come from the Book Repository. She also had other evidence that she told me about that showed others were involved. Much, of course, has been written about the assassination of JFK. In my opinion, Lee Harvey Oswald had assistance.

I asked Peter if he ever tried a shaken baby case even though I do not recall him having such a case. He stated that Bob Sicoli had tried one and that these are so emotional that you have to overcome a lot of prejudice. He pointed out that defense lawyer, Anthony Torres, defended a case involving a child that was kidnapped and more than likely murdered. He won the case and that is an extremely difficult thing to do under the circumstances. Peter mentioned that he believed the foreman on that case was a lawyer and she followed the law very closely. There was circumstantial evidence which incidentally can be very solid, but no direct proof. They never found the body and it seemed like a case where the presumption of innocence did prevail. The state did not prove the case beyond a reasonable doubt.

I then pointed out to Peter that reasonable doubt is a difficult concept for anyone to grasp. Peter did agree stating that when he started out practicing law the judge would give a definition. Peter said that you can do some things with words such as you believe to the depths of your soul. The definition is usually that a reasonable person would be convinced so as to act without hesitation in the most important of their affairs. So you can describe what that means and make some sense out of it. Peter said that unfortunately now the new JIG, which is the standard instructions in state court does not give any definition, it merely says proof beyond a reasonable doubt and presumption of innocence. These are things that have come down through the centuries, since before the beginning of our country.

I asked Peter why the definition is not discussed when the judge is instructing the jury prior-to their deliberation. I said I realize that you, as a defense lawyer, will discuss it, but why isn't it defined clearly to a jury? Peter said that because prosecutors have this sway on the committees that draft the proposed instructions. Peter said that it is actually ridiculous because if there is no description and no definition, a lot of these words can become confusing.

We continued with our discussion of reasonable doubt. I mentioned to Peter regarding Bob Sicoli, who is an outstanding defense lawyer, had a case in Brainerd whereby doubt jumped out all over the place. The prosecutor told Bob he thought he was certainly going to lose the prosecution's case and even announced it to his staff, but the guy Bob was representing was convicted.

Peter first acknowledged that Bob Sicoli is a great lawyer. He informed me that Bob has had tremendous success representing clients both rich and poor.

I inquired of Peter if he thought the system favors the rich man. Peter said that he thought largely that is the way it is, but went on to say that he didn't think it is necessarily just because the rich man has access to good lawyers, he believes it is the legal system being set up initially to protect the vested interest. In other words, if you read the cases you know they are all somewhat set up to protect the banks, the money, Wall Street; etc. I think more fundamentally from that standpoint, the law is biased in favor of the privileged.

Peter and I went on to discuss the public defender situation, a topic I have discussed with other lawyers. I mentioned to him that the cases I worked on for his law firm where he was appointed, there was a cap put on my fees. Peter informed me that he believes this is improved in federal court now. The lawyers are compensated equally for out-of-court time, however, it is not a great deal of money. In earlier

Chapter 14 - More Attorneys: Peter Thompson

years, it was such a small payment for their services that it would barely cover the attorney's overhead. Peter went on to say that he believes in state court it is still a problem with compensating outside lawyers because they do have full-time public defenders. He stated that unfortunately they carry far too many files and it is virtually impossible for a public defender to devote the time and attention needed in a felony case. The preparation they do, based on their case load, prevents them from turning every stone over.

Many lawyers have been on the public defender panel in Hennepin County; Bob Sicoli and Mark Wernick have been on the panel. Those are cases whereby there is more than one defendant involved in a case, and because of a conflict of interest that would arise in the public defender's office, the case is assigned to a defense lawyer on the panel. Peter pointed out that Mark Wernick did a terrific job representing clients he was assigned. He had a sufficient amount of time and the energy to present a high quality defense. If you are carrying 100 files that are awaiting trial as public defenders do, those lawyers must figure out a plea bargain and get on to the next case. It limits their time to go to trial. Peter added that there are some outstanding lawyers in the public defender's office, but their burdens are extremely heavy.

When it is public money appropriated by the legislature, and cuts must be made, then it often falls on the public defenders. Prison funds are often cut and it is just a difficult system to overcome.

Another subject that has interested me has been *pro bono* work; that is free representation of those in society that cannot afford a lawyer, but would like a top notch attorney to represent them. Peter and I agreed that doing *pro bono* work is appropriate and is needed in the criminal defense arena. Every defense lawyer I have worked with has done quite a bit of *pro bono* work.

In this book I mentioned Ralph Duke, who was represented by Howard Bass *pro bono*. I also worked *pro bono* for approximately three years on that case. If you are working in the system, it is almost a duty in a sense to give something back.

Whatever happened to Lady Justice?

Peter has been a *pro bono* lawyer for those engaged in the peace and justice protests. His major efforts were on behalf of protestors at the School of Americas, and also at Allina Tech. He said the nature of the clients was absolutely wonderful. He represented a number of priests, nuns and good lay people who all believed in the sanctity of life and the evils of war. Incidentally, Peter is not a Roman Catholic, but has a degree in Theology. Peter is one of the most tolerant, gentle human beings on earth.

Peter went on to say that the nuns, priests and lay people that have protested and trespassed non-violently, are sentenced to three months in jail for first time offenders and six months for second time offenders. They are charged with misdemeanors. In Minnesota, particularly in state court, the sentences have been very lenient and the judges hand out community service for the most part. If the person charged pushes the judge by saying they are not going to do community service because they already do it by protesting taxpayers' funds and government support for building mines, then the defendant might get a week in jail. Usually they get probation and no time.

I asked Peter why the sentences are so harsh in Georgia. Peter said that he is not quite sure, but it is a military town and most of the economy comes from Fort Benning. Every year there are demonstrations that are huge, up to 10,000 people, and maybe the populace feels threatened that Fort Benning will move some of their facilities off shore. Peter said there is also a kind of southern mentality.

When Peter was down there, they had three days of trials. He said he was sitting in court when another lawyer was addressing the court and he had some spare time so he wrote a little note to the judge. In his note, he suggested to the judge that they go out to dinner and just talk about different things. Peter described the judge as being very well read and that he was a good southern gentleman. Peter felt he was a good man. The judge responded to Peter's note stating he would certainly enjoy going to dinner with him, but he had to decline because he didn't want to be criticized for socializing with a defense lawyer and open the door for other problems. Peter said that he wanted to mention to the judge that the Army is going about this in

Chapter 14 - More Attorneys: Peter Thompson

the wrong way. For example, one of his clients is an 89 year old nun, Dorothy Hennessy, and this good woman certainly did not deserve jail time for protesting the training of people who went back to their countries and often engaged in murder, rape, and beating of their own citizens. Peter mentioned that Senator Tom Harkin from Iowa worshipped the ground the nun walked on and wrote a wonderful letter for her. She was a person that had never done anything in her life that she didn't feel Jesus called her to do. Peter asked what the Army was thinking to throw this woman in jail for six months. They are shooting themselves in the foot.

I asked Peter when the School of Americas began and what was the purpose of their training? I learned that they were trained by our military people in military tactics. Even though their countries are not at war with anyone beyond their borders, our government continued to spend about $20,000,000 every year of the taxpayers' money to train Latin American soldiers. According to some people, the problems in South America are internal suppression of the poor people's movements. One example would be distribution of land, so they would be able to farm and make a living rather than working on huge corporate farms owned by the rich. This is an issue in Mexico as we speak.

Peter said what they are really trained to do is make war on their own people. There are human rights abuses that occur. The School of Americas started in Panama around 1948 or early 1950s. Panama expelled this school and announced the school was one of the greatest destabilizing influence in Latin America. In 1983, this school was brought up to Fort Benning, Georgia and it has been there ever since.

I asked Peter if the nuns that were raped and murdered in Guatemala by military people were trained at the School of Americas. Peter stated that three of the four who were convicted of those rapes and killings were trained at the School of Americas. I then asked Peter about the assassination of Bishop Romero in El Salvador. Peter stated that the majority of those who assassinated the Bishop while he was on the alter saying mass, had been trained at the School of Americas. Once again, that country was El Salvador and the Bishop had been supporting revolutionary theology. The Bishop's position was that the huge rich land owners should give a break to the peasant class and actually practice democracy because there was great poverty in El Salvador.

I remember reading about the assassination of Bishop Romero and when Pope John Paul II, the Polish Pope, had visited South America he had met with Bishop Romero and chastised him about his position. One must remember that the Pope lived through the Nazi occupation during World War II. In fact, he was in the underground and then he lived under communism and the Catholic Church is the number one enemy of communism. In the article I read, the Pope agonized over his chastisement of Bishop Romero after Romero's assassination.

My comment to Peter was that this is absolutely horrible, training soldiers who go back to their own countries and live under dictators or faux democracies and end up killing their own citizens and terrorizing others. I asked Peter why congress doesn't do something about this. His response was that congress doesn't have any guts. I agree.

Peter went on to say that congress did not even have the courage to vote in any meaningful fashion or declare war on Iraq. They keep passing the buck until someone else gets the heat. Of course, this is an ongoing story concerning the Bush administration looking for data that would support weapons of mass destruction. The U.N. inspectors were in Iraq and their intent was to keep looking, we had satellites, a no fly zone and the reason was false to enter into that war. Now many of our young men and women are dying and numerous civilians have been killed, lost their homes and means of making a living. Congress, in the meantime, runs for cover now saying this was a presidential action. We did not do a declaration of war. Nevertheless, if they had discussed and debated, they could have prevented Bush from entering into the false conflict.

Chapter 14 - More Attorneys: Peter Thompson

My comment to Peter's evaluation was; many books and articles have dissected the situation and as we speak, in hindsight, the majority of our citizens have come to oppose that war.[10]

I mentioned to Peter during our interview that all the cheerleaders for war pretty much were draft dodgers during Viet Nam. Cheney got five deferments. Rudy Giuliani, out of New York, received two deferments; the second was when he was clerking for a judge who pulled some strings and wrote a letter that he was needed in his position. Give me a fucking break! There are thousands of young law school graduates that would kill to get a job clerking for a judge. Giuliani, the serial adulterer, pulled a slick one as did others.

Peter had a long list of negative comments about Bush going back to when he was AWOL from the National Guard in Alabama. General Turnipseed was on television when Bush had his first run for President and publicly stated that Bush had not shown up for duty. I happen to be a non-combat veteran, but nevertheless, this really burned my ass.

Peter, when I interviewed him, was preparing to retire from his law profession. I reminded him of a quote from the late James Shannon, former president of St Thomas College and what is now known as St. Thomas University, and a former Bishop in the Archdiocese of St. Paul. He told a friend of mine that every once in awhile you have to burn down the store. What he meant, of course, is sometimes in your life you must change your career or make a drastic adjustment.

I really miss working with Peter Thompson as he is one of the great constitutional lawyers in the State of Minnesota and a kind and gentle human being. However, I still have the pleasure of working with his former partner, Robert Sicoli, champion of the underdog and king of the sex cases.

---

[10] The polls reveal that 78% of Americans disapprove of the Bush administration.

Chapter 15

Even more attorneys: Joseph Margolis

On September 2, 2003, I met with one of the most interesting lawyers in the Minneapolis community, Joseph Margolis, who now teaches and continues to represent clients. He was a death penalty attorney in the State of Texas. Mr. Margolis also represented successfully an Australian citizen who was held prisoner in the Guantanamo facility in Cuba. Guantanamo, of course, is extremely controversial, as it is pretty much a no man's land when it comes to charging and incarcerating criminals that are labeled terrorists. As I write this, we now have Barack Obama as President of the United States and he is addressing the entire issue of Guantanamo, torture and rendering which legally are violations of the Geneva Convention.

Mr. Margolis grew up on the east coast outside of Washington D.C. He graduated from Cornell University in 1982 and then Northwestern Law School in Chicago in 1988. He states he really doesn't know why he went to law school stating that it is complicated, but believed that since law is a service industry he had an opportunity, or perhaps an obligation to try to deliver legal services to people who cannot afford it or have been denied the benefits of legal counsel. Mr. Margolis stated that he did not necessarily grow up in a home environment that emphasized public service. He stated that his father is a Republican and fairly conservative, and his mother is a Democrat and somewhat liberal. He said he has two older brothers and they think that the work that he does on death penalty cases is crazy. Mr. Margolis said he has a younger sister who doesn't attach much weight to what he does, either. He also stated that they were not a political family.

I asked Mr. Margolis if he felt that the system leaned more toward the wealthy and that many people cannot afford to hire lawyers. Mr. Margolis' response was that he doesn't know whether or not he would say that. He certainly thought in the areas of law that he is familiar with that in general there is a relationship between the amount of money you can devote to a legal problem and the quality of the outcome that you can achieve. He said, "I certainly don't want

Chapter 15 - Even more attorneys: Joseph Margolis

to say that without exception because I think some of the most gifted lawyers I have ever met worked for people who can't afford to pay for their services." Mr. Margolis went on to say that some of the most gifted and tireless lawyers he has met are people who have worked for no pay. They belong to a non-profit organization or they were paid by the government, meaning they didn't make a hell of a lot of money.

I made a point of mentioning to Mr. Margolis that if you have an affluent client in a criminal case, they can afford to pay for experts. I inquired what the poor man does if he or she would need an expert on their case. Mr. Margolis stated that is a good illustration of how the private bar doesn't understand the law. A person is not eligible for the public defender so he or she has to hire private counsel, but may not have enough additional money for expert assistance. He went on to say that it would be a mistake for the private lawyer to say that he will not get the services of an expert. The client is indigent for the purpose of costs and the lawyer should go to the court, under the 14th amendment, and inform the judge to declare the client indigent for the purpose of costs. Mr. Margolis says his firm has done this and state and federal court and the court should pay for the experts that are needed. Just because a person has enough money to hire private counsel, but nothing else doesn't mean he should be deprived of expert witnesses.

Mr. Margolis said he knows many lawyers are not aware that they can take this type of action. I commented that this should be brought to the attention of lawyers when they attend their continuing education seminars. Mr. Margolis stated that they've done it in a number of cases and it has been very successful.

Mr. Margolis informed me that his first job out of law school was clerking for a judge in the northern district of Illinois. He was also a federal clerk in Chicago for a year. After that, he went to Texas where he worked for the Texas Capitol Resource Center. They did post conviction work on behalf of people who were incarcerated on death row in Texas, both in state and federal post conviction proceedings. Mr. Margolis said he was there for three years. They were federally funded by the same organization that still funds the federal public defender offices.

I asked Mr. Margolis if he could tell me about some of his experiences in Texas; a state that executes a lot of people. Mr. Margolis stated that they execute more people than anyone else. He went on to say that there was a mixed bag of young lawyers, some right out of law school, and the organization that he became involved in was new and he said they were baby lawyers. Mr. Margolis said that most of the attorneys he was with did not come from Texas, so they were perceived as carpet baggers even if you happened to be a lawyer who grew up in Texas. They were considered non-Texans and he stated that it was a black mark against you, and they would try to make up for their lack of experience in this area of law by working hard. He stated they worked extraordinary, hours, sometimes 18 hours a day. Whenever you work in an environment like that, it is a great bonding experience, but it can be unhealthy. All of them suffered and some of his close friends went through really terrible times. For the most part, they were unsuccessful because the state kept executing people. They had some success and that would sustain them for awhile. You would be able to put off what appeared to be a certain execution and delay it for a period of months or years, and sometimes even secure ultimate relief and get a guy off death row. There were tons of cases that they worked very hard on, developed strong evidence that should have entitled the person to relief. He believes in other jurisdictions that they would have won. Mr. Margolis said that when they would lose and the person would be executed in the face of what they knew to be an unjust conviction or sentence, it would be very difficult for them. He worked for five years doing death penalty cases without interruption.

I asked Mr. Margolis if DNA was available at that time. He stated he started in Texas in 1989 and early methods of testing were available. RFL pee testing was available and they saw that in some cases, but RFL pee testing requires a whole sample of substantial size so you didn't see the kind of retesting that is going on now with people going back on old cases.

The emergence of DNA as a tool to ascertain wrongful convictions and secure the release of people is a phenomena of the next generation of DNA testing. The next testing will be PCR testing, which is much more sophisticated and uses a much smaller sample, and

Chapter 15 - Even more attorneys: Joseph Margolis

doesn't destroy the sample. We didn't see that explosion of exonerations and innocence cases until really the late 90s.

Mr. Margolis said that there have been a lot of studies concerning how many people were wrongfully executed in Texas, and it is a very controversial question. There are studies that have tried to determine the likelihood that an innocent person has been executed in the modern area, that is post 1976, and earlier years, also. There was a very famous study by a professor who is now in Colorado by the name of Michael Racliffe who, with another researcher named Hugo Eideau, had identified a number of people who were widely regarded to have been innocent but were executed.

A study was done in the early phases of capital litigation in the modern area, and there is a great deal of controversy about the number of cases of execution. People, who were executed despite significant evidence of innocence, had to do rarely about questions concerning their guilt. There has never been a case where there has been a definitive agreement in Texas, or elsewhere, that Joe-is aware of that a person, in fact, was innocent but still executed. There are a lot of cases that are very troubling in Texas and elsewhere, but the kind of post execution DNA exoneration has not come up for a lot of reasons. Many of those cases are old or didn't involve DNA testing or the evidence is not available. In some cases, the prosecutors are resisting the disclosure or release of the evidence because they don't want to determine whether he was, in fact, innocent. They want to just let that sleeping dog lie. In other cases, evidence has been destroyed after the person is executed so it is extremely difficult to prove conclusively, and you are left with these persistent questions. He said we do know that there are cases and he said he could direct me to where I could get these numbers. These cases reveal that there has been conclusive exonerations of people on death row who were carelessly close to being executed, and got a stay for one reason or another. We know that there have been, in the modern era, 103 or 104 exonerations. That is, people who were on death row, sentenced to be executed, but have since been exonerated and released from death row.

I mentioned to Mr. Margolis the work done by the Northwestern University School of Journalism and their investigation that exonerated a number of people. Mr. Margolis stated that he was delighted with the work that they had done. They were very involved in the case of a guy named Anthony Porter, who came extremely close to being executed in Chicago. The investigative group got a stay of execution because of his mental condition, Porter was mentally retarded. During the period that he was on the stay for his retardation, before the Supreme Court ruled that it was unconstitutional to execute a retarded person, he was close to being executed and, at that time, the Supreme Court would not have blocked his execution in spite of his retardation. The law has since changed. The group at Northwestern used that window of time to investigate. They were not lawyers or police officers, and not necessarily involved in the system. These folks, who did the investigation, were from the Medill School of Journalism at Northwestern. Mr. Margolis said that they were just kids and not only did they establish Porter's innocence, they found the person who actually committed the crime. Mr. Margolis said that was just the tip of the iceberg in Illinois. In one period, before Governor Ryan instituted a moratorium, the Northwestern group had handled 13 executions and got 13 exonerations. Of course, what that means is that 13 people were wrongfully convicted and released. Anthony Porter, the retarded fellow, was the case that was the most prominent. Hats off to the Northwestern University School of Journalism, those young folks deserve a medal.

I asked Mr. Margolis how we account for the history in the United States of executing so many people when they don't do so in other countries. Mr. Margolis' response was that the U.S. is in the minority regarding this issue. He says there is no country in the world with a civilized government that continues to execute juveniles, meaning people who are under 18 at the time of the crime. The only other country that does not subscribe to the International Law of Prohibition against the execution of juveniles is Somalia. Somalia, as we know, does not have an established government.[11] Life in Somalia is not secure.

---

[11] For the last 18 years, Somalia has had no government.

Chapter 15 - Even more attorneys: Joseph Margolis

Our isolation with respect to the death penalty is really remarkable. Why that is, is that the case is complicated. We have a long-standing infatuation with the death penalty and our enthusiasm for it waxes and wanes and goes through cycles. We are now in a time of re-evaluation. Generally speaking, the majority of people, if you took a poll would support the death penalty, however, if you put something in the poll such as "Would you prefer life without parole and the prisoner cannot be released, instead of the death penalty?" The majority of people prefer this option. I think it is because of nagging concerns about the reliability and realization that innocent people are sometimes convicted and sentenced to die. The realization is that this disproportionately has an impact on people of color, or people who cannot afford competent council, which leads to evidence of misconduct when the prosecution relies on false evidence or fails to disclose exculpatory evidence. [12]

An example may be an eyewitness who picked out someone other than the defendant in a line-up, and this evidence is ignored. Stories recur and enough of these accounts come out that people think about actually killing the defendant. Mr. Margolis believes that is why we are seeing a decline in executions.

Mr. Margolis continued by saying that you don't just find these death penalty conflicts in Texas. There is no public defender system in Texas, and that is one of the problems. Every attorney is appointed if the client cannot afford private council, and the majority of people with capital cases are represented by private lawyers who are appointed by the court. Therefore, the first thing the court controls is how much the attorney is getting paid, some jurisdictions in Texas such as Dallas, fund council fairly well. The result is that you have competent lawyers who want to take these cases and can devote the time because they know they will be compensated for their time. Capital cases can take literally thousands of hours and months of work, if not years. You can't do these cases unless you are

---

[12] In layman's terms, exculpatory evidence should be looked for by police investigators. This is evidence that may tend to exonerate the defendant. In my experience, police or FBI never look to exculpatory evidence, but it is their duty to do so.

Whatever happened to Lady Justice?

independently wealthy, or you are paid on a regular basis and paid a reasonable amount of money. Dallas does well and San Antonio does it well. So it is not an accident that you don't get as many capital cases out of those jurisdictions.

Houston, by contrast, funds cases in a very haphazard way. Some judges, who control their own courtroom will fund adequately. Other judges will fund poorly, thus you get terrible representation before those judges. I have seen cases that have been handled in two to three days, less time than you would spend on a gross misdemeanor case in Minnesota, and that is very scary. There is a lot of criticism about the south, but I have seen incredibly bad lawyers in California. So there are good lawyers and bad lawyers. The single most reliable predictor of whether a guy is going to end up on death row is the quality of the attorney. If you have a good attorney who is working the case hard, the guy on trial is most likely not going to end up on death row.

I asked Mr. Margolis if, over the years, he has seen much prosecutorial abuse or police misconduct. He responded by saying that the capital cases create this intense pressure on the actors in the system to secure a conviction and a maximum sentence that the law will allow. In a capital case, that is the death sentence, they are often, but not always, extremely volatile crimes that are involved. That is not always the case, but these cases generally create a great deal of antipathy and the public becomes inflamed. Often you will see cases that are interracial and, in some parts of the country, that creates a great deal of emotion. You will sometimes see quintessentially innocent victims, child victims, and this can be very traumatic, therefore, a great deal of pressure is exerted, even on well-intended and otherwise honorable prosecutors and police officers. I have noticed that we tend to think, when we talk about prosecutorial misconduct and police misconduct, of the road police officers on television who plot a circuitous route to frame an innocent man. That happens, but it is very rare.

Clarence Bradley, in Texas, is an example. Clarence Bradley was framed by an unethical police officer. It is a matter of record now. But this is not the norm. The norm, I think, is an indictment of the system. There are police officers who don't believe themselves to be

Chapter 15 - Even more attorneys: Joseph Margolis

bad cops, but who cut corners because they think they got the right guy. They let that subjective judgment cloud their investigation and as a result they don't look at the case objectively and independently as though each new day they are trying to solve the crime. They look at it as they got the son of a bitch, and how they can guarantee the case will be fool proof and to get a death sentence. That is where they make mistakes that lead to innocent people being convicted and people being wrongly sentenced for crimes much more serious than the crime for which they were responsible.

I made the comment to Mr. Margolis what I call this tunnel vision and, in the course of my 40 plus years of investigating, I have seen the total ignoring of exculpatory evidence. Margolis' comment was that it is exactly tunnel vision. They have this person in the back of the squad car and this is the guy.

Mr. Margolis went on to say that sometimes laziness is involved. There is a culture among police that contributes to the idea that whatever sort of excuse the defendant is giving them, it is some cock and bull story. Sometimes it may be a lack of proper training of investigators, and even a lack of adequate resources. I think that the police, particularly in major cities, have a very tough job and they have to stack cases on top of each other, and there is always a case waiting for them. If the case is not closed, the stack just gets higher and higher resulting in a great deal of pressure on police and prosecutors not to scrutinize cases more closely. That is one of the reasons why you don't shut off avenues of post conviction investigation because you don't know how long it is going to take for the truth to come out.

Mr. Margolis does not understand why it takes 15, 18, 20 years for a case to work its way through the system. There are a lot of reforms that have been put in place relatively recently that restrict the ability of a death row inmate, or someone who is doing a life sentence to come back and demonstrate his innocence. Those are misguided. They were born out of frustration from the length of time it takes for some of these cases to go through the system. Therefore, the government says they are going to put time limits on the process and there will be finalities so the victims can reach some closure. Those efforts are just misguided. First of all, it does not work. The cases do not move any faster. The longest delay comes from cases when they are sitting in some judge's chambers waiting for a ruling. That has not changed things. What it does, is it cuts down on the lawyer's opportunity to find the new evidence that sometimes can be difficult to uncover and to demonstrate a person's innocence. You do not speed up cases due to these misguided changes, but you do increase the likelihood that there will be a wrongful execution.

Like I have done with other lawyer interviews, I mentioned the Plookie Duke case where I came up with approximately 21 affidavits, including numerous recantations, but the 8th Circuit, without comment, simply denied Howard Bass' appeal.

Mr. Margolis made an excellent observation and talked about the very famous case involving Ruben Hurricane Carter, a champion boxer. He was exonerated while serving a life sentence in New Jersey. It is widely acknowledged that Carter was innocent, but served quite a number of years in prison. Denzel Washington played Carter in a movie about him. Naturally, his boxing career was over. Margolis stated that the conviction almost killed Carter, and the judge who granted relief in his case, granted a writ of habeas corpus, has since stated, after he retired, that if he were presented with Carter's case today, with the same facts, identical facts, that under the current law, he, the judge, would not be able to grant relief. Carter would still be doing a life sentence. Not because he is suddenly guilty, but because the judge would no longer have the power because the law had changed. How many other Ruben Carter's are there? That is the question that is impossible to determine because until you have someone granting relief, unless you have the kind of exonerations that you uncover that can lead to release such as DNA, some of these guys in prison are stuck. Mr. Margolis said that there was misconduct by the police in Carter's case, and jailhouse snitches were induced to lie and had false identifications.

Wewent on to talk about government snitches that were either paid in cash, or had their sentences greatly reduced for their testimony. Mr. Margolis said he had a case concerning a guy doing a life sentence in Minnesota, based largely on testimony of his informant. Mr. Margolis' client was Alonzo Ferguson and he was convicted

Chapter 15 - Even more attorneys: Joseph Margolis

mostly on the testimony of a guy named Johnny Edwards, who was an informant.[13] Mr. Margolis said Edwards testified in a number of cases at a time when the Minneapolis murder rate had spiked and was dubbed Murderopolis by the New York Times.

Again, as we have talked about earlier, there was pressure on the city to solve these cases and Edwards got in trouble and was looking at a lot of time for himself. He went to the prosecutors and made a deal to save himself time in prison, and told the authorities he knew all of these former Blood brothers and they all confessed their murders to him, Johnny Edwards. Johnny became the star witness in approximately a half-dozen prosecutions and all those cases unraveled. There were a number of acquittals.

By the time Alonzo's case came to Mr. Margolis, Alonzo was the only one remaining in custody as a result of Johnny's testimony. Johnny finally recanted and acknowledged that what he had said was a lie. We were able to secure relief for the client, but it was a terrible struggle. The prosecution fought to the very last moment. Judge Bush, in Hennepin County, granted Alonzo a new trial and the prosecution did not appeal that judgment. If you ask the prosecutors, I am sure they would say it was a miscarriage that my client was released. Even though Johnny Edwards was the key to their case, Johnny was not a reliable guy, nevertheless, he was part of the case against Alonzo. It is rare, indeed, that a prosecutor will say that they got the wrong man.

I asked Mr. Margolis if he knew Karla Faye Tucker, who was executed in Texas. She had been on the Larry King show, which was rather remarkable that he was able to pull that interview off, but I was quite impressed by her. Mr. Margolis said that by the time Karla was executed, he may have left the state. Mr. Margolis said, "I was in Texas for many years, when I represented my first client, Betty Beaks. Whenever I would visit Betty, I would frequently see Karla and got to know her. I never represented her, but we got to know one another."

---

[13] I interviewed Edwards regarding a different case while he was incarcerated in Stillwater. Edwards was involved with a gang called the Bloods.

I mentioned to Mr. Margolis that I saw the interview and she sounded like a person that may have been involved in Alcoholic Anonymous. On television, she admitted her crime, admitted her past horrid behavior, but she did not whine. She took responsibility for what she had done and she was doing excellent work on behalf of many of the prisoners. She was only asking to remain in prison the rest of her life. Nevertheless, she was executed. I asked Mr. Margolis what his feeling was concerning Karla Faye Tucker.

Mr. Margolis said he learned, and never had a doubt that Karla had a horrible life. The first time she was in an environment where she was physically safe was when she was in prison. It was finally in prison that she gradually started to become the person she was capable of being. She became a very different person than the person she was when she was out doing drugs and other things. Karla had been abused and, naturally, was involved with some terrible people before she was charged with murder. I don't say that this as an excuse for her, I say this as an explanation for the difference between who she was and who she became. It was demonstrated to me, and I don't think anybody doubted her sincerity. It just didn't make any difference to the state if she was executed.

Chapter 16

Women and the Law

Nancy Berg-The Polish Cannon

I call my dear friend, Nancy "the Polish Cannon" because in doing battle with her, one is liable to be blown away. She is smart and tough as nails. She is thoroughly prepared in negotiations and in the courtroom. Nancy is an acclaimed family court lawyer, has clients as far away as New Zealand and London, England. This is how we met.

Back in the 70's Nancy was a single mother. She had a son named Zack, who was very young at the time. She was trying to support her two-person family. She attended Antioch College on the North side of Minneapolis. Their main campus was in Yellow Springs, Ohio, and they had satellite colleges throughout the country. They also had a law school in Washington, D.C. The college in Minneapolis, accredited of course, was designed primarily for adults who had been out of the main stream. The emphasis at the school was law, justice studies, and sociology, and that was what attracted Nancy. She had been doing youth work in the area of drugs and sex education with teenagers. The director of Antioch College, Gwen Jones Davis, suggested upon Nancy's graduation that she apply to law school. I was adjunct faculty with a lawyer by the name of Bob Appert and Nancy was in our class. After she graduated and went onto law school, she worked part time with me, but she really needed a full time position. She went to work with the City Attorney's Office and went onto a tremendous career in family law.

Nancy is a great example of an individual who basically struggled and fought to carve out a professional career. She had no finances, and was supporting a very young child, but she didn't let that prohibit her from going forward. I asked her about her early experience in law and she told me the following: she worked a year as a contract employee with the City Attorney's Office and said it was an excellent experience. She was very complimentary about the attorneys she worked for, Bob Alton and Manny Serstock, stating that they were great mentors. She would go to court with some of the old-time

Chapter 16 - Women and the Law

prosecutors, learned who the judges were, met law clerks and did a fair amount of criminal work. Nancy said she really cut her teeth on the William Mitchell Law School sex harassment case. She and another lawyer, Chuck Galtier, sued the college, but ended up settling the case out of court. There were approximately 11 women that Nancy and her colleagues represented and it may have been one of the first sexual harassment cases in the state of Minnesota. Nancy said they were laughed at by a lot of people in the legal community and veiled threats and pressure from outside, influential people, were brought against Nancy and her partner. She reminded me that Warren Burger, who was a Supreme Court Justice, was a graduate of William Mitchell and word came out that he was very unhappy with this lawsuit. Nancy stated messages were passed onto her that her legal career would soon be over. There was a great deal of pressure brought to bear. I asked Nancy if she complained to anyone about this conduct. Nancy said that would have made things worse because the powerful people in the system would have denied that subtle threats were passed. She said she just lived with it. Nancy said that a lawyer is an officer of the court, part of the system and often the system doesn't treat people fairly.

When Nancy was in law school she stated that about one-third of her classes were women. She graduated in 1980. Today, about fifty-one percent of the law students are female. I asked her what some of the obstacles were for women in law school in 1980. Nancy said she believes the biggest obstacle was sexual harassment. My question to her was it by professors, fellow students, or administration? Nancy stated by prominent men in the legal community. I must add here Nancy was just knocked-down cute and is still an extremely good-looking woman. I directly said to Nancy, "Were a lot of men in the system hitting on you?" She said, "Yes, indeed." She told me she had one judge who would pat her on her thigh and told her instead of prosecuting hookers, she could make more money out working the scene. She reminded me of a judge who made a comment to a beautiful, black female lawyer, and his comment hit the newspapers. I personally do not recall the article, but she told me that a judge used basically the same line with attorney Pamela Alexander and she made a complaint to the Ethics Committee. The judge was sanctioned for that and Nancy said, "Can you imagine the courage it took for a young, black woman back in 1982 or 1983 to take on a judge?" Incidentally, Pamela Alexander went on to become a judge herself in state court, but is now retired.

Nancy stated that the women who entered the law field around her time also learned how to manipulate their way out of inappropriate come-ons by men, but the young woman today seem to be almost defenseless in those circumstances, which is very interesting. Nancy's point is, any young woman still has to put up with guys stepping over the line, and they don't seem to have the tools to handle the situation. It isn't easy to prove a sexual harassment case. We both agreed that fortunately things have greatly improved for women in all areas.

Nancy represents both men and women in divorce cases which can become extremely emotional. She stated that if you are looking for truth, you won't find it in a divorce case. She has seen people lie through their teeth, hide assets, and make false claims in an effort to have a spouse charged on a crime and it is all very traumatic for the children involved and extended families. Nancy did qualify that statement by saying, "Certainly, not all divorces are made in hell. There are many, many people who act in a civilized manner and have their children as their number one priority." Nancy states that is very difficult to find assets if they are off-shore. She knows this because of some international work she engaged in. She stated foreign banks do not make it easy. The United States government has a better opportunity than an attorney in the private sector. Nancy stated, "That in family court, truth is perception and we focus on what's best for the child, what's a fair resolution?"

Nancy described to me some absolutely horrible cases that involved false allegations, a lying mother having her husband prosecuted and telling her children exactly what to do in court. For example, in one particular case, Nancy said were the children told not to look at their father. One child was male, 14 years-old and the female was 15 years old. The boy looked directly at his father and mouthed I love you. The 15 year-old female did the same thing. After Nancy won custody for the father, who had been incarcerated for five months, the children told Nancy that they were told by certain people in authority that if they returned to their father's home country of Nigeria, they would

Chapter 16 - Women and the Law

have their genitals mutilated. I was damn-near speechless. I shouldn't have been because I worked on the Scott County cases which I talk about in this book.

Nancy said the various agencies involved have their own agendas. In the case that she illustrated, it involved the criminal courts, the civil courts, child protection, and counselors from the woman's home shelter. Nancy stated in that particular case, she really believes the woman who accused her husband had serious mental issues. Nancy stated that back in the 1980's, there seemed to be an unwillingness to look at the big picture because of all the turf issues between the agencies. Nancy stated that she saw some research way back that indicated children who had been put in "protection" by the child protection system had claimed that if an incident would ever happened again in their home between their father and mother, they would not tell anyone because they would rather live in an abusive situation than deal with the action of the state. Nancy said that no one has addressed that issue to this day.

Nancy stated that in our education system, we do not teach our students how it will be as a parent. She said we need emphasis on communication along with other instruction. Parenting after all is the most important thing we have in society and proper values and instructions should be paramount.

Nancy informed me that Minnesota is a no-fault divorce state. She believes this went into effect in 1976 or 1977. Obviously it wasn't designed to benefit one spouse or another. It was designed relieve lawyers and judges from the hideous task of hearing and considering the seeming evidence where one party had to prove breach of the marriage contract. This turned out to be a two-edged sword. She gave the example of a husband and wife moving from California to an affluent suburb in Minnesota. The husband spends a great deal of money to build a beautiful home for his family then discovers the wife was having an affair in his own bed, with the contractor. It is hard to explain to the man that not only does he have to pay her half the value of everything in the estate, but she is also going to get the house and kids because she is a stay-at-home mom and he's required to pay spousal maintenance to maintain her standard of living, therefore, the no-fault statute presents this dilemma.

Nancy states that family practice is pretty much still a step-child of the legal system. Very few judges are willing to sit on the family court bench. Nancy said that no one likes a divorce lawyer and she has had clients tell her that they would rather see a proctologist than see her.

I suggested to Nancy that family court law was maybe just too emotional, complicated and traumatic for most students coming out of law school to even consider it. Nancy's response was, "One must have a strong personality. By nature, the force of my personality is strong and I make it clear to the clients that I am captain of our team. The reason they are paying me money is for my judgment and direction, all based on the experience and if they don't follow my direction, they can look for some other counsel."

Nancy was on the Hennepin County Ethics Committee for 18 years. She chaired the committee for six years. It is apparent that she has a wealth of knowledge in the law. Nancy said that when lawyers get in trouble ethically, more than likely they failed to establish boundaries with a client.

Nancy stated like any profession, the law has its share of lunatics.

In the final analysis, Nancy does not blame the system *per se*. She states that too many parents choose to put their needs before the needs of the children. No one forced two people into the marriage, no one forced them to have children and no one forced them to get a divorce. Nancy said, "How can we ask a judge sitting on bench, who doesn't know this family and has a limited amount of time in a trial to hear all the evidence, which isn't even designed to get at the truth?" "The rules of evidence often limits certain things and too often you get this distorted version of the truth and the judges are expected to make a decision."

Marriage is a lot of work, but many people don't realize it. Our culture is fragmented. Many people are only concerned with their own happiness and that even when they get a divorce, they're still not happy. Nancy states, "There is no quick solution and we don't spend enough money on education, maternity leave, early childhood education, and of course, educating young people what it means to be married."

My suggestion to Nancy because she has handled so many cases, and has a fascinating life experience, she should write a book. I am truly proud and honored to have Nancy Berg, a Polish cannon as a friend.

Karen Hanson

I asked Karen Hanson what influenced her in her youth to become what she is today. Karen said, "I would attribute it to three people in my life; my mother, my father, who died when I was eight, but I knew a lot about his activism and of course a lot of it I heard later from my mother, and then my grandfather." She said her grandfather helped raise her after her dad died, but her father had been arrested several times after the depression when the Social Security Bill was being pushed. She said, "We lived in a railroad town. Of course, Superior was totally a railroad town — passenger trains going through there constantly. So my father would - he was working to get the Social Security Bill passed around 1934 and he could go into a park, stand on a soap box and hand out literature — he could do all those things and not be arrested, but once he went onto the trains, they would arrest him."

She said that it was after the depression and when her parents had very little money, her mother would have to pay to get him out of jail, but her father felt so strongly about it. Her mother and father were members of the Socialist Party, before Roosevelt, after that they became Democrats. She said her parents were very active in the co-op where everything is about sharing. They shared the profits, etc. She said all of them together had such an influence on her life.

Karren said her grandfather was very political and had a fourth grade education. She said she remembers when she spent summers with him and there were lawyers from Chicago that would come to spend the summers at resorts on Lake Superior, and they would come to her grandfather's house and they would talk about politics. She said her grandfather always made her a part of it. She always had to sit there and listen. She said he would turn the news on. He would wake her up at 6:00 in the morning with the news on the radio. He always made her aware of world events. She said she always knew what was going on. She said when she was in the fourth grade, that is when she realized that her views were different than most. She said, "I marched to the tune of a different drummer."

I told her that my grandfather was a delegate to Roosevelt's convention and he was a labor leader and got a dollar a year, but he was a quiet man. I recall listening to Roosevelt myself. Karen said that it was part of her every day existence, it was very important.

Karen said her grandfather had an enormous influence on her all her life. She said when she was in school her teacher called her mother one day, and this was when Chiang Kai-Shek was so famous and Madame Chiang Kai-Shek was on the cover of Life Magazine. Karen said she went to school and said Chiang Kai-Shek is the devil. She said the teacher called her mother asking her where Karen was getting this information, Karen's mother said," Out of the Capitol Times in Madison." She said her mother taught her not to always read main stream media that you have to look at other forms of information; it has to come from other newspapers. And then you have to learn who tells the truth and who doesn't.

I inquired of Karen about the years she became involved in protesting for peace, protesting against various wars and her involvement in other activities — humanitarian, civil, justice. I asked her when she first got arrested for protesting and what was going on at that time. Karen said that during her first years of marriage they were living in Detroit Lakes, Minnesota and the Vietnam War had begun. Karen said that she was sort of an outsider as far as politics goes. She said she would always be pushed into a corner because she didn't agree with most of the way people think. She would not have dreamt of going out in the street and protesting, as she said, she would have been all by herself. She said they would go to parties and she would argue politics and she would ask George why he didn't stop her. She said, he would say, "Why, you are the one making a fool of yourself," and because he said he knew it would never stop.

When George got a job at the University and they moved to Minneapolis, she said it was like heaven to her because she became so involved at the University and national affairs. She said she started taking classes such as history classes and then she changed her major. She first started majoring in East Asian Studies, but then she

Chapter 16 - Women and the Law

took a class in human rights issues in Latin America and she got totally turned on to human rights in Latin America. She said one of the professors she had for six different classes. She said she became very involved and started traveling to Central America, but during that time she was also involved in League of Women Voters. She said she was involved with them for quite a long time until she realized that she was getting tired of no action, just talk. She said she thinks they do a lot of good, but she was ready to protest and that was during the time that many of us found out that — and of course Lori was involved in this, too. Vinnie said, "Lori is my dear wife of many, many years." She said they first started finding out that Honeywell was making parts to atomic weapons and also making cluster bombs. She said when she was in El Salvador, she saw pictures of people's bodies ripped apart by cluster bombs. She said that cluster bombs are not meant to destroy buildings, they are meant to destroy people.

She said she remembers the first time she went to jail her son, Tony, could come see her, but her other kids had to visit her through a wire-mesh partition, but Tony was only 14 so the inmates on Saturdays could come into one room and play with the kids. She said Tony is now 38, so the first time she was arrested was 24 years ago.

My wife was arrested a couple times with Karen but was never sentenced to jail. I inquired that her jail time was at the Hennepin County Workhouse. I asked her what her feeling was about the justice system. She said that she was arrested 16 times. I informed her that Erica Bouza had been arrested along with you on a number of occasions.

She said the first time she went to jail was for one week; the second time they found her guilty, she went for two weeks; and then the third time that they found her guilty, she had an option of going back to jail, which would have been a longer term, or serving 120 hours of community service. So she said that is how she got involved with the Diabetes Institute because for her community service, they let her do a fundraiser for diabetes.

Karen said that after that many times of being arrested and going before a judge, you get to know which judge is going to make sure you are found guilty and which are going to believe that you are serving the higher good. She said you walk into a room and if you see Kevin Burke as your judge, you know it is going to be fair. She thinks he is one of the fairest judges. She said she doesn't recall some of the names of the other judges, but she said you knew that you were going to be found guilty when you saw that judge because if he had a trial by jury, they had a way of when you served as your own attorney, or pro se, when you said something on the witness stand he would roll his eyes and throw his head back to make the jury know that he thought you were lying. She said it is absolutely a stroke of good fortune if you get a fair judge.

I asked Karen if she ever went to School of Americas in Georgia. She advised that she has never done that. I asked her if she knew Attorney Peter Thompson which she said she did. I informed her that he represented some lay people and some nuns and priests who were protesting there.

I asked Karen when she was sentenced how the authorities treated her at the work house, if they treated her any different from a shoplifter, a prostitute, etc. She said the guards aren't any different than anyone else. If they hate what you are doing, they are not going to be very civil.

I asked her if there was anything that she or any other inmates did to upset the guards. I asked her if there was any example of what would displease your keeper. She said it is hard because the one way that they are so different from the other inmates and that they didn't really feel threatened by us. She said she never felt threatened. She said she was able to be visited by her state representative. She said the women that you worried about were the women in there who had nobody and were treated abominably. She said there are no bars on the doors, just a little opening. She said your cell is not across from anybody so you can't stare at anybody. She said a gal that was across from her that she had gotten a chance to talk to during mealtime, had tried to commit suicide one night. She knew about her and knew she didn't have anybody and she had been looking for her father. Karen said this woman had never known her father and wanted to find him and when she found him, he didn't want anything to do with her. She said this woman had tried to commit suicide and

Chapter 16 - Women and the Law

the guards had no compassion for any of these people. I asked if they were female guards. Karen informed me that they were female guards.

Karen said there was a woman next door to her who had pulled out all her hair and she obviously had nobody. She said she remembers she had set fire to something and so she was in isolation and when they would bring her food, she would throw it back out. Then she said if a guard went by she would say you are too fat, how can you even go out in public you are so fat. Then she'd be back in isolation. She said that anyone who would do that to themselves needs psychiatric treatment, they don't need to be locked up. Karen said when she left she wondered if that woman would be there forever.

I inquired if the other inmates treated her decently. She said they did. She said none of these people committed horrific crimes. She said when she was in there for three weekends, she went to church services to get out of the cell. She said she went to the Catholic, Lutheran and African American church. She said when you went into the black church, the soloist, pianist and preacher had all served in jail terms themselves and understood. They had a deep understanding so when you got into that room there was a lot of soul searching and a lot of dialogue going on and that is when we learned about the other prisoners. We learned more about them in that room.

She said when she went to the Lutheran church she and Erica played Bingo, but Erica had never played before so they started laughing. She said the woman who was running the church game, said," If the two of you laugh one more time you're out of here and you're not coming back."

She said when she went to the Catholic Church there was a lot of guitar playing and singing.

I asked Karen if any of these people got counseling while they were in jail, such as the woman who pulled out her hair. Karen said she had no idea. She said she never saw the woman out of that cell ever.

I asked Karen if she looked back on this as a positive learning experience. She said she does because you learn how people can get caught into a trap of criminal activity, or haven't done anything that bad and they end up in a situation like that. They have nobody. She said some of us are so lucky that we have family members that are there for us and that's what you find out. She said there are so many people that are suffering that are not bad people.

I asked Karen concerning her political activities or social engagements if she thinks that women should be more represented in all areas of society, not just in congress or city council. I asked her if she feels there has been improvement in better treatment of women. Karen said that the one comment she would have to make is that she believes there should be more women in congress, but she also said she has a sense that women are no different than men; power does terrible things to people. She said she saw that when you talk about prison and the female guards are treating women with disrespect, it's because they have that power. She said that is scary to her because some of the women in power have been just as evil as the men. I told Karen that there have been some great women, too. She said we all are products of our history.

She said she had wonderful men in her life — her grandfather believed in justice for everybody and women's rights. She said he was such a strong advocate and so was her father. She said her mother and father were very strong believers in the co-op system. She said her mother was a secretary and her father worked for the newspaper. She said when things were really bad, the co-op had a policy where only one member of the family could work and you could decide between the two of you which job was the most important. She said her husband was one of the first advocates of women's rights in the use of gyms in schools. She said this is her background and this is what she has been exposed to every day so she says she is not a strong feminist. She said she had some women judges that were not so great. I told Karen that I was surrounded by great women such as sisters, mother, aunts, etc.

She stated that she was an atheist all her life. She said she did go to church when she was younger because her friend's all did. She said when she started getting arrested and going through her trials, she

Chapter 16 - Women and the Law

got to know a lot of Catholics. She said she had one case where it was a Catholic priest and all nuns and herself. Karen said they were absolutely the most wonderful people she had met. She said her son, Tony, was having lung surgery and she told them before she went to the judge that this judge was going to find them guilty because she had him before. She said her son's having surgery and that she can't afford to go back into jail for three weeks so she said she'd take community service. She said the priest said to pray together before they went up to the courtroom. She said she thought they would pray that the judge would find us not guilty, but they all put their arms around me and prayed that my son would have a successful surgery. She said that opened her eyes to what religion was all about, that this is what it is meant to be.

I was raised as a Catholic and this is irrelevant, but I am no longer practicing that religion. I do recognize the good things that the authentic clergy and nuns have done. In other words, they have followed the teachings of Jesus. When it comes to the institution, forget about it.

Karen said she has been arrested with Sister Bridgette and others and said they are fantastic women — these women are saints. She said they have lived their lives searching for truth and reaching for justice.

She said the last time she was arrested was over the Iraqi war. She said you start to worry because you look back and you have 16 arrests, but 8 convictions which were misdemeanors. She said she never did damage to anything and she did it knowing full well that she would pay a price. She said you start to worry that one of these days that the next time it happens it isn't going to be that easy.

I asked Karen her thoughts on the protests over the Republican National Convention. She said she believes strongly that there were provocateurs that were involved, that it was a set up. She said she marched and there were thousands of them marching peacefully. She said now you are finding that out.

I told Karen that Peter Thompson had told me that the judge sentenced the priest and you knew from the get-go that the priest was going to be sentenced. I asked Karen how much she knew about the School of Americas. She said that she went on three human rights commissions in Central America. She said one of the times she went with the mayor, and a congressman, and because they were with us, we met with presidents of some of these countries.

I asked Karen by meeting with these people if she knew what they wanted changed in their countries. She said they asked for more money from the U.S. government.

She said they got a chance to meet with judges and there groups of farmers marching into town to protest. She said they saw rifles pointed at them from every direction.

Karen said they were going to visit a woman in prison. They snuck into the prison on visiting day to visit her. She said they were warned to never give up their passports. One of the people in their group could speak Spanish but they separated them from us and took their passports. Then they went to visit this woman who had been raped by the guards, had a child in the prison and had broken her legs. She said what they had learned by talking to various people was that a lot of the officers who were in charge of torture and the killing of the nuns in El Salvador had been trained at the School of Americas.

She said when they got to Nicaragua they went into a village where the torturers had cut off the tongues of men in front of their wives, had killed all of the school teachers that they could put their hands on who were teaching in literacy programs and all of the people that had trained these people. She said a girl told her that she went there recently and that they've changed the name of the school to make it sound like a technical college or something, but haven't changed any of their tactics. She said she doesn't know but would be very interested to know who exactly they are training right now — if it's the same torturers that are working with our CIA. She said it is getting scarier and scarier to get arrested in those places.

I told Karen that we could talk for days about the state of the nation and the terrible position that the Bush administration put this country in. Now the recession is worldwide and the Israeli/Arab situation, and we could go on forever about this. I asked Karen if she

Chapter 16 - Women and the Law

thought the articles of impeachment presented by Dennis Kucinich and John C should have been implemented. Karen said, "Definitely."

I asked Karen her feeling about Nancy Pelosi, not getting behind us. She said she is no longer a fan of Nancy Pelosi. She said she cut off any debate over it and she thinks Barack Obama is going to have major challenges to face. She said she wants to give him the chance to get into office, but there are some issues that we are going to have to hit the streets again. She said we are absolutely going to have to hit the streets again if he doesn't do something. She said one of them is the Israeli/Palestinian situation. She said this cannot continue.

I asked Karen based on her dialogue with people in Cuba, South America and all over, is it your opinion that most people just want peace and they want to live their life? Karen said that she's been to Cuba six times and the Cuban people always say they really like American people, they'd like to get along with Americans. It is going to be interesting to see what Obama does about this. She said she was just listening to Sean Penn who was just on Charlie Rose and Charlie Rose said I understand that you just met with Raul Castro. He said he's met with Raul Castro and Fidel Castro and Chavez in Venezuela-and he said our press has turned them into villains, it's our press that's done that. She said these people want what is good for their country and she believes that Fidel Castro is a benevolent dictator. She said it will be interesting to see what Obama does. She said the drugs they get mostly come from Sweden and we've stopped shipments and done so many things so they can't get drugs. She said they all get free medical care which people in this country should have and they all get free education and they all get the basic foods. She said she thinks a lot of people would like to live like that in this country right now.

I advised that there are 40 million uninsured for health and it seems national health care is working all right in Sweden, Norway, Finland, Germany, England, etc. The people I met in Brazil, Mexico, Europe and the Caribbean, they liked Americans but did not like our policies, the way the country is run.

Karen said she has people coming into her shop from all over the world because a lot of their kids are students here. She said they had their fingers crossed that Obama would win. She said there is hope all over the world but he's going to have to be a miracle worker, but at least the rest of the world looks at us differently right now.

I asked Karen if she felt that it is the alleged leaders, those that hold the power, are the ones that continuously make the world a negative place? Karen said she thinks it is very difficult and she thinks it is going to be harder and harder because you can't just blame your leaders, you have to blame the people. She said you have to blame the media. She said the latest news you get is that this is going to be the first generation that is going to be less educated than their parents and it's because education is going to be so costly that people can't afford to send their kids to college. The more uninformed you are the more things are not going to change. She said we can pat ourselves on the back by putting Obama in office, but how did he get into office? She said he got into office because the economy is so bad. If the economy had not taken a downturn then McCain and Palin might have won the election.

I told Karen the realization that people like Cheney, Rumsfeld, etc, have been lying and the problem with the American public according to Ken Keller is that they are really ignorant about what is going on in their own country. So many people are so busy working and trying to make a living and they don't take the time to evaluate the issues. In Italy for example, they used to have a 90 percent turnout for voting, and in Brazil you are fined if you don't vote. I asked Karen her thoughts about making it absolutely mandatory for an adult to vote. She said she thinks there are a lot of people that shouldn't be voting. She said she thinks they should take a test to see what they know because it is really scary. She said a lot of people didn't even know who Franken and Coleman are.

Pamela Spaulding

Pamela Spaulding, a partner at the Meshbesher & Spence law firm, was interviewed by me on January 31, 2005. I had explained to her that when I was young, as an investigator it was rare to ever come across a female lawyer. Therefore, I am interested in the explosion of women attorneys and, of course, in how and when she decided to enter the field of law.

Chapter 16 - Women and the Law

Pamela Spaulding was born and raised in Cold Spring, Minnesota which is a small town located roughly 15 miles from St. Cloud, Minnesota. She took the normal path of any student in elementary school, her school happened to be St. Bonifice, a Roman Catholic school in Cold Spring. She then went on to Ricori High School and after that went to Mankato State University. Her degree was in Political Science with a minor in philosophy.

Pam stated that there weren't any lawyers in her family. She said she didn't know she wanted to be a lawyer until she arrived at Mankato State University It was at the university that she first became interested in the law. She started out in a paralegal program. She was the first person in her family to get an education beyond high school, so college was not even talked about when she was growing up.

While taking this paralegal program, she became active in trying to get the American Bar Association to approve the program. Unfortunately, the program was not approved at that time. Her advisors told her that if she were to consider a career as a paralegal, she would have to go to an American Bar Association school or change her major. Her advisor, Dr. Hunter, at Mankato State University directed her to more of a broad political science tract and Pam said she just decided to go on to law school.

Pam first clerked at the Meshbesher & Spence law firm in the Business & Commercial Litigation Department working with Dan Boivin and Gus Nicklow. When she passed the bar exam in 2001, she was hired as an associate in the Personal Injury Department, because that was the department where an attorney was needed. I knew at the time that the market was very tight for young lawyers; the State of Minnesota does have a surplus of lawyers so Pam deserves kudos for being hired by the Meshbesher firm. Needless to say, they are always inundated with applicants.

Pam went on to say that she believes her graduating class from law school was 51% female, but that classmates she is in contact with are not doing litigation. Pam is a litigating attorney and she is in the courtroom on a regular basis, whereas most of her graduating colleagues are involved in transactional type work.

Pam has been involved in over ten trials and she informed me that the only female attorney she saw in court was from Chicago. Pam said that even though the numbers are getting better concerning women lawyers, there aren't as many females found in the courtroom. Pam said that there are reasons for this, as some women in the work force make the choice to be more active with their family and litigation is an extremely time consuming practice. Courtroom lawyers, during trial, are not only working in the courtroom, they are also doing work at night preparing for the following day. In addition, the initial preparation for a trial is very time consuming.

I asked Pam if she thought we had too many lawyers in the State of Minnesota. She commented that the number may be increasing because of the number of law schools. The state now has four law schools and there is always the possibility that two of them may join forces. Hamline University has a law school and, of course, they draw from their own students. William Mitchell offers evening classes and some day classes, but the undergrad base for Hamline is quite strong. The University of Minnesota would remain as it is. Pam said she suspects that if caps on damages go through the legislature, there will be more attorneys looking for jobs.

I asked Pam if the bar association would be able to get their side of the story out to the legislature and the public regarding limitations on jury awards for damages. Pam said that there are organizations such as the American Trial Lawyers Association that is nationwide, and the Minnesota Trial Lawyers Association that do some lobbying on behalf of attorneys. She stated that lawyers pretty much rely upon their associations to do what they can. However, insurance companies have far more money for lobbying, and they have great influence with the legislators. Pam said that the media seems to be listening to the anti-lawyer people and that there is a certain degree of hostility toward attorneys. She felt that when John Edwards, a lawyer of enormous success, was in the legislature he could have gotten the attorney's side regarding awards out to his fellow legislators and the public. She was disappointed with his efforts.

Pam said that it is quite amazing that the attack on lawyers and frivolous lawsuits has been very severe. The way they characterize some suits as being frivolous is wrong. Any lawyer is going to tell you that the last thing they want is to become involved in a frivolous lawsuit because lawsuits cost money, time, and preparation. If the case is not going anywhere, and going to be thrown out of court, it is a disservice to your client and yourself. Pam said there are filters set up in the system to allow valid lawsuits to go forward and the ones that do not have merit, to be filtered out. Of course, that is not what is being talked about in the media.

What the media talks about are lawsuits that have large verdicts and cases like the McDonald's hot coffee case. There were numerous articles written about the perception of that particular case and many stated it was not a justified lawsuit. In the McDonald's coffee case, information was not out there concerning the extent of the woman's injuries, and the fact that the judge reduced the verdict. In addition, the demand by the plaintiff's lawyer on behalf of the burned woman was by no means excessive. The insurance company did not want to pay so the plaintiff went forward and prevailed. Details of some of these large suits are too often left out and the public is led to believe that buckets full of money are being awarded for bullshit cases.

Pam states that she takes a lot of cold calls from people who think they have a cause of action. However, she informs these people that they have to have two things: 1) damages and 2) liability.

Pam and I discussed medical malpractice cases and she informed me of the following: In the State of Minnesota, there is a statutory requirement that you must have affidavits signed by medical experts within that field and they have to be able to define what the standard of care is in the particular case that you are presenting. It must be described if it is a case against a doctor how that doctor deviated from the standard of care and how the deviation caused your client's injury. If these things can't all be done, and causation is often a difficult thing to prove, your case will be kicked out of court. Therefore, it costs a lot of money to get someone who is considered a medical expert, and often times it is an additional expense where you may have to go out of state simply because in your own community one doctor does not like to testify against another doctor. The attorney needs to work with these doctors to get the affidavits to meet the statutory requirement and this entire process is extremely expensive. Therefore, medical malpractice cases must have merit before they can go forward.

Pam's firm, Meshbesher & Spence, has accumulated costs in the $100,000 area before even going to trial on a medical malpractice case. This is quite a sum of money so the risks are great. Pam stated that there are those people that would wish to do away with a contingency payment system, but this would prohibit the poor from hiring an attorney on an hourly basis. Not many people can spend out of their own pocket up to $100,000 to get their case ready for trial.

Pam went on to say that usually attorneys are having a difficult time getting doctors to write what they call a narrative report about the injured client.

The attorney asks for a medical opinion such as what exactly are the client's injuries, the extent of their injuries and questions of permanent damage. These reports are very important to negotiate a settlement on behalf of the client. Pam pointed out that certainly the majority of cases do not go to trial. If the majority went to trial, the courts would be totally overburdened.

The client has a right to know as part of his or her claim the nature and extent of the injuries. Pam said that it is ironic because the goals of the doctor and the attorney are to help the client. Once an injury case settles, it alleviates a great deal of anxiety on the part of the injured person. If the injured person is hurt because a negligent party caused his or her condition, then the only means of compensation is monetary.

Again, the public does not get all the information concerning personal injury cases; many are blown out of proportion concerning awards. Pam said that she doesn't have the statistics, but knows that the number of personal injury lawyers is very small compared to the corporate and Wall Street lawyers, and other areas of legal practice. The public doesn't realize that the lawyers making huge amounts of money are those involved in corporate contract disputes, the Wall Street lawyers working with the overcompensated CEOs, banking and many other areas. Some of the 'silk stocking firms' as Vinnie calls

Chapter 16 - Women and the Law

them charge $500-700 an hour and bill for every paperclip. Yet it is the criminal defense lawyers and the personal injury lawyers that are called ambulance chasers and hustlers.

I asked Pam if she could speak about a medical malpractice case that she was involved in that went to trial. Pam said the case can be discussed openly because there is a court record and she went on to describe a very tragic death of a child.

Pam said their client consisted of a family with a mother, father and two sons. The child that was the youngest, three years old, went to the hospital for a tonsillectomy and this took place in a small area hospital in Hutchinson, Minnesota. Pam said there was negligence on both the part of the surgeon who performed the tonsillectomy and the nurse anesthetist that anesthetized the child. The first mistake was that the surgeon made a certain number of cuts and ended up removing not only the tonsils, but the adenoids when the parents only consented to a tonsillectomy.

The surgeon had testified that when he entered both tonsils and adenoids were inflamed and they needed to be removed. The surgeon made a certain number of cuts, but he didn't remove the same number of pieces of tissue from the child and so two chunks of tissue the size of gummy bears fell into the child's airway and eventually blocked the boy's airway. The nurse anesthetist made the mistake of pulling the only airway, the endotracual, and when he tried to place it back in, he shoved the two pieces of tissue further down. Basically the child suffocated on the operating table and died.

Pam stated that they received in excess of $1,000,000 by verdict but in the final analysis, no amount of money can compensate for the negligent death of a child.

Pam went on to say that people should remember or think about an important aspect of a product liability case or a drug case. If there were not attorneys behind these cases, many products would be unsafe and there would be no one to make certain these products are safe. Lawyers can be bashed all over the place, but if it were not for attorneys bringing cases against manufacturers, drug makers, food producers, etc., where would society be?

Have people forgotten Ralph Nader? Ralph Nader went after one of the automobile manufacturers for unsafe vehicle and ultimately published a book titled 'Unsafe at Any Speed'.

Pam commented to err is human and I added to forgive is divine. Pam said there is some documentation that there are only a small amount of doctors who commit the bulk of malpractice. One of the problems is that doctors will move sometimes from state to state or out of their own community and their peers do not forewarn the next clinic or hospital that they are hiring an incompetent doctor; that this particular person should be watched over closely or not allowed to even operate.

Pam pointed out that the costs for medical malpractice account for less than two percent of the health care spending, but typically that is blown out of proportion by the insurance companies.

I asked Pam if there were any other specific comments she would like to make concerning the system and she said that she didn't think so. She said we could go on all afternoon discussing specific cases, but it would become redundant.

Pam then asked me if I got any good stuff. My reply, of course, was that I had and I complemented her on her being an excellent lawyer and told her it was just fun hanging out with her for a bit.

My interview with Pam took place some time ago and since then, I read a very sad account titled "Seeking Relief." This article was in the Minneapolis Sunday paper dated February 8, 2009 and written by Janet Moore. This pertains to a medical product liability case and a Supreme Court ruling which I find to be horrible. I am going to conclude this section by quoting from Janet Moore's article.

This pertains to a woman by the name of Liz Fossum who had an implanted defibrillator and it repeatedly shocked her heart. The woman said it felt like a horse was kicking her in the chest.

The 68 year old grandmother from Golden Valley now knows that part of her heart device, an insulative wire made by Medtronic, Inc.,

Chapter 16 - Women and the Law

had been recalled by federal regulators because a small number had malfunctioned, occasionally causing unnecessary shocks.

Months later, physically worn out and emotionally fragile, Fossum decided to sue the Fridley based medical tech giant in a product liability case. But a U.S. Supreme Court ruling last year — heralded by the Bush administration and the med tech industry alike — would have a crushing effect on hundreds of similar lawsuits. The high court restricted legal options for patients who claim they have been injured by a defective device. If the Food and Drug Administration, "FDA", approved the device following a rigorous review, the court said then a suit by a patient could not be filed under state laws.

Several hundred cases filed by patients who claim they were injured by the Fideles stent. They were consolidated in U.S. District Court in St. Paul. A federal judge dismissed them as a result of the Supreme Court's decision. Cases filed in state court, including Fossum's, by the Minneapolis law firm of Zimmerman & Reed now remain in limbo.

It was a stinging rebuke. Fossum said "I feel like I've been shocked all over again." The rulings have left hundreds of patients in legal purgatory, unable to get their day in court.

"The Supreme Court decision left consumers without any ability to get compensation for injuries caused by certain defective medical devices," said Representative Henry Waxman, a Democrat from California, in a statement to the Star Tribune paper.

The article goes on and talks about another individual who was so traumatized by his defective defibrillator that he ended up in a psychiatric ward.

To me, this is just an example of the attitude of the corporate world which has always been supported by the Republican Party. Considering who we have on the Supreme Court bench, particularly Antonin Scalia, his lapdog, Clarence Thomas and a few others, they are always going to support the rich and powerful.

The message to Mrs. Fossum and to the rest of us seems to be coming from the Supremes in Washington, "Tough titty folks, shit happens."

Christine Friendt

I was born in Lake Forest, IL and moved to MN when I was seven. I grew up in Ramsey, a small town near Anoka. I graduated from Anoka Sr. High in 1988 and at that time, we had the largest graduating class in the state with about 950 students. I went to college at the Univ. Of WI — Eau Claire and graduated in four years with a major in Criminal Justice and a minor in Sociology. When I graduated in 1992, I was unable to secure a job within my field. I worked odd jobs (pre-school teacher, waitress, movie theater manager) until 1994 when I found my first job in a law firm. I got married in May of 1994 and began my new job in June 1994. I was hired by Schwebel, Goetz and Sieben as an "office assistant." When I applied, it was with the understanding I would be able to move up within the company. Unfortunately, I became "stuck" in my position. I began attending paralegal school at Inver Hills Community College and graduated right before my daughter was born in December 1995. By then, I had left Schwebel and had a job as a paralegal in a small work comp firm, Meuser and Associates. I worked there for just under a year and when they didn't have enough work for me, I found my job at Meshbesher & Spence, Ltd. I've been with the Meshbesher office since June 1996.

My duties as a paralegal are very diverse. Basically, I am the client's "crutch" helping through their time of difficulty. I may be a counselor one day and the next I may be fighting with an insurance adjuster getting them to pay the benefits that are owed to my client. The next day, we could be in front of a Judge/Jury fighting for someone's future. I review cases, medical records, calculate special damages (bills/wage loss), investigate claims, etc.

I felt somewhat lucky to be where I am. I feel Meshbesher is a widely respected firm and that is extremely important to me. The attorney I worked for at Schwebel was later indicted for embezzling money from his injured clients and sent to prison. When I worked at Meuser, I felt there were aspects of the firm I did not agree with and didn't

Chapter 16 - Women and the Law

feel the firm earned the respect I wanted from my job. Unfortunately, I feel many law firms set the tone for the legal field and insurance companies.

Contingency fees, in my opinion, are the first step in tort reform. Having contingency fees in place, doesn't guarantee, but definitely, deters lawyers from taking cases that are merit-less. Anyone can represent someone who is willing to pay them(win or lose), but with the way it is now, where lawyers don't get paid until there is a recovery, it makes most of them think twice before taking a case. A law firm cannot afford to take on merit-less cases. If people could just pay a lawyer to represent them, regardless of whether their case had merit or not, there would be more frivolous lawsuits. Unfortunately, I believe the market is completely saturated with attorneys and there are attorneys out there who are trying to get started and need to make a name for themselves and may be more willing to take a chance on a questionable claim. On the flip side, having to wait years to get paid. It can cause some law firms to decline legitimate cases because they simply can't afford to hold onto those costs for 3-5 years. This can cause problems too. "Justice" has always intrigued me and knowing the difference between right and wrong can be costly, but I believe it is important. Insurance companies don't work for "justice", they are working for profit. Their mind set is "What is cheaper TODAY?" They are not looking at the big picture, they are looking at their bottom dollar.

Caps on non-economic damages places more emphasis on what someone earns than what they contribute to their family. For example, if President Bush were to die from a medical error, his family would be entitled to millions. But, if a stay at home mom dies (or a child) who is not bringing in any income, the family would be capped at $250,000.00. This would have to be spread over all family members. For the Republicans to preach family values as being so important, wouldn't you think they would want to reward a mom for making the decision to stay at home and raise her kids? If anyone thinks a cap would result in insurance companies just paying out the limits, I can't believe that to be true. In other words, an insurance company knows if a child dies and they are responsible, the most they will ever have to payout would be $250,000. So, what is the incentive for them to settle? They can drag the case to trial (which will take years) and pray for a defense verdict, but the reality is, even if the verdict comes back at 10 million, it would immediately be reduced to $250,000. Instead of reducing litigation, the caps would INCREASE litigation. The notion of "frivolous" lawsuits and capping damages is counter-productive. To cap someone's damages for a "frivolous" claim is silly because a frivolous claim will never reach that dollar amount in damages. The insurance companies bear some responsibility in this notion. Instead of "paying off" someone with $5,000 (the cost of defense), they should be taking a stand on those cases and setting a standard they are unwilling to pay when a case has no merit. Unfortunately, some attorneys make their living off these types of cases. Many of those, not all, are frivolous. This would in turn leave more money available, in the long run, for the legitimate claims. What Bush was trying to do is cap the catastrophic injuries (brain injuries, paralyzed, amputations and death) and those lawsuits (as long as they meet the thresholds of a lawsuit) are the farthest from being frivolous. If a case doesn't have merit, it gets thrown out or court or a jury would side with the defense.

Society and insurance companies are used to putting dollar values on things — I've heard "insurers have to pay for these extreme verdicts" — did anyone freak out when the Florida hurricanes destroyed homes that were worth 10 million dollars? There was a loss, and the home owner had secured insurance to pay for their loss. Obviously, their premium was higher than for someone whose home was worth $200,000, but that's exactly why we have insurance. We do not place a dollar value on a human life and quite honestly, because it's priceless. Hospitals expend many thousands of dollars trying to save a life and then when someone dies, the insurance companies try to minimize the value of that life.

The insurance/legal profession works both ways. Lawyers start high with their offers and insurance companies start low, that's just the way it is and both sides know it. It's like buying a car from a dealer—there is always room for negotiation. I think there is a happy medium and it just has to be found. If a lawyer starts off with an outrageous demand, the insurance company can't take that lawyer seriously and they lose credibility and vice versa.

Chapter 16 - Women and the Law

The justice system is NOT broken, but it has been abused by some attorneys and also by insurance companies. For the most part, the system works. There are so many checks and balances in the current justice system. For example, contingent fees (deter frivolous lawsuits), if a case does not have legal merit, a Judge can throw it out before it gets to trial, the jury — having 6-8 jurors decide on the value of one's loss keeps the verdicts "fair" — if you have one juror who says $1,000 and another say $1 million, they have to work together in order to come up with a fair and just verdict and that verdict has to support the evidence that was presented during trial.

There are ways to abuse the system and that can be frustrating. The legal system can be used to stall the inevitable and insurance companies use this on cases where they know they are going to have to payout millions. By "using" the system to get through the process, the insurance company has the time to make back their money through investments. It prolongs the agony of the injured party (or family). I believe the mind set of an insurance company is to frustrate the injured party into settling for less. By "dragging" it out, the injured party can't move on, the lawyers involved haven't been paid and the insurance company holds all the cards and the defense attorneys submit their bill each month and get paid for "dragging" things out. Even after a verdict, insurance companies will use the costs and interest as negotiating tools. They will say "we'll pay you the verdict if you waive your costs and interest." On a significant claim, this amount can be equal to what the insurance companies' initial offer was in the first place. They act as if offering $250,000 is a lot of money, but then when they negotiate after a verdict and expect our client's to just "write off" $250,000 in costs and interest, then it seems "reasonable" to them.

John Edwards book "<u>Four Trials</u>"— Wonderful! This book was an easy read and very informative. I could easily relate to what was being written because we've had similar cases and had similar experiences with insurance companies. I believe the book gives a lot of insight for those who may not know what goes on during the legal process. The news media love to broadcast huge verdicts and many times it's without facts explaining the case. People fault John Edwards for making millions, but instead, this book shows the hard work involved and the dedication it takes to represent someone who can't represent themselves. Mainstream America thinks you walk into a courtroom and just "ask nicely" for 10 million dollars. Most people do not understand and the number of hours it takes to prove each and every part of your case. People also do not realize that verdicts come from numbers "proven" at trial. Evidence has been shown to juries which justify why an injured party needs money (for medical expenses, wage loss, medical supplies, etc). An expert has to be brought in to prove each aspect of the case. Even an award on emotional damages has to be proven. Although, there are no numbers which can be given to a jury, an attorney still has to prove the loss was real and worth something. This may be the most difficult part of the case. This is definitely the most difficult for the injured party or family.

There are unethical attorneys, but there are also unethical doctors, chiropractors, insurance adjusters, corporate executives, elected officials, etc. Society loves to hate lawyers. We are an easy target and each time I hear of an attorney being unethical, I hope and pray he gets disciplined because they bring down the good we do. Unlike when doctors are caught being unethical, their insurance companies and employers "protect" them. The general public doesn't get to find out. I believe there are a lot of misconceptions out there about our legal system and until someone is forced to go through the process, they have no idea what it's really all about. The legal profession has a huge hurdle to overcome in order to get their message about fairness and truth. Controversy sells and people are intrigued by scandals. I believe the only way we get our message across is to continue to educate our clients, so they can educate their friends. We must, as a collective unit, continue to fight for fairness and truth and justice. We must remain honest and fight for what's right. I don't know how to change the public's view of what we do, but I sure know, the clients we help are always grateful. Our biggest cases — millions of dollars — they don't complain about attorney's fees, they don't complain about our services, they experience the "game" firsthand and so very thankful for what we have been able to do for them.

Summary

I do not belong to a mutual admiration society and in fact I am not one for joining clubs or organizations. In my section on women this is

Chapter 16 - Women and the Law

by no means a love fest with those I have interviewed or written about. The point here is the legal system needs and should always value these outstanding women who contribute enormously. I cannot mention every female I have met that works in the civil and criminal areas of the law, I can only emphasize the majority of them, are outstanding in their career.

Ms. Christine Friendt, a paralegal who I met at the Meshbesher firm some years ago is another example of a woman who understands what's going on in civil claims. Unfortunately she left the Meshbesher firm to take a similar job elsewhere but a position that would allow her to do much of her work out of her home. She lives in a suburb of St. Paul and has a long commute to Minneapolis. She is married and has two young children in the home so this lessened some of the pressure on her being able to do some of the work out of the residence. She's completely trustworthy, responsible and tenacious as many people well know.

Ms. Kathleen Weiker and Jody Spaude are cut from the same cloth as Christine, being well-balanced and always up to the challenge. The same can be said for Janna, Julie and anyone else I know in the Meshbesher office. They deserve support and recognition.

From Genesis until modern times women have been blamed far too often for the problems of this world. From Genesis to the inquisition women have been burned as witches and found to be powerless but having the ability to manipulate men into committing dastardly acts. This is a contradiction in terms, if they had power from early days on it would have been a better world and if they were easily able to manipulate men by their seductive powers it doesn't say a hell of a lot for a strong man. Around 1484, when many witch hunts were going on due to the Inquisition there was a hunt for these witches who were arrested and burned. There was a manual written in 1486 entitled, "Malleus Maleficarum" meaning "the hammer of the witches." The authors of this manual were highly regarded German Dominican priests. They were educated for the times in which they lived. They wrote that women were incorrigibly imperfect. "All witchcraft comes from carnal lust which is in the woman, insatiable." Bite on that, ladies, and even in this day we see women subjected to all sorts of abuse.

Whatever happened to Lady Justice?

I often wondered in the Islamic world when a martyr dies they allegedly go to heaven and are given 74 to 101 virgins. What about the female martyr, what the hell does she get? In addition among women in Islam they are not even allowed to pray with the men. The same occurs with the Orthodox Jews and of course in the Catholic Church women are virtually powerless. A woman has yet to be ordained and certainly in my lifetime I'll never see this. They have no input regarding Vatican and encyclicals, changes and policy or even minor decisions.

I can only hope that my daughter and granddaughters are standup gals, and will never let anyone push them around or physically or mentally abuse them. I am confident that there will be improvement in society but I am not confident there will be any improvement in the aforementioned religions.

The women I interviewed for this book work in the legal profession and they are just the tip of the iceberg concerning the outstanding women I know. We are witnessing a rise in the status in importance of women in our society and also the importance of women in other western industrialized countries. Unfortunately in the Mid East countries, women continue to be oppressed. In the legal community, along with medicine, business, science and government, there has been a steady increase of accomplished females in all those fields. We have seen in the last 25 years or so an emergence of women in sports and politics, along with skilled labor and technical areas. Our country should sing for joy over this as we need this talent in the world. In my opinion based on history and life experience, women over thousands of years have always been dominated by the males in control. Recordings of the past are called HISTORY not HERSTORY and this speaks volumes.

There have been women who have had the negative characteristics of their male counterparts, but by and large women of the world are not the mischief makers. Certainly I would not have enjoyed hanging out with Cleopatra, Katherine the Great, or Ann Coulter, but then again I wouldn't want to go out for a drink or coffee with Genghis Kahn or Hitler.

Chapter 16 - Women and the Law

It is my contention that if a male grew up with an outstanding mother, terrific aunts, sisters, grandmothers, nuns and female friends, he would have an appreciation for women and greatly benefit from those relationships. My lovely wife of 50 years, Lori Marie, has been a great happening in my life and, of course, I love her. My friends have often said, "Vinnie, how could you be so damn lucky to have married that woman?" Luck of the Irish perhaps, or maybe she wanted to take on a difficult project. My list of women who have helped me and encouraged me throughout my life is very long and I salute all of them.

Chapter 17

Hold that tiger!

On July 22, 2001, Mrs. Mary Hartman and her daughter Emily had gone to an unusual private zoo in Racine, Minnesota which is located in Mower County in the Southeast part of the State. Mrs. Hartman was interested in sponsoring an animal; this particular wild animal park was regularly looking for donations. On the morning of July 22, 2001 while being escorted inside the area, a tiger knocked down a gate and attacked Mary Hartman's daughter dragging her over 100 feet. This is the beginning of a rather bizarre and convoluted case whereby Mary Hartman was charged with a gross misdemeanor, several counts alleging a high-speed chase of a truck that transports wild animals, stocking and careless driving. My interview on April 27, 2005 with Mrs. Hartman will present the events and the status of a civil suit that she has made against Mower County for what I will call a great deal of hanky-panky within the system.

Mrs. Hartman, who needless to say, I called Mary, Mary Hartman – based on the T. V. series a number of years ago featuring Louise Lasser, one of Woody Allen's ex-wives. To be sure, Mary has been teased over the years because of her name, but she is nowhere near that fictional television star. I would compare Mary Hartman more with Erin Brockovich, who had a traumatic experience dealing with a claim in the civil arena and Ms. Brockovich had been battered around by the system until she obtained an outstanding lawyer who ultimately captured that elusive ephemeral thing we call justice. Julia Roberts made a movie about Ms. Brockovich and the film was excellent. What movie isn't good with Julie Roberts in it? The movie truly focused on what a remarkable person Ms. Brockovich was because of her tenacity and her refusal to cave-in to the powerful chauvinistic, corrupt and incompetent people she was facing. Mary Hartman was, and is, out of the Erin Brockovich mold, beginning with her seeking of information concerning the wild animal kingdom on a domestic level and rules and regulations governing the licensing and breeding of these beasts. Mary and her daughter returned to Bear Cat Hollow on July 22, 2001 to take part in a special tour by the owner, Mrs. Kraft. Mrs. Kraft opened up the animal pens and Mary

Chapter 17 - Hold that tiger!

and her daughter were taken to various places on the Bear Cat Hollow grounds. In the new cat barn, Emily was attacked by a white tiger that had been behind fencing in the new large cat barn. Mary said there were about 15 large cats behind fencing with about an 8 foot wide alley way between the cages. Mary believed the fencing reached all the way up to the roof top.

Mary said they were at Bear Cat Hollow for about 10 minutes when her daughter had been attacked by this whiter tiger called Como. According to Mary, the tiger had stood up against the fencing and the gate was leaning and it sprung open. The gate had hinges and pins, later it was discovered through investigation that it had been assembled improperly.

The tiger that escaped and attacked Emily dragged the child quite a distance in the barn. Emily suffered a large puncture wound in her back, was bleeding, and went into shock. There were other tigers that got out, in the area, the entire situation was traumatic and frightening for everyone. Mrs. Kraft, according to Mary, was obviously concerned only with herself stating "Oh, we are going to lose everything." Mary said Mrs. Kraft was afraid she was going to be sued and Mary said it was the furthest thing from her mind and on no occasion was a lawsuit or claim ever mentioned by Mary. Mary, of course, was focusing on her daughter who was taken to a hospital emergency room.

I asked Mary if Mr. or Mrs. Kraft, any of her staff, or her son ever contacted the hospital or Mary to express their concern for the injured child. Mary said "No, never." She stated she called the Krafts to see how Nancy Kraft was doing and also encouraged Nancy Kraft to come to the hospital.

A person by the name of Kenneth Aaron, who was on the Board of Directors at Bear Cat Hollow, phoned Mary and inquired if Emily had been screaming when the tiger dragged Emily out of the barn. This seemed to be a rather bizarre question to ask Mary. Aaron also asked if Mary would sign a waiver of liability for the USDA? Mary's response was "I don't need a waiver, this was an accident."

Whatever happened to Lady Justice?

The Mower County Sheriff's Department sent an officer to Bear Cat Hollow and the officer also came to the hospital to take a statement from Mary. The deputy was Martha Anderson who said she forgot her camera and did not take any pictures of Emily or photographs of the scene at Bear Cat Hollow, specifically of the gate, hinge, pins, etc. The hospital took medical photographs of Emily. No formal statement was taken from Mary, the officer only took notes.

When Mary arrived home on a Wednesday night in July 2001 after the attack, she phoned the Rochester Police Department and spoke with an officer by the name of Dwight Parker. Mary reported that shortly after the attack on Emily and when this became news on a statewide level, she received some threats that someone was going to shoot her. She inquired of the office how she should handle this because this was the point where her family was receiving harassing phone calls in addition to those threats. Mary and her husband suspected someone connected with Bear Cat Hollow and animal rights people were doing this mischief, the type of people who cared more about animals than an injured child that had been attacked by a wild animal. Almost immediately there had been talk about anesthetizing the white tiger that attacked Emily. That did not sit well with many people in the wild animal community.

To further exacerbate Mary and her family problem, they were watching the news one day and the chief deputy from Mower County, Teresa Amazai, was on television along with Nancy Kraft. Nancy Kraft told the news reporter that Emily was only nipped by Como, and that the tiger dropped her immediately upon command. There was only a minor injury to Emily, and that Emily was in great condition. This is absolutely a lie and the police report was erroneous. Regarding the gate that the tiger knocked down, later on in the investigation we learned that the hinge was not broken but that the hinge had been put on improperly. By this time, Howard Bass was representing Mary and he was her criminal defense lawyer representing her regarding false charges by Mower County against her. Through Mary's civil lawyer who was representing Emily for her injuries, he was able to obtain the hinge and pins— I personally delivered this hardware to a company called Twin City Testing. Twin City Testing does work in the forensic area and the final result of their tests revealed that the original hinge was not given to us. Bear

Chapter 17 - Hold that tiger!

Cat Hollow had submitted a new hinge, tried to make it look as if it had been on the gate for a long period of time, which of course was a false representation. Twin City Testing used an electron microscope and a forensic metallurgist who provided the report that the Krafts had substituted hinges.

During the course of our investigation, it was learned that the Krafts, Nancy, her husband Ken and their son had used harassing tactics against people who complained about Bear Cat Hollow. Racine, Minnesota is a very small town with a population of approximately 350 people, but they do have a city council and a mayor. Many people in the past wanted Bear Cat Hollow closed down because of the foul odor emanating from their grounds and also numerous animals had escaped from the facility and wandered around town. Mary states that there were about 19 animals that got out of that pretend sanctuary or zoo. A woman who resided in town with her family, Ilene Tjepkes, complained along with Mr. DeGice, but their complaints were in vain even though they attended council meetings. The mayor, Gary Landgrebe, who is now deceased having been killed in a helicopter crash, appeared to be a personal friend of the Krafts. Ilene, who went by the name Gidget and lived across the street from Bear Cat Hollow, stated that at least three times a week the mayor would be at the Kraft residence. Gidget, along with others, thought there was some type of a special relationship between the mayor and the Krafts because their concerns were never addressed, there were safety issues concerning the Bear Cat Hollow facility along with the sanitary and foul odor issues. Gidget requested Mary assist in gathering information pertaining to private zoos and animal parks and to bring forward the incident that happened to Emily. Mary was encouraged to attend some council meetings. She had attended a total of three meetings and at no time did she make threats against the council or state that she was going to bring a lawsuit against the Krafts and Bear Cat Hollow. Mary stated to me that after a February 12, 2002 meeting at Racine, the mayor would not let anybody speak up and that's when the people came to her stating she needed to help get Bear Cat Hollow closed.

On February 24, 2002, Mary picked up Mr. Clyde Boone, a member of the Racine community, and they drove to the home of Gidget to leave a packet of information she had put together regarding animal

Whatever happened to Lady Justice?

sanctuaries. Again, it should be pointed out that Mary was continuously being harassed by phone calls, letters, nasty letters to her daughter, and, in fact, her home had been broken into. Mary claims her computer had also been broken into.

Mary picked up Clyde Boone in her Subaru vehicle, was in route to Gidget's residence across from Bear Cat Hollow when she received a cell phone call from Gidget. Gidget exclaimed that there was a big semi-truck parked in front of the residence of the Krafts on a public road that was entirely blocking one lane of traffic on the road. The time was between 8:00 and 8:30 P.M. and, of course, it was very dark outside. Mary proceeded, but was cautioned by Gidget to be careful. Mary turned down Main Street in Racine, which would have been a right turn, approached Bear Cat Hollow toward Gidget's residence and she and Clyde Boone saw this truck parked in her lane, lit up like a Christmas tree. Mary stated there was a car coming toward her and the oncoming car had the right-of-way so Mary slowed down. The car that was approaching the semi was going at a low rate of speed and suddenly two men leapt out in front of the car. Mary said they had their fists up and they were yelling, one looked like the mayor, Gary Landgrebe. The car then moved toward the ditch along side of the road and then the driver accelerated, went in the ditch, then back up on the road.

Mary said she navigated her Subaru going around the truck and pulled into Gidget's driveway where she and Clyde Boone entered Gidget's home. Gidget stated she could hear the commotion on the road outside. Gidget immediately called 911 and spoke with a dispatcher. Almost at that moment, Clyde Boone received a cell phone call and it was from his son, Chad, stating that he was the one that drove around the truck on the roadway, reporting that two guys jumped out and were yelling. Clyde and Mary, of course, had witnessed the action.

Clyde Boone had previously told Mary that the sheriff of Mower County suggested to him and his family that they record license plate numbers of vehicles that they suspected had no business being in the area. They were also instructed to take photographs of any suspicious vehicles. Clyde's mailbox had been vandalized in the past

Chapter 17 - Hold that tiger!

and he, of course, had reported his porch being broken into by a bear that escaped from the Kraft facility.

Chad Boone knew his father and Mary were heading to Racine where the truck was blocking the road and he had taken a camera and a friend with him to get a picture of the illegally parked truck in front of the Kraft residence. Chad and his friend made an initial pass by the truck, snapped some flash pictures, went down the road to make a u-turn and then headed back toward the truck. When the truck operator and his passenger later that night spoke to a police officer, they claimed they had heard gun shots. This is complete nonsense, of course. A camera flash really makes no noise.

When Mary and Clyde left Gidget's residence, they pulled into Racine and parked on a side street that had a view of Main Street that led to the highway. A few moments later, the truck appeared, stopped at the intersection of Highway 18, took a left and proceeded south, quickly speeding up. Mary and Clyde were attempting to get the license plate number of the truck, but Mary stated she was less than mile behind the truck and the truck reached a speed, according to Mary, of at least 80 mph. Clyde got on his cell phone talking to his son and calling off mileage markers as the truck began to pull quite a distance ahead of him and Mary. Mary and Clyde had no idea what these truckers were doing, but she believed that Gidget's call to the dispatcher alerted the proper authorities. Clyde Boone also called 911 reporting what was taking place.

It wasn't long before Mary and Clyde arrived-very close to the Iowa border so she called the Howard County, Iowa police dispatch. Clyde took the phone and was giving mileage markers, temporarily lost contact but reported to Mary that a deputy was coming over and that Mary and Clyde should stop pretty soon. By this time Mary and Clyde crossed the Iowa border and they stopped a short distance outside of Chester, Iowa. She said the truck was stopped way ahead of them. Mary said at no time did anyone from the police dispatcher's office tell them to cease their surveillance of the truck. They told Mary to maintain a visual until the police pulled the truck over.

Mary states that after about 35 minutes of waiting, a police officer finally came to her vehicle. She stated she reported what had transpired, that they were told to follow the truck by a Minnesota police dispatch, and she said she believed the entire matter had something to do with the exotic animal industry. She also informed the officer that this animal industry, based on her research, had often engaged in illegal activity. She also told the police officer she had been receiving calls from a woman in Alabama named Caroline Adkins who we later referred to as the Southern Bell. Adkins was involved in animal zoos and sanctuaries and claimed also to be an informant for the federal government. Mary told the police officer that Adkins had phoned Mary reporting that the Krafts were preparing to move a number of illegal animals at some point in time. Adkins must have gotten Mary's name from the Krafts because Caroline, our Southern Belle, frequently spoke with the Krafts.

The police officer reported to Mary that he got a report that she had guns in the car and that Mary and Clyde shot at the truck. Mary, without requesting a search warrant, offered to have her vehicle thoroughly inspected inside and out. They had no weapons and were totally cooperative with the authorities.

The insane part of this entire episode is that Mary and Clyde were charged with stalking, harassing, speeding, and careless driving by the Mower County prosecutor. By the time she was charged, Mary had retained a family friend to represent her daughter, Emily. The civil lawyer phoned Mary and informed her that the county attorney, Pat Flannigan, on Monday morning after the Sunday incident that he was going to make charges against Mary. This is barely 24 hours after Mary and Clyde's adventure, and prior to any official reports being drawn up. It took 12 days for Mary to get any paperwork on these charges and the charges came by mail. Mary and her husband then contacted the Meshbesher & Spence Law Firm, and eventually met with attorney Howard Bass and I was assigned to the investigation.

Concluding remarks

There is a possibility that a news reporter from the Minneapolis Star and Tribune may do a lengthy story on the Hartman case and Mower County. Both Nancy Kraft and Kenneth Kraft have been convicted in

Chapter 17 - Hold that tiger!

Federal Court and sentenced to prison, albeit medium length sentences, where I am sure age of the defendants was taken into account. Nancy Kraft was sentenced to 18 months. I don't know what the status is of their scuzzy son, who has a criminal history, and in my opinion attempted to interfere with my investigation in Racine. It's unknown whether or not Mrs. Hartman will ultimately be successful in her case against Mower County, but several police agencies have been brought into this case. It's interesting to know that it took Mary Hartman an inordinate amount of time to convince the FBI and other agencies that something was truly amiss in Mower County, Minnesota. I would like to emphasize there are many wonderful people in that County just like every other County in the Country, but it only takes a few to totally fuck up a system. I will reserve comments about prosecutor Flanagan other than to say, he commuted down to Mower County as an assistant prosecutor, he wasn't cutting up in St. Paul, then he threw his hat in the ring, nobody knew anything about him, but may have voted for him because of an Irish name. In my opinion he is stupid, mean spirited, and abusive of the power he has. Mrs. Hartman, if she does go forward with her book, will tell you how I really feel about him and of course her analysis of this poor excuse of a human being.

There is a moral to this non-fictional story and that is never let people in power beat up on you. Perhaps I identified with Mrs. Hartman because I've always hated bullies and I am totally abhorrent to situations where people are picked on, dragged through the mud and sometimes wrongfully charged with crimes. I sued the Minneapolis paper over a case— which I am outlining in this book due to the fact that there were publications and lies about Ron Meshbesher and myself. Incidentally Mr. Meshbesher dropped his case because he is a public figure and has a different standard.

I went forward and the great attorney Joseph Friedberg negotiated a settlement on my behalf. I am not allowed to talk about the dollar figure, but that's not the point, they gave me money and the reason is that they were wrong, it wasn't just to get rid of a pain in the ass mug like me. That's a story for another time.

Conclusion

I cannot write or speak about attorneys I have not worked with. Nor can I justify writing about cases I have not been involved in. Historians such as Doris Kearns Goodwin, David McCullough and Howard Zinn write about history only after thousands of hours of research. This book is written about people I know and worked with and events of which I have been involved.

I will say there are excellent criminal defense lawyers in this state who I know only by name. Lawyers such as Peter Wold, Fred Bruno, Craig Cascarano and John Brink are highly regarded by their peers. Earl Grey is an excellent attorney who has had a great deal of publicity due to the nature of his cases. All of these lawyers are in the top echelon of criminal defense attorneys in a five state area. Bill Mauzy for example is now involved in the highly publicized Denny Hecker car dealership case. Hecker is being accused of defrauding one of the major car manufacturers out of many millions of dollars. Hecker is fortunate to have Mr. Mauzy on his legal team. Early in my career as an independent investigator I worked a number of cases for Bill Mauzy and he told me once that we had a great deal of success working together. That was quiet a compliment. I like him and I think he is a terrific lawyer.

Needless to say, these highly confident lawyers have used investigators, two that I know are Mike Grostyan and a gentleman by the name of O'Keefe. Why state the obvious, they must be very good at their work or these attorneys would not assign cases to them.

Most investigators in my area pretty much work alone, but the two investigators I know very well I have had the pleasure of working with from time to time. Jacqueline Stone who I wrote about in the Scott County sex cases and who is now a public defender investigator is absolutely superb. The other investigator is in-house civil investigator for the Meshbesher & Spence firm, Thomas McAlpine. McAlpine, who I hung a handle on and is often known as "Little Tommy Tinker," is a person who can get his foot in the door of a witness and that I can assure you is half the battle. On criminal cases it is often difficult to convince a witness to speak with the defense. On many occasions a witness who is supposed to be independent will claim he already

Chapter 17 - Conclusion

gave a statement to the police and would rather not go through it again. Tom has the ability to at least explain his position to a witness. He exudes sincerity and trust. People are generally comfortable talking with Tommy. He works primarily on civil investigations but on many occasions has assisted me in the computer area or when we are under a time restriction. He is always dependable and willing to participate. We also have a good time working together; his sense of humor is biting and quick.

Tom had been working in an administrative capacity 20 years ago at the Meshbesher firm when I first met him. We became friends and getting to know him I thought this guy would be very good as an investigator. He came out with me on some cases, and when a position opened up he asked the partners for the job as in-house civil investigator and he was ultimately signed on. That's the end of the story. I can only say even though he busts my hump on a regular basis, I love the guy, even though he has no respect for the elderly.

Who knows what the future holds in the American Justice System. My sense of this system is the government would just as soon see criminal defense lawyers fade away. The cost of a defense nowadays has certainly risen from the old days, more and more people because of the economy are only able to get a public defender. But the public defender's office is strapped for funds and because they are extremely overburdened, it's tough for them to hire experts and spend as much time and money as they would desire to represent a client. One of my second concerns about the public defender's office is many of these departments use retired police officers to do their work. I personally think there is a mind set among these cops that every person charged is probably guilty. But enough of that.

Often we hear the waverers, the propagandists talk about the United States being the best system in the world. How do we know unless we've lived under a different system? Sweden, Norway, Denmark, England, Australia, New Zealand, and Germany: all these countries have a criminal justice system and unless you live and work in those countries, it's absurd to take the ethnocentric position United States is the best. The U.S. executes more people than any other western world country, including Russia, for crimes of murder and kidnapping. Why is it that they did away with the death penalty in England? The

Scandinavian countries are not sentencing people to death or life plus on cases. I am certainly not against incarceration for crimes but our prisons are full of people that used drugs and were apprehended on several occasions but committed no violent offense. This country keeps stacking criminals or alleged criminals like cord wood and if you look at the statistics the majority of people in prison are black, Hispanic, American-Indian and, of course, all are poor.

The politicians that scream for law and order every time an election comes up give no thought to ideas about the correctional system that would be beneficial to society.

Alcohol causes more death by motor vehicle than should ever be tolerated in the society. The statistics are tragically overwhelming. Marijuana on the other hand does not seem to be a factor in the area of transportation but yet there are those that become apoplectic when someone says we should legalize this mood altering substance. In my 45 years as a criminal defense investigator I have never had a case where the client robbed a bank, raped a woman, assaulted someone or murdered someone under the influence of marijuana yet the politicians wee-wee in their pants when someone suggests this drug should be legalized and sold over-the-counter to adults only. My position is two-fold. The tax derived from the legal sale of marijuana for recreational use would be enormous. The second point is when you take the profit away from drug dealers, they have nothing. This may sound extreme but if cocaine were controlled and sold in a legal environment what would happen to the drug dealers? Most of them would really go under. Think of it this way, if I stood on a street comer and sold Hershey bars for the same price they are sold in stores I'm just not going to make a living.

Well, I know this, in my life time and the way it is in Washington, D.C., we are just not going to see any rational improvement in the Criminal Justice System. Sometimes I'm happy to be in the winter season of my life because it is rich man's justice, and that's the way it is always going to be.

See you next time I hope.

Appendix: Images and articles

This section contains a number of newspaper articles about Vinny's work, and photographs of some of the people interviewed in this book.

> Vince Carraher is one of the very best investigators I have used for over 40 years. He has a knack of getting even the most recalcitrant witness to answer his questions. His gregariousness is real and people feel it. I have frequently referred to Vince as the poor man's Columbo. He probably cracked more cases than Columbo – without a script.
>
> *Ron Mechbah*

Vinnie and his wife, Lori, 2009

Chapter 17 - Appendix: Images and articles

RUBÉN ROSARIO

Unproven accusations devastate a teacher

He says acquittal hasn't brought justice

At a workshop session on sex offenders last week in Miami, a police chief shared a cautionary tale:

"I had some young gals in a middle school in my city who reported they were sexually assaulted by a teacher, and I had parents demanding that I arrest this teacher immediately," said Port St. Lucie, Fla., chief John Skinner, who has 121 registered sex offenders living in his city of 140,000.

Mathew Curran

"Well, it turned out these three young ladies had concocted the story because they felt the teacher was a geek. That gentleman was devastated. ... So, there are some real issues out there on the part of law enforcement in ensuring that we do the right thing and conduct an accurate investigation."

He might as well have been talking about the plight of Mathew Curran, a 53-year-old former St. Paul schoolteacher now in self-imposed exile in Ireland. There is no worse crime to be accused of or shake off than child molestation. Curran, acquitted of such a crime this summer, knows this full well.

"I was roasted and ripped in the press, and my picture was all over the place before I was even charged," Curran wrote in an e-mail sent last week. "My reputation was over. I was devastated. My family was outraged."

He is a very bitter and angry man. And he may have good reason to feel that way. The troubles began May 5 when police approached Curran at Farnsworth Aerospace Elementary Magnet School in St. Paul and asked him to come downtown to answer a few questions.

Curran said he was stunned to learn that a 9-year-old girl in his fourth-grade class had accused him of fondling her during a kickball game on the school's grounds and on two prior occasions. The incidents supposedly took place in front of up to 26 schoolmates.

Aware of the severity and the potential damage such a charge can bring, Curran said nothing and asked for a lawyer. He was summarily arrested and jailed, according to the case file.

On July 11, two months after the arrest, Ramsey County District Judge Paulette Flynn acquitted Curran of fifth-degree criminal sexual conduct. There was no trial, as we know it — no jury, no witness testimony at all. In an unusual proceeding, both sides agreed to submit written evidence and have Flynn issue a ruling from the bench, which took about five minutes.

Justice served? Ask Curran.

"My reputation was annihilated," he wrote last week.

He felt very much the town pariah after his arrest. It led the night TV news broadcasts and made newspaper headlines the following morning. He was placed on paid administrative leave. He lost a friendship of 30 years. Most of the teachers at the school did not directly contact him. The teachers union, he says, kept a distance.

"One teacher sent me a postcard expressing support, but explained that the reason why she didn't sign it was because she feared reprisals back at the school," Curran said in a recent phone call.

He took pains to avoid eye contact at neighborhood grocery stores. When encounters were unavoidable, he felt the need to explain himself and the "absurdity" of the charges. He drew emotional support from his 22-year-old son, relatives and a small circle of teacher friends.

To an outsider, the case appeared weak at best.

Curran had no criminal history or similar complaints lodged against him during his 18 years as a teacher. He did have one previous arrest — for civil disobedience during a protest rally in front of Honeywell's headquarters in the 1980s.

Prosecutors insist dismissal of the charges was not proper in Curran's case.

"Our office determined there was probable cause to charge the defendant based on the victim's statement and the police investigation," said Jack Rhodes, chief of staff of the Ramsey County attorney's office. "Based on that information, the prosecution and defense determined that the case should be presented directly to the judge for a determination of the facts."

Curran's lawyer, Dan Guerrero, said police and prosecutors did not question or interview the many children who supposedly were present when the alleged molestations took place.

"That one just boggles my mind," he says.

The prosecution trial list on file is absent of any such witnesses, outside of the alleged victim's parents, brother, case investigators and the school social worker who reported the girl's accusations to police.

Meanwhile, defense investigators found a substitute teacher at the school who remembers watching the kickball game for nearly half an hour from a third-floor window.

The woman, who knew of Curran but was not a friend or acquaintance, said "she never saw Curran push a child to the ground or touch a child in any way inappropriately," according to the case file.

Questions also were raised about the state of mind of the child accuser, described in the case file as a "special education student with a history of behavioral problems."

According to the file, the girl had once accused another teacher of being a spy and once insisted that a football game between the Packers and the Vikings took place in "outer space."

Curran's move to Ireland was planned even before his arrest. He planned to retire at the end of the academic school year and had submitted a resignation letter two weeks before the allegations surfaced.

He says he had grown disillusioned about teaching and wanted to pursue a writing career — a lifelong ambition.

Although he finds fault with a system, a school district and news media that he says convicted him before a hearing, the one person he does not blame for his ordeal is the child.

"I'm not angry at her," he says. "Make no mistake. There are far too many sick and guilty adults in our midst perping against children. The question I am ultimately left with, however, is why me?"

Article in Pioneer Press: Unproven Accusations.

This is not the entire story, but reveals incompetent police work, frightened teachers, weak principals, chicken shit unions and school administrators. I had a tough time getting teachers to talk with me – the sub got the word out. This could be you!

Whatever happened to Lady Justice?

Investigator Testifies At Thompson Hearing

By J. C. WOLFE
Staff Writer

A principal state witness in the T. Eugene Thompson murder trial hinted recently at having been in the home of the slain Carol Thompson, according to testimony taken today in Thompson's appeal hearing in Hennepin District Court.

Vincent B. Carraher, an investigator for Ronald I. Meshbesher, attorney now representing Thompson, took the stand and told of an interview he had Feb. 12 with Willard Ingram, one of those who testified in Thompson's trial about the efforts to hire the killer of Mrs. Thompson.

Carraher said he met Ingram in a Chicago motel after he had been located there through a man identified as Donald Larson of Minneapolis.

The investigator said he tried to talk to Ingram about the murder case but "anytime I'd get into a sensitive area he'd change the subject."

HE ADDED THAT Ingram kept switching the conversation to the subject of sex and at one point blurted out, "I can see that Thompson broad now . . . and the sheets around her."

Meshbesher asked Carraher if Ingram had intimated that he was fearful of trying to help out in the Thompson appeal. The witness replied: "He said to me, 'What if I attacked your wife? You'd want to kill me, wouldn't you?'"

The investigator said Ingram then added, "If Thompson ever gets out, I'll get killed."

The present hearing of the one-time St. Paul lawyer, who was convicted in 1963 of having his wife killed, is based in part on the claim that state witnesses, including Ingram, offered false testimony in return for leniency in criminal cases against them.

Another of those was Dick W. C. Anderson, the confessed slayer, who said he was paid for the job by Norman J. Mastrian, later convicted as the middleman in the conspiracy.

Carraher said Ingram told him he knew Anderson and had been on several burglaries with him. He also said Ingram claimed he hated Mastrian "because I was cheated out of $40,000 worth of ice in a jewelry burglary."

Ramsey County Atty. Wil-
Turn to Page 2, Col. 4

Article about Vinnie testifying in the Thompson Case.

Chapter 17 - Appendix: Images and articles

1996 MPLS article on Vinny.

Grand Jury Make-up Criticized in Motion

By GWENYTH JONES
Minneapolis Star Staff Writer

More than 40 per cent of the last Hennepin County Grand Jury consisted of corporation officers or high executives, the attorney for a Minneapolis man accused of murder alleged today.

The Grand Jury, which completed its six-month term last week, had indicted Dr. John R. Mitchell, 34, 5601 Woodlawn Blvd., for first-degree murder in the death last Christmas night of his wife, Nancy, 34.

Mitchell's attorney, Ronald Meshbesher, challenged the indictment on the ground that the Grand Jury did not represent a cross-section of the community. His challenge will be argued before District Judge Thomas Tallakson, April 4.

In an affidavit attached to the motion, Vincent R. Carraher, an investigator for Meshbesher, said he was able to determine the occupations of all but 12 of the 120 persons on the master list from which the Grand Jury was chosen by lot. He found occupations of all 23 persons who actually served on that Grand Jury, he said.

Of the Grand Jury members, Carraher said, five, or 21.8 per cent, were corporation presidents, or vice-presidents, five were "corporation executives or high officers," and five were union executives or business agents.

Of three housewives on the jury, Carraher said, one was the wife of a corporation president, another the wife of a union executive.

Other jury members were two retired persons, one wage earner (a mechanic), a

Meshbesher

University of Minnesota office manager, and a real estate investor.

Of the 120-member jury panel, Carraher said, 22, or 18 per cent, were corporation presidents; 23 were vice-presidents or other high executives of corporations; six were self-employed proprietors of businesses; 15 were union executives;; 13 were retired with their former occupations unascertained; four were school principals, teachers or professors; one was a special agent of the Internal union executives; 13 were retired airlines mechanic, and 14 were housewives.

Of the housewives, eight were wives of professional men or business or union executives, Carraher said. There were no unskilled laborers on the panel.

Meshbesher's motion argued that Carraher's analysis indicated that the "vast majority" of the names put on the master panel by district court judges, and of those actually named to grand juries, are persons from "higher than average social and economic strata."

Meshbesher said that in the last six years the names of 101 persons have been put on the master panel at least twice, 49 persons at least three times, 16 persons four times and two persons five times.

One person has been named to the grand jury four times in the last 10 years, Meshbesher said.

Whatever happened to Lady Justice?

Private eyes: Glitz and glamour are rare

Although most private detectives work in areas of insurance fraud or personal injury, some investigators, such as Vincent Carraher (left), specialize in criminal cases. Carraher has worked on some of Minnesota's most infamous cases, including the Virginia Piper kidnapping and the Elizabeth Congdon murders. Here, he confers with defense attorney Ron Meshbesher at Meshbesher's office.

By Sheila Evertz

The trench-coated figure sits alone at the dingy nightclub bar. Working in the hazy underworld of intrigue and glamour, the slick private eye lights a cigarette and takes a drag. A distant foghorn blows. Then she walks in.

He squints and takes a long, hard look at the tall, cool blonde. He has seen her somewhere before.

Cut.

The lives of private detectives still make great grist for the movie and television mill. Writers will probably never stop grinding out scripts featuring Sam Spades, Philip Marlowes and Mike Hammers. They're the ones with the questionable pasts, full of larcenous possibilities.

They're also fictional.

About 235 private detectives are licensed by the state of Minnesota, according to Marie Ohman, administrator of the state's Private Investigator and Protective Agent Servicing Board. But of those real private eyes, few are as exciting as their television counterparts.

There just aren't any real Maddie Hayeses or David Addisons moonlighting among the shadows and back alleys of Downtown.

Minneapolis private investigator Scott Harr said his job is the most misunderstood profession in the world. "And it's because of TV. We're always battling these misconceptions. It's not (like) detective shows. It's not glamorous."

True-life detective work may not be as glamorous as television portrays it, but it still can be satisfying and exciting, according to local private eyes.

Article about Vinny in Skyway News, 1987 (page 1). Pages 2 & 3 follow.

Chapter 17 - Appendix: Images and articles

Private eyes

From Page 1

Minneapolis private detective Vincent Carraher has helped solve some of the most infamous cases in Minnesota, including the Virginia Piper kidnapping case and the Elizabeth Congdon murder.

Another Minneapolis detective, LarriAnn Hartman-Mosedale, occasionally goes on tense foot chases with two of her four yelping bloodhounds, all certified man-trailers, to track down missing people or missing bodies. She carries tiny cameras and listening devices and has small peepholes drilled into her van.

Still, the majority of private detectives in the Twin Cities are just typical family and business people, Ohman said, and most specialize in such areas as personal injury or insurance fraud.

Most, but not all. Some of the cases Carraher takes on involve violent crime. That's fine with him. A former insurance adjuster, he gave up the job to work as an investigator for Ron Meshbesher during the local defense attorney's early years.

After 11 years with Meshbesher, Carraher left the firm because he spent too much time on cases dealing with personal injury rather than crime. Now he conducts criminal investigations for some of Minneapolis' most prominent legal firms, including Meshbesher, Singer & Spence Ltd.

Carraher's first big investigation came in the early '60s with the case of the late Jack Mitchell. Mitchell, a chiropractor accused of strangling his wife and burning his house down, was convicted of manslaughter. He insisted he was innocent; Carraher believed him.

"I was chastised by Ronnie (Meshbesher) for becoming too involved with the case," Carraher said.

Despite Meshbesher's criticism, Carraher still becomes emotionally engaged in his cases.

"Vince is a good guy. People trust him and confide in him," Meshbesher said about his friend. "But he's too sympathetic. I've seen him cry at trials." Meshbesher said no one does better work than Carraher. His dogged efforts have produced clues, evidence and witnesses that have often tipped the scales of justice in favor of the defense.

Carraher feels that too often the scales are loaded on the side of the state; he is critical of the jury system, arguing that the brightest people never serve on a jury and that the prosecution has more power than the defense. So impassioned are his views on the American justice system that he is writing a book about them.

"The government is so powerful. They have so many resources," Carraher said. "I don't want to sound like a Don Quixote. . . . They refuse to let me just go out and work within the system. That just [angers] me and I work all the harder."

Although Carraher said he must struggle harder than the prosecution to unveil new information, his resources are many. Private detective Harr, who sometimes teams up with Carraher for a case, said no matter where the two go, Carraher seems to know everybody. Carraher said he has friends all over, including the police department.

Television detectives are often depicted as having an adversarial relationship with the cops. That portrayal isn't always accurate, at least not in Minneapolis, according to Randy Spence, a law student and staff investigator for Meshbesher's firm.

The Minneapolis police share information and cooperate with defense investigators, even though they have busy schedules, Spence said.

Minneapolis Police Chief Tony Bouza said he has had no problem with local private investigators. "Our paths hardly cross," he said. "There is no Sam Spade problem in our town."

Although the work is similar, police detectives and private detectives cannot do their jobs the same way, Bouza said, noting that private investigators are freer to conduct investigations than are the police.

"We can only do what the law empowers us to do," Bouza said. "An individual has a right to disappear on his own. We can't go looking for someone's 25-year-old daughter."

Meshbesher disagreed, saying it is the police who have greater freedom in conducting investigations and can get information to which private citizens are not privy.

Private investigators cite the Minnesota Data Privacy Act as an example of a law that often hampers the ability to gather information. The 19?? law prohibits the public from gainin? certain information about priva? citizens. Minnesota police, howeve? can employ a provision of the act th? grants them access to confidenti? information during an investigation

Legal considerations aside, secret? following someone around can al? present ethical issues.

In March, St. Paul city officials hired? private investigator to follow tv? building inspectors who we?

Private investigator LarriAnn Hartman-Mosedale and Ralph, one of her four "certified" man-trailing bloodhounds, are often hired by outstate police departments to find missing evidence and missing bodies.

Whatever happened to Lady Justice?

Private investigator John Jones dusts a telephone for fingerprints.

Tiny cameras, tape recorders and listening devices are all part of LarriAnn Hartman-Mosedale's arsenal to gather evidence and information.

Minneapolis private investigator Scott Harr does research in defense attorney Ron Meshbesher's office library. Harr worked as an investigator for Meshbesher while attending law school, but gave up a law career to start his own investigative agency.

Finding a faster way to make money is important to private detectives. In Minneapolis most investigators charge from $25 to $50 an hour, plus expenses. But for many investigators, clients can be few and far between. To defray costs and for convenience, some detectives, like Harr, work out of their homes.

Many Minneapolis agencies are one-person shops, said Ohman of the state board of investigators. But some investigators have as many as 20 people working for them.

Most people who apply for a license are starting their second or third careers, and many are former law-enforcement officers or insurance investigators. Because the Minnesota board requires that applicants have three years of investigating experience before it will issue them a $500 private investigator's license, former police officers and FBI and CIA agents often have an edge.

Some investigators say police officers don't make good detectives. Jones thinks they can be too aggressive.

"Police officers get an authoritarian-type attitude," he said. "An investigator needs to be gentle — be able to get people to open up."

Harr, a former police officer, agreed that social skills in the business are far more important than brute interrogation, but he disagrees that cops make poor investigators.

Harr, 30, left police work to attend William Mitchell College of Law. While a student, he was an investigator in Meshbesher's office. After passing his bar exams last year, he passed up the law career and began an investigative agency at his Bloomington home.

Besides the license fee, a new investigator must also post a $5,000 bonding fee and must pass a test of character and integrity, Ohman said.

The last requirement for licensing states that an applicant must not have any felony convictions or weapons charges on record.

The Minneapolis Police Department does not know how many local private detectives carry guns. But laws regulating gun use by private detectives aren't any different than for a private citizen, said Sgt. Glen Lang of the department's licensing division. The chief of police issues handgun licenses on an individual basis, for employment or personal safety purposes only.

Carraher and Harr both said they don't like guns and don't carry them. There have only been a couple of incidents where either of them felt he was in danger.

Carraher said he has rarely been frightened. During the male prostitution case that centered on Judge Crane Winton, a young lover involved in the case called and threatened Carraher's daughter. The threat didn't scare the investigator; it made him furious.

Another time he had a client in prison who threatened him, but that didn't shake him either. "He was just a bully boy," Carraher said.

The people who do make him nervous, Carraher said, are professional drug dealers. "They're notorious for snitching; they'd snitch on their mothers," he said. "And they're dangerous."

But not even drug dealers dampen Carraher's enthusiasm for his work. "They're the most noxious subculture of person I've ever come across — but I'll help defend them."

suspected of conducting private business on public time. The detective found no evidence of wrongdoing, but union representatives for the inspectors criticized the city for spying on its own employees. They said supervisors, not private detectives, should have investigated the employees' behavior.

Private detectives say they don't judge their clients' motives. They say they are simply finding facts and digging up clues. They have no control over how those facts are used once they are uncovered.

"I never feel bad about my work," said Mosedale-Hartman, owner of Bloodhound Investigations. 3054 Bloomington Ave. Before Mosedale-Hartman accepts a client, she tells him to get legal advice first. "Anything I turn up is going to probably end up in court anyway."

Domestic cases are considered the stickiest of investigations. Investigators like Carraher and Harr won't touch them. Still, the cases remain fairly common. Even with no-fault divorce, husbands and wives still have each other followed.

John Jones, a Minneapolis private detective for 25 years, will occasionally take a domestic case.

"No-fault divorce has not changed the types of cases that I get," Jones said. "When a woman has her husband followed, she still asks the one question women asked me 20 years ago: 'What does she look like?'"

Private detectives now specialize in new areas such as computer theft and computer espionage. Mosedale-Hartmann said. Such specialties can be lucrative.

Chapter 17 - Appendix: Images and articles

THE MINNEAPOLIS STAR
Mon., Jan. 12, 1970

State weighs Dr. Mitchell parole plea

The Minnesota Pardon Board today took under consideration the request for parole by Dr. John Mitchell, a Minneapolis chiropractor convicted in 1967 of killing his wife.

Ronald Meshbesher, attorney for Dr. Mitchell, presented to the board the results of a lie detector test given to Dr. Mitchell last summer by members of the University of Minnesota police department.

Lt. A. G. Kirby of the university police told the pardon board that he and three other test examiners all agreed that the results of Dr. Mitchell's test indicated he was telling the truth when he said he had not killed his wife, Nancy.

Mrs. Mitchell's body was found in the family home Christmas Day 1966, shortly after a fire broke out in the dwelling.

Medical evidence presented at the trial indicated that she died of strangulation. Dr. Mitchell denied he had strangled his wife and suggested she had strangled herself.

He was convicted of first-degree manslaughter and sentenced to 15 years in Stillwater Prison.

His appeal of the conviction was turned down by the Minnesota Supreme Court.

Meshbesher also presented three witnesses to the board who had not testified at the trial.

The witnesses, all acquaintances of Mrs. Mitchell, said that in the months shortly before her death, Mrs. Mitchell often spoke of death and her intent, if she was going to die, to take her husband and child with her.

Members of the pardon board are Gov. Harold LeVander, Chief Justice Oscar Knutson, and Atty. Gen. Douglas Head.

Pardon Board Hints It Won't Accept Lie Test From Mitchell

By BOB LUNDEGAARD
Minneapolis Tribune Staff Writer

The Minnesota Board of Pardons dropped some strong hints Monday that it would reject John Mitchell's request for a pardon.

The Minneapolis chiropractor, serving a 15-year sentence for manslaughter in the 1966 strangling of his wife, sought the pardon on grounds that he passed a lie-detector test last July.

"This seems to be an extraordinary request," Gov. Harold LeVander remarked to Mitchell's attorney, Ronald Meshbesher. "You want us to release him on evidence that no court has ruled admissible."

Meshbesher said there was no other place to turn. He added that Mitchell has maintained his innocence.

"Well, don't they all?" asked Chief Judge Oscar Knutson, another board member.

"But there were no witnesses to the crime. He has no other way of demonstrating his innocence," said Meshbesher.

"That's true of 99 percent of criminal cases," replied Judge Kutson. "There usually aren't any witnesses to murder."

Meshbesher also called on several witnesses for "corroboration" of the test results. In general they said that Nancy Mitchell was despondent shortly before her death and had threatened to kill herself.

"Why didn't you offer this during the trial?" Judge Knutson asked of one woman who appeared before the Pardons board. "You knew this case was going on. The papers were full of it."

When the chief judge had finished, Atty. Gen. Douglas Head, the third board member, gently suggested to the witness, "Maybe you could complete what you were going to say."

An Edina dentist who had known Nancy Mitchell for years, Dr. Raymond Peterson, said she had "constant premonitions" about death and told him she was "not going to die alone."

He said he related the conversations to investigators from Meshbesher's own law office but was never called to testify at Mitchell's trial. However, his daughter said she testified to substantially the same conversations.

"Apparently the jury didn't believe you," said Judge Knutson.

"That's a little harsh," interjected Head. "There's not necessarily anything inconsistent."

He suggested that the jury might have believed that Mrs. Mitchell had such premonitions but that she still had been strangled.

The board took the application under advisement.

THE MINNEAPOLIS TRIBUNE
Tues., Jan. 13, 1970

ST. PAUL DISPATCH
Fri., Jan. 16, '70

Dr. Mitchell Fails To Get Pardon

The state Board of Pardons today denied a request for a full pardon for Dr. John Mitchell, Minneapolis chiropractor who was convicted for the 1966 strangling of his wife.

Mitchell had asked for the pardon at the board's meeting last Monday.

His lawyer sought the pardon based on evidence that Mitchell had passed a lie-detector test administered last July in Stillwater State Prison where he is serving a sentence of up to 15 years for the first-degree manslaughter conviction.

Commenting on its denial, the Pardon Board said: "A polygraph test (lie detector) is not acceptable in court as evidence and until it is, the case having been tried by a jury and reviewed by the Supreme Court, the Board of Pardons is in no position to grant a pardon on this basis."

The Pardon Board consists of the governor, the attorney general and the Minnesota chief justice. To grant a pardon all members of the board must agree.

The lie-detector test given to Mitchell was conducted by two University of Minnesota police officers who are qualified to give the tests.

Mitchell's lawyer, Ronald Meshbesher of Minneapolis, said Mitchell's responses to questions during the test proved he did not slay his wife, Nancy.

Articles on Dr. Mitchell, 1970

Whatever happened to Lady Justice?

Supersnitch Scandal:

DRC article on snitches used in the Duke case.

Mistakes were made, Says DEA Chief Hutchinson - But no one made them

DRCNet and The November Coalition have reported on several occasions the strange odyssey of Andrew Chambers, a St. Louis native who went from being the Drug Enforcement Administration's star informant to one of its biggest embarrassments. Over a 16-year career, Chambers received more than $2 million in DEA funds - his reward for helping to arrest more than 400 people in 31 different cities. He also committed perjury on the witness stand dozens of times, lying about his arrest and conviction record, his tax payments and his level of educational achievement. According to a DEA internal investigation obtained by the St. Louis Post, some DEA agents and supervisors knew of Chambers' mendacious ways, but failed to reign him in.

Now, DEA administrator Asa Hutchinson has announced that no DEA employees will be disciplined for letting Chambers get away with serial perjury. In an interview September 28, he told the St. Louis Post that no agents would be punished because it was "a failure of policy versus a failure of personnel." Hutchinson also pleaded that the 9,000-strong agency had been duped by the crafty Chambers. "Chambers abused his position with us, and we didn't have the systems in place to keep the checks and balances on that," he excused.

According to the agency's own records, however, it did have the ability to have high-level headquarters officials wage a two-year court battle to keep Chambers' criminal record, and his repeated lying about it on the stand, secret.

Hutchinson told the Post that the agency had made reforms in the wake of the Supersnitch scandal: The agency has now set up a central registry to track snitches who testify in more than one place, said Hutchinson, and all agents have been ordered to turn over complete records on their informants to both prosecutors and defense attorneys.

Hutchinson also defended the use of informants, saying they were "crucial" not only to the war on drugs, but now to the war on terrorism. "You've got to use informants, otherwise you can't get the job done," he said.

A DEA press spokesman in Washington confirmed Hutchinson's

Dean Steward is not satisfied with the results. He is the Los Angeles public defender who broke the scandal by pursuing a three-year battle with the DEA and the Justice Department. "I'm stunned that so much government wrongdoing meant so little to the government," he told the Post. "Had this been a major corporation, heads would roll," he added.

337

Chapter 17 - Appendix: Images and articles

Ralph 'Plookie' Duke

Billboard put up for Ralph Duke

CRIME	+	PUNISHMENT	=	JUSTICE
OVER $100,000 OF YOUR TAX MONEY	+	NO TIME	=	DAVE DURENBERGER, U.S. SENATOR
GOVERNMENT DRUG STING	+	NO TIME	=	JOHN DELOREAN, CAR DEALER
GOVERNMENT DRUG STING	+	LIFE + 40 YEARS	=	RALPH "PLOOKIE" DUKE

BLACK + CRIME = TIME
WHITE + CRIME = NO TIME

Vinny with Attorney Jerry Singer.

Vinny and Attorney Helene Hoppla.

Chapter 17 - Appendix: Images and articles

Attorneys Bob Sicoli (left) and Peter Thompson (right), 1991.

Attorney Howard Bass and his wife, Kim.

Judge Bruce Hartigan, 1983.

Bruce Hartigan and Attorney Ken Meshbesher.

Chapter 17 - Appendix: Images and articles

Judge Mark Wernick, 1999

Judge Jack Nordby, 1995

Whatever happened to Lady Justice?

Vinnie with Ron Meshbesher, 1995

Ron Meshbesher in his office, 2008

Chapter 17 - Appendix: Images and articles

Dan Guerrero, Attorney Kate Flom, Jill Lindeman

Vinnie and friends, Meshbesher office, 1988

Whatever happened to Lady Justice?

PAUL HOLDEN ANDERSON

Associate Justice
Minnesota Supreme Court

Age: 59; born 5/14/43
Married to Janice M. Anderson; two daughters

EDUCATIONAL BACKGROUND:

B.A. Degree, cum laude, Macalester College, 1965

J.D. Degree, University of Minnesota, 1968

LEGAL AND PROFESSIONAL BACKGROUND:

- Associate Justice, Minnesota Supreme Court, July 1, 1994 - present
- Chief Judge, Minnesota Court of Appeals, Sept. 1992 - June 30, 1994
- Associate and Partner, LeVander, Gillen & Miller Law Offices, South St. Paul 1971 1992; specialized in real estate, estate planning, probate, business law, and construction litigation
- Special Assistant Attorney General, Criminal Division and Department of Public Safety, Office of Minnesota Attorney General 1970-71
- VISTA (Volunteers In Service to America) attorney, 1968-69; served as a neighborhood attorney for New Haven Legal Assistance, New Haven, CT

FORMER MEMBER AND/OR OFFICER:

- Dakota County Bar Association; board member and president
- Independent School District #199: board member & chairman of board
- Community Services Advisory Committee, Independent School District #199, member and chairman
- Independent School District #199 PER Committees 1982-84
- Deacon and Ruling Elder, House of Hope Presbyterian Church, St. Paul

Chapter 17 - Appendix: Images and articles

JAMES H. GILBERT

as a Civil Trial Specialist.

JAMES H. GILBERT
Associate Justice
Minnesota Supreme Court

Education and Professional Background

B.A. political science, minor economics and J.D. from the University of Minnesota (1969 & 1972). Began his legal career at Meshbesher and Spence law firm in Minneapolis, practicing in commercial litigation, real estate law and some criminal defense and bankruptcy and related appellant work; family law and probate law (1972-1997). Served as shareholder, vice president, secretary, director, and head of the Business Law Department. Managing Partner from 1984-1992 and CEO from 1996-May 1997.

Admitted to practice in Minnesota and Wisconsin, U.S. Courts for the State of Arizona, the 8th and 10th Districts United States Court of Appeals, the United States Tax Court and the United States Supreme Court. Certified by the Minnesota State Bar Association

Appointed by Governor Carlson to the Minnesota Supreme Court and sworn in as Associate Justice on January 29, 1998. He was elected in November 2000 to serve a six-year term. He presently serves as liaison to the following Supreme Court committees:

- Client Security Board
- Lawyers Trust Account Board
- Alternative Dispute Resolution Committee
- Board of Continuing Legal Education
- Legal Services Advisory Committee
- Supreme Court Drug Court Initiatives
- District Liaison: Second and Fifth Judicial Districts

Professional Associations, Societies and Activities

- Member (1991) and chair (1992-1997) Judicial Merit Selection Commission for State of Minnesota
- Member: Minnesota Courts Strategic Plan (1996-1997)
- Member: Minnesota State Bar Association (1972-present)
- Orono City Park Commission (1988-1991)
- Orono fast pitch softball coach (1991-1998)
- Serves as a non-voting member of the Board of Directors, Minnesota D.A.R.E., Inc. (Drug Abuse Resistance Education) 9/98 to present

Whatever happened to Lady Justice?

PRESIDENT'S COLUMN

RONALD I. MESHBESHER

"Informers are worshipped in the temple of justice even as the devil has been worshipped by pagans and savages—even so. In this wicked country, is the informer an object of judicial idolatry—even so is he soothed by the music of human groans—even so is he placated and incensed by the fumes and by the blood of human sacrifices."

—John Philpot Curran
Irish Barrister (1802)

"Criminals are likely to see and do almost anything to get what they want, especially when what they want is to get out of trouble with the law . . . this willingness to do anything includes not only truthfully spilling the beans on friends and relatives, but also lying, committing perjury, manufacturing evidence, soliciting others others to corroborate their lies with more lies, and double-crossing anyone with whom they come into contact, including—and especially—the prosecutor. A drug addict can sell out his mother to get a deal; and burglars, robbers, murderers and thieves are not far behind. They are remarkably manipulative and skillfully devious. Many are outright conscienceless sociopaths to whom 'truth' is a wholly meaningless concept. To some, 'conning' people is a way of life. Others are just basically unstable people. A 'reliable informant' one day may turn into a consumate prevaricator the next."

Are these the rantings of a NACDL member who is punchy after being clobbered all week by several snitches in a drug trial? Not at all. They are the considered statements of Stephen S. Trott, Assistant Attorney General in the Criminal Division of the Justice Department, and are based upon, by his own admission, "personal firsthand experience of eighteen years as a prosecutor." The statement is contained in a supplement to a lecture on the successful use of snitches and informants that Mr. Trott delivered to Justice Department prosecutors in January, 1984. He felt his observations so important that he admonished his fellow prosecutors to read the passage and commit it to memory. He then proceeded to encourage the use of snitches, suggested that negotiations for the deal not be tape recorded because it might "sound bad," and recommended that prosecutors hold back part of the deal, such as a delayed sentencing until after the informer has testified.

Many criminal defense practitioners have refused to represent snitches, recognizing the logical conclusion that follows from Mr. Trott's insightful observation: that if informers will lie and sell out their friends and loved ones, why not their lawyers.

Stool pigeons (am I dating myself?) have been around for a long time. Under Thirteenth Century English law an approver (informant) would be executed if the person he informed upon was acquitted. Some have suggested that resurrection of this practice would eliminate the problem of dishonest informants. J. Edgar Hoover once said that the use of informers is as old as man with the first recorded use being found in the Old Testament. He then went on to say in a 1955 speech before the International Association of Chiefs of Police that there is a communist inspired conspiracy to discredit the use of informers so as to deprive law enforcement of this time-tested valuable tool. A visit to a NACDL board meeting where the laissez faire spirit of free enterprise flourishes should be enough to dispel that allegation. The fact that governments have used snitches for a long time does not justify their continued indiscriminate use. Old process is not necessarily due process.

The difficult task is convincing our courts and juries of the actual hazards of testimony that the government has purchased by offers of freedom to the witness and not infrequently by actual cash payments. Some of the statements contained in Mr. Trott's paper may furnish ammunition for fruitful cross-examination or support for an argument in an appellate brief. Some recent cases have questioned plea agreements with informants that provide for favors contingent upon the results of the informant's testimony. It is not unusual to see vague plea agreements that call for the government to inform the sentencing judge of the "quantity and quality" of the informant's future testimony at trials of alleged cohorts. Such language may be used as a basis to suppress the snitch's testimony. Trial judges should be urged to give detailed cautionary jury instructions about the dangers of informant testimony as opposed to the sterile ones found in most pattern jury instruction books.

Recently a defendant/snitch in a child sexual abuse case in Minnesota was unable to make an in-court identification of a defendant whom he had previously fingered. He later recanted, admitting that his statement to the authorities was a lie provoked by a persistent prosecutor's offer of a lenient sentence if he helped to make the state's case. By exposing and cataloguing these incidents, we may be able to get the attention of the courts throughout the nation. Perhaps then informers will no longer be "worshipped in the temple of justice."

April 1985/the CHAMPION 1

Appendix: Duke Evidence

Exhibits

Drug Enforcement Administration, Office of Inspections, Management Review: Utilization of CS-84-036739 (IN-00-S906) (extracts).

Page (5) A guy named Virgil Kirkwood, Ralph Nunn a/k/a Monte Nunn, Loren Duke Ramone Hutchinson, Marcel Duke, Kim Willis Danny Givens, and a host of others put up the money to purchase the drugs offered by government informant Andrew Chambers.

Page (9) Mr. Dugas said that Yeoman said on the witness stand that he made a purchase of one kilo from Ralph Duke, and that was the end of it.

Page (3) I also learned that he had his face slashed in USP Florence Colorado.

Page (10) Walker did testify against Ralph Duke's girlfriend Vicki Hammer.

Page (11) Why would Ralph Duke, an alleged kingpin with incredible amounts of money, houses and fancy cars need about 30 people to kick in $100.000 dollars to buy 30 kilos of cocaine?

Page (14) Before trial, Ralph Duke's lawyer Joe Friedberg specifically requested from prosecutor Jon Hopeman Chambers complete background records, at which time prosecutor Jon Hopeman told Duke's Attorney Friedberg that Chambers had no criminal record or criminal background. Prosecutor Jon Hopeman stated in his opening argument to the jury that Andrew Chambers is a young man who works as a confidential informant, he has never been arrested, he's never been convicted of any crime's, he doesn't use drugs, he doesn't even drink. This is what was told to the jurors who convicted Ralph Duke. According to the post-conviction evidence that was discovered through Attorney H. Dean Steward in the internal DEA report on Mr. Andrew Chambers, at the time that prosecutor Jon Hopeman made his statements to the jury that convicted Ralph Duke, Mr. Chambers had been arrested 11 times from 1978-1989. You can see from the exhibits that the prosecutor lied to the jury in the Duke trial.

UNITED STATES DISTRICT COURT DISTRICT OF MINNESOTA

AFFIDAVIT OF·F. CLAYTON TYLER

UNITED STATES OF AMERICA; Plaintiff,

v.

RALPH CHAVOUS DUKE, Defendant.

STATE· OF MINNESOTA, COUNTY OF HENNEPIN, ss.

F. Clayton Tyler, being first duly sworn upon oath, deposes and states-that:

1. I am an attorney licensed to practice law in the State of Minnesota.

2. I represented Ralph Duke, the above-named defendant, in his direct appeal of his 1990 conviction for federal drug offenses.

3. To the best of my recollection, while listening to oral arguments before the Eighth Circuit on a co-defendant's appeal, I heard Assistant United States Attorney Denise Reilly tell the court of appeals that one of Mr. Duke's co-defendants had informed her that Mr. Duke was not involved in the 20 kilo sting operation, for which Mr. Duke was ultimately convicted.

4. When I, requested a copy of that oral argument tape recording, I was informed that the tapes had already been destroyed.

5. Attached hereto as Exhibit A is a letter I sent to Mr. Duke on December 14, 1993, in which I advised him of Ms. Reilly's statements to the Eighth Circuit and of the unavailability of the oral argument tapes.

FURTHER AFFIANT SAYETH NOT.

Subscribed and sworn to before me this _26_ day of _March_, 2001.

Marina Goutman
Notary Public

F. Clayton Tyler

Declaration of H. Dean Steward

I, H. Dean Steward, having been duly sworn, declare:

1. I am an attorney licensed to practice law in the states of California and Hawaii. I have been an attorney since 1979.

2. I am a former Deputy Federal Public Defender for the Central 8 District of California. In that capacity, I began representation of Daniel Ray Bennett in the Central District of California in January of 1997. Mr. Bennett was charged in US v. Stanley, et. al.

3. As part of my representation of Mr. Bennett, I began to investigate Drug Enforcement Administration informant Andrew Chambers. Over the last 4 years, I have continued to investigate both Chambers and the DEA in their use of him. I have continued both the investigation of Chambers and the representation of Mr. Bennett, even though I left the Federal Public Defender Office for private practice in April of 2000.

4. I have been sharing much of the information I uncovered with other defense lawyers around the country. Specifically, I shared much of the information I had on Chambers with attorney Howard Bass of Minneapolis, Minnesota starting in December of 1999.

5. In February of 2001, I informed Mr. Bass that I had learned of a 157 page internal DEA Report on Chambers, and I promised to share the report with Mr. Bass if I could get it. I then began efforts under the Freedom of Information Act to secure a copy of the Report.

6. In May of 2001, I was able to secure a copy of the Report. The copy I received from DEA is heavily redacted, and missing several pages.

7. In August of 2001, I supplied a copy of the Report to Mr. Bass. I believe that this Report is still not available to the public.

I declare under penalty of perjury that the foregoing is true and correct.

Dated: October 8, 2001

H. Dean Steward

California State Bar #85317

Chapter 17 - Appendix: Duke Evidence

UNITED STATES COURT OF APPEALS FOR THE EIGHTH CIRCUIT
AFFIDAVIT OF JACK NORDBY

United States of America, Respondent,

vs.

Ralph Chavez Duke, Petitioner.

STATE OF MINNESOTA, COUNTY OF HENNEPIN, ss/

Jack Nordby, being first duly sworn upon oath, states and deposes as follows:

1. I am currently employed as a Hennepin County District Court Judge, chambered in Minneapolis, Minnesota.

2. In 1993, I was employed as an attorney at Meshbesher & Spence, Ltd., in Minneapolis, Minnesota. Sometime in either September or October 1993, Kenneth Meshbesher, a senior partner at that law firm, asked me to represent Ralph Duke on a federal habeas appeal to the Eighth Circuit Court of Appeals.

3. I ascertained that Mr. Duke had filed a §2255 motion *pro se*, while incarcerated at the Leavenworth U. S. Penitentiary, on January 6, 1993. Another Leavenworth inmate had furnished Mr. Duke with materials from his trial indicating that Andrew Chambers lied about his criminal record at Mr. Duke's trial. United States District Court Judge David S. Doty denied Mr. Duke's *pro se habeas* petition on August 16, 1993.

4. While still *pro se*, Mr. Duke filed a motion for reconsideration of Judge Doty's order on September 2, 1993. Concerned about perfecting a timely appeal, despite the pending *pro se* motion for reconsideration, I filed both a notice of appeal and a motion to proceed *in forma pauperis* with the Eighth Circuit on October 13, 1993.

5. Mr. Duke filed an affidavit in support of the *in forma pauperis* appeal motion on October 22, 1993, and Judge Doty granted that motion on November 8, 1993.

6. I moved the Eighth Circuit to appoint me as Mr. Duke's counsel under the Criminal Justice Act on December 1, 1993, and the Court of Appeals granted that motion on December 22, 1993.

7. I filed appellant's brief with the Eighth Circuit in Mr. Duke's habeas appeal on March 8, 1994, and argued his case orally to the Court of Appeals on October 11,. 1994.

8. I never requested and, consequently, never received any money for representing Mr. Duke under the Criminal Justice Act or from any other source.

9. Further your affiant sayeth naught.

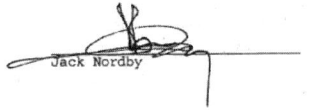

Vincent Carraher Affidavit of December 18, 2001.

David Rovella, "Some superinformant: Lies, rap sheet of DEA's million-dollar man start a legal fire." National Law Journal.

Michael Sorkin and Phyllis Librach, "Top U.S. drug snitch is a legend and a liar," St. Louis Post Dispatch, January 16, 2000.

Michael Sorkin and Phyllis Librach, "Drug agency suspends informer known to lie in court," St. Louis Post Dispatch, February 6, 2000.

Michael Sorkin and Phyllis Librach, "Lying by informer causes U.S. to drop drug charges against four in Miami," St. Louis Post Dispatch, March 7, 2000.

Michael Sorkin and Phyllis Librach, "Prosecutor who used informer draws scrutiny," St. Louis Post Dispatch, March 15, 2000.

Michael Sorkin and Phyllis Librach, "Snitch made millions and says he spent it all," St. Louis Post Dispatch, March 25, 2000.

"Warnings about Chambers," St. Louis Post Dispatch, March 28, 2000.

Michael Sorkin and Phyllis Librach, "DEA report says agency knew about snitch's lies but didn't act," St. Louis Post Dispatch, April 2, 2000.

"The high price of using snitches," St. Louis Post Dispatch, April 7, 2000.

Michael Sorkin and Phyllis Librach, "Drug agency investigates own cover-up," St. Louis Post Dispatch, May 27, 2000.

"DEA cover-up?," St. Louis Post Dispatch, May 3, 2001